D1203950

THE SELF UNDER SIEGE

How much of our identity or 'self' is truly representative of our own wants, needs, and goals in life and how much does it reflect the desires and priorities of someone else? Are we following our own destiny or are we unconsciously repeating the lives of our parents, living according to their values, ideals, and beliefs? In this thought-provoking book, noted clinical psychologist Robert Firestone and his co-authors explore the struggle that all of us face in striving to retain a sense of ourselves as unique individuals.

Through numerous case studies and personal stories from men and women who participated in a 35-year observational study, the authors illustrate how voice therapy, a methodology pioneered by Dr. Firestone, is used to illicit, identify, and challenge the destructive inner voice and to change aversive behaviors. The theory they describe integrates the psychodynamic and existential approaches and is enriched by research findings in the neurosciences, attachment research, and terror management theory (TMT).

An important addition to the area of personality development theory, this book offers a new perspective on differentiation and the battle to separate ourselves from the chains of the past. It will provide psychotherapists and other mental health professionals with the tools needed to help clients differentiate from the dysfunctional attitudes and toxic personality traits of their parents, other family members, and harmful societal influences that have unconsciously dominated their lives.

Robert W. Firestone, PhD, is a clinical psychologist and author. He has been affiliated with the Glendon Association as its consulting theorist since its inception. His innovative ideas related to psychotherapy, couple and family relationships, suicide, parenting, and existential issues have been the inspiration and cornerstone of Glendon's research and many publications.

Lisa Firestone, PhD, is a clinical psychologist and the Director of Research and Education at the Glendon Association. She also maintains a private practice in Santa Barbara, CA. Since 1987, she has been involved in clinical training and applied research in the areas of suicide and violence.

Joyce Catlett, MA, is an author and lecturer. Since 1979, she has collaborated with Robert Firestone on writing 12 books and numerous articles. She currently lectures and conducts continuing education workshops at universities and mental health facilities throughout the United States and Canada.

THE SELF UNDER SIEGE

A Therapeutic Model for Differentiation

Robert W. Firestone, Lisa Firestone,
and Joyce Catlett

NEW YORK AND LONDON

First published 2013
by Routledge
711 Third Avenue, New York, NY 10017

Simultaneously published in the UK
by Routledge
27 Church Road, Hove, East Sussex BN3 2FA

Routledge is an imprint of the Taylor & Francis Group, an informa business

Library of Congress Cataloging in Publication Data
Firestone, Robert.
The self under siege : voice therapy and differentiation / Robert W. Firestone, Lisa Firestone, Joyce Catlett.
p. cm.
Includes bibliographical references and index.
ISBN 978-0-415-52033-1 (hardback)
1. Self-actualization (Psychology) 2. Differentiation (Cognition)
3. Voice. I. Firestone, Lisa A. II. Catlett, Joyce. III. Title.
BF637.S4F5619 2012
155.2'5—dc23
2012006273

ISBN: 978-0-415-52033-1 (hbk)
ISBN: 978-0-203-12242-6 (ebk)

Typeset in Garamond
by Apex CoVantage, LLC

Printed and bound in the United States of America by Sheridan Books, Inc. (a Sheridan Group company)

I dedicate this book to Lisa Ann Firestone, my beloved daughter and esteemed colleague.

–Robert W. Firestone

CONTENTS

FOREWORD

Phillip R. Shaver, PhD

Separation theory, as described in this book, explains the underlying dynamics of attachment in a way that contributes to our understanding of how insecure attachment patterns are transmitted through generations of family life. Robert Firestone and his co-authors illustrate the theory and methodology with personal narratives gathered from participants in a 35-year observational study of more than 100 individuals and families that encompassed three generations. In this book, they describe the self under siege from interpersonal, societal, and existential perspectives and use voice therapy techniques and methodology to challenge internalized destructive elements of the personality.

For the past few years I have been using educational DVDs from the Glendon Association–the professional home of the authors–in my undergraduate courses, "Personality Theories" and "Psychology of Emotion." One of the DVDs deals with the intergenerational transmission of self-critical and self-destructive "voices" in the minds of parents and children, as described in Chapters 3 and 4 of the present volume. Because Robert Firestone encourages people to vocalize their internal voices in the second person ("*You're* the stupid one, you're the ugly one; your brother [who committed suicide] was the good one"), viewers of the DVD can hear the shocking cross-generational similarities between parents' and children's self-attacks. In the case I've just quoted, for example, both the speaker and her pre-teenage daughter say, independently and tearfully, "I was *never* supposed to be born!" Every time I see this DVD and hear the echoes of the mother's self-reproach in her daughter's words, I have to suppress tears (while teaching a large lecture class) even though I've seen the DVD many times.

As explained in *The Self Under Siege,* saying one's internal self-critical voices aloud evokes powerful emotions in both speakers and listeners. We observers get to see otherwise rational, articulate, well-composed individuals flush red, shout angrily at themselves, and burst into tears when what they have just said strikes home full force, activating a flood of painful memories. The speaker immediately realizes that "this is what he or she (usually the speaker's mother or father) said to me!" Another example (from another woman), "Change that face! Change that face!... and [regretfully] I feel that way about my son: Change that face!"

Under other circumstances, the same person can discuss her problems in a calm, intellectualized way (as I, a university professor, usually talk about psychological theories and clinical examples in my classes). Without the voicing procedure, an observer would never guess how vulnerable people are to self-criticisms when they hear them spoken out loud, often echoing their parents' words. Several of the participants in these videos experience and exhibit a second burst of strong emotion when they realize that they are hurting their children in the same ways their parents hurt them, despite their obviously benevolent intentions.

Because the large sample of individuals with whom Robert Firestone and his associates (in the case of this book, his daughter Lisa Firestone and colleague Joyce Catlett) have studied over the years are generally healthy, attractive, intelligent, socially engaged, and financially comfortable, the ambitious students in my university classes, with whom I share the Glendon videos, easily identify with them, cry with them, and marvel that such enviable-looking, presumably privileged people can harbor such cruel and destructive self-critical thoughts. With reflection and discussion, however, the students realize that they have similar voices in their own minds and wish they could get rid of them. Readers of this book are likely to have the same experience. Certainly I gained insight into my own childhood interactions with my parents–remembering more of them than I thought I could–while reading this book.

One of the commendable features of Firestone and associates' voice therapy is that, unlike generic cognitive-behavioral therapy, it is based on a realization that many of the irrational thoughts, beliefs, and expectations that hamper a person's progress toward autonomy are personal and unique. Although many of these negative thoughts could be described in general terms–as putdowns, devaluations, demolishers of hopes and dreams, and "contingencies of worth" (Rogers, 1961)–the emotional impact of stating the thoughts out loud and directing them at oneself is much more powerful and insight-provoking than the general 'cognitions' or statements one finds, for example, in Albert Ellis's books (e.g., 2001) about rational-emotive therapy. A person's particular self-criticisms–unique because they are the words or inferred attitudes of his/her parents–pierce one's heart in a way that general statements do not.

I think it's important to consider, as I just suggested, that some of the voices may be based on inferences rather than verbatim parental statements. It seems unlikely, for example, that the girl who said she was never meant to be born was literally told so by her mother. The voices may, in some cases, be verbalizations of inferred parental attitudes and actions, to which children react emotionally as if actual verbal criticisms had been directed at them. It's now clear in both academic psychology (e.g., Hassin, Uleman, & Bargh, 2005; Kahneman, 2011) and clinical psychology (e.g., Fonagy, 2008; Fonagy, Gergely, & Target, 2008; Renn, 2012) that many mental processes are implicit rather than explicit, intuitive rather than rational, and automatic rather than consciously considered. In the case of emotional wounds caused in childhood by parental failures of empathy and emotional support (failures that marital therapist Susan Johnson, 2008, calls "attachment injuries" when they occur in the context of adult marriage), many of the injuries occurred before the victims could understand emotions or describe them in words.

One of the regrets I have about my own father having died before we could have adult discussions about his life experiences and the reasons for his attitudes, is that I–now a parent of teenagers myself–realize that my inferences about what my dad thought, wanted, and needed were probably incorrect in some important cases. Certainly, I now remember many of his positive, supportive behaviors that I didn't recognize or acknowledge when he and I were battling during my adolescence and I was trying to establish myself as my own person.

It's important to consider that many childhood attachment injuries are not discrete, one-time events, like a single car accident. Renn (2012) and others have emphasized that instead, or in addition, many are "cumulative developmental traumas":

> When this context [the child-parent relationship] is characterized by dramatic or cumulative developmental trauma, the attachment system is hyperactivated and the capacity to mentalize [understand and articulate one's own and others' intentions and feelings] is compromised (Fonagy, 2008). As a consequence, the child relives the traumatic experience in the mode of psychic equivalence, characterized by a frightening correspondence between internal reality and external reality, instead of in the pretend mode characterized by play, imagination, and metaphor, [thereby blurring the ability] to differentiate inner reality from outer reality (Fonagy et al., 2004; Fonagy & Target, 1996). A compromised capacity for mentalization [has] implications for self-organization, self-agency, impulse control, and affect regulation.... Stressful interpersonal contexts in later life may activate representational models developed in...an early relational context and again compromise the capacity to mentalize (Fonagy, 2008; Renn, 2006). (Renn, 2012, pp. 20-21)

These confusions of past and present experiences create difficulties in close relationships–between marriage partners, and between them and their children–as Firestone et al. explain in Chapter 5. Voice therapy helps to identify components and hints of the representational models that plague individuals and ruin their relationships. They make the models and their historical roots accessible to adult analysis and correction.

Part of the process of adult analysis and correction described in this book are conversations and nonverbal interactions between participants and facilitators (usually Robert Firestone in the videos I've watched and in most of the examples in this book). He appears to be an unusually thoughtful and empathic person who is fully present with these individuals, helping them to explore their experiences and perceptions and gain a new perspective on themselves. These interactions remind me of a passage in one of psychoanalyst Thomas Ogden's (2012) essays on seminal works in psychoanalysis:

> Psychological growth...involves a form of acceptance of oneself that can be achieved only in the context of a real relationship with a relatively psychologically mature person. A relationship of this sort (including the

> analytic relationship) is the only possible exit from the solipsistic world of internal object relationships. Self-acceptance is a state of mind that marks the (never fully achieved) relinquishment of the life-consuming effort to transform unsatisfactory internal object relationships into satisfactory (that is, loving and accepting) ones. With psychological growth, one comes to know at depth that one's early experiences with one's unloving and unaccepting [parents] will never be other than what they were. It is a waste of life to devote oneself to the effort to transform oneself (and others) into the people one wishes one were (or wishes they were). In order to take part in experience in a world populated by people whom one has not invented, and from whom one may learn, the individual must first loosen the unconscious bonds of resentment, addictive love, contempt, and disillusionment that confine him [or her] to a life lived principally in his [or her] mind. (Ogden, 2012, p. 75)

Watching the video-recorded groups facilitated by Robert Firestone, watching an interview with him conducted by Lisa Firestone, and realizing that these people have stuck with him for years and contributed to his vision–all of this indicates that he is the kind of "psychologically mature person" that Ogden wrote about.

Reading this book led me to a number of theoretical ruminations about such concepts as repressed emotion. The emotional eruptions that follow the second-person articulation of self-critical voices in the Glendon videos are so dramatically abrupt and forceful that people are often stunned by their vulnerability to what has issued from their own mouths, as if by parental ventriloquism. These eruptions are reminiscent of Freud and Breuer's (2004/1895) early discoveries concerning repressed or suppressed memories, which led to Freud's concepts of repression, catharsis, and return of the repressed. Repressed, suppressed, or unrecognized emotions are still central to many approaches to individual and couple psychotherapy (e.g., Johnson, 2008a, 2008b; Renn, 2012), but voice therapy offers additional insights concerning suppressed emotions and the nature of repression.

The term "repressed emotion" has always bothered me, because emotions, as studied in contemporary psychology, are in-the-moment physiological and behavioral reactions which, as such, cannot possibly be stored in a Mylar bag buried deep in the brain. (I sometimes ask my students where "repressed emotions" might reside in the brain, and they sometimes imagine a place where emotions can be pushed down into a container and locked in by a tight lid, similar to pushing a spring-loaded Jack-in-the-box back into its container. But what we mean by emotion–autonomic arousal, discrete facial expressions, emotion-specific actions or action tendencies–is not something, per se, that can be held in a neural Jack-in-the-box container.)

Emotions are evoked by cognitive appraisals of events and experiences (Lazarus, 1991; Scherer, Schorr, & Johnstone, 2001) or by conditioned stimuli associatively connected with such events and experiences (LeDoux, 1996). I suspect, therefore, that what a traumatized person learns to inhibit or exclude from awareness is not the emotions themselves, but the appraisals that trigger them. When a person voices painful attacks on him- or herself in voice therapy, the painful emotions are evoked again, anew, and the pain, humiliation, loss of support, and lack of love are powerfully reinstated.

The similarities and differences between Firestone's approach and those of Freud, Rogers, contemporary cognitive-behavioral therapists, and today's positive psychologists were brought home to me again and again while I was reading this book. Unlike the general trend in today's psychotherapy toward focused, short-term, and often (in my opinion) superficial psychological or questionable medical interventions (encouraged or mandated by insurance companies), Firestone et al. have chosen to explore psychological concepts in depth over a period of years with the same group of people, and eventually with their children as well. Firestone et al. therefore know each of these people as whole, developing, contextualized human beings, making it possible to tackle such large life issues as marriage, sexuality, parenting, work, aging, and mortality. Perhaps by virtue of being well educated and professionally successful, they are interested in more than simply eliminating neurotic 'symptoms.' They are motivated to progress toward goals of the kind that Rogers (1961) called the "fully functioning personality" and Maslow called self-actualization.

Contemporary positive psychologists (e.g., Seligman, 2002, 2011) have revived some of the spirit of Rogers' and Maslow's humanistic psychology, but–in line with contemporary psychology's fragmentation and thinness–positive psychologists seem to favor lists of disconnected virtues and simple exercises to promote "happiness." They have not offered a new approach to depth psychology or considered how their contributions might be integrated into a depth psychology.

Only in books by Irwin Yalom (e.g., 2002, 2008) have I found a contemporary approach to mortality, psychotherapy, and self-development of the kind provided by Firestone and his associates, but Yalom does not have the advantage of having observed the individuals described above Moreover, Yalom tends not to connect his hard-won personal insights with contemporary research, whereas Firestone et al. achieve great clinical depth while linking their ideas to the latest empirical research on, for example, terror management theory (an empirical approach to existential anxiety; see Greenberg, Koole, & Pyszczynski, 2004; Greenberg, Pyszczynski, & Solomon, 1997; Shaver & Mikulincer, in press), attachment theory (my own field of expertise; see Cassidy & Shaver, 2008; Mikulincer & Shaver, 2007), social cognition, and social and affective neuroscience.

I know from having met and talked with Lisa Firestone and Joyce Catlett at professional conferences, that they are continuously engaged in learning about recent developments in research and in making their clinical and empirical discoveries available to researchers. Their ability to rely on their experience observing and participating with individuals and families without the pressure felt by academic psychologists to obtain federal research grants and specialize in tiny topic areas allows them to think broadly, roam across specific research areas, and seek theoretical integration and tools for individual and social development.

While reading this book I was carried back in memory to my long-standing interests in existential philosophy, psychoanalysis, humanistic psychology, transformational leadership theories, and political and social change. At the same time, I was reminded of important discoveries in contemporary psychology. The authors are thoroughly familiar with research and theories concerning child-parent relationships, marriages, sexuality, depression and suicide, defenses, culture, and the construction, across developmental periods, of a self. Their insights trace back to Laing's (1971, 1972) classic writings on the divided self, which I hadn't thought about in years, and to Roger's (1961) idea that internalized parental conditions of worth, in contrast with unconditional positive regard, distort a child's path to autonomy and healthy self-regard. There are interesting connections between their theorizing and Kohut's (1971, 1977, 1984; Kohut & Wolf, 1978) self psychology, which focuses on ways to foster healthy self-esteem (or "healthy narcissism," as Kohut called it). Firestone et al.'s emphasis on relationships and larger social groups can be viewed in connection with the huge turn toward relational approaches to psychotherapy (promoted for example by Mitchell, 2003). Because Firestone et al. have observed for years the same group of parents and children as they moved through different life phases, they are able to keep sight of the larger picture of human social life as well as the complexity and uniqueness of every individual.

The simultaneous consideration of *both* individuals and relationships is important. There is a tendency in contemporary relational theories in psychoanalysis to be so self-congratulatory about focusing on relationships, including the one between the therapist and client, that the inner life of individual minds is somewhat neglected. There is a similar tendency in cultural psychology, at least in my university (where 35 percent of the students are of Asian ancestry), to celebrate collectivism while denigrating individualism. Because Firestone et al. are interested in the self, in self-limitations rooted in past relationships, and in helping a person relinquish what Firestone calls "fantasy bonds" or imagined connections with previous relationship partners and move toward greater differentiation and autonomy, they are champions of the individual mind while realizing that it is, in part, a product of social relationships, both constructive and destructive. This emphasis on individual development goes hand-in-hand with an acknowledgement of human mortality and existential anxiety. The authors are partially rooted in Western existential philosophy, which was based on recognizing that each individual has only one life to live, and the freedom and responsibility to live it authentically (or not).

In focusing so intently on individuals and the desirability of differentiation, individuation, and autonomy, this book is strongly "Western" in its orientation, perhaps even specifically American. Although I am aware of modern critiques of American individualism, I found myself, while reading this book, quite proud of being a child of the Enlightenment, of the Declaration of Independence, and of the 1960s human potential movement (now viewed critically by many conservative Americans, but clearly the precursor of classic humanistic and contemporary positive psychology). This "Western" framework is appropriate for the educated residents of Santa Barbara, California (where the Glendon Association is located), at least those who, like me, are seeking what Maslow (1971) called "the farther reaches of human nature."

Despite my own affinity for this "Western" orientation, I wonder how the authors' ideas will fare in other cultures. Would participants in collectivist societies accept the notion of differentiating themselves from family members and pursuing their own inclinations? Would Tibetan Buddhists–another example–wish to develop them*selves* within a philosophy that emphasizes "no self" and "nonattachment" (Sahdra, Shaver, & Brown, 2010). I don't mean to prejudge these matters, but teaching, as I do, at a university with as many Asian and Asian American students as European Americans makes me realize how conflicted the Asian students often are about embracing American norms and ideals, on the one hand, while attempting to please their parents and extended families, on the other. I have, for example, had more than one student talk to me during office hours about their wish to attend graduate school in psychology despite their parents' insistence that they become doctors or dentists, or take over a family business. One of them decided a few years ago to attend graduate school in clinical psychology despite her father's claim that he would never to speak to her again if she did, and for years she has stayed in a hotel when she returns to her California hometown. Her mother comes over for meals and catch-up discussions while her father keeps his promise never to speak to her again. Hers is definitely a "self under siege," but my culture and her father's culture have different ideas about how to end the siege.

The previous paragraph is an example of the many internal dialogues I've had with myself while reading this thought-provoking book. Because of its breadth, depth, and seriousness, readers will be both educated and spurred to think further–in fact, to develop them*selves* further, in line with the authors' intentions. If self-development and self-actualization are your own personal goals, reading this book will greatly facilitate your journey.

REFERENCES

Cassidy, J., & Shaver, P. R. (Eds.), *Handbook of Attachment: Theory, research, and clinical applications* (2nd ed.). New York: Guilford Press.

Ellis, A. (2001). *Overcoming destructive beliefs, feelings, and behaviors: New directions for rational emotive behavior therapy.* Buffalo, NY: Prometheus Books.

Fonagy, P. (2008). The mentalization-focused approach to social development. In F. N. Busch (Ed.), *Mentalization: Theoretical considerations, research findings, and clinical implications* (pp. 3-56). New York: Analytic Press.

Fonagy, P., Gergely, G., Jurist, E. L., & Target, M. (2004). *Affect regulation, mentalization, and the development of the self.* New York: Other Press.

Fonagy, P., Gergely, G., & Target, M. (2008). Psychoanalytic constructs and attachment theory and research. In J. Cassidy & P. R. Shaver (Eds.), *Handbook of Attachment: Theory, research, and clinical applications* (2nd ed., pp. 783-810). New York: Guilford Press.

Fonagy, P., & Target, M. (1996). Playing with reality: I. Theory of mind and the normal development of psychic reality. *International Journal of Psychoanalysis, 77,* 217-233.

Freud, S., & Breuer, J. (2004). *Studies in hysteria.* (Trans. R. Bowlby). New York: Penguin. (Orig. published in German in 1895, with Breuer as first author)

Greenberg, J., Koole, S. L., & Pyszczynski, T. (Eds.). (2004). *Handbook of experimental existential psychology.* New York: Guilford Press.

Greenberg, J., Pyszczynski, T., & Solomon, S. (1997). Terror management theory of self-esteem and cultural worldviews: Empirical assessments and conceptual refinements. In M. P. Zanna (Ed.), *Advances in experimental social psychology* (Vol. 29, pp. 61-141). San Diego, CA: Academic Press.

Hassin, R. R., Uleman, J. S., & Bargh, J. A. (Eds.). (2005). *The new unconscious.* New York: Oxford University Press.

Johnson, S. M. (2008a). *Hold me tight: Seven conversations for a lifetime of love.* New York: Little, Brown.

Johnson, S. M. (2008b). Couple and family therapy: An attachment perspective. In In J. Cassidy & P. R. Shaver (Eds.), *Handbook of Attachment: Theory, research, and clinical applications* (2nd ed., pp. 811-829). New York: Guilford Press.

Kahneman, D. (2011). *Thinking fast and slow.* New York: Farrar, Straus, and Giroux.

Kohut, H. (1971). *The analysis of the self.* New York: International Universities Press.

Kohut, H. (1977). *The restoration of the self.* New York: International Universities Press.

Kohut, H. (1984). *How does analysis cure?* Chicago: University of Chicago Press.

Kohut, H., & Wolf, E. (1978). The disorders of the self and their treatment: An outline. *International Journal of Psychoanalysis, 59,* 413-425.

Laing, R. D. (1971). *Self and others.* Hammondsworth, UK: Penguin.

Laing, R. D. (1972). *The politics of the family and other essays.* New York: Vintage.

Lazarus, R. S. (1991). *Emotion and adaptation.* New York: Oxford University Press.

LeDoux, J. (1996). *The emotional brain.* New York: Touchstone.

Maslow, A. H. (1971). *The farther reaches of human nature.* New York: Viking.

Mikulincer, M., & Shaver, P. R. (2007). *Attachment in adulthood: Structure, dynamics, and change.* New York: Guilford Press.

Mitchell, S. A. (2003). *Relationality: From attachment to intersubjectivity.* New York: Taylor & Francis.

Ogden, T. H. (2012). *Creative readings: Essays on seminal analytic works.* London and New York: Routledge.

Renn, P. (2006). Attachment, trauma, and violence: Understanding destructiveness from an attachment theory perspective. In C. Harding (Ed.), *Aggression and destructiveness: Psychoanalytic perspectives* (pp. 57-78). London: Routledge.

Renn, P. (2012). *The silent past and the invisible present: Memory, trauma, and representation in psychotherapy.* New York: Routledge.

Rogers, C. (1961). *On becoming a person.* Boston, MA: Houghton Mifflin.

Sahdra, B. K., Shaver, P. R., & Brown, K. W. (2010). A scale to measure non-attachment: A Buddhist complement to Western research on attachment and adaptive functioning. *Journal of Personality Assessment, 92,* 116-127.

Scherer, K. R., Schorr, A., & Johnstone, T. (Eds.). (2001). *Appraisal processes in emotion: Theory, methods, research.* New York: Oxford University Press.

Seligman, M. E. P. (2002). *Authentic happiness: Using the new positive psychology to realize your potential for lasting fulfillment.* New York: Free Press.

Seligman, M. E. P. (2011). *Flourish: A visionary new understanding of happiness and well-being*. New York: Free Press.

Shaver, P. R., & Mikulincer, M. (Eds.). (in press). *Meaning, mortality, and choice: The social psychology of existential concerns.* Washington, DC: American Psychological Association.

Yalom, I. D. (2002). *The gift of therapy: An open letter to a new generation of therapists and their patients.* New York: HarperCollins.

Yalom, I. D. (2008). *Staring at the sun: Overcoming the terror of death.* San Francisco: Jossey-Bass.

PREFACE

The authors have always been interested in psychotherapy as a lifestyle pursuit of self-awareness, self-understanding, and personal autonomy. Our primary concern has been to define and preserve the essential humanity of our clients and ourselves, and in particular the human spirit. In this regard our goals for psychotherapy reach beyond helping disturbed or maladapted individuals in overcoming their problems and include helping normal individuals in their process of self-actualization. Our primary interest has been in understanding and overcoming people's resistance to finding a freer, more fulfilling life. It was inevitable that our quest would lead us to identify and challenge the primary forces that act as a barrier to self-differentiation.

Differentiation ultimately means being human to the fullest extent—that is, becoming an independent person who functions primarily in the adult mode, lives with integrity, and has an inclusive worldview. It is crucial at this juncture in our evolution to develop a new humanitarian perspective not only to transcend destructive familial and social influences that reinforce the individual's defensive mode of living but also to preserve the species in relation to climate control, warfare, and other crucial problems facing humanity.

The Self Under Siege[1] describes the struggle that all people face in striving to retain a sense of themselves as unique individuals. Not only are we affected by environmental and existential challenges, but we also exist in a social structure that imposes serious restrictions on some of our most important human qualities—the capacity for sustaining personal feeling, the desire to search for meaning, and the ability to live in harmony with other people. The result is that we are all plagued, to varying degrees, by an internal dialogue or thought process that is critical, restrictive, and, at its worst, self-destructive. Indeed, the self *is* under siege in almost every aspect of an individual's daily life. As e. e. cummings accurately observed, "To be nobody-but-yourself—in a world that is doing its best, day and night, to make you [into] everybody else—means to fight the hardest battle which any human being can fight; and never stop fighting" (from "A Poet's Advice," cited by C. Norman, 1958).

The book sets forth a new perspective on the process of differentiation and provides an innovative method for freeing oneself from the enemy within. To a certain extent, all people experience a split within their personality. Early in their development, they incorporate critical attitudes and self-destructive elements into their personalities and remain undifferentiated, to varying degrees, from these internalized harmful influences throughout life. We describe the dynamics of this essential division between destructive tendencies and life-affirming, goal-directed tendencies. The division of the personality fosters a self-hating voice within the child that attempts to destroy the project of being and becoming oneself that gives human existence its most significant meaning. Only by learning to understand and cope with one's internal demons in the form of these negative thought processes can one aspire to emancipation and personal freedom.

I (the first author, Robert Firestone) have spent the majority of my professional life developing and exploring voice therapy procedures and separation theory to help people in the process of individuation. My work has proven to be a valuable laboratory for understanding psychopathology as well as the core problems normal individuals face in their relationships and careers. Furthermore, my methodology has enabled clients to progress beyond previous limitations in traditional talk therapy and overcome the most serious obstacles to their personal development.

The book describes a developmental perspective and outlines factors that oppose differentiation in the family of origin, the couple, and the new family constellation. It postulates the concept of the fantasy bond, an imaginary connection or fused identity with mother, family, country, and religion that people invoke to heal the wounds of emotional pain, frustration, separation anxiety, and death anxiety. The fantasy bond offers a false sense of safety and security and a feeling of pseudoindependence but at the same time predisposes maladaptive responses. We focus attention on destructive societal influences and the social pressure to conform to conventional ways of living that are based primarily on a defensive orientation that supports the destructive thought processes. We elucidate how psychological defenses that were once adaptive for the child become self-limiting and dysfunctional in later life.

Later we outline the problem of passivity and submissiveness to authority figures and the damage caused by pathological leadership and the misuse of power. We go on to describe the concept of personal power as a positive manifestation of power, relating to a person's self-confidence, maturity, sense of autonomy, and integrity. Last, we indicate that the fear of death is the ultimate enemy of differentiation, because when we become afraid, we tend to retreat from life and desperately rely on defenses that include subordinating ourselves to other people, painkillers and addictive habit patterns, and fantasy processes. In the last chapter, we describe the characteristics of the ideally differentiated person, the therapeutic value of friendship, and the special significance of depth psychotherapy.

In developing their treatment program, the authors utilized findings from a 35-year observational study of more than 100 individuals and families who contributed significantly to the development of the new methodology. Through the personal narratives of these participants and clinical case studies, we illustrate how voice therapy, a cognitive-affective-behavioral methodology, was used to access, identify, and challenge destructive thought processes and change maladaptive behaviors based on their prescriptions. The theoretical approach described in this book has been enriched by findings from the neurosciences, attachment research, and terror management theory, which validate many of the first author's basic tenets.

In conclusion, most people are unaware of the extent to which their behavior is governed by a destructive thought process that not only causes considerable pain and personal limitation but inclines people to be trapped into repeating negative aspects of their parents' lives. They can best challenge these insidious effects by identifying and understanding the source of their self-critical, self-attacking thoughts and endeavoring to change behaviors based on the negative voices that they harbor. Bear in mind that it requires complete dedication to fight one's way out of these maladjusted patterns. Our ultimate goal is to help the individual remain independent, open, honest, deep feeling, vulnerable, and able to operate with integrity from his or her own value system.

ACKNOWLEDGMENTS

We wish to express our appreciation to Tamsen Firestone for her significant contribution to the development of this work from inception to completion. She applied her considerable talents for rewriting and editing at each stage and offered suggestions for improving the narratives and case studies that illustrate the voice therapy methodology. We are also grateful to Jo Barrington and Susan Short for their excellent editing skills. We wish to thank Anne Baker, who worked closely with us to reference and complete the final draft of this work. Our thanks go to Jina Carvalho, who is responsible for disseminating an expanding number of written, filmed, and digital resources to mental health professionals and the general public, and to the Glendon Association staff, Nina Firestone, Sarah Eichenbaum, Maureen Sullivan, and Geoff Parr.

We are grateful to the men and women whose stories portray the challenges involved in moving toward higher levels of differentiation and more humane ways of being and living. We acknowledge their openness and courage in revealing their personal journey in life. They have been strongly motivated to make the insight and understanding that they have gained over the past three decades available so that others might benefit from their experiences.

We wish to express our appreciation to Rick Roderick (1949–2002) for his inspiration for the title of this book, which was also the title of a brilliant lecture series he presented on existential philosophy, "The Self Under Siege: Philosophy in the 20th Century" (1993), produced by the Teaching Company.

The names, places, and other identifying facts in the personal stories contained in this book have been fictionalized, and no similarity to any persons, living or dead, is intended.

1

INTRODUCTION

Can human beings be persons today? Can a man be his actual self with another man or woman?... Is freedom possible?

—R. D. Laing, *The Politics of Experience*

Each person has a unique set of genes that distinguishes that individual from every other human on the planet, with the exception of identical twins.[1] This identity is affected by the impact of interpersonal stimuli that are either favorable to the development of the personality or damaging to it. In order for people to live their own lives and fulfill their destinies, they must differentiate themselves from destructive environmental influences. To the degree that people can retain significant aspects of their unique identities, they are able to live truly individualistic and creative lives.

Painful events and negative programming during the developmental years constitute the most serious threat to the evolution of the authentic self. Psychological defenses, which were once adaptive as an attempt to dull or block out early interpersonal trauma, later become limiting and dysfunctional and, at their worst, can predispose psychopathology.

To lead a free life, a person must separate him- or herself from negative imprinting and remain open and vulnerable. This differentiation is difficult to accomplish and requires considerable effort because, as children, people not only identify with the defenses of their parents but also tend to incorporate into themselves the critical or hostile attitudes that were directed toward them. These destructive personal attacks become part of the child's developing personality, forming an alien system, the anti-self, distinguishable from the self system, which interferes with and opposes the ongoing manifestation of the true personality of the individual. Remaining undifferentiated renders one unable to fully accept the gift of life and, instead, leaves one merely living out the life of another.[2]

In addition, children must contend with the anxiety surrounding their evolving awareness of a finite existence. Death fears reinforce the psychological defenses that they formed earlier in life and thereby intensify the division within the personality between the self and anti-self systems. To a large extent, the impact of death awareness affects a person throughout his or her life span.

Last, the self is under siege by social imprinting from the society at large. In the struggle to achieve and maintain autonomy and a strong sense of self, one must resist the tendency toward unnecessary conformity and avoid becoming a passive part of a group process. Society represents, in part, a pooling of the individual defenses of its membership; its collective attitudes, politics, and philosophies reflect back on the individual. These social pressures impose limitations on a person's unique approach to life and sense of freedom and pose a significant threat to his or her individuality. It is a full-time job to cope with alien elements from both interpersonal sources and societal influences.

THE STORY OF KEVIN

We refer here to the example of Kevin and a conversation the first author (R. Firestone) had with this 3-year-old boy because it inspired us to further explore the problem of self-differentiation and eventually influenced us to write this book. From 1977 to the present, we have used a technique called voice therapy to help individuals identify the destructive thoughts, attitudes, and beliefs that were interfering with their personal growth and movement toward autonomy and independence. The technique, which uses a dialogue format, enables people to expose their self-attacks and cope with alien elements of their personalities. In essence, the methodology challenges the enemy within that predisposes much of a person's misery and malfunction in life. Voice therapy exposes the split that exists in each person between the real self and the incorporated negative parental attitudes that make up the anti-self. My interaction with Kevin reinforced my focus on helping people access and separate from alien elements of their personalities and underscored how critical it is for each of us to develop and maintain an independent, authentic, and differentiated sense of ourselves.

Kevin's parents, Jenny and Michael, were distraught because their son exhibited violent behavior and impulsivity and would savagely attack other children without provocation. Seemingly out of nowhere, he would suddenly hit or try to bite a younger child. He was agitated a good deal of the time, continually pretended to be an aggressive animal like a dinosaur or a tiger, and threw a serious tantrum if interrupted. He manifested certain risk-taking behaviors and appeared unconcerned about things that would frighten most children. There were times when he would hit himself in the face with his fists while saying he was bad. At other times, for no apparent reason, he would suddenly collapse on the floor and scream out.

His parents discussed their concerns with me and spoke of their fear that Kevin's violence, lack of control, and bravado might, in part, be related to genetic factors (Fowles & Kochanska, 2000).[3] Jenny and Michael felt unable to cope with the situation, and Jenny had asked a friend of the family, Amy, to help her with Kevin. Although Amy was a sensitive and warm individual who had an easy way with children, she could not feel for this boy, and he provoked uncharacteristically angry emotions in her. Over time, she had become worried and discouraged.

One day, Amy spoke to me about her worries about Kevin. She described his demeanor as being unpleasant and said that he appeared to be unlovable. She provided me with valuable insight into the family's dynamics. She said that, although she knew Jenny felt loving toward Kevin, she would often act strangely with him. She would engage in scary games, jumping out at him and making mean faces. While Jenny thought they were playing and having fun, the child appeared to be terrified.[4] Amy also mentioned that, in her opinion, Jenny seemed immature and misattuned to her son and had difficulty being nurturing.

Kevin, a nice-looking boy with blond hair, was small for his age. On the day that I met him, he looked like he felt angry and scared. It was obvious to me that this child was of exceptional intelligence. My initial reaction to Kevin was similar to Amy's experience of him. He gave me an uneasy feeling, and it was hard to warm up to him. I found him unlikeable, a rare feeling for me to have toward any child. Then I decided that I wanted to get to know him better, so I sat down next to him and started to talk with him.

To keep his attention, I encouraged him to look at my eyes. We engaged in some friendly small talk, and then I asked him about the things that scared him. His face looked serious, and, in an earnest voice, he began to tell me a story. He said that there were two Kevins—a regular Kevin and a Kevin witch—as well as a Mommy witch. Based on what I knew about the fantasy bond, I conjectured that the Kevin witch was the destructive aspect of Jenny's mothering that he had assimilated. I intuitively challenged him, saying, "There is only one Kevin." Kevin responded, "No, there are two Kevins." To this I repeated, "There is only one Kevin."

He objected for a while, but I repeated the sentence over and over. Suddenly he caught on and his eyes lit up. He jumped out of his chair and said, "This is what Mommy does." He imitated his mother, raising his arms in a menacing manner and making an angry, distorted face. Then he said, "Let's attack the Mommy monster!" and started pummeling a pillow, hitting it with his fists. I supported him in expressing his anger. I said that he was killing the monster but that I would protect him. After the outburst, Kevin felt particularly relaxed and self-possessed; his face had changed and he looked sweet. I felt warmly toward him.

Following this conversation, Kevin's family told me that he seemed more lovable and relaxed. His outward behavior was friendlier and more affectionate, which was significantly different from his usual demeanor. Whereas in the past he had frequently referred to himself as a bad boy or a monster, his parents reported that he had begun referring to himself more often as a good boy.

My unusual encounter with this child and its positive outcome impressed me. I was surprised that I could verbally communicate with someone so young. I pondered the significance of our conversation and interpreted the exchange as follows: When I said that there was only one Kevin, I was really saying that the Kevin witch represented the threatening persona of his mother that Kevin had incorporated into himself. In his fantasy of fusion with his mother, he saw himself as the monster. That is the reason he judged himself as bad and why he acted out elements of the raging, incorporated monster on other children. When he made the separation from the Kevin witch and conceptualized himself as simply Kevin, he was able to mobilize his anger toward his mother and he felt relief.

When children are especially frightened or hurt, they incorporate the aggressor (the person causing them emotional pain) into themselves. This is a psychological survival mechanism that reduces intolerable stress. Because of this incorporation process, Kevin had a split within himself that was part him (the self) and part his scary mother (the anti-self) that was alien to him and aggressively directed outward toward other children. After Kevin made the separation from his internalized parent, he seemed like a different person. He maintained a pleasant disposition with only occasional outbursts of anger. When these fits did occur, they were much more moderate and he was reachable. Following my conversation with Kevin, he and his parents entered into an ongoing treatment program, and Kevin continued to make progress. Nonetheless, my brief exchange with him was exceptionally significant and meaningful both to Kevin and to me.

To a considerable extent, people become carbon copies of one or both of their parents. To the degree that they manifest their parents' positive qualities, this identification becomes a harmonious, integrated part of the personality. However, parents' negative characteristics, points of view, and maladaptive psychological defenses become a separate, nonintegrated, alien aspect of the personality that has a destructive influence.

For example, my father was a good-hearted medical doctor who believed in helping people and felt love and respect for his patients. I have embraced a career in a helping profession as a psychotherapist and manifest a similar concern for my clients. On the other hand, my father exhibited a mean, hypercritical attitude toward me as a child, and, to my own detriment, I have internalized this destructive pattern. To a considerable extent, my self-critical attitude and self-depreciation have played a part in limiting my capacity to enjoy life.

Perfect parenting is impossible. Because of the power differential between parent and child and the child's utter helplessness and dependency, some degree of trauma is inevitable. A certain amount of parental misattunement and failure to repair these disruptions are unavoidable, even in the best of circumstances. This is because, despite parents' best intentions, their unresolved trauma is usually unconsciously—or sometimes even purposefully—acted out on their offspring. This negative imprinting tends to have a significant effect throughout the lifetime of the individual and can far outweigh positive influences. For example, casual irritability or anger on the part of parents (particularly when disciplining their children) may have a dramatically frightening effect on the child who experiences the parents' mean face and angry disposition as life-threatening.

We place a great deal of emphasis on the material about Kevin because, to varying degrees, all people experience a split in their psyche that is similar to his. Fonagy and his colleagues (Fonagy & Bateman, 2008) have described how this split leads to the development of the "alien self":

> To achieve normal self-experience the infant requires his emotional signals to be accurately or contingently mirrored by an attachment figure.... When a child cannot develop a representation of his own experience through the caregiver's mirroring interactions, he internalizes the image of the caregiver as part of his self-representation. We have called this discontinuity within the self the "alien self." (pp. 142–143)[5]

Our real self is under siege by our anti-self. To the extent that we retain the critical attitudes and destructive elements we have incorporated into our own personalities, we remain undifferentiated from our parents throughout our lifetimes. For most of us, there is very little awareness of the negative elements that we have assimilated and that are now manifested in our personalities. These characteristics are hurtful to ourselves and others, particularly those closest to us.

In a very real sense, we have both a positive and negative identity, and we are very different people depending upon which side is dominant. The negative identity is most likely to emerge and become ascendant when we are under stress or are particularly fearful. On those occasions, we symbolically reconnect to the people who caused us psychological pain and anxiety in our developmental years by acting out the destructive behaviors that they directed toward us.

To summarize, to the extent that we are possessed by this alien aspect of our personality, we exist as divided selves. This incorporated personality represents the dark side of parents or caretakers—in essence, the worst attitudes and behaviors that were directed toward us as vulnerable children. Left unchallenged, the anti-self operates as an extensive alien viewpoint that has an impact on us throughout our lives. This process is damaging to both individuals and their relationships, and, sadly, most of us remain largely unaware of its insidious effects. These incorporated attitudes promote a defensive lifestyle that predisposes misery and maladaptive behavior, opposes individuation and self-realization, and serves as the core resistance to psychotherapy and a happy and harmonious life.

THE SELF AND IDENTITY

According to Kerr and Bowen (1988), "Differentiation is a product of a way of thinking that translates into a way of being" (p. 108). "The more differentiated a self, the more a person can be an individual while in emotional contact with the group" (p. 94). And "This process of change has been called 'defining a self' because visible action is taken to which others respond" (p. 107).

Philosophers and psychologists have long debated the nature of the self. Many contemporary Eastern thinkers believe that one's perception of having a self is merely an illusion. A number of Western psychologists, including social constructivists, claim that the self can only be studied or understood in the context of the social environment, pointing out that others tend to reify the concept of self. With respect to this ongoing debate, developmental psychologist Daniel Stern (1985) asserted, "Even though the nature of self may forever elude the behavioral sciences, the sense of self stands as an important subjective reality, a reliable, evident phenomenon that the sciences cannot dismiss" (p. 6).[6]

Erik Erikson (1963) frequently used the terms *identity* and *self* interchangeably, describing identity as dynamic, fluid, and capable of being transformed in significant ways throughout a person's lifetime. "As proposed by Erikson, identity helps one to make sense of, and to find one's place in, an almost limitless world with a vast set of possibilities" (Schwartz, 2005, p. 294).

> For Erikson, personal identity represents one's set of goals, values and beliefs. What is most important...is the extent to which this set of goals, values and beliefs are internally consistent and, taken together, form a coherent sense of self. (Schwartz, Zamboanga, & Weisskirch, 2008, p. 635)[7]

Jeffrey Arnett (2000) has proposed a new stage in identity formation: emerging adulthood, which spans the years between 19 and 29. In this distinctive stage, "changes in worldviews are often a central part of cognitive development....It is notable that emerging adults who do not attend college are as likely as college students to indicate that deciding on their own beliefs and values is an essential criterion for attaining adult status" (p. 474). Erikson's and Arnett's formulations are congenial with my (R. Firestone's) own way of thinking about self and identity. In my conceptualization, the self system, in contrast to the anti-self system, is composed of the unique wants, desires, goals, and values that hold special meaning for the individual as well as the specific manner and means that the individual uses to fulfill these goals.

In this regard, the essential questions regarding identity are these: How much of our identity or self is truly representative of our own wants and goals in life, and how much does it reflect the wants and priorities of someone else? Are we following our own destiny, or are we unconsciously repeating the lives of our parents and automatically living according to their values, ideals, and beliefs?

Most people rarely, if ever, consider these questions in relation to how they are conducting their lives. They implicitly trust that their thoughts, beliefs, and feelings are their own and fail to recognize that they may be channeling someone else's thoughts and feelings. They perceive themselves as integrated or whole rather than as divided or of two minds.

In our experience, we have found that most people are initially unaware of the extent to which their lives have been preempted or taken over by an incorporated parent whose thoughts, beliefs, and feelings are actually antagonistic to their own desires and goals. Most people are compliant and rarely deviate from the beliefs and opinions held by their parents and tend to live conventional and predictable lives. They fail to recognize their lack of differentiation or the fact that they are reliving someone else's life rather than living their own life. Others adopt a defiant stance in opposition to their parents' ideas and values and approach life mistakenly believing that their defiance and rebelliousness are their real identity. However, compliance and defiance are both driven by the views, behaviors, or lifestyle of one's parents, and neither is truly representative of one's own identity or self. It is of the utmost importance to take both of these contingencies into consideration when approaching the project of differentiation.

Our aim in this book is to help readers identify and break with external and internal negative influences—that is, to emancipate themselves from imagined connections with parents, to unlearn destructive aspects of early programming, and to learn to embrace more life-affirming ways of satisfying needs and pursuing goals. The process of differentiation is arduous work and a lifelong project, because as people give up habitual ways of living, which are based on their parents' defensive prescriptions about life, they will inevitably experience the anxiety aroused by a heightened awareness of their aloneness and vulnerability. Nevertheless, working through these issues is a worthwhile endeavor, because it enables a person to live a full and integrated life.

THE PILOT STUDY

Because we recognized the value of differentiation and wished to broaden our perspective on the subject as it related to individuality, personality dynamics, and psychotherapy, we formed a group to study the process. The experimental population referred to in the preface was originally made up of more than 30 professionals and close friends who volunteered as subjects because they wished to develop themselves further. Our motivation was twofold: to learn and expand our psychological knowledge and to further develop ourselves personally.

We decided to use the methods of voice therapy, which involves a dialogue format whereby subjects express critical attitudes toward themselves and others in the second person. For example, instead of saying, "I'm stupid" or "I'm shy," a person would say, "You're stupid" or "You're shy," as though someone else were expressing the thought. In revealing critical attitudes toward others, instead of saying, "He's taking advantage of me," a person would say, "He's taking advantage of you." We knew from past experience with the technique that when people entered into this type of dialogue, considerable emotion was manifested and participants were able to separate out alien and dysfunctional elements of their personalities. They were also able to understand where and how they developed their negative point of view toward themselves and others and to grasp the extent of the destructive effect it had on their personal lives and careers.

Other voice therapy procedures involved answering back to the critical attacks on self and others, planning corrective suggestions for behavioral change based on countering the negative voices, and implementing these suggestions on the action level. In prior studies, we found that these procedures not only constituted an effective method for understanding maladaptive aspects of personality but also served as an effective psychotherapy procedure that demonstrated positive results for a variety of psychological disorders.

In the current study, we asked the subjects to represent one or another of their parents or significant family members in the voice therapy format. They would reveal the person's critical attitudes and point of view toward them as though that person were speaking to them directly. For example, a participant might start by saying, "This is my mother's point of view," and then begin the dialogue as follows: "You always were an angry child. You never were any good; I always resented you." The process of expressing these negative parental points of view enables the participant to come to understand his or her destructive attitudes.

Five basic steps were involved in the subjects' attempts to differentiate from their incorporated malevolent voice attacks: revealing the destructive ideation and feelings that were directed toward them from a particular parent in the form of a dialogue as described above; developing insight regarding the sources of the attack; answering back by stating their own point of view; recognizing the impact of the voice on present-day behavior; and planning and implementing constructive action that challenged and countered the internalized point of view.

In the process, subjects not only identified the enemy within but also became aware of the myriad negative ways that they had become like their parents. They recognized that they manifested many of the unpleasant and noxious characteristics of their parents in their interactions with other people. In this manner, destructive thoughts and actions are passed on through the generations with painful residual effects. For example, parents who were themselves victims of a variety of abuses in their developmental years innocently or not so innocently pass on these abuses to their own children.

There are two aspects of the imprinting process that indicate the seriousness of a lack of differentiation. The first and most important is that the introjection of negative, self-destructive attitudes and related defenses bears a primary causal relationship to psychopathology. The second concern relates to the problem of formulating one's own goals, values, and ideals, thereby establishing a separate and unique identity. Without differentiating from parents or caretakers, we may never succeed in living our own lives.

An Example

To illustrate the concept of differentiation and our therapy approach to the subject, one can consider the following case material, which involves Vivian, a 26-year-old woman who had moved with her husband and young daughter to California from their home state of Kentucky. Even though she had been eager to relocate her family to the West Coast, after the move, instead of feeling happy and optimistic, Vivian was extremely self-critical and somewhat pessimistic about her life.

In dealing with her self-hating thoughts, Vivian utilized the methods of voice therapy to formulate and verbalize her mother's attitudes toward herself, her husband, and her daughter as though her mother were speaking about her and them. Her mother's basic attacks have been excerpted from the material that Vivian presented, and the following passages contain an abbreviated version of her expressions in the group discussions.

> About herself [in a snide tone and pronounced Southern accent]: You're weird. You're not like other women; you're not feminine. You were such an ugly little girl! You were so shy and backward, no wonder you didn't have any friends! And you think it's going to be different here? It's not, because you're still like that!
>
> About her daughter: So you have a daughter! Big deal! You don't know anything about taking care of a child. And she looks just like you. She's ugly,

> creepy, just like you. She'll never have any friends. She's going to turn out unlovable, just like you!
>
> About her husband: Do you really think he has loving feelings toward you? Why would he? You're so ugly, creepy, and unlovable. You know why? Because he's a creep, just like you. And why would you want to be with him, anyway? He's weak and wimpy.
>
> About herself: Who do you think you are, saying these things? Nobody wants to hear you! I'm not interested in what you have to say! Why don't you just keep your mouth shut? In our family, we're quiet about these things, and you should be quiet, too. Just shut up!

In describing her insights after expressing her mother's negative views about these areas of her life, Vivian said,

> I can see that even though I left my mother in Kentucky, she is still in my thoughts even though I'm in California. It's like she moved with me. I actually think that the attacks are stronger because I physically left her. Her voice is telling me that I am the same person she said I was as a child. And she's not just attacking me; she's attacking the people I love and the people who love me.

After discussing her insights, Vivian was encouraged to answer back to the criticisms and attacks on herself and her family.

> I feel like I could go on and on saying my mother's attacks on all areas of my life, but right now I feel so angry. I just feel like saying back: "Goddamn it! Fuck you. You're wrong about me! I'm not an unlovable, creepy person. That's such bullshit! You may have seen me that way, but that's not who I am. And I don't see my daughter that way, either. I love my husband. I love my daughter. And they love me. You're wrong about me and about my life!"
>
> My mother was the one who didn't have friends, who didn't have a husband, who didn't love her daughter. That's true of her, not me. I feel like I'm so different from her, I mean at the opposite end of the spectrum. I appreciate being able to say this, to stand up for myself. I think that it was also important for me to say rationally what I felt about her attacks.

Follow-Up

Over a period of several months working with this form of voice therapy dialogue and expanding on these formulations, Vivian came to understand the division in her personality. She challenged thoughts that were critical of herself, her husband, and her daughter. In talking about her goals, she thought of actions to take to go against her voice attacks. She made an effort to express affection toward her husband and made sure to set aside time each evening for conversation with him. She was compassionate and patient with her daughter and offered her support as she adjusted to a new school. As a result, Vivian's mood improved considerably; she felt happy and more herself. Her progress was a direct result of her ongoing use of voice therapy methods to gradually differentiate her own point of view and behaviors from the cynical, hostile attitudes of her mother.

The original investigation that we undertook several years ago to examine and analyze the voice has been supplemented by the more recent pilot study. Our basic conclusion from both explorations is that we can access the internalized destructive thought process and accompanying affect with this dialogue format. We can understand its roots and further the process of differentiating from the damaging effects of negative programming internalized during the developmental years.

Voice therapy has proven to be valuable both as a research tool and as a therapeutic methodology. It has led to the development of scales for assessing the potential for self-destructive behavior and suicide risk: the *Firestone Assessment of Self-Destructive Thoughts* (Firestone & Firestone, 2006), and for violence risk, the *Firestone Assessment of Violent Thoughts* (Firestone & Firestone, 2008a, 2008b). Items on both scales are made up of actual voice statements revealed by subjects during observational studies. Results of reliability and validity studies show that the scales effectively discriminate between suicidal or violent individuals and nonsuicidal or nonviolent subjects at a high level of significance.

In conclusion, a destructive thought process exists within all of us, and we are plagued to varying degrees by an internal dialogue that is harmful, restrictive, and, at its ultimate extreme, self-destructive. By identifying the voice and going against its dictates, we can begin to address the questions posed earlier: Are we living our own lives and pursuing our own dreams, or are we repeating patterns of the past and reliving our parents' lives? Are we being ruled by the ways our parents, other people, and the world have viewed us or by attitudes that express our real self? The more we are able to break with our parents' negative prescriptions for living and differentiate our own point of view from the views they imposed on us, the greater the opportunity we have for fulfilling our personal destiny in life.

2

A DEVELOPMENTAL PERSPECTIVE

> There are those who say that man will never find a way to be scientific about himself. I believe this is as shortsighted as his own emotionality. . . . I think the differentiation of self may well be one concept that lives into the future. It merely begins to define how one human life is different from all those in the immediate environment.
>
> —Michael Kerr and Murray Bowen, *Family Evaluation*

INTRODUCTION: SEPARATION AND DIFFERENTIATION

Life can be conceptualized as a series of progressive weaning experiences as originally described by Otto Rank (1936/1972). It begins with birth, then continues with separation from the breast, from the mother, from parents; the first day of school, leaving home, getting married, pregnancy, becoming a parent, saying good-bye to one's children as they leave home, becoming a grandparent; and it ends with one's death, the ultimate separation. As we evolve as individuals and become more independent, we become aware of moving away emotionally from some sense of security in the family. Each separation experience creates a new situation that is both exciting and frightening. It heralds growth and new frontiers but at the same time symbolizes the loss of parental support, which fosters separation anxiety.

A distinction can be made between the concepts of separation and differentiation: the former refers to physical distance or geography, whereas the latter refers to distinguishing oneself as a unique individual. In this sense, leaving home is very different from forming a separate identity or individuating. A person may seek independence by leaving one's family of origin but will most likely maintain destructive parental attitudes and prohibitions that are binding and that negatively impact the emergence of one's personal freedom or independence.[1]

Differentiation is a universal struggle that all humans face if they wish to fully develop themselves as individuals. The process of differentiation encompasses four tasks. A person needs to: (1) break with internalized thought processes (i.e., critical, hostile attitudes toward self and others); (2) separate from negative personality traits assimilated from one's parents; (3) relinquish patterns of defense formed as an adaptation to painful events in one's childhood; and (4) develop one's own values, ideals, and beliefs rather than automatically accepting those one has grown up with.

One must identify one's critical, self-destructive attitudes; understand their source; and challenge them by changing the relevant behaviors. People must come to the understanding that they do not have a fixed identity. They have the power to identify and alter features of their personalities that they find negative or unpleasant. Later, as individuals develop their own values and ethics from within, they can begin to "chart the course of their lives in a manner that is both harmonious and well integrated" (Morrant & Catlett, 2008, p. 350). Differentiating from parental introjects and psychological defenses based on the emotional pain of childhood is essential not only for neurotic or seriously disturbed individuals; it is a central developmental issue in every person's life.

Our distinctive DNA code is the organic basis of our personal identity or self.[2] Very early in life, this innate distinctiveness gives rise to our awareness of being separate and alone. This sense of aloneness stimulates a desire for affiliation or belongingness as a survival mechanism. It is impossible for the newborn to begin to develop a self or identity in a vacuum. The self emerges only in relation to another person or persons.[3]

Developmental psychologists as well as neuroscientists emphasize that the development of the neonate's brain and personality is environmental-dependent—that is, the growth and development of the self are completely dependent upon inputs from the environment, specifically upon stimuli from other humans (Perry, 2001; Schore, 2003b; Siegel, 1999; D. Stern, 1985). Our need for social affiliation and attachment is expressed through the pursuit of love and personal contact; however, when this need is not fulfilled in childhood, we often choose to rely on fantasy processes to compensate for the emotional deprivation we experienced at the time (Firestone, 1985).

POSITIVE AND NEGATIVE ENVIRONMENTAL INPUTS THAT AFFECT THE DEVELOPMENT OF THE SELF

From the beginning, the parental environment has a profound impact on the baby. In an optimal setting, infants encounter attuned responses from caring adults that promote a feeling of safety, which in turn facilitates learning and the further development of the core self. These positive inputs originate in interactions with parental figures who are able to provide their children with a secure base from which to explore their world as they grow and develop. Ideally, parents would be warm, affectionate, and sensitive in feeding and caring for their offspring and offer them control, direction, and guidance as well.

Unfortunately, even in a relatively benign atmosphere, a certain amount of damage occurs because of the infant's heightened reactivity to sensory inputs—for example, overstimulation and understimulation (D. Stern, 1985).[4] The prolonged dependence of the human infant on his or her parents for physical and psychological survival provides the first condition for defense formation. According to Guntrip (1961), the infant's need for "reliable maternal support" is so absolute and failure to provide it so nearly universal that "varying degrees of neurotic instability…are the rule rather than the exception" (p. 385).

Because the infant or young child lacks worldly experience and a sense of proportion and because of the size differential in relation to the parents, the same events that might seem relatively trivial or insignificant to adults are often highly dramatic to the child. The desperate need for love and care from a parental figure makes negative experiences appear more exaggerated and dangerous from the child's vantage point. Anger or irritability on the part of parents may be seen as life-threatening from the child's perspective but register only on the periphery of parents' awareness.[5] As Winnicott (1958) observed, seemingly innocuous interactions with an insensitive parent can seriously impinge upon the child's "going on being." Even "good-enough" parents, who can be characterized as effective in relation to their child-rearing functions, have certain limitations and deficits that are damaging to the child's emerging self.

The extreme sensitivity of the child to harmful influences that are practically imperceptible to an outside observer is documented in the first author's film, *Invisible Child Abuse* (Parr, 1995). The film offers many examples of relatively healthy individuals who were nevertheless seriously impaired in certain aspects of their development by innocent or not-so-innocent hurtful actions on the part of their parents. In the film's conclusion, I (R. Firestone) said,

> The fact is that all the participants in the film were scarred in ways that negatively impacted their development in the incidental process of growing up. Because of the lack of understanding of children and parent-child relationships, subtle forms of emotional abuse largely go unnoticed or at the least are misunderstood.
>
> It's a certain kind of insensitivity, a certain kind of "lack of feeling"—basically not seeing the child as a person with tender emotions and a vulnerable nature. These are not the kinds of things that most parents or people would even think were that hurtful until you actually see the damage done to the individuals involved and observe their limitations in how they conduct their lives.

Parental Ambivalence

Parents have a fundamental ambivalence toward themselves that is also manifested in a basic ambivalence toward their offspring. These conflicting feelings and attitudes coexist within all people in all societies (Firestone, 1990a; Hrdy, 1999, 2009; Rohner, 1986, 1991).[6] In research conducted in 35 cultures, Rohner (1986) examined parents' attitudes and found that they existed on a continuum ranging from parental warmth and acceptance to indifference, rejection, and hostility. Both positive and negative attitudes could be measured *intergenerationally* (in both parent and child). The patterns of parental rejection assessed by Rohner and his associates included hostility and aggression, dependency, emotional unresponsiveness, negative self-evaluation (negative self-esteem and negative self-adequacy), emotional instability, and a negative worldview (Firestone & Catlett, 1999).

Just as parents indicate positive and negative feelings toward *themselves,* they display both tender, nurturing impulses *and* hostile feelings toward their children. Mothers and fathers have a natural desire to love and nurture their children; however, at times, they harbor unconscious resentment and anger toward them—both profoundly affect their children's ongoing development. Because negative, hostile feelings toward children are generally socially unacceptable, parents are resistant to seeing these aggressive feelings in themselves and attempt to deny or suppress them. However, the negative side of parents' ambivalence is expressed in both critical attitudes and punitive behaviors that the child is highly sensitive to.

In addition, people who are inward, withdrawn, or self-protective tend to be limited in their ability to adjust to the responsibilities of parenthood. For example, a parent may pass on his or her self-protective way of dealing with life by being either overly protective or neglectful in relating to the child.

Children are also extremely sensitive to how their parents feel toward *themselves.* They feel relaxed and secure in an environment in which their parents have positive regard for themselves. However, if their parents have low self-esteem, strong feelings of inferiority, or unresolved feelings of loss or trauma from their past, children intuitively sense their parents' state of mind and feel threatened in their own security (Firestone, 1990a).

A parent's ambivalent feelings and attitudes—his or her state of mind—are picked up by the infant or child at the neuronal level, via brain-to-brain communication, during feeding, play, and other social interactions (Cozolino, 2006; Schore, 1994; Siegel, 1999; Siegel & Hartzell, 2003). According to Cozolino, the growth of the infant's brain "depends on interactions with others for its survival" (p. 6).

> When good-enough parenting combines with good-enough genetic programming, our brains are shaped in ways that benefit us throughout life. And the bad news? We are just as capable of adapting to *unhealthy* environments and *pathological* caretakers. The resulting adaptations may help us to survive a traumatic childhood but impede healthy development later in life. Our parents are the primary environment to which our young brains adapt, and their unconscious minds are our first reality. (p. 7)

Emotional Hunger

Most parents believe that they love their children even when their child-rearing patterns would be described as angry, indifferent, neglectful, or even abusive. Parents' internal image or fantasy of love allows them to imagine that their actual behaviors are affectionate and caring. In addition, they often confuse their own intense feelings of need and anxious attachment for genuine love. They fail to make a distinction between emotional hunger, which is a strong need caused by deprivation in their own childhoods, and genuine feelings of tenderness, love, and concern for their child's well-being.

Emotional hunger may be expressed in anxious overconcern, overprotection, living vicariously through one's child, or an intense focus on appearances. Parents who behave in this manner exert a strong pull on their children that drains a child of his or her emotional resources. The residual effects of parental hunger on adolescent and adult personalities are often evidenced in an inward, self-protective orientation toward life, fear of success, severe anxiety states, or passive-aggressive tendencies (Firestone, 1990a).

Parental Withholding

Many parents inhibit or hold back their affection and other positive qualities from their loved ones, particularly their children, despite their best intentions to love and care for them. Because of their own defenses, they are often also unable to accept love and affection from their children. To be refractory to a child's loving responses is especially damaging in that it denies the child a sense of him- or herself as a feeling, loving person (Firestone & Catlett, 1999).

The child who is being withheld from is left feeling emotionally hungry and tends to form an anxious/ambivalent attachment to the withholding parent.[7] In many cases, children who are hurt in this way stop wanting affection (become self-denying). At the same time, they tend to hold back their natural feelings of love and affection toward their parents. They unconsciously block the flow of their natural feelings, increasingly rely on fantasy for satisfying their needs, and develop a defensive posture toward life for the purpose of keeping real experiences predictable and manageable and maintaining their psychological equilibrium, however negative it may be.

Attachment, Attunement, and Misattunement

The newborn needs close contact with a consistent caregiver to ensure its survival and adequate protection from separation experiences and other stimuli that might overwhelm its immature system. According to Bowlby (1982), attachment develops out of an evolutionarily determined behavioral system within the infant that functions to keep it in close proximity to an adult, protects it from harm and intense anxiety states, and later facilitates its exploration of the environment.

The formation of an optimal or secure attachment is largely dependent on the parents' responses to cues or signals from the infant indicating its needs. When parents are sensitively attuned to the baby, they adjust the intensity and emotional tone of their responses to accurately match the child's feeling state and needs. Obviously, no one can ever be completely consistent in adjusting his or her responses to these cues; in fact, research has indicated that attuned interactions occur in only one out of three of parent-infant exchanges (Siegel & Hartzell, 2003).

Interactions with well-meaning but emotionally immature parents who themselves have suffered a good deal of unresolved personal trauma and loss in their own upbringing are detrimental in innumerable ways to the healthy growth and development of children (Cassidy & Mohr, 2001; Main & Hesse, 1990). In general, parental deficiencies lead to both harmful, insensitive treatment and repeated failures to repair disruptions in attuned interactions between parent and child. These conditions intensify the child's feeling of isolation and fear of abandonment. In such circumstances, children are diverted from what would have been their natural developmental pathway and they go on to lead primarily defended lives.[8]

Bowlby (1988) proposed the concept of developmental pathways based on the biologist C. H. Waddington's (1957) theoretical model and distinguished it from the Freudian concept of libidinal phases. In explaining this concept, Bowlby wrote,

> At conception the total array of pathways potentially open to an individual is determined by the make-up of the genome. As development proceeds and structures progressively differentiate, the number of pathways that remain open diminishes.
>
> A principal variable in the development of each individual personality is, I believe, the pathway along which his attachment behavior comes to be organized and further that that pathway is determined in high degree by the way his parent-figures treat him, not only during his infancy but throughout his childhood and adolescence as well. (p. 65)

If a parent is able to successfully repair disruptions in attuned interactions with the child, the child gradually learns to regulate his or her emotions. Repair involves the parent acknowledging the disruption, taking responsibility for it, and providing a reasonable explanation for what happened that would validate the child's reality. The child is then able to make sense of his or her emotional reactions and can begin to construct a coherent narrative of the event. When parents admit their error and try to make restitution, their child is also less likely to blame him- or herself, idealize the parent, or internalize an image of being the "bad child."[9]

The Impact of Misattunement on the Child's Developing Brain

Preliminary studies in the neurosciences suggest that children as young as one year are able to accurately perceive a parent's purpose or intent from the parent's facial expression and tone of voice, perhaps even in the absence of other, more overt expressions of aggression (Cozolino, 2006; Schore, 1994, 2003a, 2003b; Siegel, 2001).[10] During a misattuned or otherwise frightening interaction with a parent, an infant can detect, through specialized cells in its brain (the mirror neuron system), the parent's emotional state and intentions at that moment in time (Iacoboni, 2007; Rizzolati, Fogassi, & Gallese, 2001).[11]

According to Badenoch (2008), "With the discovery and exploration of *mirror neurons* in the last decade, we are becoming aware of how we constantly embed within ourselves the intentional and feeling states of those with whom we are engaged" (p. 37). For example, D. Siegel (personal communication, September 4, 2009) speculated about what an infant or young child might experience during a fear-provoking interaction with an angry parent. Taking the role of the infant in this scenario, Siegel said,

> What this looks like from my mirror neuron point of view is you [the parent] come at me, really angry and you're terrifying me with your fury. Now I see your intention. You may not want this intention to be there, but it is. Your intention is to hurt me. Even though it's not your global intention, at that moment, you have it because of your own unresolved trauma. And I look at you and my mirror neuron grouping makes the assessment that the intention of this caregiver is to do me harm.
>
> What is a child supposed to do when his mirror neurons, like sponges, are soaking up the intention to be harmed by the one who's supposed to protect? He fragments. And in that fragmentation is dissociation of the usual continuity of the self.

Research studies in interpersonal neurobiology indicate how the child's developing mind adapts to a parent's feeling state and intentionality (Cozolino, 2006; Siegel, 2004; Siegel & Hartzell, 2003).[12] The data tend to support my (R. Firestone's) conceptualization of the process of introjection and its role in the transmission of negative parental attitudes, abusive child-rearing practices, and blatant or more subtle forms of neglect from one generation to the next.[13] It has become increasingly clear that the way parents interact (or fail to interact) with children becomes hardwired in their children's brains, often before they are even capable of formulating words to describe what they are experiencing (Schore, 2003a).

THE FORMATION OF THE SELF AND ANTI-SELF SYSTEMS

> The weak and undeveloped personality reacts to sudden unpleasure...by anxiety-ridden identification and by introjection of the menacing person or aggressor.
>
> —Sandor Ferenczi, "Confusion of Tongues Between Adults and the Child"

When parents are out of sync with the child—particularly when they become angry, punitive, or emotionally unavailable—the child stops identifying with him- or herself as the frightened, helpless victim and identifies instead with the angry or avoidant parent. This identification partly alleviates the child's fear, yet it also leads to a split in the personality portrayed by R. D. Laing (1960) as follows: "The splitting is not simply a temporary reaction to a specific situation of great danger, which is reversible when the danger is past. It is, on the contrary, a basic orientation to life" (p. 83).

During those interactions, which are terrifying from the child's perspective, children disconnect from themselves and cease to exist as a real self, as a separate entity.

In identifying with the punishing or neglectful parent, they incorporate not only the anger or resentment that is being directed toward them but also any other emotion the parent is feeling at the time, such as guilt or fear. The child takes in a complete representation or internal image of the parent's emotional state at that specific moment. The reason children incorporate these angry, hostile aspects of the parent into themselves is that it is too threatening for them to see the danger as coming from the very person they are dependent upon for survival. Because of their pressing need for love and their utter helplessness during their formative years, children must see their parents as adequate, good, or caring and concerned and must deny any of their inadequacies, weaknesses, or lack of caring and concern for their well-being.

Rather than acknowledge that they are at the mercy of an out-of-control or negligent parent, children come to see themselves as at fault, worthless, and bad (Arieti, 1974; Bloch, 1978; Harter, 1999). Similarly, rather than perceiving their parents as incapable of loving them, children come to see themselves as unlovable. This idealization of parents is an essential element of the self-parenting system; "to parent oneself successfully in fantasy, one must maintain the idealized image of one's parent" (Firestone, 1997a, p. 88).

Fonagy et al. (2002) have described this conceptualization of the defense of identifying with the aggressor in explaining how failures in parents' attunement or "affect-mirroring" lead to the formation of an "alien self" within the child. Fonagy has asserted,

> The alien self is present in all of us, because transient neglect is part of ordinary caregiving; it is pernicious when later experiences of trauma in the family or the peer group force the child to dissociate from pain by using the alien self to identify with the aggressor. Hence the vacuous self comes to be colonized by the image of the aggressor, and the child comes to experience himself as evil and monstrous.... [Later, there is a] vital dependence on the physical presence of the other as a vehicle for externalization [projective identification]. (p. 198)

In general, children incorporate their parents not as they are most of the time, but as they are at their worst.[14] When faced with parents' overt or covert aggression or indifference, children try to make the best adaptation possible in order to maintain some form of rationality. However, their efforts to remain intact produce a division within the self or personality (Firestone, 1997a) (see Figure 2.1).

We refer to this as the "division of the mind," a primary split between forces that represent the self and those that oppose it. These propensities can be conceptualized as the self system and the anti-self system, respectively. The two systems develop independently; both are dynamic and continue to evolve and change over time. They are susceptible to influence from significant people throughout one's adult life (Firestone, 1997b).

The self system consists of the unique characteristics of the individual, including biological, temperamental, and genetic traits, and his or her harmonious assimilation

Division of the Mind

Self System

Parental Nurturance/Genetic Predisposition/Temperament

Attunement, Affection, Control

Other factors: effect of positive experience and education on the maturing self system.

Greater Degree of Differentiation

Unique makeup of the individual–harmonious identification and incorporation of parent's positive attitudes and traits.

Personal Goals/Conscience

Realistic, Positive Attitudes Toward Self Realistic evaluation of talents, abilities, etc.… with generally positive/compassionate attitude toward self and others.	**Behaviors** Ethical behavior toward self and others
Goals Needs, wants, search for meaning in life	**Goal Directed Behavior**

Anti-Self System

Destructive Parental Behavior/Genetic Predisposition/Temperament

Misattunement, lack of affection, reject, neglect, hostility, permissiveness

Other Factors: Accidents, illnesses, traumatic separation

The Fantasy Bond

The Fantasy Bond (core defense) furthers a self-parenting process made up of both the helpless, needy child, and the self-punishing, self-nurturing parent. Either may be acted out in relationship context. The degree of reliance on this defense is proportional to the amount of damage sustained while growing up.

The Self-Parenting Process

Self-Punishing Voices		Self-Soothing Voices	
Voice Process	**Behaviors**	**Voice Process**	**Behaviors**
1. Critical thoughts toward self	Verbal attacks—a generally negative attitude toward self and others pre-disposing alienation	**1. Self-soothing attitudes**	Self-limiting or self-protective
2. Micro-suicidal injunctions	Actions contrary to one's own interest and goals, and one's own emotional/ physical health	**2. Microsuicidal injunctions (seductive/self-indulgent thoughts)**	Addictive Patterns Actions contrary to one's own interest and goals, and one's own emotional/ physical health
3. Suicidal injunctions-suicidal ideation	Actions that jeopardize one's health and safety; physical attacks, physical attacks on the self and actual suicide	**3. Aggrandizing thoughts toward self**	Narcissism/Vanity, acting superior to others and demanding they treat one as such, and punishing those who don't
		4. Suspicious, paranoid thoughts toward others	Alienation toward others & hostile attitudes toward others, aggressive behavior toward others

Figure 2.1 Division of the Mind

of the parents' positive attitudes and traits. Parents' warmth and nurturance, as well as their ability to repair misattunements, support the development of vital functions of the prefrontal cortex in the child's brain: body regulation, attunement, emotional balance, response flexibility, empathy, self-knowing awareness (insight), fear modulation, intuition, and morality (Siegel, 2007, 2010). The effects of ongoing psychological development, further education, and imitation of other positive role models throughout an individual's life span continue to contribute to the evolution of the self system.

One's personal goals—the basic needs for food, water, safety, and sex; the desire for social affiliation, achievement, and life-affirming activity; the expression of love, compassion, and generosity; and transcendent goals related to seeking meaning in life—are all aspects of the self system. Positive environmental influences allow the evolving individual to formulate his or her own value system and to develop the ability and courage to live with integrity—that is, according to his or her ethical principles.

The anti-self system refers to the accumulation of negative introjects—that is, the buildup of internalized parental hostility and cynicism that represents the defensive aspect of the personality. This alien self develops as a defensive response to the destructive side of parents' ambivalence: their rejection, hostility, neglect, and unresponsiveness. In addition, parents' emotional hunger, overprotectiveness, ignorance, and lack of understanding of a child's nature negatively affect the child's development. Moreover, many parents unconsciously dispose of traits they dislike in themselves by projecting them onto their children, and their children internalize these projections as part of their self-concept. The anti-self system is also affected by other negative events that can occur early in life: birth trauma, accidents, illnesses, traumatic separations, and the actual loss of a parent or sibling (Firestone & Firestone, in press).

The defensive process operating within the anti-self system is influenced primarily by interpersonal pain, which is reinforced and compounded by the suffering inherent in the human condition (e.g., poverty, economic recession, crime, natural disasters, illness, physical and mental deterioration, and death). Once the defensive solution is formed, people protect it at the expense of limiting their lives and goal-directed pursuits.

This antagonistic part of the personality predominates to varying degrees at different stages throughout the life span. Depending on which system or state of mind is ascendant in the personality—self or anti-self—a completely different point of view will be expressed. Individuals are very dissimilar when they feel like themselves, which is generally more relaxed and likable, than when they slip into the anti-self system and are more reactive, hostile, or toxic to those around them. Often when a person is under stress, there is a breakdown in the self system, and the anti-self prevails. As R. D. Laing (1960) observed,

> A most curious phenomenon of the personality . . . is that in which the individual seems to be the vehicle of a personality that is not his own. . . . There

> seem to be all degrees of the same basic process from the simple, benign observation that so-and-so "takes after his father," or "That's her mother's temper coming out in her," to the extreme distress of the person who finds himself under a compulsion to take on the characteristics of a personality he may hate and/or feel to be entirely alien to his own. (p. 62)

In this statement, Laing described the component of the anti-self that develops through the processes of introjection and imitation. To preserve the imagined fusion with the idealized parental figure, children unwittingly imitate their parents' undesirable traits and behaviors. The imitative process represents an attempt to cover over what would be a more realistic perception of parental weaknesses and inadequacies. In protecting their parents' image, children displace their parents' real inadequacies and negative traits onto other people and perceive them as more hostile or untrustworthy than they are. In addition, children tend to emulate and internalize their parents' negative, pessimistic views about life, which gradually correspond to their own distrust of others. Their identification with the idealized parent is strong, whether or not the family situation is frightening or punitive. However, the more that children feel powerless and victimized, the stronger their identification with their parents and their need to idealize them.

THE FANTASY BOND

Early in the developmental sequence, the infant experiences a primitive anxiety reaction when he or she is exposed to traumatic events or a sense of aloneness or separation. Some of these experiences are inevitable in childhood—for example, when the mother leaves the room for a few minutes to warm the baby's bottle. Lacking any realistic sense of time, the baby feels abandoned for what seems to be forever. Alone, hungry, and desperate, the infant screams in frustration, fear, and protest. The infant attempts to cope with the painful separation anxiety and hunger pangs by utilizing its emerging powers of imagination to create an internal image of the mother, or more specifically, the mother's breast, in its mind.

The reaction to excessive frustration, separation anxiety, and personal trauma is to seek fusion. The image of being merged with the mother, the fantasy bond, in some measure heals the fracture brought about by separation and alleviates anxiety and frustration by partially gratifying the infant's emotional and physical hunger (Firestone, 1985). Indeed, the antidote for real separation is imagined fusion.[15]

This fantasized connection, together with rudimentary self-nurturing, self-soothing behaviors, such as thumb-sucking or rubbing a favorite blanket, becomes part of a self-parenting process that leads to a false sense of self-sufficiency. Infants and young children are able to develop this posture of pseudoindependence and omnipotence because they have introjected an image of the good and powerful parent into the self and feel that they need nothing from the outside world. However, at the same time that they find comfort and security from the introjection of the parent, they have necessarily also incorporated the parent's rejecting attitudes and hostile views toward them and come to see themselves through unfriendly eyes.

The self-parenting process is composed of a self-nurturing component and a component that is self-accusatory and attacking. Both components derive their special character from the internalization of parental attitudes and responses. Children learn to treat themselves much as they were treated by their parents—that is, both nurturing themselves with self-aggrandizing thoughts and self-soothing addictive habit patterns and punishing themselves with self-critical thoughts and self-destructive behavior.

The degree to which the child, and later the adult, comes to rely on these self-parenting behaviors and fantasy processes is proportional to the degree of stress, frustration, and emotional pain that the child experienced during the formative years. Extensive research has shown that the cumulative number of aversive incidents (neglect, abuse, witnessing violence, poverty, etc.) experienced by children is directly proportional to the severity of their physical and mental health problems as adults. In one study, Felitti et al. (1998) reported "a strong graded relationship between the breadth of exposure to abuse or household dysfunction during childhood and multiple risk factors for several of the leading causes of death in adults" (p. 245). In addition, these researchers specified self-soothing addictive behaviors, including smoking, alcoholism, and drug abuse, as mediating factors between the original aversive experiences and elevated rates of early mortality.

The extent and specific kinds of maltreatment experienced by children may also be reflected in the specific types of attachment patterns they form with the parent or caregiver—for example, whether they develop an insecure/anxious, insecure/avoidant, or disorganized attachment to their caregiver (Mikulincer & Shaver, 2007). According to J. Solomon and George (2011), "A recent meta-analysis of the conditions under which disorganized attachments [considered as more pathogenic than two insecure categories] are most likely points strongly to families in which there has been maltreatment or where there is high cumulative stress" (p. 14).

The self-parenting process becomes the core psychological defense, and the child comes to be increasingly dependent on it as a way of compensating for whatever was missing in the primary relationship with his or her parents. The introjected parental image takes on the significance of a survival mechanism in the child's mind. It prevails as a part of the child's evolving personality and interferes with the emergence of a separate identity. Illusions of fusion that originally reduced the child's anxiety impair the adult's ability to differentiate from self-limiting internalized parental influences.

THE IMPACT OF THE CHILD'S EVOLVING AWARENESS OF DEATH

> The wish for fusion and merger denies the reality of separation and, thus, the reality of death.
>
> —James B. McCarthy, *Death Anxiety*

Early separation experiences and interpersonal pain in the family lead to the formation of psychological defenses to ward off anxiety, frustration, and distress. Later in the developmental sequence, these defenses are intensified and confirmed and become rigidified when the child first becomes aware of death. Usually between the ages of three and seven, children discover the fact of mortality—first their parents' and then their own (Firestone, 1994b).

The awareness of their parents' vulnerability to death affects young children in two ways: (1) On a survival level, the anticipated loss of the parental figure fills them with feelings of terror associated with being abandoned in their helpless state, unable to physically survive on their own. (2) On an emotional level, the prospect of losing the source of warmth, affection, and love evokes deep sadness and pain.

The anticipated death of one's parents is so traumatic that the child desperately relies on the fantasy bond to maintain an illusion of connectedness that gives him or her a sense of pseudoindependence and a perceived ability to deny the truth of his or her parents' ultimate fate.[16] Later, when children are faced with their own mortality and the fact that there is no recourse, the realization completely shatters their world (Firestone & Catlett, 2009a). Their illusion of self-sufficiency is destroyed, and they experience overwhelming anxiety. They are confronted with the tortuous truth that their life, which once seemed so permanent, is only temporary. Everything dies, the stars die, and so will the child. Death is separation for eternity. As Lifton (1979) wrote,

> Separation is the paramount threat from the beginning of life and can give rise, very early, to the rudiments of anxiety and mourning.... Still extremely dependent upon those who nurture him, the child continues for some time to equate death with separation. (p. 68)

Unconsciously, children deny the reality of their personal death by regressing to a previous stage of development, to a phase before death was a reality to them. While they accept the idea of death on an intellectual or conscious level, from a deeper psychological perspective they attempt to escape from a situation that they recognize as hopeless by holding on tenaciously to the familiar defensive solution. Thus, the fantasy bond or self-parenting process is strengthened and becomes more deeply entrenched as a core defense when the child confronts the death issue.[17]

Defenses Against Death Anxiety

In their attempts to deny or negate the fact of death, many children transfer their fears of dying into obsessive thoughts about bad guys or monsters that are out to harm them. Some children regress and become more infantile or engage in forms of magical thinking. Others become distrustful, hostile, or distant toward their parents and others. Perhaps more significant is the phenomenon that children learn to imitate the habitual, defensive behaviors and lifestyles that they observe their parents utilizing in an attempt to deny their own existential realities. For example, a child may emulate his or her parents' avoidance of death by adopting their belief in an afterlife or their belief that death only happens to old people or bad people or to people who don't take good care of themselves. They may sense their parents' reluctance to talk about the subject and become silenced themselves, suppressing their questions about the subject and eventually colluding with them in denying the reality of death.

The fantasy bond provides children with an illusion of immortality that helps dispel their existential terror. The imagined fusion with parents, as manifested in introjected parental traits, attitudes, and behaviors, remains the most powerful and effective means for denying awareness of death throughout an individual's life. Although these defenses come into play to prevent children's fears of death from surfacing, these feelings are still preserved in the unconscious. Whenever these imagined connections are threatened, the underlying death anxiety is reactivated. People tend to revert to a defensive posture before their anxiety becomes fully consciousness (Arndt, Greenberg, & Cook, 2002; Pyszczynski, Greenberg, & Solomon, 1999).[18]

In our experience, we have observed a direct relationship between death fears and attempts to reconnect with the introjected parent. The observable manifestations of this trend include (1) the individual beginning to exhibit some of the undesirable traits and behaviors of his or her parent; (2) the individual experiencing an increase in self-attacks and distrust of other people; (3) the individual feeling more like he or she did as a child, stuck in a familiar negative identity; and (4) the individual intensifying real-time contact with family members and tending to back away from close associations in his or her current life that have proven to be more respectful, warm, and loving.

Once children become conscious of mortality, their defenses go beyond an attempt to protect themselves from interpersonal hurt or rejection. Now, the core defense is also directed toward protecting against the anxiety and dread surrounding their newfound knowledge of death. From this point on, the principal fear underlying a person's resistance to change and differentiation is usually associated with the painful awareness of one's finite existence and essential aloneness in the world. How a person deals with this existential crisis is a primary determinant of the course of his or her life. The enemy of differentiation is the awareness of death.

The Core Conflict

There is a core conflict within each person that centers on the choice between contending with painful existential realities and avoiding them. The question is whether to live with emotional pain or to escape into an unreal world. We are all presented with this fundamental dilemma and face a no-win situation. The resolution of this conflict toward a more defended way of life has a profoundly detrimental effect on an individual's emotional health and overall functioning. First, there is a considerable loss of freedom and a diminution of personal experience. Second, anger, which is a natural response to frustration, shame, or anxiety, is obscured and tends to be internalized or projected outward. Internalized anger leads to self-denigration, whereas its projection onto others leads to a sense of victimization and counteraggression or eventually to a paranoid focus on other people or events.

Third, the defended individual is not well integrated and, as a result, cannot communicate honestly. For example, if people fail to acknowledge their genuine wants and priorities, then they deceive both themselves and others about their true intentions. If they fail to pursue the goals they claim to want, then their behavior contradicts their expressed wants. This form of internal inconsistency accounts for the prevalence of duplicitous or mixed messages in both personal communications and in society at large, statements that confuse each individual's sense of reality. Last, the defended person's life is distorted by a desperate clinging to addictive attachments and a reliance on self-soothing, self-nourishing habit patterns, which contribute to strong guilt reactions. Because defensive patterns spread and eventually become habitual, there is a progressive debilitation in broad areas of functioning. People not only lose energy and develop symptoms of distress, but they also lose the ability to identify the underlying causes of these symptoms (Firestone, 1997a).

In contrast, less defended, more differentiated individuals have a greater potential to experience all of their emotions, including an increased capacity to feel the joy and happiness of life, and a higher tolerance for intimacy. Yet at the same time, they have a heightened awareness of the inevitability of loss through death. They are also more vulnerable to the pain inherent in living and appear to be more sensitive to events that impinge upon their well-being. People who are relatively undefended feel more integrated, are better able to live more fully and authentically, and tend to be more humane toward others (Morrant & Catlett, 2008).

In contemplating the choice between living defensively and living with a minimal amount of defensiveness, one is faced with a number of salient questions: Why should one invest in close relationships and devote oneself to humane pursuits and transcendent goals when all will be lost in the end? Wouldn't it make more sense to put these disturbing matters aside and numb oneself to the realities of aging and death? Why not cut off these torturous feelings, defend oneself, and put ideas about death and dying out of one's mind?

The problem is that people cannot selectively avoid emotional pain and suffering without losing their real feeling and uniqueness as separate individuals. Making the defensive choice dehumanizes the individual and, as noted, results in a corresponding loss of personal identity. In addition, people cannot be innocently defended; their defenses hurt other people, especially those closest to them.

SUMMARY

Each individual is unique. Differentiation from the negative attitudes and undesirable traits of one's parents and other significant figures in one's childhood is essential for optimal functioning. In the course of a person's development, experiences of personal trauma and separation anxiety lead to fantasies of fusion and psychological defense formation. This defensive fantasy process is reinforced by the child's developing awareness of death. From that time forward, death anxiety is the driving force behind the defense system; as such, it presents the core resistance to change in psychotherapy and to movement toward higher levels of differentiation.

No parental environment is perfect, and families vary considerably in terms of the emotional damage they impose on their offspring. The more trauma children experience, the more they rely on the fantasy bond and imagined fusion. In this sense, parental misattunement, particularly during the early developmental years, is a primary determinant of how much an individual will suffer from the presence of psychopathology and from an inability to differentiate.

The imagined connection to one's parents leads to the incorporation and introjection of the parents' points of view. Whereas parents' positive traits and attitudes are easily assimilated and identified with, the negative aspects of their point of view function as an alien element of the personality, the anti-self system. This malevolent portion of the self is maladaptive and self-destructive and, at its extreme end, suicidal.

The resultant effect of these diverse forms of programming on the ability to maintain one's unique outlook and set of values is powerfully undermining. Few people survive the process and succeed in remaining creative, independent, and inner-directed versus outer-directed. Yet to fulfill one's personal destiny and to make full use of one's life and lifetime, one must make every effort to differentiate. One must brave the anxiety and sense of aloneness that are inevitable in living as a separate individual; the reward of doing so is experienced in maintaining a liking and respect for oneself and in the satisfaction of living an honest, autonomous, and meaningful life.

3

THE VOICE

Our life is what our thoughts make it.

—Marcus Aurelius, *Meditation*

The concept of the voice refers to malevolent internal thought processes and attitudes toward self and other people that oppose the self-realization of the individual. These attitudes and feelings are the antithesis of a unique and positive self-differentiation. Voices relate to destructive ideation that criticizes and punishes the individual and maintains negative, cynical, and hostile attitudes toward others.

When confronted with intolerable psychological pain, the child tends to fragment or depersonalize in an attempt to avoid complete ego disintegration. As described in the previous chapter, the anti-self system refers to an alien element of the personality that evolves from parents' negative attitudes and personality characteristics that were incorporated under stressful conditions during the formative years. James Grotstein (1981) depicted this rupture of the self and the resultant effects on one's personality and life as follows: "'Split-off' really means that a part of one's being has undergone alienation, mystification, mythification, and re-personification—in effect, has become someone else, an alien presence within" (p. 11).

People are reluctant and frightened to be aware of the essential division within their personalities. They are threatened to discover that they have irrational, destructive thoughts and derisive attitudes toward themselves and others that conflict with their basic orientation toward life. Rather than recognize this split within the self, they accept the internal voice as their own point of view. Unaware and unwilling to tolerate this lack of integration, they tend to compromise their basic aliveness, spontaneity, and individuality and conduct their lives in a manner that is largely dictated by the incorporated voice process (Firestone, 1997b).

THE CONCEPT OF THE VOICE

A man about to give a speech starts thinking, "You're going to make a fool of yourself. You're going to sound stupid. Who wants to listen to what you have to say anyway?"

A woman preparing for a date tells herself, "What makes you think he'll like you? You'd better think of something interesting to talk about or he'll be bored."

During sex, a man thinks, "She really doesn't like making love with you. You're so awkward."

An alcoholic tells himself, "What's wrong with taking another drink? You've had a hard day. You deserve it." Later, in the throes of a hangover, he thinks, "You weak-willed jerk. You let everyone down again. You have no self-control."

A woman checks into a high-rise hotel, steps onto the balcony to look at the view and thinks to herself, "What if you fall? What if you jumped off?"

In each case, a seemingly innocuous thought process affected the person's actions. The man preparing to give a speech felt increasingly nervous as he took the podium and stumbled over his first few statements. The woman who experienced self-doubts about her upcoming date felt awkward and was subdued when the couple met. The man making love did have difficulty sexually after running himself down as a man. And the woman in the hotel did step back from the edge even though she was barely conscious of the internal warning.

These examples represent only the tip of an iceberg, because there are more serious voices and outright aggression toward the self that exist below the surface. The voice is often experienced as a running commentary in one's mind that interprets interactions and events in ways that cause pain and distress. It explains situations in pessimistic terms based largely on painful experiences that occurred in an individual's past. The voice is analogous to a lens or filter that casts a gloomy light on the world.

Much of the distress and pain that people suffer is not so much caused by the actual occurrences as by what they are telling themselves about their experiences. These self-attacks or voices vary along a continuum of intensity, ranging from mild self-reproach to strong self-accusations and suicidal ideation. The pattern of destructive thinking about the self predisposes microsuicidal and suicidal actions. Self-destructive behavior, like self-destructive thinking, exists on a continuum that ranges from self-denial, self-defeating behavior, and substance abuse to direct actions that cause bodily harm.

As noted in Chapter 1, our empirical research indicated a close relationship between internal voices and self-destructive lifestyles (Firestone & Firestone, 2006, 2008a, 2008b). The findings revealed that people have two diametrically opposed views of themselves, their career goals, and their interpersonal world. They have a point of view that reflects their natural strivings and aspirations (e.g., their desire for affiliation with others, their drive to be sexual, and their urge to be creative); at the same time, they hold an opposing point of view that reflects their tendencies toward self-limitation and self-destruction. The alien view also includes cynicism and hostility toward others. Both types of negative attitudes are moderated by the voice process.

DEFINITION OF THE VOICE

The voice refers to the language of the defensive process. It is a well-integrated pattern of negative thoughts that is at the core of an individual's maladaptive behavior. It can be thought of as "an overlay on the personality that is *not* natural or harmonious, but learned or imposed from without" (Firestone, 1988, p. 33). In defining the voice as basically negative and reflective of the anti-self system, we exclude from the concept positive thoughts or attitudes about oneself, creative thinking processes, constructive planning, and any realistic self-appraisal. Although the prescriptions of the voice can at times seem to be aligned with moral principles, the process is not primarily concerned with values and ideals. The voice does not have a constructive influence on a person's morality. Instead, it interprets moral standards and value systems in an authoritarian manner for the purpose of self-attack and recrimination. It transforms normal ethical concerns into rigid attitudes and dispenses harsh punishment for any infraction (Firestone, 1997a).

Even seemingly positive self-nurturing voices that may appear on the surface to be supportive are indications that an individual is fragmented or removed from him- or herself. For example, thoughts supporting vanity or an inflated self-image represent a compensation for deeper feelings of inferiority and a negative conception of self, which are also mediated by the voice. When destructive thought processes take precedence over rational thinking, the self can become the object of a false buildup and an attack.

In *The Divided Self,* R. D. Laing (1960) described the nature of this largely malevolent "observing self" and its origins in childhood:

> This *identification of the self with the phantasy of the person by whom one is seen* may contribute decisively to the characteristics of the observing self. . . . This observing self often kills and withers anything that is under its scrutiny. The individual has now a persecuting observer in the very core of his being. (p. 126)

The voice has a dual focus. It not only serves the function of attacking the self, but it is also directed toward attacking others. Just as individuals have a split view of themselves, they possess two opposing views of the significant people in their lives. In general, negative views of others correlate with one's self-critical attitudes. In exploring the dual nature of the voice, we have observed that whenever people were basing their actions on a hostile view of themselves, their interactions with loved ones tended to be angry, intrusive, or provoking. As our study progressed, it became increasingly evident that harsh, judgmental views of other people as expressed by the voice correlated with self-attacks (Firestone, 1988).

The voices we are referring to are not experienced as actual auditory hallucinations, as in psychosis, but instead represent an identifiable system of critical and aggressive attitudes, which, when accessed in the voice format, take the form of a negative dialogue about or toward the person. These voices may be conceptualized as a way of talking to or coaching oneself as though from an external point of view (Firestone, 1988). The content and sources of the voices as they exist within the personality are made up of (1) the internalization of parents' (and other significant figures in one's early environment—siblings, relatives, teachers, peers) destructive attitudes toward oneself and others; (2) an imitation of one or both parents' maladaptive defenses and views about life (relationships in general, religious beliefs, political ideologies, etc.); and (3) a defensive approach to life based on emotional pain experienced during one's formative years (Firestone & Firestone, in press).

When people verbalize these voices or self-attacks in the second person, the amount of aggression they express toward themselves contrasts with their affect when they simply enumerate their self-criticisms in the first person. As they express themselves in voice therapy, participants frequently blurt out vicious self-accusations in a powerful, passionate language that is accompanied by strong anger and deep sadness, often including intense, primal crying. In some instances, the verbal condemnations are actual duplications of phrases or sentences people's parents had verbalized. At other times, the self-criticisms portray the emotional atmosphere in which people were raised and correspond with the images they had of themselves in their families. Usually, individuals themselves make the association between the voice's brutal attacks and the covert or overt malice that was directed toward them at times as children.

One woman who was recently laid off because of company cutbacks began by expressing her voice attacks calmly: "You're such a failure. Look, you can't even keep a job. Sure, they said it was because of cutbacks; but the real truth is that you weren't good enough!" Gradually, her verbalization accelerated, and, directing an angry diatribe against herself, she yelled, "What made you think you could make it in the business world? You can't; you don't have what it takes! And now everyone knows it! You just humiliated yourself in front of everybody. Just go away and hide, just get rid of yourself!"

IDENTIFYING THE VOICE

There are several distinct methods a person can use to become aware of unconscious or barely conscious voice attacks. One approach is to participate in an ongoing voice therapy group (Firestone & Catlett, 2009b; Firestone, Firestone, & Catlett, 2003). As participants listen to others verbalize *their* voice attacks, they become aware of their own self-attacks and voices. They tend to identify closely with both the content and emotions that are being expressed.

Because this type of therapy experience is not always practical or available, we can suggest other ways in which an individual can work to identify the destructive voices that influence his or her life (Firestone, Firestone, & Catlett, 2002).[1] For example, a person can recognize what he or she is criticizing him- or herself about and express these criticisms in the voice therapy format. Instead of saying, "I'm a failure" or "I'm inadequate," the individual would say, "You're a failure" or "You're inadequate," to himself or herself.

Another method for uncovering voices is to formulate, in words, the angry or critical point of view of one or the other parent about various aspects of one's life. As people articulate what they imagine their father or mother would think about the fundamental issues in their life, they become conscious of the voices that lead to personal torment. In this exercise, they come to recognize how they are critical, disapproving, or even hating of themselves.

Another effective strategy for revealing the voice is to become aware of changes in one's mood or state of mind. A sudden or gradual transition to feeling bad or depressed may indicate that the process of self-attack has been activated. People can slip into a bad mood or become upset following a seemingly innocuous, everyday interaction. The fact that they shift from feeling relatively content, optimistic, or relaxed to feeling irritable, down, or disturbed is an indication that they have begun to interpret a situation through the filter of the voice.

Simply realizing that one is involved in a self-punishing process is helpful for beginning to counteract the effects of the voice. However, it is also beneficial to recall the time period when one's feelings changed and to look into the situation or personal interaction that was taking place then. In reviewing the details of the incident, people can try to recollect what they were telling themselves about themselves or about another person.

Thus, people can examine how they are living and focus their attention on aspects of their personal and professional lives that are causing them particular concern or distress. They can then investigate what they have been telling themselves about these issues and events. People can also look for contradictions between their actions and their stated goals. These discrepancies are often caused by unconscious, destructive attitudes toward themselves. By identifying the voices that are influencing their behavior, people are able to gain insight into areas of their lives where they have been having trouble.

For example, a man who had been progressing well in therapy reported that he had begun to feel somewhat down at some point during the previous week. He traced his change in mood to a conversation he had had with his partner's mother several days prior to the session. His therapist inquired as to what he might have been telling himself either during the conversation or afterward, including any self-attacks or criticisms of his partner's mother. He said,

> My partner and I were having lunch with his mother, and eventually the conversation got around to her asking if she could borrow some money from us. Looking back, I realize I had so many different reactions. I had a lot of nasty thoughts toward her, which I am ashamed of. But if I say them as a voice, they are: "God, listen to her complain! She's such a victim of life. Don't give her a dime. Give her an inch and she'll take a mile in relation to money. She'll take advantage of you. And she's always intruding into your life. What a meddling bitch! She's always trying to get in the middle of everything. If you let her have her way, she'd end up ruining your relationship!"
>
> I recognize those thoughts as being so much like the way my mother viewed people, and she acted them out freely. She didn't trust anyone; she thought everyone was out to get her. And she treated people with disrespect. I remember her telling me how certain people had taken advantage of her and ruined her life. Even though there are times when my partner's mother is intrusive and tries to interfere in our lives, she's certainly not as horrible as my voice makes her out to be.
>
> And then, after I had that angry reaction to her, I started being critical of myself. If I said my thoughts as voices, they would be, "You're such a bastard! Why can't you be nice to her? Can't you take pity on her for once?

> Don't you have any feelings? Where's your heart? So what if she wants to borrow some money? You can afford it. You're so tight." It's interesting, but that's what my mother always accused me of. I remember her telling me how cold-hearted and tight I was.

Events That Trigger Self-Attacks

Both negative and positive events in life can trigger destructive thoughts and feelings of self-hatred. Illness, financial setbacks, failure at work, and rejection are situations that activate self-accusatory thoughts and feelings. With regard to the negative events, personal rejection plays the most significant part in people's adverse reactions in relation to themselves. In essence, conditions of rejection and abandonment typically turn an individual against him- or herself. Rather than face the angry and aggressive feelings toward the person who is rejecting, one's anger is often turned on oneself. The threat of loss causes people to redirect anger inward in a subtle, yet desperate, attempt to hold on to the person who is rejecting them. This process starts in childhood, when, as explained in Chapter 2, children internalize hostile, rejecting attitudes toward themselves rather than recognize the negative characteristics of their parents.

In considering the positive events, an unusual success, accomplishment, or special fulfillment in a personal relationship can precipitate strong self-attacks and guilt feelings. Significant positive transitions and changes in one's circumstances often precipitate the voice process. When people are actively pursuing their personal or vocational goals, they may be relatively free of voice attacks for an initial period of time. However, when they become self-conscious about positive changes in their life, particularly if they have surpassed a rival or a parental figure, they tend to turn on themselves and "interpret events and circumstances in a manner that disrupts the ongoing movement" (Firestone, 1988, p. 39). The more aware individuals become of expanding their life experience, they more they are susceptible to self-critical thoughts, warnings, and dire predictions of the future—for example, "Better be careful. Things can't go on like this. The ax is bound to fall!" Indeed, any event or experience that arouses guilt and separation anxiety may trigger voice attacks.

Projections Based on the Voice Process

Recognizing the division within oneself is often so disconcerting and painful that, in an unconscious attempt to disown one's voice attacks, a person may project them onto other people and then feel criticized by them. In general, individuals find it easier to fight against an outside enemy than to struggle against an internal one (Firestone, Firestone, & Catlett, 2002). However, left unchallenged, this projection process becomes increasingly maladaptive and leads to basic misperceptions and distortions of reality; in turn, these can lead to problems in one's personal relationships and work situations. Thus, it becomes essential for people to recognize that they often project their own self-attacks onto others.

In a discussion group, Shawn revealed that he was insecure when it came to women and dating.

> I'm fine when I'm around my friends; I'm totally myself, even when I'm around my women friends. But whenever I go out on a date or start to have that kind of interest in a woman, I am a mess! I absolutely know that she's thinking negative things about me. I don't just think that I'm imagining it; I'm completely sure of it. So I thought it would help for me to say what I believe she is thinking as a voice:
>
> "You are so immature and boyish. I would never take someone like you seriously as a boyfriend. I could be friends with you, but I could never consider you as a real man. You're like a little kid! The thought of being sexual with you is out of the question. As a matter of fact, it's disgusting."
>
> What I am saying really feels like the way women see me. It's hard for me to see these attacks as coming from me, as coming from what I think about myself. What are my attacks on myself as a man? "You're not a man. You're weak. You're short; you're inadequate. You don't have what other men have. You don't have what women are attracted to. You are too small! You're too small to satisfy a woman!"
>
> Those attacks feel more at the heart of the matter for me. And they have nothing to do with women. They are what my father thought about himself and what he thought about me. He was small and he ridiculed me constantly about being short. The truth is, with all of this going on in my head, I don't have a clue about what women really think of me.

DIMENSIONS OF THE VOICE

The voice acts to bind adults emotionally to their parents by supporting the internal parent that continues to advise, direct, control, and punish them. As Fairbairn (1952) emphasized, "No one ever becomes completely emancipated from the state of infantile dependence...and there is no one who has completely escaped the necessity of incorporating early objects" (p. 56). Significant aspects of the voice process also pertain to the quality of the relationship and patterns of attachment one developed with parents during the formative years.

There are distinct similarities between the voice and defensive aspects of internal working models described by attachment theorists (Bowlby, 1980; Bretherton, 1996; Bretherton, Ridgeway, & Cassidy, 1990; Fonagy et al., 2002; Main, Kaplan, & Cassidy, 1985).[2] Critical views of the self, distrust of others, and expectations of rejection resulting from early experiences with insensitive, misattuned, or rejecting parents tend to become core beliefs or schema that have an effect on one's behaviors in adult relationships. Findings from attachment research (Maier, Bernier, Pekrun, Zimmermann, & Grossmann, 2004; Pietromonaco & Barrett, 2000; Shaver & Clark, 1994; Shaver, Collins, & Clark, 1996) have shown how internal working models mediate people's attachment patterns and how they influence the way that each partner interacts in an intimate relationship (Mikulincer & Shaver, 2007).

Other researchers have investigated specific cognitive and emotional processes that make up these models. For example, "Collins and Read (1994) have suggested that working models shape behavior primarily by shaping the way people think and feel about themselves and their relationships" (Collins & Allard, 2004, loc. 1603). Some of the cognitive processes that comprise internal working models include "selective attention, memory encoding and retrieval, social construal, and emotional response tendencies" (loc. 1630–1632).

Imitation of a Parent's Psychological Defenses, Undesirable Traits, and Toxic Behaviors

As noted, we not only incorporate parents' critical, hostile thoughts toward ourselves as well as toward other people, but we also imitate parents' psychological defenses, undesirable traits, and toxic behavior as well as incorporate their basic attitudes toward life and their overall point of view.

Carla, 35, was typically a generous person who enjoyed thinking of ways to help her family and friends. Recently, she became aware that she had started feeling stingy—for example, she felt resentful when asked for small favors. She was ashamed that her immediate response was to want to say an emphatic "No!" Carla was motivated to explore the reasons for her uncharacteristic tightness. She recognized that this recent trend toward negativism was similar to her mother's ungenerous, withholding way of being.

In a discussion group session, Carla examined this connection and the underlying attitudes that influenced her actions.

> Here's a typical example of how my mother was: she was a good cook but any time we said we liked a particular dish she had cooked, she would hardly ever prepare that dish again. The more my mother was praised for a particular dinner, the less frequently she would prepare it, especially when we asked for it. The household joke between my father, my brother and me was to never compliment her on a meal we liked. Sure enough, it worked, because she would make that meal again. She was that way about everything: if we liked it or wanted it, she stopped offering it.
>
> It's obvious that I carry some of that with me today. At first, I thought it was just procrastination, but then I realized that it was more than that. If my husband and kids liked something I did, I would put off doing it again. I began to see that I have been procrastinating more and more these days and that my procrastinations are very pointed. I can see that I have been doing it with friends, too. And when I think of the voices behind it, they start out sounding sort of reasonable like, "Your request is an interruption. I don't have time for you now!" Then it gets angrier, like, "Don't you tell me what to do! You have no right! Stop interrupting me! I can't be bothered with

> you! What's the matter with you? Why me? If you want it so bad, go get it yourself. Get out of my space, don't BUG me!"
>
> While I was saying that voice, I realized that I was saying exactly what my mother would have said to us. I really see how my behavior is like hers in so many of these instances. And I haven't been aware of it. It causes me so much sadness to think of how I was treated by her and to think of how I am treating the people I care about the same way. It's not the way that I want to be with the people I love.

Introjection of a Parent's Overall Point of View and Basic Attitudes Toward Life

Marty, age 55, spoke about feeling discouraged and old. He was overweight and out of shape. He was divorced and lived alone, and he said that, basically, all he did was go to work and then sit at home and watch TV. In a group, he explored what his voices were telling him about his current situation.

> "What are you doing here? What are you complaining about? You're overweight? What's the big deal? You look like a man your age is supposed to look. You're out of shape? What? Do you think you're still young? Face it; you're old. You're too old to play sports anymore. You want a girlfriend? Those days are over, buddy! So just stop whining and complaining. Look at how I lived my life! I wasn't running around making a fool out of myself. I accepted the way my life was when I was 50. What are you talking about improving it? It's too late; accept it."
>
> Wow! I had no idea that those thoughts were going on in my head. They totally express my father's philosophy about life: by the time you're 50, you're stuck with the cards that life has dealt you. I was very aware that as he got older he had no interests. He wasn't at all active. And he had no sex life with my mother; that was obvious. That's how I have ended up living.

In the course of identifying the negative thoughts that supported their undesirable traits, participants in our study learned why and how they acted out toxic personality traits in everyday interactions. As they became aware of the voices that reflected their parents' attitudes about life, they gained insight into the connection between their parents' attitudes and the views they had incorporated as their own. Becoming conscious of the dimensions of the voice enabled people to regain feelings of compassion for themselves and to begin to alter their negative traits on an action level.

The Voice Supports the Self-Parenting Process

The voice controls both components of the self-parenting process: the self-protective, self-nourishing, self-aggrandizing component and the self-hating, self-punitive component. Voices that are self-nurturing have overtones similar to those expressed by an overprotective parent—for example, cautioning, directing, advising, controlling, and praising an individual in a way that ostensibly has his or her best interests at heart. For example, some common self-protective prescriptions are

> Why stick your neck out? You'll only get hurt in the long run.
> Be careful; you can't trust people. People are just out for themselves.
> She's just interested in you for your money.
> Why work so hard? You're not appreciated anyway.

Some self-nurturing prescriptions are

> What's wrong with taking another drink or two?
> Go ahead and eat that doughnut!
> You're under a lot of pressure. Smoke a cigarette; it will relax you.

Often when these prescriptions are acted on, especially those that encourage addictive behaviors, they are followed by voice attacks saying,

> You're so weak. You have no willpower.
> You're never going to change.
> You might as well give up on yourself.

Thoughts that build up a sense of self-importance—voices of vanity—function as a compensation for low self-esteem and feelings of inferiority:

> You're indispensible to your company. Look at how much you've contributed!
> You're smarter than other people.
> You can do anything you set your mind to.

Self-protective, self-nurturing, and grandiose voices have an adverse effect on an individual's well-being. They are not expressions of concern; rather, they are manifestations of self-limiting, self-denying, and self-hating attitudes and have an underlying tone that is malicious.

Throughout a person's life, the self-punishing aspect of the voice process acts as a malevolent and disapproving parent. At times, self-attacks expressed by individuals in our study escalated into injunctions to hurt the self. These types of voices are obvious and apparent in suicidal individuals who exist in a trancelike state, besieged by negative attitudes, self-destructive ideology, and intent to do bodily harm.

> I made a mistake at work last week. It was minor and I corrected it right away. There were no consequences as a result of my mistake. But by the weekend, I realized that I was going crazy in my head about it. Even though it had been resolved, I was obsessing about what I had done. That made me think that I must be having voices about it. So, what would they be?

"You fucked up, you know. Sure it was a little mistake. There is no such thing as a little mistake! Failure is failure! And what about next time? Next time it will be a bigger mistake. You are on your way to failure! You're going to fuck up this job!"

This makes me think about my mother. She was constantly driving herself and all of us kids to be successful. She wanted us to be super-achievers. To get the highest marks. There was absolutely no room for error in her world. The attack gets even stronger: "You are going to humiliate yourself and you're going to humiliate me and your family! You are bringing us shame! [Loud, rageful yelling.] You little shit! You don't deserve to live! You should just get out of here, get rid of yourself!"

What's so amazing to me is that I have tried really hard to be different from my mother; I have made a conscious effort to not put pressure on myself. And I have been different from her, especially at work. But I realize that I still have her voice in my head telling me that I'd better not fail.

The Voice Supports the Fantasy Bond

The voice process operates as a secondary defense that supports the primary defense, the fantasy bond. As such, the voice reinforces fantasies of fusion with an internalized parent that directs, controls, and punishes. Although the fantasy bond is developed in the family of origin, it is extended and replicated in adult associations and is a major force in couple and family relationships (Firestone, 1985, 1987). In that sense, fantasies of fusion with the new significant figures in one's life are as strong and as debilitating as the original fantasy bond.[3] These new bonds act to maintain an equilibrium between the past and the present and to protect the status quo at the expense of a better life. The voice supports each aspect of the fantasy bond: (1) the idealization of parents and family; (2) negative attitudes toward the self; and (3) the projection of parents' negative traits onto other people.

Idealization of Parents and Family

Most people tend to idealize their parents as part of the primary defense, a process that occurs at the cost of harboring negative attitudes toward self. As children, they believe that even if their parents are punitive or rejecting, it is not because they (the parents) are inadequate or malevolent but because they (the children) are bad. This idealization is reflected in voices of a superior internalized parent:

I always said you wouldn't amount to anything.
You were always just a joke. No one else will take you seriously either.
I told you that you were stupid. What makes you think you'll be able to understand this?
You are basically unlovable; that's what's wrong with you. No one can ever love you.

As part of the idealization process, people accept their parents' verbal protestations of love and concern at face value. For example, "Your father really loves you; he just doesn't know how to show it." These translate into rationalizations and feelings of guilt that people carry with them in the form of a voice telling them,

> Look how much we've done for you! You are so selfish and ungrateful.
> What did you ever do for us? And now you're going off to live your own life with no concern for us.
> Everyone thinks that we are wonderful people. There is nothing wrong with us; obviously, the problem is you!

To compensate for feelings of helplessness and loneliness, children take some comfort in identifying with the "good" parent, and their vanity is stroked by belonging to a "good" family. Identification with the image of one's family as strong, right, and superior to other families represents the child's intense need for a sense of security. As noted, vanity is also an attempt to alleviate inner feelings of inadequacy and badness. Voices that represent this type of idealization are

> The car our family drives is better than other families' cars.
> We belong to the good political party; the other one is bad and will ruin the country.
> Our religion is the right religion; anyone who adheres to a different religion is a strange kind of person.
> Our family's ethnic background makes us superior to other families.

The idealization of parents is supported by many conventional views that prevail in society, such as unconditional parental love, implicit beliefs that children belong to their parents, and the tenet that parents should always be respected. (See Chapter 5, this volume.) The assumption that parents have proprietary rights over their children has its source in the illusion of connection between parent and child. Societal views promote voices such as

> What is wrong with you? You should respect your parents.
> Who are you to question your parents' love for you?
> How can you think that your parents weren't acting in your best interest?
> Mothers are innately nurturing and loving toward their children.

Voices not only support this idealization process as a part of the original fantasy bond in the family, but they go on to support it in couple relationships. When people exhibit hostility toward themselves and maintain a distorted self-image, they are usually insecure and desperate in their personal relationships. Just as they idealized their parents in order to retain a sense of safety and security, people build up their mates and tend to exaggerate their positive qualities. The need for security compels a person to form an imagined connection or fantasy of love with their partner, even in a situation where real love is absent and the relationship is empty or dysfunctional. Voices that support the idealization of a partner in a relationship are

> What is she doing with you? She is too good for you.
> You will never be able to hang on to someone as good as him.
> Something's going wrong between you. It must be your fault, because she is much better at relating than you are.

Over time, as partners come to see each other's weaknesses and foibles, they become disillusioned and disappointed in one another. When the idealization is shattered, each develops critical and rejecting attitudes toward the other. In fact, anything that fractures the idealization disturbs the security of the fantasy bond, which, in turn, leads to anxiety and hostility between the partners.

Negative Attitudes Toward Self

The idealization of the parents leads to deprecating feelings about the self (Arieti, 1974; Bloch, 1978, 1985; Firestone, 1985; Oaklander, 1978, 2006). As noted in Chapter 2, destructive thoughts and attitudes toward oneself are inextricably tied to an internalized exaggerated positive image of one's parents. Maintaining a negative self-concept predisposes inwardness and a defensive orientation. Examples of voices that lead to low self-esteem are

> You're a loser.
> You can't do anything right.
> You're different from other people.
> You don't fit in; you don't belong here.

Voice attacks also predict rejection by others. The anticipated rejection justifies avoidant behavior and interferes with developing and maintaining close personal relationships. Anticipations of rejection often become a part of a negative internal working model that develops in response to experiences of deprivation, rejection, or indifference in an early attachment relationship. These negative expectations regulate the person's beliefs about, and attitudes toward, him- or herself and others and thereafter shape his or her style of relating (dismissing, preoccupied, or fearful) in a new attachment relationship. For example, Bretherton (1996) found,

> If the parent has frequently rejected the infant's bids for comfort or interfered with the infant's exploration, he or she is later likely to construct an internal working model of self as unworthy or incompetent and a complementary working model of the parent as rejecting. (p. 5)[4]

These negative attitudes toward self and others prevent people from feeling vulnerable. When they have been hurt in a relationship, their voices warn them not to take a chance on being hurt again, further reinforcing their feelings of worthlessness.

The Projection of Parents' Negative Traits Onto Others

To preserve the idealized image of their parents, children may dispose of their parents' actual negative traits by projecting them onto the world at large, particularly onto other people. As adults, their experience continues to be distorted by their projections. They tend to twist the attitudes and intentions of others and respond to them with negative or fearful expectations. This propensity to project the undesirable traits of the parents onto other persons is especially evident in couples' relationships. For example:

> He isn't attracted to you.
> Don't trust her; she doesn't mean what she is saying to you.
> He doesn't value you.
> She is insensitive to you.

Eventually, people succeed in provoking the very treatment they fear or expect; they evoke negative responses similar to those they experienced in their original family. Indeed, one of the primary reasons relationships fail has to do with the self-critical attitudes that each person brings to the relationship. In troubled relationships, both partners are often responding to voices that depreciate and devalue them and make them feel bad or alienated from each other.

Exposure or feedback directed toward any of the three aspects of the fantasy bond—the idealization of parents and family, maintaining a negative self-concept, and the displacement of negative parental traits onto other people—challenges the defensive process and is usually perceived as a threat. In therapy sessions, resistance is often mobilized whenever these challenges arise, and they must be worked through to achieve a successful psychotherapy.

SUMMARY

Negative voices represent an internal enemy that influences much of people's unnecessary pain and frustration. Incorporated critical and self-destructive attitudes play a significant part in a person's maladaptive responses to life circumstances. People's decisions, when based on the voice, are neither rational nor in their interest.[5] When the voice predominates the thinking process, individuals turn their backs on their own motives and wants. Listening to the voice and believing its warnings interfere with self-expression and diminish rather than enhance one's sense of personal identity (Firestone, 1988). Before people learn to identify the internalized parental prescriptions that guide them, they find it difficult or impossible to differentiate their real wants and desires from the destructive prescriptions of their voices.

In a therapy setting, separation theory and voice therapy encourage movement toward differentiation because they challenge core defenses, strengthen a person's self system, and lead to a gradual relinquishing of the voice as a prescription for living. The next chapter describes the specific techniques of voice therapy: identifying the contents of the voice's malevolent counsel, expressing the associated feelings, understanding the source of one's self-attacks, and taking concerted action against its flawed advice. The therapist who practices voice therapy must be particularly sensitive to the self system (clients' unique points of identity) in order to help clients give appropriate value and importance to their existence.

The significant aspects of the process that lead to increased differentiation and a less defended lifestyle include: (1) mastering one's self-attacks; (2) controlling addictive, self-defeating, and self-destructive behaviors advocated by the voice, thereby weakening the influence of the anti-self system; (3) learning to satisfy one's wants and to fulfill one's goals in the real world; and (4) developing a coherent narrative about one's personal history and constructing a life plan based on one's own values and point of view. In applying our approach to psychotherapy, consider the major goals to be helping clients remain vulnerable and fully open to their experience and feelings, assisting them in developing the capacity to respond appropriately and with feeling to both positive and negative events in life, and supporting them in their pursuit of a free and independent existence.

4

VOICE THERAPY

> The voice process becomes an autonomous but alien governor of the mind, a ghostly and ghastly inner officialdom that runs almost every aspect of our lives. It gives an illusion of security but we do not so much live as are lived by the voice process.
>
> —Chris Morrant, review of *Creating a Life of Meaning and Compassion*

SEPARATION THEORY

The theoretical approach underlying voice therapy is referred to as separation theory because it focuses on breaking with destructive fantasy bonds and parental introjects, thereby facilitating movement toward individuation (Firestone, 1997a). Separation, as conceptualized here, is different from isolation or withdrawal; rather, it involves the preservation of a strong identity and distinct boundaries while simultaneously maintaining close relationships with others. In contrast, the undifferentiated individual lives an inward existence characterized by imagined fusion with another or others that necessarily limits his or her capacity for self-expression and self-fulfillment.

Separation theory is a broadly based, coherent system of concepts and hypotheses that integrates psychoanalytic and existential systems of thought.[1] As noted, the conceptual model explains how early interpersonal pain and separation anxiety lead to the formation of defenses and how these defenses are reinforced and elaborated when the child becomes aware of his or her personal mortality. Psychoanalysts and object relations theorists have described the impact of interpersonal trauma on both children and adults, whereas existentialist psychologists have explored issues of being and nonbeing (Firestone & Catlett, 2009a). Neither theoretical approach deals sufficiently with the fundamental concerns of the other, and to neglect or minimize either one imposes certain limitations on our knowledge of human behavior. Both theoretical frameworks need to be recognized in order to fully understand the forces within people that are opposed to their ongoing development and movement toward individuation.[2] In describing the basic tenets of separation theory, Beutler (1997) wrote,

> This approach is integrative even beyond the blending of the psychoanalytic and existential views.... Its ties to existentialism and humanism are in its acceptance of the viability of the emerging "self," its observation of the preoccupation of humans with death, its assertion that people must

transcend the desires for immediate gratification, and its view that there is an inevitable drive of the organism to become a differentiated system. (p. xiv)

HISTORY OF THE DEVELOPMENT OF VOICE THERAPY

No treatment could do any good until I understood the voice and saw that it was running me, that I was an automaton. . . . I feel as if I've been reprieved from a lifelong sentence.

—James Masterson, *The Real Self*

Voice therapy is a cognitive/affective/behavioral methodology that brings internalized destructive thought processes to consciousness with accompanying affect in a dialogue format such that an individual can confront the alien components in his or her personality.[3] In the process of giving language or spoken words to thoughts and attitudes that are at the core of people's maladaptive behavior, voice therapy techniques expose fantasies of fusion; critical attitudes toward self and others; and addictive, self-limiting patterns of behavior that interfere with their movement toward autonomy and independence.

The first author's (R. Firestone's) life's work has focused on the study of resistance in psychotherapy and people's fundamental resistance to a better life. I was searching for an explanation as to why most individuals, despite emotional catharsis and intellectual insight, still hold on to familiar, destructive patterns and seem unwilling to change on a deep character level. On the basis of my observations of individuals in both clinical and nonclinical populations, I hypothesized that most people reject, manipulate, or control their environment to avoid personal interactions that would contradict or disprove their early conception of reality. They "tend to cling to childhood labels which seem to be branded: the clever one, the stupid one, the beauty, plain Jane, the troublemaker, and so on" (Morrant & Catlett, 2008, p. 354).

During the early 1970s, while conducting group therapy sessions, I became interested in the emotional pain that people experienced when they received certain kinds of feedback. Initially, I thought the old adage "the truth hurts" was the explanation for these reactions. However, I noticed that even when the criticism or negative feedback was inaccurate, there were many times when it would still have a painful effect. Investigating further, I found that most people judged themselves in ways that were not only distorted but were often harsh and self-critical. Any external criticism that confirmed a person's negative internal views of him- or herself would tend to trigger a self-hating thought process. My associates and I thought it would be worthwhile to explore this phenomenon further by investigating self-critical thinking and the kinds of events that aroused this self-attacking process (Firestone, 1988).

When individuals began to verbalize their destructive thoughts, it quickly became apparent that it was not so much the external criticism or unpleasant incidents in their lives that were causing them distress; instead, it was more what they were telling themselves about the incidents. It was their voice's interpretation of the feedback or situation that was making them feel bad. Participants became aware that many of their personal interactions were being filtered through the distorted lens of the voice process, which gave their interpersonal communications a negative emotional loading. This helped them to understand why they then sometimes responded in a manner that hurt their loved ones or pushed them away.

Since 1977, we have conducted more structured investigations of the voice. As noted in Chapter 3, when participants expressed their self-attacks, they often blurted out malicious statements against themselves in powerful language and with strong, angry affect. We were surprised by the intensity of the aggression that accompanied these outbursts, and it indicated the depth and pervasiveness of the voice process within the personality. We also observed that notable changes often occurred in individuals' physical appearance and expression while they were verbalizing their voice. At times, people adopted postures and mannerisms that were uncharacteristic of their own style of relating. Frequently, they assumed speech patterns, colloquialisms, and regional accents that were similar to those of their parents, often the parent of the same sex. It was as though the parental figures were living inside the person and could be brought out by this method.

We learned that when the voice predominates over more rational thought processes, a person is generally cut off from feelings and is more likely to manifest toxic traits and behaviors in personal interactions. When people view events from the negative perspective of the voice, they respond differently than when they are themselves or closer to their feelings. When they are in the negative state, they are usually acting out their most undesirable characteristics. In describing this, R. D. Laing (1960) noted, "Someone else's personality seems to 'possess' him [the individual] and to be finding expression through his words and actions, whereas the individual's own personality is temporarily 'lost' or 'gone'" (p. 62).

When we began utilizing voice therapy methods in our psychotherapy practices, we observed that, as our clients used the dialogue format to verbalize their self-attacks, they gained clarity and insight and were able to understand the connection between their destructive voices and the harmful behavior patterns that resulted. Therefore, they were better able to identify and control the negative manifestations in their personalities. In addition, by expressing the emotions associated with their destructive thought patterns, clients were able to relinquish deeply held misconceptions of self, allowing them to experience increased feelings of compassion for themselves (Firestone, 1997a).

VOICE THERAPY METHODOLOGY APPLIED TO THE PROCESS OF DIFFERENTIATION

Following our initial investigations, we became interested in expanding the methods of voice therapy in ongoing discussion groups to facilitate the process of differentiation.

The techniques directly access the damaging point of view of the internalized parent and further the differentiation process.

Steps in the Therapeutic Process

The steps in voice therapy as applied to the process of differentiation include:

1. Identifying the maladaptive point of view incorporated from the parent during childhood, giving words to the hostile voice attacks on self and others, and releasing the associated affect.
2. Identifying the sources of the voice in the family background.
3. Answering back to the incorporated alien point of view and to the attacks on self and others. There are two aspects of the answering-back process: (a) countering each charge by answering back with strength, anger, and emotion and (b) offering a rational and realistic evaluation of one's actual point of view.
4. Understanding the impact of the destructive thoughts or voices on present-day behavior, therapeutic goals, and the desire to change.
5. Challenging the negative traits and behaviors that reflect the internalized parental point of view by collaborating in the planning and implementation of corrective suggestions. These suggestions are directed toward taking action against the dictates of the voice by both eliminating destructive habit patterns and initiating positive steps toward attaining one's goals and priorities in life. Often when an individual challenges the critical voice by answering back or taking action, there is a temporary increase in voice attacks or rebuttals that must be dealt with as the therapy progresses. In addition, people tend to experience varying degrees of anxiety as they alter the aversive behaviors and traits they internalized under stressful conditions during their formative years.

The above steps are not necessarily discrete or undertaken in the order delineated here. Usually it is necessary to go through them a number of times, because it takes patience and dedication to change well-established defensive patterns. In a psychotherapy setting, it is important to alert clients to the anxiety that arises at crucial points in the therapy. They not only must learn to deal with the guilt and anxiety of separating from the voice but must take the necessary risks involved in self-actualization. "Only by coping with the anxiety generated by positive changes can a person hold on to the psychological territory he or she has gained" (Firestone, 1997a, p. 193). The process tends to be repetitive rather than linear, and there are ups and downs in the therapy, but, overall, there is a movement toward progress.

In the following pages, two personal narratives elucidate the specific steps in the methodology of voice therapy, describe the results, and discuss the typical resistances encountered in this process.

BRAD

Brad, 47, was a business executive who had enjoyed considerable success in his career. At the time that he entered therapy, he had a pronounced tendency to be driven in his work and could be considered a workaholic. Brad had difficultly expressing his feelings and was often overly intellectual and analytical in his personal interactions. In a more relaxed state, he was friendly and had a good sense of humor. Divorced after several years of marriage, he tended to be mistrustful of women.

He had become increasingly sedentary and passive in his life. He had, in effect, given up his friendships because of working for inordinately long hours and, as a result, was somewhat isolated and dejected. Brad was gradually losing confidence in himself and retreating from his position of leadership in his business. He had begun to notice that he was behaving in a domineering and vain manner at work, which reminded him of certain qualities in his father that he found particularly objectionable. Recently he had been careless with his personal finances and, like his father, had gotten into debt. At this point, Brad sought psychological help. He was determined to overcome these increasing manifestations of his negative identification with his father and to regain the ground he had lost in both his personal and professional life.

Family Background

An only child, Brad was raised by a narcissistic, intrusive mother who built up his vanity and lived through his accomplishments. As an adult, he was deeply humiliated on numerous occasions by her intrusiveness and extravagant praise. For example, when Brad was promoted to chief executive officer, she appeared uninvited at a company dinner and loudly praised his business acumen to everyone within earshot. Even though he distanced himself from his mother, his fear of her gave her considerable power over his life. Brad went so far as to never answer his phone at home, instead always letting it go to voice mail, for fear that his mother might be on the other end of the line.

Brad's father, on the other hand, was hypercritical of his son and constantly ran him down. A bitter, cynical man, he rationalized his sadistic behavior by saying it was his attempt to counteract his wife's coddling influence over his son. Brad's father claimed that he wanted "to keep her from turning the boy into a sissy." He treated Brad with disdain, depreciated his successes, and was harsh and verbally abusive.

Both of Brad's parents suffered from chronic illnesses throughout his childhood, and during their long stays in the hospital, Brad was left on his own to care for himself. At one point, his father was so debilitated by recurrent sickness that he was forced into bankruptcy. When his father wasn't ill, he worked long hours and had no friends or social life.

Applying Voice Therapy Methodology

In this example, we will illustrate the steps in Brad's personal development using excerpts from selected tape recordings to demonstrate how he progressed over the next several months.

Step 1: Identifying the maladaptive point of view incorporated from the parent, expressing the hostile voice attacks on self and others, and releasing the associated affect. In this step, we suggest that participants verbalize the maladaptive point of view of one or the other parent as though the parent were directly addressing them. The process of articulating the thought content of one's self-attacks in the second-person format brings powerful feelings of anger and sadness to the surface, where they can be fully experienced and expressed. We encourage the expression of feeling with statements like, "Try to say that with more feeling," "Say it louder," "Say it the way you hear it in your head." This release of feeling facilitates the process of separating one's own point of view from the hostile thought patterns that make up the incorporated alien point of view toward oneself (Firestone, 1988, p. 205). Our emphasis on the affective component is congenial with the psychotherapeutic practice of a number of other clinicians who recognize that accessing clients' emotions is a key element in an effective treatment program (see J. Beck, 1995; L. Greenberg, Rice, & Elliot, 1993).[4]

In the early group meetings, Brad formulated the problem areas he wished to address and the behaviors he wanted to change. One of the first actions he decided to challenge was his tendency to work at the expense of his personal and social life.

BRAD: I've always seen myself as a loser. I think that's why I have been so desperately focused on making money. It would finally prove that I'm not a loser.

R. FIRESTONE: Try to verbalize the attack that you're a loser as though someone else were talking to you. Start off by saying, "You're a loser" and go on from there.

BRAD: "You're a loser; you're such a loser! You can't do anything right. You are a lazy, good-for-nothing! You're a failure!" Anytime I have a success, I think it's just that I was lucky.

R. FIRESTONE: Say that as a voice attack.

BRAD: "You were just lucky this time. It's not because of anything that you did. You're still a loser; you'll always be a loser!"

R. FIRESTONE: Where do you think those attacks come from?

BRAD: That's an easy question to answer: from my father. It was obvious from as early as I can remember that he thought that I was a nothing. He was constantly making degrading comments about me. He would call me a lazy, good-for-nothing, little shit.

R. FIRESTONE: Try to express the way he felt about you as voice.

BRAD: Okay, let's see. It would be like, "You are nothing but a little shit! You are a lazy good-for-nothing. You think you can be somebody? Well, you can't! You think you are worth something? Well, you're not! You think you can be a success in life. Forget it!"

R. FIRESTONE: Keep going....

BRAD: "You think you are so great? You think you can be better than me? Well, you can't! You're just like me! You're no different from me. You're no better than me!" [Long pause, sad expression.]

My father thought of himself as a failure, and he thought that way about me. He saw me as worthless and a failure just like him.

R. FIRESTONE: He projected his doubts about himself and his own shortcomings onto you.

BRAD: Exactly. When I think more about those particular voice attacks, I realize that my mother had those same hostile, degrading thoughts about my father. That was the point of view that I picked up in my family: that men are fuck-ups. My mother and father both thought of my father as nothing but a failure, that he couldn't make any real money, that he would never be a success, that he couldn't do anything right. I identified with the attack on my father, and felt like I was a fuck-up, too.

R. FIRESTONE: What voice attacks would be coming from your mother?

BRAD: Those are easy; she actually said those out loud. "Look at your father! He is such a failure. He can't do anything right. His whole life he has been a failure and an embarrassment to me. He's supposed to take care of me and make me proud. But he has always failed me. You're better, you could be the one, you're special. You've got to succeed and make me proud."

Step 2: Identifying the sources of the voice in the family background. In this step, participants discuss their spontaneous insights and analyze their reactions to verbalizing the voice. One advantage of this methodology is that individuals rapidly achieve their own insights and draw their own conclusions from saying the voice and formulate their own ideas about the origins of their distorted views and attitudes. In a therapy setting, the lack of interpretation on the part of the clinician reduces transference reactions, establishes a feeling of equality between client and clinician, and tends to place the responsibility on the client to work through the material that has been uncovered.

After verbalizing his parents' points of view toward him, especially his father's attitudes, Brad gained insight into one of the reasons he had retreated from a position of leadership.

> You know, I'm beginning to see that when I became more successful, at a certain point, I started to become more like him. This is so clear to me now. This is especially apparent in the financial problems I started having. I never had those kinds of problems before; that had been a particularly easy area for me. It's like I began to sabotage my success. It was like I was too guilty to be that much more successful than him.

Brad recognized that surpassing his father in the business world had symbolized separating from him. However, after he achieved significant success, he was too fearful and guilty to maintain his separateness and he reverted to defensive behaviors that emulated his father's lifestyle and way of doing business.

Step 3: Answering back to the alien/incorporated point of view and to the attacks on self and others. There are two possible components to this step. Each component can be used on its own or with the other to facilitate further differentiation. People can deal with a particular voice attack by responding emotionally and angrily. They can also put into words a rational or realistic appraisal of their point of view and their behaviors from an adult ego state.

Sometimes people answer back to the voice and challenge it directly as though they were addressing an actual person. Because they tend to attribute their voice attacks to specific parental figures who were hurtful to them, they often find themselves talking directly to their parents in a form of psychodrama (Firestone, 1988). These expressions tend to be intensely angry and may reflect the reactive rage of a child against a parent, whereas rational statements about oneself reflect a more adult or mature posture. This is not to say that a person's answer to the voice spoken from the adult mode will not contain strong anger and outrage at the abuses suffered in growing up.[5]

After answering back to the voice, individuals then objectively evaluate any element of truth in the self-attack, without being harsh or judgmental toward themselves, so that they can formulate a realistic plan of action to change destructive behavior patterns or negative traits.

Subsequent to expressing his parents' demeaning attitudes toward him, Brad was aware of a strong urge to contradict their distorted views.

R. FIRESTONE: How would you answer back?

BRAD: First of all, in response to my father's attacks I would simply say, "You are wrong about me. I'm not what you say I am. You don't even know me. I am hard working; I have been working since I was 14 years old. I am certainly not lazy. And I am not a failure or a loser. You are the failure; not me. Don't put that on me; that's how you felt about yourself. Those attacks have nothing to do with me."

My response to my mother feels angrier. I felt a lot of pressure from her to perform, and I felt like I could never measure up. "I'm not interested in what you have to say about my father or about men in general. You were a bitter, victimized, childish woman. In your inflated, egotistical view of yourself, no man was good enough for you. I'm not here for you. I have my own life. Fuck you." [Loud, angry voice.]

Step 4: Understanding the impact of the destructive thoughts on present-day behavior, personal and professional goals, and the desire to change. In this step, people become cognizant of how the internalized parental views and self-attacks influence their current behavior and impose limitations on their lives. In answering back to his father's attacks—and, in particular, after expressing anger at his mother's buildup and exploitation—Brad gained considerable insight into why he had always felt under such pressure to work compulsively to achieve success. Trying to fulfill his mother's exaggerated expectations was a way to compensate for feelings of inadequacy and low self-esteem brought about by his father's criticality. Brad's new understanding regarding the factors involved in his retreat from success also provided the impetus he needed to want to change the undesirable behaviors and traits in himself that were similar to those his father had exhibited.

Step 5: Collaborating to change behaviors through the planning and implementation of corrective suggestions. Because the methods of voice therapy challenge core defenses and one's basic self-concept, the process of initiating behavioral changes that expand one's boundaries exposes many misconceptions about oneself. It leads to differentiation from the imitation of parents' destructive traits and behaviors and is a vital part of our overall approach (Firestone, 1988). Corrective suggestions bear a direct relationship to the maladaptive behavior patterns that are influenced and controlled by the person's voices. They act as a catalyst to help people approach new and unfamiliar situations in a more open and less defended manner.

There are two types of corrective suggestions: (1) relinquishing addictive, self-defeating, self-destructive behaviors and lifestyles along with altering personality traits mediated by the voice and (2) taking emotional risks by initiating positive actions that are potentially more satisfying and fulfilling.

After countering his father's view of him as lazy and achieving insight into the reasons he had felt so driven in business, Brad outlined a plan designed to break into his compulsive work pattern. He began by taking one day off from work each week to relax and socialize with friends. This change in routine precipitated considerable anxiety and triggered new voice attacks, which he dealt with in the discussion groups.

In general, when a corrective suggestion is implemented, anxiety is aroused because taking constructive action disrupts defenses that were once survival mechanisms that provided a sense of safety and security. Nevertheless, when people maintain the new behavior and resist reverting to the old patterns, their self-attacks gradually diminish.

Subsequent Developments

Using the Methodology to Address Brad's Tendency to Be Miserable

Step 1

BRAD: The other day, it occurred to me that I wasn't miserable about anything. Not that everything is okay, you know, with my financial situation being what it is, but I actually felt happy. Then by the next morning I was feeling down, and so I knew I must be attacking myself. My father was never happy. He was always miserable, and I wondered what he would have said about my life today or about the fact that I wasn't miserable that day. I think it would go something like this: "So you think you can be free from misery for a couple of days? Believe me, you can't. You're going to be miserable soon enough! Let me tell you something about life: it's fucked!"

That voice from my father is quick to come into my mind. And the word "miserable" is key, because that's the word my father often used to describe how he felt.

"My life was miserable! I had to stay with your mother for years, and for your sake. I was stuck with her and I was stuck with you, you miserable kid! I had no life because of you. I had no fucking life. And you know something, that's the way life is!" [Angry, yelling, then a long pause.]

R. FIRESTONE: You're saying that the basic belief that you've been carrying around with you is your father's idea that life is miserable. You also said that your father blamed you for his misery.

BRAD: Yeah, and he constantly complained about how stuck he felt, and he made sarcastic remarks about me being able to get out and go places.

R. FIRESTONE: How did those go?

BRAD: They were like: "It must be nice to have no worries or responsibilities; to be free to just run around and have a good time. You certainly have it made, don't you. You don't have a care in the world. For you, life is just about running around with your friends. Who do you think you are anyway? You're just a spoiled kid. You were always spoiled. And you aren't any different in your life today."

Step 2

I'm beginning to notice how easy it is for me to find things to be miserable about. But it's really his attitude that makes me look at life that way. I realize how deep-seated those voices about life being miserable really are. It isn't just a passing thought. I think that's another way I've imitated my father's negative views about life. Without realizing it, I became miserable and unhappy and pulled away from my friends.

Step 3

R. FIRESTONE: What would you say back to the voices you verbalized?

BRAD: [Angrily.] Don't you tell me what life is about. Just because you made a miserable life for yourself doesn't mean that is the way life is. And it certainly doesn't mean that I have to live my life that way. I'm happy! I have friends! I enjoy my life!

In a more rational way, I would answer back by saying: My life is not at all like yours. I am basically happy. I enjoy my work. I've become more active again and I enjoy sports. And I have friends in my life who I care about and who care about me.

Step 4

R. FIRESTONE: What effect do these voices have on your everyday life?

BRAD: I believe that my father's prescription for life still influences me in subtle ways I am just now beginning to wake up to. It's not only my mood, but it's also the activities I choose to be involved in, actually the lack of activities. By not challenging that point of view, I actually thought that I preferred doing things alone, but that's not really me.

Step 5

So I've actually decided: I'm not going to be miserable. Whenever I catch myself starting to get miserable, I am going to stop and look for the voices that are behind that feeling. Because I know that it's not coming from me. That's the way he felt about life; that's not how I feel. Also, I plan to be more active in pursuing my social life, spending more time with my friends, which is really my choice.

Using the Methodology to Address Brad's Issues With His Mother

Step 1

BRAD: I was thinking more about the voices I have, and I am really aware that they come from both sides. I've looked into the ones that come from my father; you know the ones like "You're a piece of shit! You're not a man! You're a failure and everybody can see it. You're nothing." Looking at the voices from my father has really helped me to be free of his attacks on me.

But I know I haven't fully investigated the voices that come from my mother. I've talked about how she gave me a huge buildup. My God, she acted as though I could walk on water. Those voices are the ones that are behind my vanity: "You're so great! They don't understand how great you are. How really great you are! You're just brilliant. I always said you could be anything; you could be president of the United States!" But I have a feeling that on a deeper level, there are more attacks and that I've been scared to look into them. I think they have to do with my sexuality and me being a man.

R. FIRESTONE: Are you aware of how they might go?

BRAD: All I can think of right now is this one thought: "You're so cute. You're so cute." There's more to it: "You're not like the other boys. You're not disgusting like they are. You're so cute!" That keeps going over and over in my mind. It's embarrassing, and I'm also afraid of those thoughts.

R. FIRESTONE: Keep going with them....

BRAD: "You're just the way I like you! So sweet, so cute; just like a little girl. You're my little boy. Not a disgusting man! You're all for me. You don't have anything masculine about you. My little angel; all mine. You're part of me. You belong to me! Don't you see that? I've got you. I got you! [Voice gets louder, face grimaces.] You're my little girl! You're not a man. Men are horrible!" Aaaugh! [Sounds indicating disgust, then deep crying, followed by a long silence.]

Step 2

I've always been afraid of those voices. The whole time I was growing up, I was afraid that I was going to turn out to be homosexual. I was sure that I was going to be effeminate and gay. It was always a worry of mine and even though I never had any homosexual feelings or indications of being gay, I always felt that that's what I was destined to become. And the whole thing was supported by my father calling me a "mama's boy."

Sometimes the things that my mother and father said to me became my own voices. But also the way they looked at me and the way they acted toward me turned into voices. My mother's voices about me also imply that she was humiliated because I could never be the kind of person she wanted me to be, because I could never be great enough. Nothing would do the trick; nothing would satisfy her. That's one of the reasons I've always felt inadequate. I realize that during the time I was doing badly in business, I was also acting vain and officious, trying to cover over my feelings of failure and inadequacy.

Step 3

BRAD: I'd like to answer back to those voices, "I'm not a girl. I'm a man. I'm not cute and sweet. I'm not weak! I am strong and masculine. And there is nothing wrong with that! Being strong doesn't make me horrible. Being a man doesn't make me horrible. I'm a decent person. I have feelings. Just because I'm a man, it doesn't mean that I don't have feelings. I do! I'm not horrible."

I started feeling shaky, feeling my own anger. I can almost see her in front of me and I felt like I could kill her. I feel strongly that her treatment of me was vicious and inexcusable.

R. FIRESTONE: Keep going with it....

BRAD: "I am so angry I feel like I could kill you, you vicious bitch! That is no way to treat a boy. You tried to emasculate me. You wanted to castrate me! Well, it didn't work! I am a man. And I stood by while you ran down my father! And he stood by while you emasculated me. Well, no more! I am not going to listen to you and your disgusting views of men anymore. You are a destructive, man-hating bitch. I am done with you!"

That felt so good. It felt so good saying those things. I feel like I finally stood up to her. I did something that my father never did; not for me or for himself. What a relief.

Facing his rage toward his mother, answering back to her point of view about him, and describing his insights about her treatment of him strengthened Brad's identity and helped dispel his doubts about himself as a man. As a result, it became easier for him to again assume leadership in the work arena, and in his personal life, he became increasingly open and trusting in relating to women.

Using the Methodology to Address Brad's Feelings About Being Labeled "Cold and Heartless"

As he uncovered more voice attacks, Brad came to understand how his parents' illnesses and repeated hospitalizations contributed to his adopting an inward, pseudoindependent orientation, shutting down his feelings, and becoming increasingly isolated from his peers. He recalled that, as a child, when he wasn't working his paper route, he would lock himself in his room and read for hours. He recognized that being passive and seeking solitude were core defenses that had been powerfully reinforced by his parents' extreme unsociability.

At one point, approximately a year after Brad began participating in the group, his father died. Although it was not unexpected, Brad was nonetheless shaken and experienced a combination of sadness, guilt, and anxiety. He felt a strong pull to retreat to his former passivity and withdraw from his friends, but he struggled against these regressive tendencies. After several weeks, he again began to explore memories of his childhood.

Step 1

BRAD: When I look at my childhood, and all of the craziness that went on between my parents and then add to that their illnesses and then add to that the ways they each related to me, when I look at all of that, I think it's no wonder I withdrew into myself. And then both of my parents reacted to my withdrawal by accusing me of being "cold and heartless." They said that I was devoid of feeling; that I didn't care about them; that I was not capable of loving anybody. They would always say, "Oh that Brad; he's just cold and heartless." And do you know, I believed them.

R. FIRESTONE: What are the voices that go along with that way of seeing you?

BRAD: Like I said, "You're just cold and heartless. You can't love anyone. You have no feelings. You aren't even human. You don't care about anybody. You're not even from this planet. You don't feel anything toward anybody."

Step 2

The sad thing is that because of the way they acted, I thought of myself as cold and heartless for years, and I acted on that. In a way it always felt more natural to me to be cold and heartless than to think I could have feelings toward people. For a long time, I acted like I didn't have human emotions. I wasn't sociable or friendly with people; I wasn't fun or affectionate with friends.

Step 3

R. FIRESTONE: How would you answer back to those attacks?

BRAD: "I am human. I do feel. I feel a lot. And I care a lot. And I have deep feelings. I feel sadness and pain; not just mine but other people's, too. And besides that, I act as though I care. I am kind and friendly to people. I'm not an alien. I'm tired of feeling like I'm looking in from the outside, looking at humanity from the outside. I'm not any different from anybody else." [Sad, quiet.]

Step 4

R. FIRESTONE: How have those voices affected your behavior since your father died?

BRAD: I think that my father dying was really a final separation from him. It was the end of any hope I had that he might someday see me for who I really am. Also I felt even more guilty about surviving him than I had about surpassing him in business. I felt anxious and disoriented, and basically I began conforming again to what my parents, especially my father, thought about me. The truth is that in not being sociable and friendly, I was acting more like them. While my father was alive, he had no friends, only business associates. Actually, neither of them had any friends, and they certainly didn't know how to have fun. There was an unspoken code in my family: "We're not social animals, we don't go out there and go to parties and socialize with people. We keep to ourselves." And I found myself adhering to that viewpoint again.

Step 5

Suggestions that would have the effect of increasing Brad's sociability and activity level, particularly in the aftermath of his father's death, continued to be crucial to his progress in separating from behaviors that duplicated his father's reclusiveness and passivity. For example, during one group meeting, Brad said he had always wanted to learn how to drive a powerboat. He complained that even though a friend who owned a boat had offered to teach him, he could never find the time.

One of the group participants recommended that Brad call his friend, set aside a specific time to go boating, and even invite other people to join them. The fact that Brad's friends responded favorably to his invitation moved him beyond the limitations he had previously imposed on himself. He then had to cope with the voice attacks triggered by this disturbance to his psychological equilibrium. In general, renewed attacks or rebuttals from the voice tend to occur as individuals take action to separate from the negative parental prescriptions that have guided their lives.

> I began to have strong voice attacks right after taking the boat out for the first time. I felt awkward with my friends and self-conscious when handling the boat. Then I realized that it was such a point of departure from my father. He never even learned how to drive a car. So I really was separating from him.
>
> I also decided to act on the assumption that I do fit in, that people do like me, and I've been acting more friendly toward people, being more sociable, based on that assumption. And my friends have responded to me in a very positive way. But then, again, I had intense self-attacks afterward. They went something like this,
>
> "Do you really think that this is going to do any good? Don't you understand that certain things are just in a person? Everyone knows you and

> there's no possible way that you are going to get rid of this thing in you. You've been stuck with it for all these years. Nothing is going to change! I know you and what you are trying to do. But don't forget that I know who you really are. You can't fool me! You can fool everybody else, but you can't fool me! You can't fool yourself either, because you know it's deep inside you." [Yells loudly.]
>
> My first answer to that voice is that, "You don't fucking know me! You never saw me for who I really was!" To answer more rationally, I'd say, "I really feel good about the possibility that I can get rid of this underlying feeling I have of being an alien, of being cold and heartless, not like other people. I'm optimistic; I can get rid of this negative feeling that's been inside of me, always pulling at me. I feel like a normal person."

Follow-Up

The process of identifying his self-attacks and challenging his parents' prescriptions for living eventually freed Brad to see himself in a different light, to enjoy his friendships, and to develop and sustain a close, loving relationship with a woman. Recently, Brad summarized what he had learned while participating in the group discussions:

> This process has had an amazing effect on me. Thoughts and feelings that tormented me all my life have disappeared and haven't come back. That's not to say that I don't have any negative feelings about myself, but I now know where they come from and how to deal with them. Some major self-attacks have disappeared—for example, I don't see myself as a loser anymore.
>
> I know that my life would not have changed if I hadn't changed my behavior. I don't always follow all the corrective suggestions to socialize and maintain my friendships, but when I do, the actions I take eventually cause the voices to diminish. I'm not always sociable, but I'm much more so than I was. Before, when I was working insanely to compensate for my father's voice about me being lazy, I was also avoiding having a personal life. And that has drastically changed.
>
> It's funny but when I first started challenging the critical voices, it was like there was a void left where the negative thoughts had been. Then I realized that when I'm just being myself without the companionship of those voices and that hostile point of view, I have a sense of simply being a person, alone, in the world.

AMANDA

Amanda, 32, had put a great deal of effort into creating a life for herself that was different than the one she had grown up in. She had moved to a city, done well in a job that she liked, and met a man who was kind and loved her. Eventually they married and had a baby boy, Sami. Even though Amanda had everything she had always dreamed of, she had become aware that she was unhappy in her life. She had become negative and critical toward her husband, Jason. She had a tendency to have melodramatic reactions when she was under stress. At times, she felt overwhelmed by caring for Sami and resented him. The worst of it was that these were traits that she had strongly disliked in her mother. At this point, she began to participate in the discussion groups because she was motivated to control her emotionality and negativity and to regain her sense of herself.

Family Background

The oldest of three sisters, Amanda was raised in a small Midwestern town, and her parents were well respected in the community as "good, decent, God-fearing" people. As far as her family was concerned, Amanda was the only flaw in their otherwise perfect life. From the time Amanda was born, her mother had considerable difficulty relating to her. She complained that there was "something off-putting" about Amanda, making it hard for the mother to respond to her infant's physical needs or to show her affection.

Amanda's mother acted out her hostility by being punishing and physically abusive of the young girl when she was alone with her. Amanda's father, an ambitious and wealthy industrialist, was often absent from the home and was unaware of his wife's mistreatment of their daughter. While aggressive in his work, in his personal life he was passive. He was intimidated by his wife, easily manipulated by her hysterical outbursts, and frightened by her harsh, degrading attacks on his "weak character."

When she was 5, Amanda was made responsible for her younger sister's care. Whenever the little girl got into trouble or hurt herself, their mother blamed Amanda. When her sister attempted suicide at the age of 15, their parents held Amanda responsible. As a teenager, Amanda was careless and took unnecessary risks, exhibiting a pattern of self-destructive behavior and repeatedly placing herself in dangerous situations. In her late teens, she chose to walk alone late at night in a neighborhood she knew to be unsafe and she was raped. When she was 20, she had a boyfriend who was physically abusive. She eventually broke away from this relationship and began to create a more constructive life for herself. She moved, pursued a career, fell in love, and began a family.

Applying Voice Therapy Methodology

In the following pages, we provide excerpts from Amanda's expressions in the discussion groups. The material has been edited considerably due to the length of her verbalizations of the voice. In her expressions, Amanda revealed a remarkably clear picture of what she experienced in relation to her mother. She articulated these voice attacks in diverse ways: through sarcastic innuendoes; cold, punishing accusations; and long-winded outbursts of irrational rage against herself.

Using the Methodology to Address Amanda's Reluctance to Trust Anyone

AMANDA: Over the last year, I have felt more and more isolated. I've been remote from my husband and my little boy. But recently I've been so emotional and I have been overreacting to everything. I haven't wanted to talk to anyone about these feelings because I felt there was no one I could really trust. I've begun to think that if I could just get away for a while, I could figure everything out by myself. Jason [her husband] encouraged me to talk in this group, but I have to tell you, I am reluctant about it.

R. FIRESTONE: What are you telling yourself about people that makes you feel distrustful?

AMANDA: Lots of things. I'm even attacking myself for saying what I'm revealing right now.

R. FIRESTONE: Try to put what you're thinking into the form of a voice attack.

AMANDA: Let's see, the attacks are something like, "Don't let people get too close. People are dangerous. They'll hurt you. You can't trust anyone; no one will understand how you are feeling. Why are you revealing this to the group? They only pretend to care about people? They don't really care about you. They won't understand you."

I can almost hear my mother's voice as I'm saying these things. "Don't trust anyone! Don't talk to anyone else. I'm the only one who could possibly care about you. You can't trust anyone outside of our family. You should just get away from people!" [Angry tone.]

R. FIRESTONE: What are you feeling?

AMANDA: I feel so ashamed to have these thoughts. I'm afraid of making everybody feel bad toward me, of provoking them, but I think that's a voice too, like "You're so provoking. Of course they don't like you, the way you're talking!" [Pause.]

R. FIRESTONE: What else did you think?

AMANDA: I know that's not the way I really think. My mother distrusts everybody; her point of view is the opposite of how I really feel. But I'm also shocked at how much I want to be alone and push people away when I feel down. The voice is basically telling me to take my problems and keep them hidden. But that's what I've been doing my whole life; keeping everything inside. But it's making me sick! I don't want to do that anymore; I want to talk about myself so I can feel better.

R. FIRESTONE: What would you answer back to her? How do you really feel?

AMANDA: I'm angry at my mother's advice. I don't agree with how she sees people. My answer to her would be, "I'm not going to be quiet! I can trust these people; they are interested in getting to know me. Who do you think you are anyway, advising me? You're the one I can't trust, not them! You hurt me! So just shut up and get out of here."

Addressing Issues in Amanda's Marriage

In subsequent group meetings, Amanda became more familiar with her mother's distorted attitudes toward men, particularly toward Jason.

AMANDA: I've started to become more aware of how critical I am of Jason. It's gotten to where I am critical of every little thing he does. Especially if he is coming toward me, being sweet to me. Like if he comes toward me to give me a kiss, I'll pull away. Or I'll start an argument right before we go to bed. It's so strange; I want to be close and loving, but then I act so hostile or I get so critical of him that I ruin those feelings.

R. FIRESTONE: What are the voices that you are listening to at those times when you do things to push him away?

AMANDA: I know they are very critical of him. It's like they're telling me, "How can you feel sweet toward him? How can you stand him? He is such a creep. He's so insecure. He doesn't love you; all he's worried about is if you love him. He should be strong; like a real man! If he loved you, his attention would be on you, not on himself. He's supposed to be secure and strong so that you can lean on him! That's what he's supposed to be offering you!"

R. FIRESTONE: Whose attitude are you expressing?

AMANDA: More like my mother's than mine. When I say those attacks I also want to stick up for Jason. My answer back to her is, "Don't call Jason weak and insecure. There is nothing wrong with him; he's just human. He has his problems just like anyone else does. Just like I do.

"I have faults and Jason has faults, but so what? We can work on them, we can work on them as two adults who love each other and care about each other. This world is not black and white. It's not made up of good people and bad people, or strong people and weak people. There are just people. And people can change!"

The voice from my mother telling me that I need to be taken care of makes me really furious! That is exactly what she thought about marriage: it's about the woman being taken care of. She lives like that, too; she acts like a helpless child in relation to my dad. That way of behaving makes me so angry. My answer back would be, "Don't tell me about how to relate to my husband! You have no idea what it means to be in a marriage. It's about two equal adult people sharing life—loving each other and respecting each other. It's not about one being the daddy and the other the little girl. It's not about playing some kind of unequal game like that. It's about honesty and respect and equality."

I feel like it's important for me to also answer by acknowledging how things really are, "The thing is that I know there are times when I listen to your point of view and I act childish in relation to Jason. And that pulls parental reactions out of him. But I don't like when I do that. And it has a destructive effect on our marriage; it throws things off between us and makes us not get along. So I don't want to follow your advice anymore!"

Dealing With the Rebuttal to Challenging the Voice

AMANDA: I started feeling better over these past weeks, and things have been better with Jason. Then just in the last few days I've noticed feeling childish again, you know, wanting to be taken care of by him again. And I really don't like this because it goes against everything I've been trying to do for myself lately. I feel like I've started to act more like my mother does with my father again. What happened was that I got the flu and then I started worrying that I wouldn't be able to take care of Sami by myself.

R. FIRESTONE: Say any voices that go along with that feeling. . . .

AMANDA: They go like this, "So what good is all of your talk about being independent going to do now? You're sick and you can't take care of yourself, much less your kid! Now you need Jason to take care of you. You see, I was right: the reason you need a man is because you need him to take care of you and Sami.

"And what happens if you get really sick? Then he has to take care of you. Why don't you act really sick now? So even if you aren't, act like you are so you can let him know that you need him to take care of you. It's important to make him know this!"

R. FIRESTONE: How do these voices affect you?

AMANDA: One thing that I notice is that I start to overreact to trivial things, just like my mother does, and it's embarrassing. I become overwhelmed just like a child. It gets to where I am exaggerating and reacting dramatically to every little thing that comes up in my life.

I'm realizing how much of my life I've given up in order to be taken care of. It's so childish. I've never really seen how much I've pulled on people and how bad it's made me feel. But I did come by it honestly, I'll say that for myself. I realize that I've acted this out a lot in my life and it's not nice. I'd get panicky about something and want someone to take care of me. There are definitely times when I've played the child role with Jason. It's painful because when I get into feeling childish, our whole relationship gets off. It really kills any feelings of sexual attraction I have for Jason, and any feelings of wanting to be sexual. I get into such a childish place. But I know it is something I can stop doing. I've been doing that, stopping myself from getting back into a childish state. Understanding how my voices support this behavior makes it easier for me to control it.

R. FIRESTONE: How would you answer back to your mother?

AMANDA: "I don't want to listen to you; you're still wrong. If I get so sick that I need help, then Jason will be glad to help me. Not because I am a helpless little girl, but because he cares about me. If I need help, he wants to help me, and if he needs help, I want to help him. And we both share taking care of Sami so that's never a problem. You're just looking for a way to get back at me for changing and being more independent, and for being different from you."

Following this meeting, Amanda was able to identify the voice attacks that were rebuttals to the progress she was making in challenging her critical voice and changing her negative behavior. She learned that if she held her ground and did not let these new attacks affect her actions, they would subside and she would continue to develop.

Addressing Issues in Amanda's Sexual Relationship

Amanda's relationship with Jason improved as she dealt with ways that she acted childish and unequal in their marriage. She also used the methodology to understand why she felt inhibited and held back sexually.

AMANDA: I have always felt held back sexually. I am easy and relaxed about being affectionate but when it becomes sexual, I get tense. And I don't know why; it doesn't make any sense to me. But in spite of this inhibited feeling, I usually enjoy being sexual with Jason. I'm really attracted to him and he is so loving and enthusiastic. He says he likes the way I am; he has no complaints about me. But it bothers me not to feel freer and more spontaneous. There have been times when I have been less held back, like on a vacation or something. But there have also been times when things are friendly between Jason and me, but not sexual. This really bothers me. I want our sexual relationship to be everything that it could be.

R. FIRESTONE: What are the voices that you are telling yourself about being sexual? Can you think of any that you hear when you are actually being sexual?

AMANDA: If I imagine Jason and me being together? Let's see. They would go something like this, "Look at you! What are you doing? I can't believe you like being sexual. I can't believe you like that. You're so disgusting!

"You're so dirty and disgusting; how can Jason stand your touch? How can he want to touch you? How can he not be repulsed by you? You are so dirty and gross. You have always been dirty and gross. I know because you were a dirty little girl. I was disgusted by you; why do you think I never touched you? Because you were gross! Do you really think Jason wants to touch you when you're such a dirty girl? [Derisive tone of voice.] Do you really think he wants to be with a dirty person like you? You're such a dirty little girl.

"And you know what else proves that you were dirty and disgusting? Look what happened to you when you were a teenager: you were raped! That's what you got for being so dirty; that's what you deserved. And after that, everyone could see that you were damaged goods! Everyone knew what I have known all along: you are a dirty, gross girl." [Crying.]

Saying this makes me feel so sad.

R. FIRESTONE: How would you answer back to those voice attacks?

AMANDA: I would say, "I'm not disgusting or repulsive. I'm not dirty and gross. All of those are ways that you saw me when I was little, but they aren't how I was. I was never dirty or gross. And I didn't deserve to be raped; I didn't deserve to be beaten. You had a twisted view of me and a sick view of sex! I wasn't perverted; you were. I didn't know anything different then, but I do now. And now I can fight back and reject the way you saw me.

"There is nothing perverted or dirty or gross about me sexually. I see sex as natural; it's not perverted to like sex. And I am attractive to Jason. And he is attractive to me! I like being sexual! What I don't like is your way of seeing me!"

My mother's attacks on my sexuality made me feel like avoiding being sexual with Jason, and so I did just that. I would make any kind of excuse to not make love with him. I had actually started thinking that I had a serious sexual problem, but I can see now that was wrong. Before Sami was born, I had really enjoyed our sexual relationship. How I answered back to her voice is how I really feel and who I really am as a woman.

Addressing Issues About Being a Mother

In the group meetings, Amanda investigated her feelings about being a mother and her fears in relation to her son. As she expressed her voices about motherhood, which she verbalized in a lengthy tirade, Amanda exposed her mother's profoundly illogical and unrealistic views about being a parent as well as her mother's distorted attitudes toward her.

AMANDA: When Sami was born, my biggest fear was that I would pass on to him the negative things my mother put onto me. It's funny, but right now, when I think of saying what those negative things are, I feel anxious about saying them. I'm still afraid to reveal the way she saw me. It's like I don't want anyone to see the terrible way she thought about me and also, I don't want anyone to see what my critical thoughts are toward my son. It's like these are my deepest, darkest secrets.

So anyway, this is what she would say, "I didn't want to have you. I wanted to have an abortion but your father wouldn't let me. He said it was against our religion. But I didn't care, that's how badly I wanted to get rid of you. You thought that you were different than me because you wanted to have a baby! Ha! So how do you like it now? Now that all the fanfare is over; now that everyone's excitement about the new baby is over. Now that it's just you stuck with him! Now you know how it feels to have a baby just hanging on your shoulder.

"Now you know what it's really like! You have no life; it's all about him. You have to pay attention to him. And everyone else pays attention to him, too. You don't get any attention anymore. Everyone thinks that he's the cute one. Now you know how it feels to have someone come along and demand all of your attention and then, on top of that, he takes all of the attention away from you. Now you're all alone! And you're supposed to be thrilled about being a mother."

I have to say I'm shocked by what I just said! I don't think these things consciously; in fact I've never thought any of them until they came out of my mouth just now. It feels humiliating to say all of this stuff, this point of view. It seems horrible to think of a child that way, for my mother to have thought that way about me. And to think that way about Sami is painful. I feel so sorry. [Cries.]

R. FIRESTONE: How would you answer back to that point of view?

AMANDA: I'm furious at it. My answer to that voice is, "Shut up! You have no idea what I feel as a mother! I love Sami and I don't feel like he takes anything from me. I love giving him attention; it brings me joy. Even though I have you in my head trying to convince me about your twisted way of seeing motherhood, I don't agree with you. I don't have to be the same way with my child that you were with me. I don't have to be the same kind of childish, self-centered immature mother that you were. I love my son. He is a spirited little boy and I'm so glad that I had him."

This experience, along with her participation in the group meetings, allowed Amanda to develop a coherent narrative of her attachment history with her mother. Making sense of her painful childhood enabled her to become more sensitively attuned to her son. In addition, she continued to identify the origins of her propensity to react to events in a childish, melodramatic manner and to cling to her husband whenever she felt anxious or distressed. She became an active collaborator in thinking of corrective measures she could take that would minimize her tendency to be melodramatic, including learning new ways of describing her everyday experiences in a more matter-of-fact (adult) tone of voice. She also made plans to talk frequently with a close friend about her thoughts and feelings rather than allowing them to escalate into an emotional storm as she had in the past.

Follow-Up

In Amanda's case, the methodology enabled her to understand the basic split in her thinking about herself as well as her fundamental ambivalence toward her husband and son. Over a period of two years, she separated out the incorporated elements of her mother's point of view that were opposed to her own goals and priorities. Even more importantly, exposing the voice, essentially her mother's destructive attitudes and views of life, enabled her to bring the behaviors regulated by these voices under her control and to alter traits she disliked in herself. She feels considerably better in her sexual relationship with her husband and is generally more adult in all of her personal and work-related interactions. As a mother, she is more relaxed and easy going than before and enjoys sharing the care of Sami with her husband. Her life is more stable, and the previous sense of childishness and drama is noticeably diminished in her current life.

RESISTANCE IN VOICE THERAPY

Resistance to change in therapy centers on protecting the core defense, the fantasy bond, from intrusion. Preserving a fantasy of connection with one's parents on an internal level by symbolically parenting oneself offers an illusion of protection and security. Each aspect of a person's resistance can be explored and understood in terms of how it functions to protect the fantasy bond and the self-parenting process.

Every element of the voice process functions to protect an inward lifestyle that offers an illusion of pseudoindependence, the fantasy that one can sustain oneself without needing anything from anyone else. Viewing resistance in terms of protecting clients' inwardness from intrusion enables a therapist to better predict the points at which their anxiety and defensiveness will be aroused. It is worthwhile to examine the kinds of resistance typically encountered in voice therapy. These include:

1. Resistance to utilizing specific voice therapy procedures.
2. Resistance to changing one's self-concept.
3. Resistance to formulating personal goals and corrective suggestions and taking action to implement them.
4. Resistance and regression after answering back to voice attacks.

Resistance to Specific Therapeutic Tasks

As noted previously, people are reluctant to recognize the presence of an internalized alien, hostile, or destructive point of view within themselves or experience themselves as divided or fragmented.[6] For this reason, they may find it difficult to learn to follow voice therapy procedures that separate out discordant elements of the personality. Some feel embarrassed and self-conscious to attempt to formulate their self-attacks in the second person as external attacks or voices, while others are hesitant to follow instructions to say their voice attacks louder or more emotionally. Many hold back significant feelings because they sense that they are tampering with defenses they have relied on throughout their lifetime. Some actually find the dialogue format scary because, as in utilizing free association techniques, clients can be terrified of their thoughts and feelings spilling out without control. They are concerned that if they use the technique, they will be giving too much power to the voice. Others are afraid that the self-attacks they reveal might turn out to be true.

Resistance to Changing One's Self-Concept

There is fundamental resistance to identifying voices and self-attacks that challenge a person's negative identity formed in the family of origin. Accepting positive changes in one's self-concept implies a disruption in one's psychological equilibrium, because both the idealization of one's parents and the internalization of negative attitudes toward the self are a fundamental part of the fantasy bond. A person cannot effectively parent him- or herself while maintaining an inadequate or weak internalized parental self-image.

Altering one's basic self-concept to a more positive outlook also implies changes in both behavior and the style of relating to significant people in one's current life. Because these changes arouse anxiety, many people prefer to hold on to and preserve a static, albeit negative, view of themselves.

Resistance to Formulating Personal Goals and Corrective Experiences and Taking Actions to Implement Them

People are reluctant to set definitive goals and to plan a specific course of action for working toward these goals. Strong voice attacks are aroused when people take bold steps directed toward pursuing their own lives in a manner that is free, nonconforming, and independent. In a therapy setting, although corrective suggestions are generally initiated by clients and develop out of their own motivation, the situation still lends itself to the arousal of powerful resistance. Although they initially collaborate with the therapist as an equal partner in planning corrective suggestions, clients may later reverse their point of view, distort the situation, and deal with it in a victimized or paranoid manner. When this occurs, they project their desire to change onto the therapist, perceive the therapist as having a stake in their progress, and mistakenly believe that the therapist is telling them how to run their lives and making decisions for them. Unless this issue is directly addressed and worked through, there will be little, if any, progress.[7]

Some people respond adversely to the experience of being a separate decision-making individual by regressing and attempting to form a fantasy bond with the therapist. Clients who recognize and work through these transference reactions, maintain an equal partnership with the therapist, and take responsibility for their actions are more likely to progress and achieve a higher level of differentiation.

Resistance After Answering to Voice Attacks

Resistance is often encountered after an individual directly challenges the voice by answering back dramatically with strong anger. Attacking parental introjects, much like attacking one's actual parent or parents, arouses strong guilt reactions.

The overall problem of voicing aggression toward parents and parental introjects in sessions is a serious issue in any therapeutic endeavor. When people become aware of the damage they sustained in their early development, they experience a good deal of pain and sadness. These memories and insights give rise to primitive feelings of anger and outrage. Feeling the intensity of these emotions is symbolically equivalent to actually killing or expressing death wishes toward the parents. Individuals often experience intense guilt reactions and anxiety when they awaken these emotions. To compound matters, the symbolic destruction of parental figures leaves the person fearful of object loss. The combination of the two emotions, guilt and fear of losing the object, can precipitate regressive trends in any therapy. When this happens, individual often turn their anger against themselves, take on the negative parental point of view, and revert to a more childlike mode of interaction.

We have also observed that when people attempt to differentiate themselves from their parents (for example, "I'm not like you, you bastard" or simply "I'm different"), they often revert to the very behaviors they were challenging (see Firestone, 1997a, pp. 160–163). As noted, considerable attention must be paid to the possibility of rebuttals from the parental voice directly following a person's expressing independence or rage or indicating unusual improvement.

In anticipating these regressive trends, therapists need to be sensitive to their clients' strengths and weaknesses. They need to carefully monitor clients' responses to answering the voice and their embarking on corrective experiences.[8] Therapists must be aware that clients who break with the prescriptions of the voice before they have the psychological maturity to separate from parental introjects will suffer setbacks in their therapy. It's as though they made a premature break with their family—in effect, they left home before they were ready. When this happens, the person usually regresses to feeling more dependent and afraid than before and becomes more resistant to the therapy process. Altering behaviors based on the voice represents even more of a break with the internalized parent than verbally answering back.

Another source of regression in voice therapy is the guilt caused by clients avoiding actual relationships with family members. Even after living separately and moving toward autonomy, when clients come into contact with family members, it tends to activate voice attacks, thus precipitating regression. This often happens despite the fact that the interactions themselves appeared to be innocuous, uneventful, or seemingly positive. Becoming aware of their negative reaction to these reunions can create a conflict for clients who have no desire to hurt their families yet who wish to avoid them because they are still reactive to family influences and feel bad after contact. In general, social pressure to conform and prescriptions against choosing a lifestyle that is different than one's family of origin work against constructive change and personal development.

SUMMARY

In this chapter, we have described the steps in voice therapy, a broadly based therapeutic methodology with an emphasis on cognitive, affective, and behavioral components. The technique of verbalizing the voice in the second-person format not only elicits strong affect but also appears to access core negative beliefs or schema more quickly than other methods. In addition, this format "facilitates the process of *separating* the client's own point of view from hostile thought patterns that make up an alien point of view toward self" (Firestone, 1988, p. 205). The combination of identifying automatic thoughts or self-attacks, which is a primary focus of cognitive-behavioral therapy, and verbalizing these thoughts in the second person, which is a key component of voice therapy, shifts clients' point of view in a positive direction and leads to enduring changes in their behavior.

We outlined the theoretical basis of voice therapy methodology in separation theory and elaborated upon the concept of the fantasy bond as a core defense that underlies the individual's fundamental resistance to change or progress. We presented two case histories, which demonstrated how participants work on themselves using voice therapy. The goal in voice therapy in relation to the process of differentiation is to effectively separate out those elements of the personality that are antithetical toward the individual, that adversely affect his or her life, and that impede his or her movement toward individuation.

Voice therapy techniques help strengthen people's personal identity by identifying and challenging angry, destructive thoughts toward themselves and hostile, cynical attitudes toward others by changing self-limiting and self-destructive behaviors and by supporting them in developing their own points of view, goals, and values. Last, the methodology enhances participants' ability to remain vulnerable and open to experience, helps them to stay close to their feelings, increases their capacity for responding appropriately to both positive and negative events, and enables them to live a life without maladaptive fantasies that impede the achievement of a freer, more independent existence.

5

RELATIONSHIPS

> The fear and pain of losing love is so crushing, and so basic to our natures, that just about any trade-off to prevent it can seem reasonable. And thus you have the psychological signature of the modern self: defined by love, an empty vessel without it, the threat of love's withdrawal shriveling even the most independent spirits into complacency.
>
> —Laura Kipnis, *Against Love: A Polemic*

There is nothing more wonderful than when two people love and respect one another in a close personal relationship. An affectionate style of relating is most fulfilling and rewarding and is at the core of positive couple and family interactions. Sadly, most people find it difficult to love and find it even more problematic to accept love being directed toward them. It is a significant challenge to find and maintain a kind, generous, and decent relationship in which there is respect for each person's individuality.

Indeed, intimate relationships pose a potential threat of serious proportions to one's individuality and independence. Love is a vital force in people's lives, yet it is not essential for physical survival. Despite this fact, when people feel insecure, they tend to cling desperately to each other as though the loss of a partner would be life-threatening. In a misguided attempt to find and maintain safety and security in a relationship, they are diverted from following their own destiny. Consequently, they suppress their personal interests, goals, and dreams and may even compromise their ideals and basic values. To hold on, maintain the status quo, and keep the peace, people deceive themselves, confuse their partners, and manipulate one another in ways that are destructive to their ongoing state of being.

The psychological defenses of each member of the couple constitute the greatest threat to personal satisfaction in an intimate relationship. The more defended partners are, the greater the threat to their having a successful relationship and to their own individuation process. Accepting love leads to a feeling of increased vulnerability and challenges aspects of the negative identity formed in the family of origin. As a relationship becomes more meaningful and intimate, being loved and positively acknowledged can threaten to disrupt one's psychological equilibrium by piercing core defenses. This causes anxiety, which can be relieved by utilizing distancing behaviors that adversely affect the closeness of the couple. As the relationship deteriorates, one or both partners unconsciously sacrifice their independence and individuality to hold on to an illusion of being in love.

Fantasy bonds of this sort characterize a majority of relationships in our society. Yet compensating for what is missing by resorting to fantasy processes minimizes one's chance of achieving a fulfilling relationship or marriage. Furthermore, it is exceedingly difficult to maintain one's unique identity and to avoid submitting to the numerous agreed-upon, implicit rules of coupledom that are prevalent in our culture. Even when marriages last, each person's individuality and independence can be seriously compromised. Therefore, in respectful marriage counseling and couples therapy, the focus should ideally be on saving the individuals rather than the institution.

HOW RELATIONSHIPS BECOME HURTFUL

There is so much pain and suffering in couple relationships relative to other aspects of life that it is one of the primary reasons that people seek psychotherapy (Bradbury & Fincham, 1990).[1] Relationships can be conceptualized in terms of the differential effects they have on each person's sense of self. In good relationships, each person's self-esteem is affirmed and nurtured, as contrasted with bad relationships, in which the negative attitudes and voices of the anti-self system of each partner are reinforced. In our study of couples and families, we discovered that any personal communication or interaction between partners could be evaluated either as being supportive of the self or as interfering with each person's positive sense of self and personal development.

Unfortunately, partners often interact in ways that are supportive of the anti-self of the other. For example, research shows that individuals commit the most egregious human rights violations in their closest, most intimate associations (Tedeschi & Felson, 1994).[2] In their everyday lives, partners often treat each other in ways that they would never think of treating a coworker or friend. Without even thinking, members of a couple may overstep each other's boundaries, disregard each other's autonomy, restrict each other's freedom, and discourage any movement toward independence. These disrespectful behaviors and aversive interactions bend both people out of shape psychologically in that they trigger and support destructive voice attacks in each person and precipitate a retreat to a more defended posture.

As romantic attachments evolve, people tend to progress through different phases of relating. Initially, during the falling-in-love phase, individuals are more open, more vulnerable, and less defended than they are typically. They are willing to risk more of themselves emotionally, experience a greater sense of aliveness and vitality, treat each other with consideration and respect, and are congenial in their interactions.

However, the excitement of being in love is also fraught with emotions that can be frightening. As people become aware that they are loved, they give value to themselves and the relationship and come to realize they that have something precious to lose. The fear of the possibility of future loss evoked by being loved is difficult to tolerate, particularly for those who lacked a secure attachment early in life. At the point where people begin to feel anxious or frightened, many unconsciously retreat from feeling close, gradually give up the most valued aspects of their relationships, and instead form a fantasy bond just as they did during their childhood (Firestone & Catlett, 1999).

Once a fantasy bond has been established within a couple, experiences of genuine love and intimacy intrude on its defensive function, whereas symbols of togetherness and images of love strengthen the illusion of connection. To maintain their psychological equilibrium, people unconsciously act in ways that regulate the amount of love and affection being directed toward them. Their distancing behaviors effectively diminish the positive emotional transactions—the loving, kind, and respectful give-and-take exchanges—to a level that each person is able to tolerate. They relinquish vital areas of personal interest, opinions, and unique points of view to become a unit, a whole, at one with their partner. To the extent that the individuals progressively lose their personal identities, they suffer a loss of feeling for one another and a diminution of real communication. Instead they begin to rely more and more on habitual contact, routines, and small talk about practical matters.

Destructive Behavior Patterns

Individuals in a couple who have formed a fantasy bond engage in a multitude of behaviors that are destructive to both parties. These include dishonesty, defensive reactions to verbal feedback, and actions based on obligation. Implicit rules gradually replace free choice; role-playing takes over for personal relating; and a lack of respect for each other's boundaries, goals, and priorities becomes more prevalent. In addition, partners often demonstrate attitudes of contempt, manipulate through bullying, exhibit outright hostility, or engage in passive-aggressive manipulations.

One of the most damaging behaviors in couple relationships is the attempt to control through weakness. This type of negative power involves a partner becoming tearful, falling apart, exhibiting childlike fits, whining, or sulking or, on a more serious level, threatening self-harm or suicide (M. Miller, 1995).[3] While these actions are often effective in creating guilt feelings and manipulating one's mate or family members, they are detrimental to both the relationship and oneself.

Contempt is a toxic behavior that is commonly seen in distressed couple relationships; it involves relating to another person from a superior position and in a condescending manner that denigrates and belittles the other's opinions, thoughts, and feelings. Research conducted by John Gottman (Gottman & Silver, 1999) showed that couples whose behaviors and communications expressed attitudes of contempt were the most likely to eventually divorce. Defensiveness, stonewalling, and filibustering were among the other aversive behaviors delineated by Gottman as strong predictors of marital distress.[4] Partners who are defensive respond angrily to any criticism—whether true or false, mild or harsh—by counterattacking, crying, or employing the silent treatment in an attempt to punish the other person for his or her feedback. These overreactions and punitive responses convey a message that certain subjects are taboo. All of this leads to a shutting down of the lines of communication within the couple.

Partners tend to develop implicit contracts or rules based on conventional views about the obligations inherent in the marital roles of husband and wife. A common pattern is one that is derived from traditional gender role expectations, based on stereotypic views of women as weak, childlike, and helpless and men as logical, practical, strong, and masterful (Geis, 1993).[5] The implicit contract can be expressed in more explicit terms. For example, the woman's part could be, "I'll defer to your wishes and decisions because I need to be taken care of," whereas the man's part might be, "I'll take care of you because I need to feel big and important."

Laura Kipnis (2003) has delineated more than 100 implicit rules or interdictions that are automatically accepted by couples because they offer protection from potential threats to their illusion of connection. They take a serious toll on the people involved. Her examples include the following:

> You can't sleep apart, you can't go to bed at different times, you can't fall asleep without getting woken up to go to bed... you can't get out of bed right away after sex. (p. 86)
>
> You can't go to parties alone. You can't go out just to go out, because you can't not be considerate of the other person's worries about where you are, or their natural insecurities that you're not where you should be. (p. 84)
>
> Thus is love obtained... what matters is the form... exchanging obedience for love comes naturally—we were all once children after all, whose survival depended on the caprices of love. And thus you have the template for future intimacies. If you love me, you'll do what I want or need or demand to make me feel secure and complete and I'll love you back. (pp. 92, 93–94)

In the process of playing out these roles and adhering to their unspoken rules, people substitute the form of being in love for the substance of genuine love and affection. As they enact the everyday routines, customs, rituals, and role-determined behaviors that provide the structure and form of their relationship, they gradually lose a sense of themselves as individuals.

Couples in Collusion

> When a couple's level of differentiation is low, every effort to develop an independent identity by one of the partners is perceived as a threat to the relationship. Partners respond by feeling hurt and either attack or withdraw; emotional flooding is frequent and communication is poor.
>
> —Ayala Malach Pines, *Falling in Love*

There are a number of collusive patterns of relating that have a negative impact on individuals' personalities. For example, partners who engage in parental and childish behaviors tend to become progressively more polarized in their functioning over time. The childlike partner acts incompetent, helpless, and immature, which elicits parental responses—worry, fear, anger, and even punishment—from the other. The person who has assumed the parental role denies his or her own feelings of fear and helplessness and behaves in an authoritarian, analytical manner (Willi, 1975/1982).[6]

Another pattern of collusion closely related to the parent/child mode is that of dominance and submission. When partners refuse to be equal companions in sharing their lives, they tend to manipulate and control each other through domineering or submissive behavior. Through bullying (including the use of force), the assertive, bossy, or overbearing person controls the one who is more acquiescent. The aggressive partner's responses indicate approval and disapproval and provide rewards and punishment; he or she may become verbally or physically abusive. Some use threats of reprisal, warning the other person about a potential withdrawal of financial support or actual abandonment. As Jessica Benjamin (1988) stated,

> Ironically, the fantasy of erotic dominance and submission expresses the deep longing for wholeness. But as long as the shape of the whole is not informed by mutuality, this longing only leads to an unequal complementarity in which one person plays master, the other slave.... [Thus] our deepest desires for freedom and communion become implicated in control and submission. From such desires the bonds of love are forged. (pp. 82, 84)

A more subtle mode of dominance involves a relationship in which one partner is quick to respond and is more masterful verbally while the other has difficulty organizing his or her thoughts and expressing him- or herself. In the process of being continually defined, the quiet partner suffers from a significant loss of identity and an underlying anger and becomes more and more confused and insecure. Passive aggression is then mobilized and directed toward the more verbally aggressive partner. The same dynamics are in play when one partner acts as the helper and the other as the one with problems. The helper constantly analyzes and tends to the other, and the other becomes increasingly incapacitated and resentful.

Other complementary behavior patterns that can be observed in relationships are when one partner is more extroverted, outward, and friendly while the other is more introverted, inward, and shy; when one person is outspoken while the partner is quiet or reticent; when one is active and adventurous and the other is passive or more laid-back. People involved in collusive relationships often imagine they have found their soul mate and feel that they are finally whole. However, over time, they become progressively more dysfunctional as individuals. For example, the shy person who relies on the talkative partner to interact in social situations becomes more socially awkward while his or her mate becomes more gregarious and long-winded. Once established, this mode of interacting tends to reign throughout the duration of the relationship, with occasional role reversals. The partners rarely relate to each other from an adult ego state.

It is indeed a truism that opposites attract; however, they often eventually repel as the relationship develops. The passive person becomes more passive, and the aggressive person becomes more aggressive, and they both become more resentful. They eventually come to hate the very traits that they were originally drawn to (Pines, 1999). This explains the ultimate irony that the people to whom one is most attracted are often not necessarily those who are good for one's overall development. In looking for "the missing piece," people choose someone who best fits with their defenses and destructive voices so they can reconstruct the emotional environment of their past. Thus, they find themselves involved in a process of reliving rather than living.

Patterns of Withholding and Self-Denial

One of the most hurtful behaviors that people act out in their intimate relationships is the defense of withholding. Withholding generally involves holding back positive qualities and responses that were previously a significant expression of a person's kindness and affection.[7] Withholding is a complex problem that is made up of two very different aspects: (1) passive-aggressive reactions based on anger and (2) self-denying reactions that involve a basic retreat from love, positive acknowledgment, and successes in life (Firestone & Catlett, 1999, 2009a).

Passive-aggressive withholding involves indirect ways of expressing anger that are provoking and subtly punishing in close personal interactions. Whenever there is a power differential and people find it difficult or impossible to cope with anger directly, they tend to use passive means to accomplish their goals, assert themselves, or express their feelings of resentment. People utilizing passive aggression often agree with a plan of action but later refuse to cooperate, act forgetful, are stubborn, tend to procrastinate, sabotage situations, are nonproductive or noncompliant, or simply refuse to obey rules and regulations. This type of withholding often involves control through weakness, manipulating others through falling apart, crying, behaving incompetently, or acting out self-destructive responses.

Withholding that is self-denying and self-limiting in relation to one's priorities can be considered a core defense against death anxiety. The person accommodates to death by progressively giving up life pursuits, particularly his or her highest priorities. When being loved and experiencing closeness become too frightening or stressful, people hold back positive responses in order to establish a safe emotional distance. They tend to resist involvement in emotional transactions, refusing to take love in from the outside or to offer love and affection outwardly.

There are innumerable examples of this type of withholding that are commonplace within couple relationships. In some instances, partners stop participating in what were once their favorite activities, situations that they especially enjoyed together. Early in their relationship, a woman loved to fly with her boyfriend in his small Cessna, but after they were married, she stopped accompanying him on his flights, claiming that small planes were claustrophobic and dangerous. In addition to retreating from companionship, partners may withhold physical affection and sex or put on excessive weight or otherwise change their appearance to be less attractive. One man who was initially admired by his boyfriend for his slim physique gained more than 20 pounds within a few months of their moving in together. In other instances, partners may refuse to share in practical arrangements, use work to avoid closeness, and provoke distance by pushing the other's buttons. A woman told her boyfriend how much she enjoyed his frank and open communication. Not very long after, he became more withdrawn, quiet, and indirect in their conversations. These and other similar expressions of withholding are common, yet they have a devastating effect on intimate relationships and families.

Acts of withholding often involve first offering then withdrawing support for one's mate. For example, a businesswoman, marketing expert, and web designer offered to construct a website for her husband's company. For weeks, she procrastinated and failed to meet the deadline for launching the site, a date set in stone by her husband's vendors and sponsors. When he became frustrated and angry, she acted innocent and misunderstood. Ironically, it had been her idea to undertake the task in the first place, and he was sorry that he had agreed.

In a humorous, tongue-in-cheek book, *How to Ruin a Perfectly Good Relationship,* Pat Love and Sunny Shulkin (1997) list statements representing the thoughts or voices that influence a wide range of withholding behaviors typically observed in couple relationships. Obviously, the goal for people who want to pursue positive relationships is to *not* engage in any of these behaviors but rather to take action against these directives:

> Make it a practice to be late. Be stingy with praise and appreciation. Withhold information.
>
> Withhold sex (you get extra points for this one). Refuse your partner's sexual overtures. Give up on sex. Decide you're just not sexual. Let passion die. Promise sex then don't follow through.
>
> Never let him (her) see you smiling.
>
> Exchange the gifts your partner buys for you. Deflect all compliments. Never ask for help.
>
> Control everything and everyone. Hold fast to the belief: "If you loved me you would know what I want." When your partner tries to please you, find fault with the efforts.
>
> Keep no promises. Keep your true thoughts and feelings to yourself.
>
> Pay more attention to the TV than your partner.
>
> Let days go by without a kind word or loving gesture. Take pleasure in withholding pleasure. Strike the words, "I love you" from your vocabulary.
>
> Refuse to see how your partner shows you love. (pp. 2, 3, 12, 25, 34, 37, 38, 42, 43, 44, 45, 55, 56, 59, 68, 71)

The more people prize a relationship, the more they value their own life and that of their partner, and the more they come to dread the inevitable loss of both. Indeed, affection, closeness, and a sense of intimacy often cause feelings of death anxiety to surface. In our investigations, we found that death salience tends to increase distancing behaviors between partners. When a fear of mortality is aroused, partners tend to retreat from actions of genuine closeness and unconsciously withhold affection and sexual responses. This process is difficult to measure experimentally because death awareness increases the fantasy bond. Couples may act more clingy and dependent while at the same time being able to tolerate less genuine affection, sexuality, companionship, and communication and fewer respectful interactions.[8]

For example, Janet had been married for several years to a man 15 years her senior. A close friend of theirs suddenly became ill and died. In the weeks following the funeral, Janet withdrew more and more into herself, becoming emotionally unavailable to her husband. She seemed to be losing all interest in him and even began to question their relationship. She was confused and didn't understand the rapid change in her feelings toward her husband.

Increasingly troubled by her ambivalence and conflict and concerned that her relationship was deteriorating, Janet decided to explore her voice attacks in a group meeting. As she spoke, she began to recognize that the attitudes she was acting upon reflected her mother's point of view about life and love:

> "See, I told you; it's just a matter of time before he gets sick and dies, just like your friend. How did you get yourself into this situation in the first place? Why did you marry this person? You idiot! He's just going to die and leave you and then you'll be all alone. You'll have to take care of the kids by yourself. What a selfish, inconsiderate thing for him to do, to marry you. He should have thought about this. It just shows he doesn't give a shit about you. Just look ahead down the road and see how that goes! [Louder.] Just see how that goes!
>
> "It's just going to get worse. IT'S JUST GOING TO GET WORSE! [Yells angrily.] Yeah, he might be feeling fine now, but it's just going to get worse. What do you think your life will be like then? You're going to feel awful! You're going to hate it. You're going to hate him!"
>
> At night, sometimes if my husband looks tired, I start listening to those voices telling me he's going to die and I get worried. I want to answer back to those voices and say what I really believe. "The present is precious to me, because this is what matters to me, right now. That's all there is really. I don't know about the future and I don't want to keep on thinking miserable things about it in advance when it's not happening at this moment. I don't want to ruin these moments with your negative kind of thinking.
>
> "And I don't want to give up things in my life just because down the road things are going to be more difficult. I hate that attitude. It pisses me off. That's no way to live. But that's how you live now, a drudge of a life in preparation for death. That's not living. And it's also not sharing it with anybody. I'm not going to stop my life just because I'm going to die someday. I'm not going to die ahead of time, like you have. I'm going to live my life every moment."

Janet used the methods of voice therapy in subsequent groups and was able to break out of her miserable, inward state. Once again, she felt close and affectionate with her husband. She realized how her actions had been dominated by the critical, self-protective attitudes she had internalized from her mother.

When people hold back their positive feelings and actions, it arouses anxiety and anger in their partner and creates pain and distance in the relationship. Sustained patterns of withholding contribute to an individual's feeling of pessimism and general retreat from life. For this reason, people who are withholding often experience painful feelings of self-hatred, regret, remorse, and existential guilt in relation to a life unlived.

The mechanism of withholding is basically a self-destructive process that hurts the perpetrator as well as his or her partner. It profoundly limits a person's fulfillment in life and restricts personal development. Those who are withholding and self-denying fear a loss of control; therefore, they tend to perceive spontaneous responses and free-flowing interactions with others as risky and potentially painful (Firestone & Catlett, 1999).

The motives that are behind withholding behavior are usually obscured or well rationalized, and the self-destructive aspect of the behavior is successfully repressed. As a result, there is considerable resistance and defensiveness when people are confronted about their withholding patterns. When people rely heavily on this defense, they are poorly differentiated, maladaptive in their responses, and at serious odds with themselves.

SELECTION, DISTORTION, AND PROVOCATION IN RELATIONSHIPS

> For the partner carries parents inside the self, and is not aware when their voice takes over.
>
> —Wym Bramley, *Bewitched, Bothered, and Bewildered*

Individuals who lack significant differentiation from the negative, internalized parental point of view toward themselves have difficulty living in an emotional environment that is more positive and different from the one in which they developed their defenses. Rather than change themselves and adapt to the new situation, people usually adjust their interpersonal world in an effort to maintain their original defensive adaptations, recapitulate their early attachments, and preserve their imagined connection with their parents. Within intimate relationships, partners often use the defense mechanisms of selection, distortion, and provocation for this purpose.

Selection

People tend to select as a mate someone who is similar to a parent or family member, who therefore feels familiar to them. On an unconscious level, they are drawn to someone whose defenses mesh with their own.[9] Initially this dynamic may contribute to a good deal of sexual chemistry. In addition, people choose each other on the basis of looks, personality, intelligence, suitability, success, race, religion, and other attributes. This makes the selection process a complex operation.

It is apparent that within the selection process there are high-level and low-level choices. A high-level choice would be defined as a person who meets one's highest and most stringent standards—for example, one whom they would like, find attractive, and admire and who would also choose them. Not many people are fortunate enough to be able to choose from a pool of many high-level prospects. Even with the advent of computer dating assisted by technology that purports to match people with compatible personalities, it is still rare for people to find their high-level choice. Moreover, the selections made by most men and women still come from a relatively small pool of available prospects; these selections would realistically be characterized as medium- or perhaps even low-level choices.

In an attempt to rationalize medium- or low-level choices, many people aggrandize the person they have selected and elevate the person into becoming their "soul mate" or "that one in a million." In the fantasy bond that ensues, this transition from a lower-level choice to a higher-level one involves a certain amount of self-deception and mutual idealization that ends up taking its toll on the relationship.

Most people are aware on some level that they are not necessarily the highest-level choice of their mate. This fosters a sense of insecurity and desperation in both partners and makes them fearful that the other will make a better choice at some future date. As a result, each persistently demands that their partner indicate a preference for him or her over all others, creating a pressure in the relationship for each mate to constantly reflect the illusion that the other is special. Both members of the couple tend to be punishing when confronted with evidence to the contrary.

Distortion

When people select a partner whose manner is unfamiliar to them, a person who loves and values them in a way that is essentially different from what they were used to, they may distort their perceptions of this person to re-create conditions that are more familiar, although negative. They often alter their perceptions of their mate so as to see him or her as more similar to a parent or caretaker than they actually are. Distortion also serves to preserve an idealized image of one's parents, because people can deny their parents' inadequacies, shortcomings, and aggressive tendencies by projecting these weaknesses and hostilities onto their partners. Distorted perceptions of a romantic partner are affected by cognitive schemas or destructive thought processes associated with negative internal working models.[10]

In the process of distortion, people exaggerate any faults their partner does possess and attempt to build a strong case against him or her. On a subliminal level, the partner picks up these distorted views through projective identification and eventually comes to believe they are true. Clearly, this process is hurtful and leads to escalating cycles of blame and counterblame and to long-standing grudges on both sides that are difficult to unravel. In the end, much individuality and closeness are lost.

Provocation

People often manipulate their loved ones in order to elicit familiar parental responses. They may incite frustration and rage in their partner through forgetfulness, thoughtlessness, or other passive-aggressive behaviors.[11] Eventually a partner may not only be provoked into a point of view that is alien to him or her, but he or she may actually end up verbalizing the other person's voice attacks. A person may ultimately be maneuvered into no longer being able to love or even like one's partner.

Withholding is one of the most successful means by which people provoke their partner. Feelings of longing, desperation, and emotional hunger are provoked in the person being withheld from. The awareness that feelings and responses are being withheld arouses an intensified focus on the partner who is holding back his or her natural, positive responses. The withholding partner frequently misperceives this focus as a demand or as intrusive and entrapping. He or she then reacts defensively, and the resultant downward spiral creates distress and emotional pain in both parties, strains their relationship, and increases their self-attacks.

The double messages conveyed by withholding individuals to their partners are also provoking. Their positive verbal statements contradict the negative messages their behavior is communicating nonverbally through posture, facial expressions, and tone of voice. This is "crazy-making," confusing, and hurtful to the person being withheld from. In their book *Stop! You're Driving Me Crazy,* Bach and Deutsch (1979) described partners who portray their passive-aggressive behaviors as simple mistakes, errors of judgment, carelessness, or innocent forgetfulness. They noted, however, that most people "are not usually aware that they are sending two conflicting messages" (p. 17).

For example, a man worked side-by-side with his fiancée on her landscaping project. She expressed her appreciation for his help, but soon, in spite of his interest and desire to continue sharing the work with her, he found excuses for avoiding these activities. In another example, a woman told her husband that she wanted to be closer to him and suggested they plan to spend more time together despite their tight work schedules. He agreed, and during the following weeks, he invited her to various dinners and for evening walks. But for one reason or another, she consistently turned him down. When he pointed this out to her, she rationalized her rejection of his offers by saying that her work was important to her. In both cases, the double messages were confusing and mystifying because they played with the other person's sense of reality.

When other means and methods of defense fail, people resort to provocative behaviors that create distance and help maintain the safety of their defensive solution. Combined with the selection process and distortion of their partners, these mechanisms enable people to relive the emotional climate of their childhoods in their current relationships. To the extent that partners had secure attachment patterns in their developmental years, they tend to be more differentiated and less reliant on these processes.

THE EFFECTS OF CONVENTIONAL SOCIAL MORES ON RELATIONSHIPS

Although every couple has a unique style of relating, there are many societal attitudes, standards for behavior, roles, and customs that most people accept uncritically. As noted earlier, society represents, in part, a pooling of individual defense systems (Firestone & Catlett, 1989). Once established, social mores and conventional points of view reflect back on the individual and can adversely affect the quality of his or her relationships.[12]

In relation to finding and sustaining a loving relationship, society adheres to two conflicting views: one is idealistic, and the other is pessimistic. The idealistic view is based, in part, on the assumptions that (1) one can satisfy all of one's wants and needs in an intimate love relationship and (2) there is a special person, a soul mate, out there somewhere, who is capable of fulfilling one's dreams. These unrealistic expectations cause a good deal of disillusionment and misery; they tend to reinforce people's tendencies to form a fantasy of love and elevate the relationship to something that it could never be, even in the best of circumstances. Along with these assumptions, many people believe that members of a couple "belong" to each other. They tend to give over or assign their sexuality to their partner, which, in itself, contradicts the basic truth that people's sexual attractions, like their feelings, are their own and cannot be given over to anyone else or controlled by another person.

At the same time, the cynical or pessimistic view of relationships predicts that romance is destined to fade after marriage. This gloomy forecast can become a self-fulfilling prophecy for individuals who act out their negative, suspicious attitudes toward others. The stereotypic views of the opposite sex that are prevalent throughout society support people's distrust, restrict their thinking, increase their hostility, and negatively influence their behavior toward one another (Firestone, 1985). Even though many of these destructive social mores, sanctions, and societal prohibitions remain largely implicit or unspoken, they have become the accepted standards by which people assess behavior. Despite being based on core assumptions about human nature that are blatantly false, they tend to be perceived as common knowledge. Some of these beliefs may include the following:

Humans are basically deficient in and of themselves. Most people grow up feeling that something is inherently missing in them. As noted earlier, many people imagine that to be a whole person, they need to find that special person out in the world who will make them complete. This belief intensifies their feelings of desperation to find a partner and leads to premature or unwise choices. Later they are disappointed when the feeling of emptiness persists.

An individual must subordinate him- or herself to preserve the couple, family, or society's norms; otherwise, he or she is abnormal. When people do not live up to society's expectations to get conventionally married or to live together in a committed relationship, they may be considered peculiar, immature, or deviant. Conformity and adjustment to society are seen as moral and healthy, whereas nonconformity to societal expectations is perceived as aberrant and a threat to society.

The nature of love is constant and unchanging. The idealistic, romanticized view of love as depicted by society and the media encourages an expectation that the feelings in a relationship will always stay the same. However, love, like any other emotion, fluctuates; it comes and goes, and its expression is affected by innumerable situations and internal states. Even satisfying relationships are characterized by emotional highs and lows in the ebb and flow of loving feelings between partners. When people think of love as unchanging, they find it difficult to reconcile contradictory feelings (love and hate) toward the same person.

A person's physical nature and sexuality are sinful or immoral. Any belief system or religion that conceptualizes the human body and its sexual functions as sinful or dirty has the effect of instilling feelings of shame and guilt in people that limit the course of their lives, particularly their sexuality. Negative attitudes toward the body that were formed in early childhood are later extended into the adult's sexual life. Shame, guilt, and restrictive views about sex have made it an area fraught with anxiety, pain, and guilt for many.

Rigid restrictions on sexuality seriously interfere with people's personal fulfillment and sexual maturity. Furthermore, these standards perpetuate the very destructiveness that they were originally established to control. Unreasonable prohibitions concerning the body, nudity, and sexuality tend to increase hostility, tension, and sexual abnormalities (Prescott, 1975, 1996).

People who subscribe to the popular beliefs noted above tend to become more cynical, indifferent, and duplicitous in their couple and family relationships. The pressure to conform to societal mores and expectations supports people's reliance on the fantasy bond and their tendency to emphasize form over substance in their style of relating. Insight into the societal myths and assumptions described here could lead to more relevant and informed education about relationships and challenge many of the harmful interactions that currently occur between people (Firestone & Catlett, 1999).

SUMMARY

Positive relationships can be defined as being supportive of the individuality of the members of the couple. Relationships are never neutral; those that fail in this regard have a negative effect on the differentiation process. When two people first meet and choose one another, they tend to be relatively independent, affectionate, and respectful of each other's boundaries. But quite often the individuals begin to indicate various levels of immaturity, insecurity, and fearfulness. In their desperation to find security, they resort to fantasies that make more of the situation than is merited. In trying to make things feel safe and secure, they attempt to nail things down. At this point, people form a fantasy bond.

To protect this illusion of fusion and imagined connection, people retreat to a more familiar, less personal style of relating—one that repeats the kind of attachment they originally formed with their parents. In this way, they transform the new relationship into one that more closely matches the original relationship in which their defenses were formed. When the fantasy bond is extended into an adult relationship, it exists as an implicit defensive pact between partners to protect against feelings of aloneness, insecurity, and death anxiety. Supporting the fantasy bond and its imagined safety is comforting, but it is costly and ultimately hurtful to the participants.

In maintaining the fantasy of love, the tolerance for real love and acknowledgment by partners is greatly reduced and is often replaced by a disrespectful collusion and by negative behaviors that do not fit any realistic definition of love. Most couples act toward one another in a manner that reinforces each partner's negative voices and is indicative of a lack of support for each other's goals, independence, and personal boundaries. Over time, there is generally an increase in criticality and hostility and a diminution of affection and sexuality.

The three defensive maneuvers of selection, distortion, and provocation operate to maintain both partners' psychological equilibrium at the expense of their self-realization. People tend to act out a variety of hurtful behaviors, often without awareness or intentionality. They include role-playing, exhibiting parental or childish responses, withholding positive traits and behaviors, addressing the other with disrespect and contempt, and preemptively distancing themselves from one another. These defensive actions function to keep people entwined with one another, and they come to live more as a unit or a "we" than as two individuals who move freely together in each other's company. The members of a couple tend to gradually relinquish their independence and function in a manner that is no longer separate or equal, and each loses a certain zest for life. Lastly, social mores, attitudes, and assumptions about relationships play a destructive role in affecting the quality of people's relating. The self is under siege from a host of conventional attitudes and expectations about coupling that adversely affect intimacy and sexuality.

However, there is hope in understanding these issues. In becoming aware of how they hurt each other in their relationships, people can learn to avoid destructive interactions. By being open to change and concerned with their own personal development, they can make radical changes in their intimate relationships and retain their feeling of self and their strength and individuality.

By having the courage to explore these subjects and look at their relationships honestly, couples could stop looking for definition or confirmation of themselves in the other and would no longer need to attempt to satisfy all their wants and needs in the one relationship. They could learn to "leave each other alone" in the best sense of the phrase, to treat one another with kindness and decency, and to take pleasure in seeing the other person grow and flourish.

People could take definite steps to break into the fantasy bond and recapture the feeling of friendship and love they experienced in the early phases of the relationship. They could expose their weaknesses and hostility, take back their projections, learn to be nondefensive and open to feedback, admit critical attitudes toward themselves and their partner, and face the sad feelings involved in trying to restore intimacy. They could talk openly about their fears of being alone and their fear of rejection, abandonment, and the inevitable loss through death of themselves and their partners. Both parties could move toward independence, increase their respect for each other, and establish equality and interdependence in their relationship. They could expand their interactions with other friends and family members to provide a broader basis for reality testing.

In conclusion, by breaking free from the imprisonment of their defenses, rejecting the temptation to form a fantasy bond, and separating from negative parental prescriptions, men and women can expand their capacity to both offer and accept love, sustain their feeling and passion, and find meaning in their lives (Figure 5.1).

In Figure 5.1, the circles represent the individuals and the alterations in the circle outline represent their defensive adaptations. It is obvious that A is the counterpart or fit to D—that is, A is defensively suited for D and vice versa. If A and D went to a party (all other things being equal), they would be attracted to one another and they would feel a certain sexual chemistry. This type of selection process tends to endure, and research teaches us that people are consistently drawn toward the same types (Pines, 1999). Figure 5.2 shows the close couple, and Figure 5.3 represents the couple in a fantasy bond. The latter symbolizes the couple's merged identity and their subsequent loss of individuality.

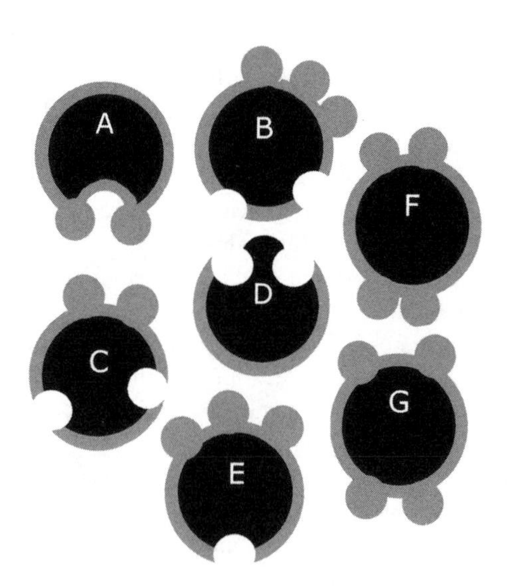

Figure 5.1 Individuals and Their Defenses

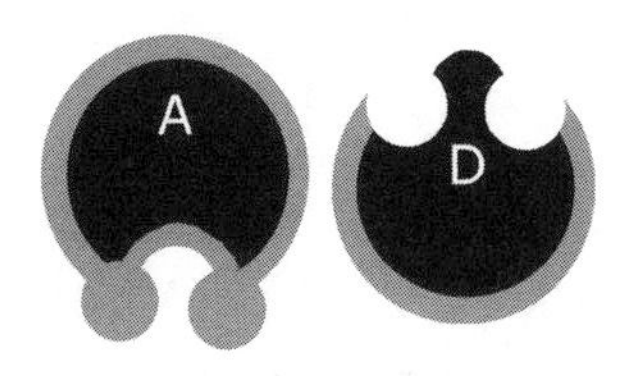

Figure 5.2 Emotionally Close Couple

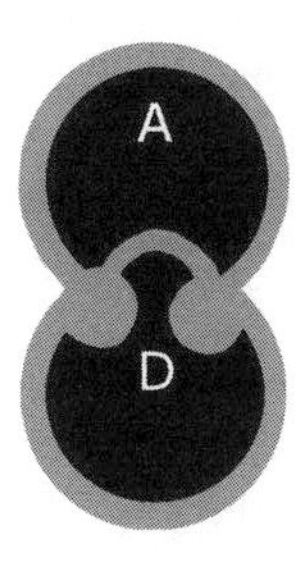

Figure 5.3 Couple in a Fantasy Bond

6

VOICE THERAPY APPLIED TO COUPLE RELATIONSHIPS

> For humans, differentiation boils down to... four abilities that support and develop your sense of self: Holding on to your self while your partner pressures you to adapt; regulating your own anxiety; staying non-reactive and engaged; and tolerating discomfort so you can grow.
>
> —David Schnarch, *Intimacy and Desire*

The internalized voices that people bring to intimate relationships are disruptive to their personal development and to their differentiation as autonomous individuals. They are the primary cause for the difficulty that people have in establishing and maintaining intimate relationships in which both partners thrive. In no other area of life do people live out their negative destiny according to past programming more than in their closest relationships. Thus, associations that could be the most rewarding often turn out to be the opposite.

In relationships characterized by a fantasy bond, both partners filter their communications through a biased, alien point of view monitored by a system of critical voices that, more often than not, distort their partner's real image and intentions. Based on this malignant coaching, the members of a couple tend to avoid or reject each other's expressions of love and use rationalizations to justify their anger, alienation, and distancing behaviors. They often project their self-attacks onto each other and then respond defensively, as though they were being disrespected or demeaned by their mates (Firestone & Catlett, 1999).

The most effective psychotherapy for couples involves each person identifying his or her critical voices and challenging their destructive effects. When utilized with couples, voice therapy helps partners gain access to the voice attacks that are influencing their alienating behaviors and creating conflict in the relationship. Patterns of dishonest communication are interrupted as each person reveals and then challenges the contents of his or her voice attacks. By identifying specific self-criticisms and judgmental, hostile thoughts about the other, each partner is able to relate more openly and closely. As they come to understand that their own voice attacks are the primary source of distress in the relationship, the focus is taken off of changing the other person and is instead placed on changing themselves. This shift in attention significantly alters people's attitudes toward their mates and enhances their own personal growth.

PRELIMINARY STUDY OF HOW VOICES AFFECT RELATIONSHIPS

In our investigation of voice therapy methodology, it was immediately apparent that destructive voices had a powerful effect on the quality of people's intimate relationships. When we utilized the procedure with couples, both individuals were strengthened in their sense of self; there was a decrease in each person's defensiveness and distortion of the other and a significant improvement in the quality of their relating, both emotionally and physically.[1]

Several years ago, we became interested in developing a scale to assess an individual's destructive voices in the context of his or her intimate relationship. The rationale was similar to the one we used in constructing several other instruments, including the Firestone Assessment of Self-Destructive Thoughts (Firestone & Firestone, 2006) and the Firestone Assessment of Violent Thoughts (Firestone & Firestone, 2008a). To obtain items for the new scale, we asked participants in a focus group to think about their intimate relationships and to verbalize their negative thoughts toward themselves, their partners, and their relationships.[2] They began by identifying the content of these attitudes and thoughts in a rational manner; however, as had been the case in our other studies, they ultimately verbalized powerful voice attacks and released intense feelings of anger and sadness.

Based on this initial investigation, we discovered the following: (1) People have considerable hostility toward self and often feel that they are unlovable. (2) Partners often have similar levels of self-differentiation and reciprocal voices; they seek confirmation of their self-worth through the other. (3) Destructive voices that people bring to the relationship, when left unchallenged, often lead to a destructive polarization in which partners play out complementary roles (e.g., parent/child or dominant/submissive). (4) People's styles of relating are often similar to the attachment patterns they formed with early caregivers. For example, Fraley (2002) has developed a prototype model that "predicts that the continuity between early attachment security and attachment security at any point later in the life course will be equivalent to a correlation of approximately .39 . . . a moderate degree of stability" (p. 135). Insecure styles of relating in an adult romantic attachment (preoccupied, dismissing, or fearful) are largely based on negative parental prescriptions, expectations regarding the availability or unavailability of a new attachment figure (internal working model), and other defensive adaptations developed in relation to interpersonal pain in the family.

Romantic attachments not only produce conditions that can reinforce destructive voices already existing within each person, but an intimate relationship also provides a format for creating new forms of negative programming and critical voices in each partner through the process of defensive projective identification (D. Scharff & Scharff, 1991; Zeitner, 2012).[3] In addition, when partners distort or provoke their mate in an unconscious effort to support their defenses and re-create their past, new voices can be generated in the person who is being misunderstood or manipulated.

In one example, a woman who was characteristically noncritical and accepting married a man who had grown up with a hypercritical mother. Because the marked difference in this character trait between his wife and his mother caused her husband anxiety, he responded by unconsciously projecting his mother's negative traits onto his wife. At first the woman was confused and annoyed by being seen incorrectly and by frequently having to explain herself and her motives. Over time, however, her husband's attitudes and behaviors evoked an entirely new set of voices in her, and she actually came to feel and believe that she was a disapproving and critical person.

AN OVERVIEW OF VOICE THERAPY WITH COUPLES

In applying voice therapy methodology with couples in a psychotherapy setting, partners identify and challenge voice attacks that govern the behaviors that are detrimental to their usual way of relating to each other. They then collaborate with the therapist to formulate goals for the relationship as well as for their personal development. This process involves planning and implementing corrective suggestions for actions that contradict the voice. It requires taking emotional risks and choosing to remain vulnerable by breaking with defenses that protect one from experiencing anxiety and other painful feelings. In applying the techniques of voice therapy to these therapeutic tasks, both parties become more individuated and pursuant of their own goals and priorities in life.

One reason that people in a couple are resistant to evolving psychologically and becoming more differentiated is that they are fearful that if they develop a more independent style of relating they will lose their relationship. They are concerned that they might not continue to be chosen or that, worse, they may no longer choose their partner. This fear results in their clinging to a familiar style of relating, no matter how negative it may be, and in that service they manipulate and control each other. However, once manifestations of a fantasy bond have been altered, as described in the summary of Chapter 5, a new, more positive type of relationship becomes possible. Individuals can reclaim the territory they have lost through the expansion of their personal boundaries and their development as individuals. In addition, when a couple participates in voice therapy, each partner is directly exposed to his or her mate's psychotherapy experience, which helps the couple to develop an empathic way of viewing one another.

The therapist may determine that the couple would benefit from first participating in individual sessions where they might feel less inhibited in expressing their angry and hostile voice attacks about their partner. After they have learned to separate incorporated attitudes from their own point of view, conjoint sessions are productive. On the other hand, treatment can begin with sessions where both partners participate. In these sessions, each partner listens in turn as the other verbalizes his or her voices toward self and other. When expressing their voice attacks toward their partner, people often speculate about which critical statements their parents or other early significant figures might hold regarding their mate's behaviors and personality traits. These hostile, cynical thoughts are generally verbalized in the third-person format, as though the negative information were being imparted to the person about his or her partner. For example, "He's so weak and pathetic!" or "She's so overbearing and bossy!"

PART I: STEPS IN THE VOICE THERAPY PROCESS WITH COUPLES

During the therapeutic process, partners first formulate the problem that they perceive is limiting their satisfaction in the relationship and then proceed through the same five steps utilized in the discussion groups, as described in Chapter 4. For couples experiencing problems in sexual relating, partners who have learned the techniques can verbalize voice attacks that lead to diminished sexual desire or that interrupt the flow of feelings during sex.

Voice therapy methodology helps each member of the couple give away his or her hostile attitudes toward the other, take back projections based on past relationships, and cease blaming and denouncing the other. In tracing the source of these destructive attitudes to early family interactions, the partners develop a new perspective on one another's problems and feel empathy for their mates and compassion for themselves. Each person learns to accommodate to the anxiety associated with taking action to challenge self-protective defenses and is gradually able to maintain the behavioral changes.

Daniel and Heather

For the first three years that Daniel and Heather lived together, they enjoyed a close, loving relationship, but over the last year, they had become increasingly estranged and their interactions were fraught with conflict, which caused them much distress. They decided to participate in a discussion group for couples to address these issues in an attempt to recapture the feelings of companionship and love that they had initially enjoyed.

Formulating the Problem

Partners are encouraged to listen respectfully to the other person as he or she expresses feelings, thoughts, and opinions about the problem they are experiencing in their relationship. In their first group meeting, Heather describes a typical interaction with her husband:

> It's gotten to where every time Daniel and I try to work on anything together or even talk about things, I feel bad. Whether we're talking about finances, or even if we're just trying to decide something simple like where to go for dinner, I end up feeling tense and nervous. Then he notices how I'm acting and says things like, "Look, if you really don't want to talk about this or do this with me, if you're going to act like that, I'd just as soon not talk at all."

> I feel especially bad with him in relation to our financial situation. He criticizes me all the time, and accuses me of not wanting to stick to our budget, but that's hard to do in these times. So my feelings get hurt and I usually just get quiet or start to cry. Sometimes I get angry at him and walk out of the room and this makes him even angrier. I end up feeling powerless, like a child. The thing that's really puzzling to me is I don't feel this way in other areas of my life. I'm a pretty level-headed person at my job, so it has something to do specifically with this relationship.

Next, Daniel describes how he conceptualizes their difficulties.

> I know I can be a critical person sometimes, and I can be impatient with people who are incompetent. But sometimes I get so frustrated with Heather it's ridiculous.
>
> [Turning to Heather.] I know that you're smart, you've taken on so many responsibilities at your work, but with me you act the exact opposite. A lot of times you act incompetent and helpless. You ask me so many questions about practical things. More and more these days, you act like a child whenever we try to do something together. I end up feeling like I'm the meanest guy in the world. We used to have so much fun doing anything together. [Sad facial expression.]
>
> But the thing that bugs me the most is the way you act about our finances. The childish way you are whenever we even talk about it, I just end up trying to deal with it by myself, but I get so angry because you keep sabotaging the budget we agreed on by spending way too much money.

Daniel and Heather had become polarized in a collusive parent/child pattern of interaction, whereas initially their relationship had been more equal. This polarization fostered defensive reactions and counterreactions in both people. Their relating became increasingly characterized by bickering and outright hostility, and there was a reduction in the respectful exchange of thoughts, opinions, and feelings between them. Heather began withholding her intelligence and competence, whereas Daniel became more authoritarian and parental.

Family systems theorist Murray Bowen (1978) has described this type of polarized relationship as being made up of an "over-functioning/under-functioning reciprocity" in which both partners are trying "to make one self out of two":

> One spouse becomes more the dominant decision maker for the common self, while the other adapts to the situation. This is one of the best examples in borrowing and trading of self in a close relationship. One may assume the dominant role and force the other to be adaptive, or one may assume the adaptive role and force the other to be dominant. . . . The dominant one gains self at the expense of the more adaptive one, who loses self. More differentiated spouses have lesser degrees of fusion, and fewer of the complications. (p. 377)

In these cases, one partner more often plays out the child part while the other plays the part of parent, thereby externalizing the self-parenting process. Neither partner is functioning from an adult ego state. As long as these types of manipulations and the corresponding reactions are operating, both partners feel inextricably bound to the other and at the mercy of voices attacking themselves and their partner. R. D. Laing (1961/1971) succinctly depicted this type of relationship in *Self and Others:*

> Some people undoubtedly have a remarkable aptitude for keeping the other tied in knots. There are those who excel in tying knots and those who excel in being tied in knots. Tyer and tied are often both unconscious of how it is done, or even that it is being done at all. (p. 158)

Verbalizing Destructive Thoughts and Releasing Feelings

In this step, both partners, in turn, verbalize (a) voice attacks toward themselves and their partner, (b) negative attitudes they believe their partner has toward them, and (c) negative attitudes they believe their parents have about them, their partner, and their life. They also express any feelings that surface while articulating these destructive thoughts and attitudes.

Each person takes full responsibility for his or her own voice attacks by acknowledging that these are not being caused by the other and reassuring the other that the attacks do not necessarily represent their actual point of view. Even if a voice attack has some basis in reality, partners are asked to focus on the source of the attack within themselves and relinquish any hostile or blaming attitudes toward the other person. Interestingly, people are rarely surprised by their mate's voices about them. Instead of feeling hurt or angry, they often feel relieved because their partner has usually been acting out behaviors based on these voices in the relationship. In this group meeting, Heather describes how she feels after an argument with Daniel about their finances.

HEATHER: It's so strange but after we have one of these arguments and I really feel like I am going to be different about our finances, it's like he doesn't believe me. I think he's cynical about me and thinks that I can't change.

R. FIRESTONE: What do you think Daniel is thinking about you at those times? How do you think he's seeing you?

HEATHER: I just know he's still putting me down in his mind. I know he doesn't believe I can change this.

R. FIRESTONE: How would you say those thoughts as a voice? Try to say what you imagine Daniel is thinking about you; say the thoughts as though he were saying them to you.

HEATHER: He would probably say something like this: "Just look at you, trying to convince me that you can manage money. You're so incompetent, so stupid. You can't fool me. I don't believe you. I've heard all this before from you."

That's the way I think he's thinking about me. Then I get demoralized and give up on trying to be different. But I don't really want to give up on changing this.

R. FIRESTONE: What are some of your other voices on the subject?

HEATHER: I know what my mother would say. First, she would feel sorry for me. She'd say something like: "You're trying so hard, and look at him, you still can't satisfy him. You still can't make him happy." But then it starts getting angry and starts attacking me: "You still can't get it right, can you? You're so stupid! You were never good at math. You're an idiot. And you think you're going to be different? You can't be any different!" [Cries softly, pauses.]

But then my thoughts quickly turn into anger at Daniel. [To Daniel.] I feel hesitant to say them in front of you [Daniel], but it's like: "Can't he see that you're trying? He doesn't even appreciate the effort you're making. He's so demanding of you! No matter what you do, no matter how hard you try, nothing makes him happy. He's so mean! He's just a mean, demanding asshole!"

R. FIRESTONE: [To Daniel.] How did you feel listening to Heather?

DANIEL: I feel a little bit shaken up, but I also feel a sense of relief. I was picking up her feelings anyway. I always sensed her anger, and the two or three times when she actually got angry and told me off, she called me names like that.

The dynamics operating in this relationship underscore the fact that both partners were using the other to validate their negative identity. Heather was using Daniel to confirm a view of herself as incompetent and stupid. She was holding on to low-grade anger and hostility toward her husband, and she acted out a childlike, victimized role in relation to what she called Daniel's "intrusive and controlling" behavior. For his part, Daniel was using Heather to support his view that he was mean by acting judgmental and condescending toward her, especially when discussing their finances.

R. FIRESTONE: [To Daniel.] What are your voices when you and Heather have those conversations?

DANIEL: When we get into those arguments, it's like I can hear my father's voice in my head, saying: "She's so careless with money. She doesn't give a shit about you or your problems. She's hopeless, or maybe she's even stupid, but anyway, you'd just as well give it up. Just give her the fucking money. You'll never get anywhere arguing with her. She's like a stubborn child! Look, just give up on her. She'll never grow up. Sure, she was a good companion and friend for a while, but look what's happened now. She's just like your mother! I had to put up with her spending and lying and conniving for years."

Those are the attacks I have on Heather, but mostly I turn on myself and have attacks that I'm stingy with money, like: "You're so tight. You're a miser with your money! Why are you so mean? You don't care about anybody but yourself! You don't give a damn about her, or about anybody! You're just like your father!" Obviously that's my mother's point of view. I think it ties into a feeling I have of being selfish: "You're so selfish, self-centered, you just want your own way all the time."

Later in this meeting, Daniel examined his anger toward Heather at a deeper level:

DANIEL: I'd like to be able to deal with my anger better so I can stop acting so parental. But when we get off track, the way Heather gets victimized is so hard for me to deal with. I really don't know how to deal with it. I start off trying to be logical but that doesn't go anywhere because she doesn't respond. And then I get angry and even if I win the argument, I lose because I've made things even worse between us.

R. FIRESTONE: What would you say directly to Heather in that situation if you were to really express your anger?

DANIEL: Here's what I'd say [loudly, angry]: You provoke the shit out of me by acting like a child. Why do you do that? Why do you insist on being a child? What are you getting out of it? You're just ruining our relationship! You're making me hate you! And I can't stand hating you; I can't stand being mad at you. Stop playing out this stupid game. We used to be equal; what the fuck are you doing? I love you. I want our old relationship back the way it was. I want you as my partner. I loved sharing life with you like that!

I feel relieved to get that out. I'm always holding that anger in and trying to act in a reasonable way. But it comes out anyway. That's why my reactions to you are so intense, and that's why you think that I act so superior. The whole thing is so reminiscent of how I felt at home with my mom and dad, listening to their arguments about money, about my mother's drinking, and her endless complaining that she never got any help from him. She was always feeling like she was being screwed over. I can really see his part in it, too. He would either placate my mother or get furious at her.

HEATHER: I felt angry at what you were saying at first, but then I felt really sad about the way things used to be between us.

Discussing Insights Brought About From Partners Expressing Their Voices

Each partner discusses the insights they developed from expressing their voices. As a result of saying their voice attacks and separating from a point of view that is not their own, people gain more clarity about their lives. Releasing their feelings often leads to their recovering implicit memories of early attachment trauma and loss. These new insights allow people to make sense of their childhoods and develop an understanding of their personal history. This helps people keep their past out of their current lives.

HEATHER: Things got really horrible after my parents divorced. My father didn't pay the child support and we were practically destitute. I remember going to bed hungry most nights. My mother was always angry; she blamed the situation on my father and on us kids. There were times that we had absolutely no money.

Then my mother would get really panicky. One day she loaded us all in the car and took us to my father's house to beg him for money and they had a huge fight in his front yard. It was horrible; I felt so humiliated and guilty. I still remember every detail of that day.

So those are the feelings that come up in me whenever Daniel and I have a discussion about money. I actually feel like I am that child again; and all I feel is the old guilt and fear. I get into such an anxious state that I don't make any sense. I just start crying and he gets furious.

R. FIRESTONE: That distortion really cuts into your relationship with Daniel. It's hard to have an equal relationship when you are thrown back into reliving your childhood. If you could learn to recognize that your emotional reactions are exaggerated because they pertain to old situations and old fears, then you and Daniel would be able to talk about your finances in a more rational way, as two adults.

HEATHER: I know what you're saying. I could learn to handle my anxiety in the moment by realizing that's how I felt as a child and not what's really happening now. When I was a little kid, it was a terrifying situation for me. But I don't have to act like that frightened child anymore. I can be aware of what I know sitting here, talking as a logical adult, that I'm not in any danger. Daniel is not going to abandon me like my father did or punish me like my mother did.

After listening to Heather describe her childhood of financial insecurity, Daniel felt empathic toward her and more optimistic about their relationship:

> [To Heather.] I really understand how you must have felt back then. I feel sorry for contributing to your feeling afraid. It's amazing how our voices fit together. When we get into those financial discussions and you go off, your reactions remind me of the childish way my mother acted and my anger toward her is triggered. That's when I'm pissed. And once I'm angry, I'm back where I was as a kid: the angry, mean person my mother accused me of being.
>
> I don't just have this reaction with Heather—it's an overall feeling I have about anger. Whenever I get angry, I immediately feel like I am a terrible person. So it's hard for me to just have clean anger. Instead of expressing my anger directly, I act like Heather says, kind of self-righteous. This is something that I really want to work on, especially in relation to Heather.

Answering Back to Voice Attacks

Partners formulate answers to their self-attacks and distorted views of the other person.

R. FIRESTONE: [To Heather.] What would you say back to the voice, to your mother's view of you?

HEATHER: My answer feels really angry. First, I would say back to her:

"You're so wrong. You're so wrong about me! You're so wrong about him! You have no idea what you're talking about. I never knew what you were going to do. I'd get hit for nothing. If any of us kids got out of line or made a mess in your perfect house, you'd go crazy! So fuck you! I was terrified of you! You just tore me apart verbally; you constantly criticized me, my whole childhood. I couldn't stand being around you. I never knew what would set you off. I always had to watch out.

"Well, I don't have to watch out anymore. So get out of my head! This is my life! I have a man who loves me and who I love. I don't have to be careful anymore. Fuck you! I always thought I had to take punishment from you. I felt like I deserved it but I was wrong. You're a sadistic bitch!

"I'm not a child who's scared of you! And you're wrong about Daniel. He's not like you at all. He's not mean and he cares about me. He's so different from you. I'm sick and tired of acting like he's scary and mean. I have such a different life than I had living with you, especially the way it was after Dad left. I hated being left with you. It was hell! So go on and live out your life alone with no one to love you. I'm not going to repeat that in my life."

After listening to Heather stand up for herself and defend him against her mother's point of view, Daniel was touched. He then answered back to his own voice attacks.

DANIEL: I feel like standing up for myself and saying back to my mother's voices: "Leave me alone! Leave me alone. Stop evaluating me. I'm not mean just because I get angry sometimes! Everyone gets angry. You're so wrong about me. Just because I'm a man doesn't mean that I'm mean. You're wrong about me and you're wrong about men! I'm an affectionate, loving person! You were never right about me."

It feels good just to hear my voice sounding loud. I used to feel louder and more self-assured. That was more like the real me. I remember expressing my feelings and my anger more directly. It was like a break with my old identity in some way, to be able to be angry and not see myself as mean. I was more assertive then, but after we started to have problems, I got worried that I was becoming an angry, mean man. Like I was believing my mother's attitude that men are mean. My rational answer to that voice attack is, "I'm not mean, and I don't feel superior to other people." I know within myself that I really care about you, Heather, I really love you.

HEATHER: [To Daniel.] I felt a lot when you were talking. I felt sad about how you were treated by your mother. I felt a lot of pain for you.

DANIEL: Thanks for saying that. I realize that I've had a block against seeing how awful I've been acting in our relationship, and looking at my part in keeping this whole thing going. As long as I believed that you saw me as mean and selfish, I couldn't see that I was making those attacks on myself. And I couldn't see that they were really how my mother saw me. I sort of understood it intellectually but I haven't been able to really see it until now.

Understanding How Each Partner's Voices Affect His or Her Behavior

Both partners make connections between the childhood experiences where they internalized their voices and the behaviors in their present-day lives and relationships that cause them distress.

DANIEL: I was afraid to confront those voices in myself; instead I saw you as the one who was weak, who was being unreasonable and childish. I really saw you as the one who had problems, not me. Then I would either try to help you or I would criticize you, but always from above. I was so damn condescending and I'm sorry for that. The way I acted really stopped you from being able to communicate your feelings and concerns to me.

R. FIRESTONE: So you focused on her problems instead.

DANIEL: Exactly. [To Heather.] If I saw problems in you and tried to take care of them, I could avoid looking at my own problems, at what I was feeling, at my own miserable attacks.

HEATHER: I realize now that when I believed what that voice was telling me about you, I felt that I had to protect myself. I didn't trust you on some level, Daniel, especially when it came to financial matters. But my distrust spread to so many other areas. I'm really sorry I wasn't able to be more trusting.

Planning and Implementing Suggestions to Change Behaviors Dictated by the Voice

Both members of the couple collaborate to identify specific behaviors based on each partner's voices that interfere with them having a close relationship. Then they plan actions to take that would counteract what their voices are directing them to do. As they implement their plans, they discuss any resistance they encounter or voice attacks that arise as a result of their taking the actions to challenge their voices. In subsequent meetings, Daniel and Heather formulated actions they would take.

R. FIRESTONE: It seems like things are going in the right direction. If you both continue to be aware of your voices, you'll be better able to communicate instead of using each other to feel bad. That's the most important part, to actually be friends and allies by not being on the defensive when you're talking about finances.

DANIEL: [To Heather.] I know that I don't have to act superior to you or be arbitrary. The truth is that I feel better when we relate as equals.

HEATHER: [To Daniel.] I feel so much more on my own side right now. I can certainly be as adult with you as I am at work. I can stop acting like I don't know anything about handling money. I really feel like working this out for myself. I want it to be like it was at the beginning of our relationship. Also, I'm determined to stop focusing so much on what you're thinking and feeling toward me, and pay more attention to what I'm thinking. I want to know how I feel toward myself and toward you.

To counter his voices about being critical, parental, and condescending, Daniel set as his goal to be more respectful and forthright in communicating with Heather. In addition, he would strive to maintain a compassionate perspective about problems she might be struggling with. In a similar spirit, Heather's goal was to behave in a competent, self-assured manner with Daniel instead of sinking into a childish state of mind.

Implications

Tracing the origins of their self-attacks to childhood experiences enabled Heather and Daniel to take back their projections and opened up the possibility for real communication. Previously, externalizing or projecting the voice was an end in itself because each partner was able to reduce his or her anxiety by perceiving the other person as his or her critical parent.

Moreover, through projective identification, Heather and Daniel acted out complementary parent/child roles and induced the same negative thoughts and disturbing emotions in each other that they were experiencing within themselves. In explaining this process, D. Scharff & Scharff (1991) noted that the partner who has disowned a part of him- or herself and who perceives it instead as in the other "so convincingly identifies the part of the self in the external object that the feeling state corresponding to that part of the self is evoked in the... spouse" (p. 58).

The cycle of blame and counterblame had become well established in Heather and Daniel's relationship. They had difficulty interrupting it because each one was strongly invested in preserving the status quo of their defensive adaptations. Through their group meetings, they were able to straighten out their complicated aversive interactions only after they had gained a comprehensive understanding of the voices operating within each of them and how these were influencing their behavior.

In the practice of couples therapy, the ultimate goal is to help individuals enhance their ability to give and accept love. In moving toward this objective, people first need to recognize the presence of internalized voices that are continually coaching them to not take chances, to not invest fully in the relationship, and to not trust others. Second, they must come to value themselves as well as their partners; this poses a problem because the ability to see oneself as worthwhile is often seriously damaged during one's formative years. For this reason, the process of freeing oneself from remnants of one's early programming, overcoming defenses, and counteracting voices is an ongoing venture.

PART II: VOICE THERAPY METHODOLOGY APPLIED TO DIFFICULTIES IN SEXUAL RELATING

Most disturbances in sexual relating can be attributed to people's tendency to view themselves and their sexuality through the distorted lens of restrictive voices that arouse guilt feelings about a natural, potentially pleasurable part of their lives. Some people experience feelings of shame in relation to sex that reflect critical attitudes toward their bodies or their innate need for affectionate physical contact and love. Indeed, voice attacks that deride and discourage the pursuit of love and sexual gratification were among the most common voices reported by participants in the focus group mentioned earlier.

When voice therapy methodology is applied to couples, clients discover what their voices are telling them about their bodies and their sexual performance, about their partner and their relationship, and about sexuality in general.[4] Recognizing the restrictions imposed on them by the voice and releasing the underlying affect supports people in moving away from these negative attitudes and prohibitions. Clients undergo a shift in their perspective in relation to sexuality; rather than seeing sex as, for example, a conquest or obligation, they come to experience it as a shared pleasure.

The patterns of chronic misattunement that often develop in a couple's sexual relating can be traced to critical attitudes about themselves and about their partners. These attacks may be manifested in two ways: (1) in negative attitudes toward oneself, one's body, and one's sexuality and (2) in negative expectations, perceptions, or distortions of one's partner. For example, a woman reported telling herself,: "Why should he still be attracted to you? You're getting fat. Plus, what's the big deal anyway? You're getting too old for sex." She also had negative thoughts about her husband: "He's not really interested in sex any more. He just falls asleep at night. When he is sexual, it's so routine, always the same." Both types of attitudes lead to behaviors that create emotional distance between partners during lovemaking. In revealing his voice attacks about the situation, her husband said, "You're too tired to make love tonight. You've been working hard all day. You come home and she expects you to be romantic! What's she been doing all day anyway? She just doesn't understand you and she never did!"

Identifying Voices During Sex

As noted, people experience many different types of voices during sex, including criticisms of their bodies, their sexual adequacy, and their own level of excitement and that of their partner. Individuals in our pilot study reported a variety of voice attacks about their bodies; for example, "Your body doesn't look normal, your breasts are too small [or too large], you look gross; keep yourself covered up! Look at your penis; it's so small." As to their sexual performance, they reported voices such as, "You're not going to have an orgasm; you're not going to be able to satisfy her." These self-defeating thoughts often leave people regarding sex as a performance to be judged instead of as a natural extension of affection and feelings of attraction. They effectively cut off sexual desire and keep people from wanting to make love in the first place.

Paradoxically, a gratifying sexual experience that is devoid of voice attacks may be followed by a barrage of voices that depreciate either the person or his or her partner or predict a negative experience in the future. Some of these voices include, "So you felt terrific? Big deal! You just lucked out. You'll probably mess it up the next time."

Or, "He didn't look all that thrilled. You probably scared him off." Or, "How do you know she had an orgasm? She probably just faked it."

Couples who have learned to express their voices in a therapy setting can apply the same process at home to reveal their negative thoughts to each other whenever they experience voice attacks while being sexual. Instead of trying to ignore the intrusive thoughts while concentrating on completing the sex act, they can temporarily stop making love, verbalize their voice attacks, and at the same time try to remain affectionate and maintain physical contact in order to preserve a sense of intimacy. As in a therapy session, the person experiencing the voice attacks expresses his or her negative thoughts in the second person. The partner listens, allowing the partner enough time to express all of his or her voices and the feelings that accompany them.

Verbalizing their attacks during lovemaking usually helps a couple sustain a level of feeling and maintain emotional closeness rather than becoming increasingly removed from each other. When these types of voices are not dealt with, they cause tension and confusion to both parties and often disrupt the sexual act. Utilizing voice therapy techniques while being sexual requires a good deal of trust on the part of both people. When this rapport is lacking in a couple, it is better for them to investigate their voice attacks about their sexual relationship in traditional voice therapy sessions in the therapist's office.

Ellen and Sam

After 10 years of marriage, Ellen and Sam sought help in couples therapy (with L. Firestone) because in recent years, they had become estranged and had begun to experience difficulties in their sexual relating. In weekly sessions, they learned how to reveal their self-critical thoughts and negative attitudes toward each other. By relating honestly in a manner that was respectful and nonaccusatory, they became more insightful into, compassionate toward, and understanding of themselves and one another. In one session, Ellen described how she and Sam had used voice therapy methods during the previous week to deal with issues that had come up when they were being sexual.

ELLEN: Sam and I were being sexual the other night and I was feeling really excited and very sexual when he was touching me. But then I suddenly started feeling distracted. Then I noticed I wasn't feeling any sensations or feelings. I was thinking of other things, like all the things I had to do the next day. And Sam picked up on the fact that I was distracted, so we stopped and talked. When I said I was distracted, Sam asked if my voices were telling me anything. Then I realized that I was very tense. So I said what my voices were. They were: "What's the matter with you? Why can't you just relax? See, now you're not feeling anything. He's going to notice."

And I was also having thoughts about Sam. I was questioning if he really wanted to make love with me. The voices about that were: "He probably doesn't really want to make love to you. He's tired. Besides, he didn't seem that happy to see you tonight. And you're the one who had to initiate sex. Can't you tell he doesn't want to be doing this? He doesn't feel that close to you anyway."

Those thoughts just crept in and started to ruin the good time I was having with Sam. I hated to be thinking those things, but I thought if I told him about them, then I would be able to feel close to him again.

L. FIRESTONE: How did you feel in that situation, Sam?

SAM: I was really glad she said something because I could feel her pulling away from me. All it did was confuse me: I didn't know what was going on and I didn't know what to do about it. When we stopped to talk, I became aware that I was having my own voice attacks, like: "What's going on here? She seems excited. She really wanted to be sexual tonight. It must be you. You're doing something wrong! Don't let her know something's wrong. Just figure out what to do to fix it!"

It was really amazing, after we said our voices and felt our feelings, we felt back to ourselves. We went back to making love and it was especially close and passionate. Just taking those few minutes to say our voice attacks turned the night around for us and we avoided what could have been a bad night.

TEACHING CORE ATTITUDES

In interacting with couples, we attempt to inspire an understanding, affectionate style of relating that is noncritical and accepting with the recognition that each person is a separate individual. Love is manifested in simple ways, in small everyday acts of kindness and consideration, in a sense of kinship and companionship, and in behaviors that contribute to a deep sharing of life's experiences. These qualities constitute an essential dimension of a fulfilling life that extends outward from the couple relationship to their children, other family members, and friends.

The philosophical approach underlying voice therapy for couples is that happiness is a by-product of extending oneself in love and generosity and of placing the well-being and happiness of the other person on a parallel with one's own. Genuine love implies finding enjoyment in the personal evolution of one's partner and in seeing him or her develop and flourish even in areas beyond one's own interest. The gratification inherent in simply loving another person is a vital component of a mature and satisfying relationship.

In the practice of a couples therapy, as the therapist interacts with each member of the couple, he or she is providing them with an example of how to relate to another person with respect and compassion and of how to be empathic and fully present while listening. The therapist serves as a role model for how to relate with sensitivity and attunement during personal exchanges as well as during stressful interactions. Clients who emulate these qualities develop a "therapeutic stance" in their personal relationships.[5] This involves the ability to remain attuned to the other person's communications and to offer appropriate responses and the skill to repair the damage done by any misattuned responses.

Couples learn to give up the need to always be right. This defensive posture leads to angry exchanges between partners that escalate from mild disagreements to outright hostility and verbal abuse. Ideally, as soon as one partner senses that a disagreement is degenerating into a battle of wills, he or she can drop the stake in winning and reach out to the other. Genuine expressions of caring in the midst of an argument are effectively disarming, as the other person feels touched by the gesture of making peace. As a result, the hostility usually dissipates. This technique of "unilateral disarmament" does not imply that one must surrender one's point of view or necessarily defer to the other's opinion; rather, it indicates that one values being close to one's partner more than winning one's point.

Lastly, it is valuable for couples to learn to endure the anxiety that is necessarily associated with personal growth and differentiation. It is important for them to stay close and hang in there rather than use distancing behavior to ease their anxiety. In this way they can maintain their gains and hold on to the new territory.

As people overcome resistance and modify destructive patterns of interaction, they not only feel more anxious but often also experience a recurrence of voice attacks. However, if they remain vulnerable and refuse to retreat, the rebuttals of the voice will eventually subside and their tolerance for intimacy will increase.

SUMMARY

Voice therapy methodology as applied in couples therapy facilitates a process of differentiation by strengthening each partner's independence, point of view, goals, and priorities and by identifying negative thoughts and prescriptions for living that encourage people to reject real expressions of love and increase their tendency to rely on fantasy.

The voice process operates to erode the equality between the two people and to weaken each partner's sense of self until the companionship and sexual attraction that originally characterized the relationship are diminished or lost. It interferes with each person's movement toward individuation and autonomy until ultimately the relationship develops into a fantasy bond in which both individuals are using the other as an instrument to reenact their past lives. This destructive pattern can be reversed as each member of the couple focuses on developing him- or herself personally. In this regard, partners must challenge the internal voices underlying negative core beliefs about themselves and their distorted views of the other.

In this chapter, we elucidated how voice therapy methodology was employed in group meetings with couples in trouble. We illustrated how utilizing these techniques allows people to free themselves of the self-defeating, restrictive behavior patterns that cause much of the distress in their intimate relationships. Recognizing the enemy within enables people to strengthen their sense of self, expand their boundaries, and significantly improve their intimate relationships. Indeed, there is no defense or relationship problem that is impervious to change, providing the partners have the courage to challenge their early programming and subsequent fantasy bonds, to maintain a sense of themselves as separate individuals, and to risk being vulnerable to both loving and being loved.

7

FAMILY DYNAMICS THAT AFFECT DIFFERENTIATION

> The degree of emotional separation between a developing child and his family influences the child's ability to differentiate a self from the family.... In a poorly differentiated family... the high intensity of emotionality and togetherness pressure does not permit the child to grow, to think, feel, and act for himself.... When the child leaves home, he replicates some version of the family relationship patterns with others.... Having achieved little emotional separation from his family, he achieves little in other relationships.
>
> –Murray Bowen, in Michael Kerr and Murray Bowen, *Family Evaluation*

This chapter explores diverse family bonds and child-rearing practices that contribute to the difficulties that people encounter as they mature, develop their identities, and strive to fulfill their potentialities as unique individuals. The positive and negative elements that exist in the father-daughter, father-son, and mother-son dyads are delineated in terms of how they either support or obstruct a person's movement toward individuation and self-realization. Each dyad or relationship is important to consider in examining family dynamics that affect the differentiation process.[1] We have set aside the next chapter to investigate the mother-daughter dyad, because in our clinical experience, we have found that this relationship profoundly influences women's movement toward individuation.

In the present chapter, we also examine the detrimental effects on the child born to parents whose relationship is characterized by a fantasy bond. In this scenario, the infant is immediately drawn into the parents' world of illusion and adapts to their inward lifestyle by imitating their defensive strategies in coping with its own expanding world. As a result, most individuals never fulfill their natural destinies because the process of forming a fantasy bond diverts them from seeking goals they might otherwise have freely chosen to pursue (Firestone, 1985).

FATHERS AND DAUGHTERS

Over the past two decades, psychologists have increasingly focused on the importance of fathers to family life and their involvement as nurturers and role models for children of both genders. According to Oren and Oren (2010),

> Fathers often provide their children the freedom to explore and promote active, physical play.... In a father's play, both father and child often become enthralled in the intensity of the experience. Active, physical play can teach children self-control, social cues about managing emotions, and recognition of others' emotional cues. (loc. 1215)[2]

With respect to the relationship between fathers and daughters, research has shown that girls who enjoy a close, trusting relationship with their father tend to feel secure, protected, and strengthened in their identity as women. According to Cramer (1997), a father's warmth and emotional investment in family life are factors that affect the development of femininity in young girls. In addition, fathers who feel fulfilled in their intimate relationship provide their daughter with a constructive example of intimate relationships and married life. Research also suggests that the quality of the father-daughter relationship is predictive of how the daughter will later relate to the people closest to her. For example, Lopez-Duran (2009) reported findings from a study investigating correlations between father-daughter bonds and the quality of daughters' romantic relationships:

> Girls with good communication with their fathers had significantly better communication with their boyfriends when compared to girls with low communication with their fathers. Girls with high levels of trust in their fathers had significantly better communication and trust with their boyfriends. (p. 1)[3]

Fathers play a significant role in facilitating the development of their daughter's independence and autonomy and contribute to her experiencing less psychological distress and better marital adjustment as an adult (Dresner & Grolnick, 1996; Flouri & Buchanan, 2002, 2003). When a father has a strong sense of self and maintains a congenial, supportive relationship with his daughter, he offers her a point of view that can mitigate, to some extent, any harmful influences of negative mothering. In this regard, Rubin (1983) cogently observed,

> In childhood, a girl handles the threat [of separation from the mother] by turning to father to help her make and maintain the necessary separation.... It's this difference, and the importance it holds in her separation struggle, that helps to define a girl's sexual orientation.... A father affirms the femaleness of his daughter. (pp. 147–148)

On the other hand, a father's absence, emotional unavailability, indifference, or overt neglect can be detrimental to his daughter's development.[4] For example, researchers who studied fathers in everyday interactions with their infant sons and daughters discovered that the fathers in their sample population were available to and involved with their sons significantly more than with their daughters (Manlove & Vernon-Feagans, 2002). Fathers who prefer the company of their sons and are less interested in their daughters often instill feelings of insignificance and low self-worth in their daughters.

A father can potentially provide confirmation of his daughter's feminine characteristics. However, he can also have a harmful effect if he behaves in ways that denigrate these potentialities. For example, several women in our discussion groups revealed that, as adolescents, they were humiliated by their fathers who insensitively teased or ridiculed them about signs of their emerging sexuality, their developing bodies, or their overall appearance. One woman described the humiliation and shame she experienced when she was 16 and starting to date.

> My father made fun of everything I wore and the guys I went out with. Once when I was dressed up to go to a party, he told me I looked like a clown and made me take off my makeup before he would let me leave the house.

Fathers who have a cynical or critical point of view toward women also have a negative influence on their daughter's feelings of self-worth. Research has shown that girls internalize their father's negative attitudes toward their mother and other women in the form of critical attitudes toward themselves (Cramer, 1997). A father can also have a detrimental effect on his daughter when he fails to convey a positive image of manhood to his children. For instance, another woman recalled being lectured to by her father about the dangers of dating "testosterone-flooded" adolescent boys.

> He told me I had to be really careful with these guys because "the least little thing you do is going to trigger them, and they're going to get out of control and won't be able to stop." Once when I was leaving on a date, I had on a miniskirt, and as my boyfriend and I were walking to his car, my father yelled out the front door, "What do you want to do dressed like that, get raped?"

Fathers who are domineering, condescending, and paternalistic in interactions with their mate reinforce stereotypic views of men as being harsh, chauvinistic, and overbearing. In addition, findings from several research studies have found "experiences of father verbal abuse and violence . . . to be related to women's alcohol problems and low self-esteem" (Downs & Miller, 1998, p. 440). Consequently, as adults, daughters of harsh or verbally abusive fathers are likely to perceive a romantic partner's strength and assertiveness as meanness and hypercriticality. Conversely, if a man is overly dependent or seeks validation of his manhood from his wife, his daughter will tend to develop a view of men as weak and ineffective or perceive them as unreliable love objects.

Some fathers experience discomfort and anxiety when their daughters approach puberty, the time when they notice that they are becoming attractive women. Fearful of any feelings of attraction they might have, these men begin to withhold their affection and withdraw from the previous closeness they may have felt with their daughter. This withdrawal is experienced as confusing, rejecting, and distressing to the young teenager.

When parents are emotionally mature and have gratifying adult sexual relationships, they are generally at ease with their sexual feelings and are able to express normal loving affection to their children. It is also natural for feelings of sexual attraction to accompany the close contact that parents have with their children (Firestone, 1990a; Friday, 1977; H. Kaplan, 1995).[5] Obviously there is a distinction between the normal attraction of fathers to daughters and any overly sexualized involvement or incestuous behavior acted out between a father and his daughter.

Emotional Hunger and Emotional Incest in Father-Daughter Relationships

For women, one of the most destructive influences on the differentiation process is a psychologically immature father overstepping a daughter's personal boundaries by turning to her for the love and support he should be seeking from an adult. Much to their own detriment, girls who are used or exploited in this manner feel a strong pull to try to gratify their father's misdirected needs (Masterson, 1985).

Fathers who are emotionally hungry often take vicarious pleasure in their daughter's accomplishments. In extreme cases, men with a confused gender identity may perceive their daughter as an extension of themselves and form a strong identification with her in an unconscious attempt to live through her. These fathers typically become angry and punishing when their daughter makes independent choices.

Emotional incest is closely related to emotional hunger. It is apparent that the father's exaggerated preference for and focus on the daughter has a definite sexual component, "even when there is no clear-cut, explicit sexual activity between the individuals" (Gartner, 1999, p. 26). This type of covert incest is acted out in sexualized affection and excitement when close to the daughter, in flirtation, sexual innuendos, inappropriate touching and handling of the girl's body and clothing, or extravagant behavior such as giving her inappropriate gifts and expressing adulation of her beauty, intelligence, or other positive qualities. These fathers are often possessive and jealous of other people in their daughter's life.

According to Love (1990), emotional incest has two defining features: "The parent is using the child to satisfy needs that should be satisfied by other adults [while] ignoring many of the child's needs" (pp. 9–10). Emotionally incestuous fathers injure a daughter's capacity for wanting and her desire as an adult to seek satisfaction in a mature, sexual relationship. The sexualized, enmeshed dynamic generates considerable guilt, anxiety, and anger in the young girl that can block her psychosexual development. In describing sexual problems common among women who were involved with this type of father, Love observed that these women tend to become involved in "brief, clandestine affairs with relative strangers" (p. 54), or, on the other hand, they become afraid of sex or have difficulty achieving an orgasm. Ultimately, they fail to establish a committed relationship characterized by emotional closeness and sexual intimacy.

In many cases, at the beginning of a relationship, these women feel sexually responsive; however, as the relationship becomes more meaningful, they start to experience sexual problems, including inhibited sexual desire. Some tend to completely repress their sexuality or fail to develop a mature, genital sexual orientation. In describing these dynamics, Helen Singer Kaplan (1995) has noted that women with this type of background usually "find nice partners, but always manage to destroy their relationships" (p. 146).

Incest and Child Sexual Abuse

Incest is far more prevalent than previously recognized. Statistics show that the majority of child sexual abuse occurs in the family and not only involves fathers but also mothers, stepparents, older siblings, and other relatives. In only 10% of cases does child sexual abuse involve a neighbor or person who is a stranger to the family. Most clinicians and researchers believe that the sexual abuse of children is underreported in the United States and in other countries as well (J. Herman, 1992). According to Putnam (2003), incidents of child sexual abuse "range from 12% to 35% of women and 4% to 9% of men reporting an unwanted sexual experience prior to age 18 years" (p. 270).[6]

In describing incest involving daughters, Freyd (1996) asserted that profound amnesia for sexual abuse often occurs when there has been a betrayal of trust in cases where the perpetrator is an attachment figure, such as a parent or caregiver. Zurbriggen and Freyd (2004) also observed that "survivors of childhood abuse by a caretaker have learned to cope with [the] social conflicts they cannot escape by being disconnected internally" (p. 145).

FATHERS AND SONS

The ways that boys are socialized and the adjustments they make as they change the object of their identification from their mother to their father exert a strong influence on how they feel about themselves as men and how they interact in their relationships and careers. There is considerable debate in the field of psychology about the specific pressures and developmental milestones that boys face in growing up. A number of theorists have asserted that society's patriarchal influences still direct the socialization of boys and girls, whereas others contend that there is little difference in how sons and daughters are being raised in today's families (Geary, 1998; Nealer, 2002; Pollack, 1998).[7]

For men, differentiation requires courage not only in challenging negative parental influences, but also in resisting external social pressures to conform to rigidly defined gender roles and conventional images of masculinity (C. Gilligan, 1982, 2011). With respect to this process, the significance of the father as a role model for the son cannot be overemphasized (Neubauer, 1986). There is nothing as positive or confirming of a boy's sense of self and masculinity as having a father who possesses strength as well as warmth; who enjoys a close, satisfying relationship with a woman; and who feels confident and fulfilled in his career.

In a chapter in his seminal book *The Role of the Father in Child Development,* Lamb (2010) reviewed several long-term studies investigating the characteristics of fathers that facilitate their son's psychosexual development. Two personal qualities were found to be crucial variables: warmth and closeness. To the extent that a father possesses these characteristics and participates in parenting functions and family activities, his son will take on these positive qualities as his own and feel integrated within himself. Lamb also found that children of both genders, and particularly male adolescents, "whose fathers either shared or took primary responsibility for child care... were characterized by increased cognitive competence, increased empathy, fewer sex-stereotyped beliefs, and a more internal locus of control" (loc. 443–452).

When fathers have doubts about their masculinity, their sons tend to imitate their father's style of relating, especially in their intimate relationships. For instance, if the dynamic between the parents is one in which the father is weak and the mother is controlling, as an adult, the son will most likely be attracted to domineering women and adopt a subservient role in relation to his partner.

All boys long for tenderness, love, and nurturance from their fathers, yet in many families, there are strong taboos against fathers expressing physical affection to their sons. According to Pollack (1998), "Because of the way we as a society view boys and men... many fathers, especially in public settings, may feel inhibited about showing the empathy they *naturally* feel for their sons" (p. 116). Unfortunately, the majority of men have taken on the stereotypic view that men are uncommunicative, harsh, and unfeeling (Kindlon & Thompson, 1999).[8] This sexist attitude is reinforced in many families who fall into the conventional pattern of using the father as the agent of discipline and punishment. As a result, sons often come to view male strength in a negative light.

In addition, because women are typically idealized as being innately maternal and loving, many men defer to their wives in relation to child-rearing practices. In these cases, the sons are likely to grow up feeling that they have no ally or protector in their father. With respect to conflicting views of masculinity that boys are presented with, Park (1995) emphasized,

> What the boy needs is a father's help in dealing with the emotional pressures that come from his mother. He needs to learn that there are other views of masculinity than those which she propounds, and that what she says to him [in this regard] has more to do with her own past experiences than with him. (p. 23)

Competition Between Father and Son

In many families, the father's unresolved competitive feelings are acted out in relation to his sons. They are manifested in intense, usually covert, feelings of envy, hostility, rivalry, and even hatred toward the son. There is often resentment of the mother's involvement with the son. All of these factors intensify the natural competitive feelings a son has toward his father and contribute to a sense of alienation that later affects his camaraderie and friendships with other boys and men. As an adult, he projects the aggression that was originally directed toward him by his father onto men in his present-day life. This leads to an exaggerated fear of retribution and a tendency to retreat from competitive situations (Firestone, 1994a).

A father's passivity, retreat from competition, and doubts about his own masculinity have a debilitating effect on his son's attitudes toward competition, particularly in sexually rivalrous situations. There is an unconscious anticipation on the son's part that both winning and losing will trigger either guilt or strong self-attacks similar to feelings and attitudes that were internalized early in life in relation to his father. In the same vein, men usually pull back after an unusual success in an area where they have surpassed their father—for example, in their careers or by finding more satisfaction in a personal relationship. These achievements often arouse anxiety about differentiating from the father's limitations, going beyond him, or symbolically leaving him behind. Men often experience powerful voice attacks that lead to regressive behaviors that act to sabotage their accomplishments after literally or symbolically triumphing over their fathers.

Mark was an outgoing man with an engaging personality. He was well liked and successful in his career, having been cited as salesman of the year by the computer software company where he worked. Less than a year later, Mark talked in a discussion group about how he had begun failing in his job. He said that he felt turned against himself as a salesman: "It's not the business or the market; it's me. I just don't feel the same enthusiasm I have always had about what I do. I don't take the pride that I used to take in my job."

When he speculated about what could have triggered this regression, someone reminded Mark about his father's death the year before. Mark went on to tell the story of how, at work one afternoon, he had received news that his father was seriously ill. That evening in his father's hospital room, Mark had attempted to lift the old man's spirits by telling jokes and humorous stories. The hospital staff was amused and several nurses were laughing when his father interrupted in a loud voice, "Don't listen to him. He's just a salesman. Mark bullshits all the time. That's what he does for a living." The room fell quiet and soon afterward, Mark said goodnight. Later that evening, his father died, and those hostile comments turned out to be his dying words to his son. When Mark came to the end of the story, he spoke with sadness in his voice, "I know that's the way he saw me my whole life." Mark verbalized the voice attacks that his father's comments had triggered in him:

> "You're only a salesman! Nobody takes them seriously. Everybody knows they're bullshitters. That's why you're good at it: you're full of shit. You're just a show off. No one respects you. Sure, they laugh at you, but you're just a clown. You're not a man. You're a joke! You don't have a respectable job like a real man. You don't do any of the things real men do!"
>
> My father always put me down; he never taught me sports or helped me in any way. He thought I was too incompetent or too stupid to learn

anything. If I was better than him in any way, he would be really competitive with me. That's where those attacks were coming from. In the hospital, he was jealous because I was getting the attention.

But then other attacks come in and go in another direction. These feel like they are from the way my mother saw me; they're like: "Go ahead, play the role of the big man. All you can do is just play the role. You can try to act smart, but we all know that underneath, you're really stupid. You're still nothing! Everyone can still see how small and weak you are. But go ahead, try and be the big man like your father tried to be. I saw through him and I can see through you!"

My voice attacks come from both sides. It's the way my father and my mother both saw me. It's also the way my mother saw my father. I want to answer back to both attacks; first the ones from my father: "First of all, I am not a bullshitter. I happen to like people and I like joking around and having a good time with them and making them feel good! When I was in the hospital, I was trying to make you feel good! I wasn't bullshitting. The truth is that you were jealous of the attention I was getting. You were always so socially awkward; you were never easy with people the way I am. People never liked you the way they like me. You stupid jerk, you could have been proud of me instead of being jealous and putting me down. I wasn't an insult to you!"

Then to my mother's voices I would say, "I'm not playing any role! I'm being myself. You see me as small and weak and stupid but I'm not. And when I am strong and being myself, you attack me for being phony. You just don't like men!" [Long pause.]

Saying these voice attacks gives me a total picture of my family, just from understanding where these attacks come from. It's interesting that my mother and father seemed to be in agreement about the kind of person I was. Also, they both seemed to believe that all men were pathetic, you know, weak and stupid.

Mark had been aware that as he had become successful, he had felt guilty about surpassing his father. He now realized that these feelings became heightened by the critical and disrespectful remarks his father made just before his death. The week following this discussion group, Mark reported that he felt energized and more confident at work; his mind was clear; and he made a few sales. Over the next few months, he gradually reversed his downward trend and was becoming successful again as a salesman.

To summarize, the psychodynamics operating in father-daughter and father-son dyads are complicated and often difficult to untangle. The style in which both parents relate to each other generalizes to become a formative influence in the lives of children of both genders. Nevertheless, an important factor contributing to men's and women's ability to develop and sustain an intimate relationship is the presence in the family of a father who is warm, empathic, and attuned to his sons as well as to his daughters. According to Lamb and Lewis (2004), "The evidence to date suggests that... paternal involvement predicts their adult children's feelings of satisfaction in spousal relationships" (p. 290).

Male Vanity and Chauvinism

Vanity is a fantasized image of the self that is formed when parents substitute empty praise and a false buildup for the real love and acknowledgment they have failed to provide to their child (Firestone, 1985, 1997a). As Lowen (1985) noted, "If [a man] believes himself to be a prince, it is because he was raised in that belief" (p. 21). Boys who have been brought up in this way often develop an inflated sense of self-importance or vanity to compensate for the underlying feelings of being unlovable or defective that this type of treatment induces. This pattern of quelling insecurity with vanity becomes a self-parenting process, a way of nurturing the self, and, as an adult, the man who is dependent on it seeks out a woman who will feed his vanity with her praise, flattery, and approval.

The man who implicitly insists on a false buildup and reassurance of his manhood often arouses resentment, anger, and rage in the woman. However, she also recognizes that the man's dependence on her buildup gives her the power in the relationship. The fact that her partner will do almost anything she wants him to do as long as she supports his vanity provides the woman with leverage. As one woman put it, "All you have to do is build him up and you will have him at your beck and call. He will take care of you and you don't have to do anything." This type of buildup is harmful to both people's sense of autonomy. When a woman surrenders her individuality and gives up her dignity and self-respect to build up a man's sense of importance, the result is a personal loss for both herself and her mate (Firestone & Catlett, 1999). A woman's dishonest adulation of her partner weakens him because it supports his belief that there are innate deficiencies that he needs to compensate for, which only increases his feelings of inadequacy.[9]

Vanity in a man and the corresponding buildup from a woman are both encouraged by the stereotypic views of male superiority and strength and female inferiority and weakness that are commonplace in many families and in society at large. Men who are vain inflate their self-image by adhering to sexist views that women are inferior to them intellectually, unreliable, and basically less important in the overall scheme of things. These chauvinistic, paternalistic attitudes are reflected in their outward behavior toward women, whether they are subtly condescending or blatantly domineering and authoritarian. The vain man often views women as fragile or physically less capable and assumes a protective stance toward them that is, in itself, disrespectful and demeaning.

The conventional notion that a man should be the ruler of his household supports male vanity and contributes to the creation of the false image of the father as being "king of his castle." This position creates an illusion of a father who reigns as the supreme authority over his family and contributes to a delusion of greatness in the man. While on some level he senses that the buildup is counterfeit, he is afraid to be without it. In families where this is operating, there is a strong pressure on children of both genders to support and protect their father's vanity. The son is often perceived as a threat to the father's supremacy and becomes the target of the father's competitive anger. The collusion between family members to flatter the father and shield him from comparisons with other men bends the entire family out of shape.

Unfortunately, children in families where this illusion of superiority/inferiority is being acted out are deprived of knowing their parents as strong and equal individuals. Rather than being offered examples of a relationship characterized by respectful, loving treatment and honesty, they are provided with role models of compensation, manipulation, and dishonesty. The boy learns to expect a buildup, and the girl learns to control with false flattery.

MOTHERS AND SONS

> The less rewarding his experience of mother… the stronger is the man's yearning for someone else to take her place.
>
> —James Park, *Sons, Mothers and Other Lovers*

The first attachment figure for both boys and girls, and the one with whom they develop their primary identification, is the mother. C. Gilligan (1991) asserted that during their formative years, children of *both genders* struggle to preserve the original attachment to their mother while at the same time maintaining their own point of view. However, the developmental tasks for men are different than those for women, because, while men first form an attachment with the mother, they then shift their identification to their father.

When a boy's mother is sensitively attuned to him and responds to his needs in age-appropriate ways, he is likely to become well adjusted, to have a secure sense of self, and to go on to form a harmonious, secure relationship with his partner (Lamb, 2010). In supporting her son's development, his mother will help him make the transition from his initial attachment to her to the identification with his father. However, for the son who has suffered from inadequate mothering, the inevitable disruption in the attachment is often experienced as a profound loss.

To the extent a mother does not possess these positive qualities—for example, if she is withholding, self-denying, emotionally hungry, seductive, or controls the family through weakness and powerlessness—her son's development and adult adjustment are more likely to be seriously compromised. When boys suppress their angry reactions to maternal withholding and internalize their aggression, their anger can surface in explosive outbursts. As adult men, the underlying anger or rage can lead them to be dominating or controlling toward women. When they act out their anger, it is often followed by deep feelings of remorse, self-recrimination, or self-hatred that can last for extended periods of time. Other boys react to a withholding mother by becoming clingy, desperate, and overly dependent. As adults, they form an anxious attachment to their partners and sacrifice their individuality in intimate relationships.

Sons raised by mothers who are intolerant of having loving feelings directed toward them tend to withhold their spontaneous expressions of tenderness and affection. They interpret their mother's reactions to mean that their physicality, body, and touch are basically unacceptable or objectionable. They suffer from not being allowed to express their natural attraction toward the first love object in their life and later on unconsciously hold back their love, affection, and sexual responses toward women in anticipation of a negative reaction.

Men whose psychological development has been negatively affected by inadequate mothering also tend to feel alienated from other men and find it difficult to relate to them beyond a superficial, friendly level. They believe that other men do not experience the same feelings of inadequacy, desperation, or fear that they do and therefore feel isolated and alone in their distress. They try to disguise these emotions by covering them up with a pseudoindependent, tough persona, but when this defensive overlay is pierced, it reveals a self-doubting, self-critical, and vulnerable person.

Overprotection and Emotional Incest in Mother-Son Relationships

Overly protective, emotionally hungry, or intrusive mothers interfere with the ongoing psychosexual development and adult adjustment of their male offspring (Gurian, 1996).[10] Investigations into the long-term effects of this type of mothering on boys have shown that this form of "psychological control was positively related to both depression and antisocial behavior" (Barber & Harmon, 2002, p. 19).

Men whose mothers were seductive tend to feel sexually inferior and have fears of being incapable of satisfying a woman. In addition, these men may become critical of sexually responsive women and find them intimidating and difficult to relate to. This type of mother-son relationship predisposes a variety of sexual problems in adult men, including erectile dysfunctions, promiscuous behavior, and a complete avoidance of sex. It stimulates intense Oedipal rivalry and leads to an increased fear of competing (Love, 1990; Park, 1995). In his research, Park (1995) described typical reactions that men have to an intrusive, seductive mother:

> Men [from these enmeshed families], who generally have so much of mother, tend to experience her presence as sometimes smothering, stifling and demanding. In their later relationships, the pull towards intimacy and sexual union is powerfully countered by the fear of being submerged or swallowed up. They cannot get close because they do not think they will survive the experience. (p. 125)

Many men transfer the fears engendered by this type of mothering to their adult relationships and often react by pulling back from emotionally fulfilling experiences. Park (1995) conjectured that on an unconscious level these men had negative expectations or internal working models that profoundly influenced their behavior:

> He may decide that the "bad" mother is always going to be acting out her baleful and dangerous desires, so that the only way to maintain his sense of self is by keeping a distance from women. For fear of what might happen, he will feel impelled to cut himself off from full intimacy. Alternatively, he can seek to master his terrors and anxieties by learning to trust the women with whom he is linked. Most men adopt a combination of these strategies. (p. 130)

Mario's father was harshly critical of him and, in particular, ridiculed his interest in music. His mother, on the other hand, attempted to live through her son's musical talent. A bitter woman who had given up a singing career for marriage, she exaggerated Mario's abilities and encouraged his fantasy about becoming a rock star. Of her three sons, Mario was his mother's shining star, her "golden boy." Her behavior toward him was erratic, alternating between a buildup with seductive overtures and a cool indifference along with rejecting responses. Apart from her focus on Mario and his fledgling musical career, her life seemed devoid of meaning. As an adult, Mario captured the tenor of their relationship in the lyrics of a song; he wrote,

> She waits for tomorrow, but tomorrow never comes.
> So she must borrow the life of her son.

Mario's sexual history included several short-term relationships, numerous one-night stands, and an occasional encounter with a prostitute. When Mario was 37, he decided to go into therapy, an endeavor he found surprisingly rewarding. After terminating therapy, he became involved with Anna, and, for the first time in his life, Mario was able to sustain a close relationship with a woman for an extended period of time. However, when the couple talked about starting a family, Mario began to encounter problems sexually. He began to take part in the group discussions. to identify the thoughts and attitudes underlying the tension he felt when being sexual with Anna:

> I've had voices lately warning me about the future and I know they are affecting me indirectly sexually. You know, warning me that I'll never be able to support a family, that we shouldn't have a baby. They go like, "You can't support a family. You're not man enough to take care of a family. You can't handle the responsibility! You'll just get overwhelmed. You can't take it! And you'll be trapped for the rest of your life." That voice about being trapped is definitely my father's point of view, it's the way he felt in our family until he finally left.
>
> My answer to those voices is "Quit warning me about the future; I'm not overwhelmed by responsibility. I could be a father. I can support a family! And I'd be a good man to have a baby with. There is nothing wrong with me."

And lately I've been having a lot of voice attacks when Anna and I are being sexual. I start to get excited but then I start thinking things like, "You'd better get an erection. What's the matter with you? You'd better make this happen. What's the deal, anyway? You're not responding. This is it! You've got to perform!" And when I do respond and we are having sex, I have other voices like, "You're going to lose your erection. You better not lose your erection." or "You aren't going to be able to come. This is taking you too long; see, you can't finish." I am so in my head! Sometimes the thoughts get so bad that I'm too distracted to carry on. When that happens, I have attacks that I'm not capable of being sexual anymore."You can't even be sexual. You're inadequate; you're just like a little boy. You're not a man. You're going to make a baby? What a joke! How are you going to do that when you can't even be sexual?" [Angry, snide, degrading tone.]

My answer to that voice is, "The truth is, there's nothing wrong with me. I'm a normal man. I enjoy sex; Anna likes being sexual with me. There is no problem here apart from you being in my head! I am a man, not a child. There is nothing wrong with me; I am a normal sexual man!"

Talking about this reminds me of when I was in high school, when I first started dating. I would be holding a girl close and feeling attracted and sexually aroused just from being close; I'd feel good. But then that feeling of excitement would disappear. I remember feeling guilty like I was doing something wrong. What were the voices behind that guilt? "That's the wrong feeling to have! You'd better stop that feeling. Hide that erection! Don't you try to have sex with her! You are so disgusting! What are you going to do? Have sex with her and get her pregnant? You'll go to hell!" That's definitely my mother's way of thinking. And she didn't just think it about me, she lived by it herself. She had nothing with my father, no affection, no sex. And she made me feel that sexuality was bad; she tried to stamp it out of me.

[Later.] I feel sad right now because my whole life I've missed out on so many opportunities to have close relationships, sexual relationships. I've missed out on having children. Whenever I started to have that level of intimacy in my life, I would start to imagine that the woman was demanding something that I couldn't give her. That's what happened with Anna. She was the one who brought up wanting to have a baby. And I wanted it, too, at first. But then I started feeling like she was pressuring me. But what really happened is that I started attacking myself and having voices that I've been really ashamed of, like the ones about not being man enough to be sexual and have a baby.

In families where a seductive mother's primary relationship is with her son, the father tends to be pushed into the periphery of the boy's life. The father often feels distressed and angry at the way his son is being indulged or overprotected, but because he is excluded from the relationship, he finds it difficult to intervene and, as a result, may develop resentment toward both his wife and son (Firestone, 1990a).[11] Pollack (1998) has attributed the father's difficulties in this situation to interference from "gatekeeper mothers":

> Gatekeeping is what happens when mothers, despite their very best intentions, unwittingly maintain so close a bond with their sons that there is simply little room left for the father to play a meaningful role—the emotional "gate" has been kept closed. (p. 125)

Men Who Identify With a Passive-Aggressive Mother

Most often children identify with the parent who they sense has more of the control in the family. Therefore, when a mother controls the family through covert negative power—for example, by being self-sacrificing, chronically ill, or self-destructive—her son often blames himself for her misery, feels sorry for her, and aligns himself with her point of view that she is a victim. In some cases, the mother treats the son as a confidante and turns to him as her "strong man," all the while complaining about the shortcomings and failures of her husband. Mothers who manipulate in this way have a devastating effect on their son by evoking fear, guilt, and anger in him.

The identification with a passive-aggressive mother contributes to the son's propensity to internalize his mother's derisive attitudes toward his father and toward men in general. Therefore, many men are turned against themselves as men, and their self-attacks reflect their mother's hostile and degrading views toward their gender. Indeed, they adopt the stereotypic view that men, including themselves, are inherently harsh, mean, and insensitive.

Men who identify with their mother in this way develop an acute sensitivity to her emotional state and, as adults, tend to be overly reactive to variations in their mate's moods and state of mind. These men are often attracted to and become involved with women who manipulate through covert negative power in a manner similar to that of their mothers. Any sign of unhappiness or misery on the part of their mate can arouse guilt reactions that lead to serious tension within the couple.

In group discussion, Rick investigated his pattern of feeling an exaggerated sense of responsibility whenever he was involved in a relationship. He verbalized his mother's point of view about men and what they were supposed to bring to a relationship.

> "You're here just to take care of a woman. That's your job as a man. You're nothing except to take care of a woman. Look at your father. He was supposed to take care of me but he didn't! [Angry.] So it's your job. You're the one who has to take care of me. It's your job to make me feel good. You had to do well in school to make me proud, so I could compete with my sisters. I needed you to take care of me!" [Angry emphasis on each word.]

My mother expected my father to take total care of her. She never learned to drive, so he had to drive her everywhere. He took her to the doctor. When she was sick, he brought her meals in bed. But she complained endlessly that my father didn't really know how to take care of her. I remember her calling him terrible names. She told me that I was much better than he was when it came to taking care of her.

So then I married someone *I* had to take care of. It's not that she was a bad person, but it is uncanny how incompetent she was. She was dysfunctional and unable to take responsibility for her life. The sad thing was that there were times when she was disrespectful of me in the same way my mother was of my father. And I felt guilty; the same way I did with my mother. I felt guilty for not wanting to take care of her; I felt guilty if I was angry at her helplessness. I felt like I was being cruel. That's why it's so hard to answer back to those voice attacks; they were supported by my wife. But I'm going to give it a try. What I'd say back is like, "I'm not here for you! I'm not here to serve you. I am not here just to make you happy. I am a person; I am here for myself. I exist! Everything isn't about you. The world doesn't revolve around you and your sickness and inability to function! And I am not cruel to say this! There is no reason that you shouldn't have functioned like an adult. I was the child; you were the parent but you tried to make it the other way around. There's nothing wrong with me. I'm just a person, a decent person. [Pauses, feels sad.] I'm a man who has feeling for people, for women. I don't need to take care of a woman to make her love me." [Yells forcefully.]

These voices are always in the background, telling me that all I'm good for is making a woman feel good; that I need to be taking care of her. I've decided to not listen to that voice anymore and I'm taking definite steps to have a different kind of relationship. First, I'm going to look for a different kind of woman than usual, someone who is equal and independent and who isn't looking to be taken care of. I'm going to change my actions and make sure not to engage in any of my usual caretaking behaviors.

Some men manifest personality traits of passivity and meekness by deferring to their partner's wishes and demands in an effort to symbolically placate their mothers. Women who select this type of man falsely equate strength with meanness and often mistake subservient behavior for sensitivity or kindness. Men who abrogate their real strength and personal power often utilize covert, negative means of control in their personal relationships, such as sulking, feeling victimized, or becoming moody and jealous. Their unhappiness, personal suffering, and self-hatred function to arouse guilt reactions and fear in their mates and associates (Firestone & Catlett, 1999). This can lead to partners competing with each other for which one will be the more unhappy, self-destructive, or confused. In this manner, men, who were initially the object of this type of manipulation, now come to play a similar game.

Men who identify with their mother's negative view of men are initially resistant to learning the specific ways they are being manipulated, mistreated, or withheld from by their partners. They become anxious and disoriented when the idealized image of their partner is challenged. They find it difficult to accept information that is supportive of them and instead defend the woman in their lives. Some men even react angrily when someone stands up for them and takes their side in relation to their mates. These reactions indicate the collusive nature of the fantasy bond that is formed in this type of relationship.

In summary, many men attempt to gratify their unfulfilled longings for affection, tenderness, and love through the relationship with their partners. Any desperation and dependency that they initially experienced in relation to their mother are later directed toward the woman in their lives. They tend to seek symbolic safety and reassurance in a fantasy bond with their partner, to their own detriment and to the detriment of their relationship (Firestone, 1985). Lillian Rubin (1983) referred to the inevitable outcome of men's futile search for the "lost mother" in their present-day relationships. According to Rubin, a man's romantic involvement with a woman

> Calls up the memory of the infantile attachment to mother along with the old ambivalence about separation and unity, about emotional connection and separateness. It's likely therefore that it will elicit an intense emotional response—a response that's threatening even while it's gratifying.... It's also what they fear. For it threatens their defenses against the return of those long-repressed feelings for that other woman—the first connection in their lives. (pp. 105–106)

THE FANTASY BOND AND FAMILY DYNAMICS

> One requires collusion to play "Happy Families." Individually, I am unhappy. I deny I am to *myself;* I deny I am denying anything to myself and to others. They must do the same. I must collude with their denial and collusion and they must collude with mine.... So we are a happy family and we have no secrets from one another. *If* we are unhappy/we have to keep it a secret/and we are unhappy that we have to keep it a secret.
>
> —R. D. Laing, *The Politics of the Family and Other Essays*

My colleagues and I have observed that the fantasy bond and the resultant idealization of the couple relationship extends to each family member, who, in turn, believes that his or her family is better than other families. Each member must faithfully adhere to family beliefs and to the parents' point of view and must not deviate from family tradition. This collusive pattern functions to support an exalted, unrealistic view of the family.

In order to protect the picture of the happy family, free speech and honest perceptions are controlled within family life. Any communication that threatens to disrupt the bond or interrupt the illusion of enduring love between parents and family members is not permitted. When personal communication is restricted in this manner, a toxic environment is created for the developing child that fosters hostility and resentment. The child must not show pain or unhappiness, because this would disrupt the positive view of the family and betray the parents by exposing their flaws and inadequacies (Firestone, 1990a). In this sense, many families take on the dimensions of an oppressive cult or dictatorship that is hurtful, both to members and outsiders.

Psychologists have described how distorted views of reality exist within many families and have explained how they are maintained and passed on to the children. In their thought-provoking book, *Invisible Loyalties,* Boszormenyi-Nagy and Spark (1973/1984) asserted, "The child's conflicts are directly connected with the interlocked, collusively unconscious, or denied processes which disrupt and interfere with growth of all the family members" (p. 251).[12]

The attitudes and defenses that each adult manifests within the couple relationship are significant predictors of the views, practices, and interactions that evolve within their emerging family.[13] The attempt to find security in an illusion of merging with another leads to a progressive loss of identity in each partner, which in turn affects the children born into such a union. To the extent that parents have formed a fantasy bond and are deceiving themselves about their loss of independence and the decline in the quality of their relationship, their interactions with their children will be dishonest and duplicitous. "With respect to communication between family members, discrepancies between words and actions are capable of creating mental disturbance in children" (Firestone, 1997a, p. 301). Moreover, when a fantasy bond within the family is operant, it leads to the substitution of role-determined behavior for genuine relating. Children learn to mistrust their own perceptions, accept their parents' role-playing as real feeling, and deny the reality that their parents may be self-serving, hostile, indifferent, or emotionally unavailable.

SUMMARY

In elucidating the impact that fathers have on their daughters, we described how positive fathering helps women differentiate and form better relationships and emphasized how fathers can either support or disparage their daughter's emerging sexuality. We indicated the detrimental effects of critical, indifferent, possessive, emotionally hungry, or sexualized fathering on women and emphasized the extent and destructiveness of childhood sexual abuse in family life.

In describing men's development, we noted how healthy manhood is related to "good enough" fathering and mothering. A boy's relationship with his father along with the early mothering he receives make up the key components of his identity and determine how well he will adapt to adult life.

In terms of father-son relationships, we examined the effects of a father's negative or paternalistic attitude toward women on his son's ability to relate intimately in an adult romantic relationship. We explored the hostile, rivalrous feelings that many fathers experience in relation to their sons and illustrated how internalized, paternal hostility aroused fears of competing that restricted their sons' natural assertiveness. To differentiate, men must work through these negative aspects of their identification with their fathers and break with their fathers' critical or hostile attitudes toward them.

The quality of a boy's relationship with his mother as his first attachment figure is vitally important to his future. In delineating the negative elements in mother-son relationships, we called attention to the harmful impact of maternal withholding, overprotectiveness, and seductive mothering on a son's psychosexual development and relationships with women.

We explained that many men compensate for feelings of inferiority by adopting a chauvinistic, macho posture, building an image of exaggerated self-importance or demanding continual validation from their partners. We pointed out how the stereotypic views of women that still exist in our society tend to reinforce men's attitudes of dominance and condescension toward women, and we explored the dynamics underlying male vanity.

To achieve equality, adult companionship, and satisfaction in their relationships, men must relinquish stereotypical and cynical attitudes they hold toward women. In addition, they must recognize the unreality of the quest for the perfect love based on unfulfilled primitive needs from childhood; abandon their idealized image of women, especially in their role as wives and mothers; and develop a realistic perspective. In our experience, we have found that as men differentiate and develop a genuine sense of self, they tend to become more attractive to women and are more capable of sustaining intimate relationships. In differentiating from internalized, negative parental views, they are more likely to be drawn to partners who are affectionate, independent, and strong and take pleasure in respectful and equal companionship (Firestone & Catlett, 1999).

Last, we described how the style of relating that evolves within the couple largely determines the quality and type of attachment parents form with their children. When a couple's relationship is characterized by a fantasy bond, their child will usually sustain damage in his or her sense of security, uniqueness, and vitality. Despite their best intentions, parents often act out abuses that they themselves suffered in the process of growing up. By contrast, in the healthy or ideal family constellation, parents would not only be loving but would also be sensitively attuned to their child's needs and manifest positive personal qualities that contribute to their child's well-being and growth into an autonomous person.

8

THE MOTHER-DAUGHTER BOND AND DIFFERENTIATION

> Whatever else the girl becomes once she is set on a path of differentiation, it has to be envisaged, first, as a separating out from the maternal role as exercised by her mother.... But implicit in that is woman's struggle to come into possession of her unencumbered truth.
>
> —Nini Herman, *Too Long a Child: The Mother-Daughter Dyad*

Although women's relationships with their fathers are contributing factors in their development, in most cases, the mother-daughter bond exerts the most powerful influence on a woman's life. To the extent that the mother has admirable qualities and is also nurturing and sensitively attuned to her daughter's needs, there is a positive identification with her. If the mother enjoys an equal and loving sexual relationship with her husband and has maintained her own independence, values, and opinions, she provides a strong positive role model for her daughter to emulate. Mother-daughter relationships that are predominantly congenial have beneficial effects on girls' development and their future relationships (Collins & Ford, 2010).[1]

Research conducted by Gavin and Furman (1996) showed that a girl's harmonious relationship with her mother, characterized by high "ratings of attunement, positive affect, and power negotiation" (p. 375), was replicated in the close relationships she formed as an adult. In another study, Carnelley, Pietromonaco, and Jaffe (1994) found that, among college women, "more positive childhood experiences with the mother were linked to better relationship functioning, including greater satisfaction, more positive exchanges, and a more constructive style of conflict resolution (i.e., more compromising and collaborating and less contending)" (p. 132).

On the other hand, when circumstances are less than ideal, the mother-daughter bond can become the most destructive influence in a woman's life. As Hendrika Freud (1997/2011) asserted in her book *Electra vs Oedipus: The Drama of the Mother-Daughter Relationship,* "Generally speaking, the bond between mothers and daughters facilitates passing on emotional health as well as pathology to the next generation via the female line" (p. 66).

The effects of "not good enough" or deficient mothering can cause lasting damage to a daughter's development and are passed on to succeeding generations. To the extent that a woman has failed to emancipate herself from destructive aspects of the bond with her own mother, she will be unable to meet her daughter's needs.[2]

Unfortunately, the negative aspects of the daughter's bond with her mother may outweigh any positive maternal influence and contribute to maladaptation in the daughter's adolescence or adult life (Fenchel, 1998; Firestone et al., 2006; Welldon, 1988).[3]

THE PSYCHODYNAMICS OF THE MOTHER-DAUGHTER BOND

> The daughter/mother bond is not only symbiotic; it is powerfully ambivalent, incorporating both the comforting and alarming, the good and bad.
>
> —Liam Hudson and Bernadine Jacot, *Intimate Relations: The Natural History of Desire*

The process of differentiating from the imagined connection with the mother is perhaps the most difficult developmental task that women encounter. Beginning with the earliest weaning experiences, this process continues throughout the life span and is often accompanied by considerable anxiety, guilt, and emotional pain. To whatever degree a woman is duplicating her mother's negative traits and behaviors in her own life and relationships, she has not separated from the fantasy bond with her mother and has not yet become her own person.

In *Mothers and Daughters and the Origins of Female Subjectivity,* psychoanalyst Jane Van Buren (2007) described the harmful effects on daughters who continue to hold on to the imagined connection with the mother. She went on to delineate the challenges that women face when they break out of this merged identity and move toward increased autonomy and higher levels of self-differentiation:

> Crucial questions that relate to mothers and daughters in the inner world are:... Am I able to maintain a sense of judgment conviction about the ethical nature of my society, my family and myself? Am I able to develop and stand by respect for myself as a person and a woman? (p. 148)

Similarly, Chodorow (2001) has emphasized that a girl's strong identification with her mother can lead to difficulties as she strives to become an individual in her own right: "It seems likely that from their children's earliest childhood, mothers and women tend to identify more with daughters and to help them to differentiate less, and that processes of separation and individuation are made more difficult for girls" (p. 85).

Another factor that makes differentiation a particularly thorny problem for women is that for centuries they have been subjugated by a patriarchal society. C. Gilligan (personal communication, August 2008) has described the effects of this pervasive cultural influence on both men's and women's personality:

> What does patriarchy mean? It's a hierarchy, which means a rule of priests in which the priest is a patriarch. So it divides some men from other men,

> the men from the boys, like African American men were called boys, not real men, it divides all men from women, and places fathers over mothers and children. And in fact, in making those separations, it divides everyone from parts of themselves.

Historically speaking, biological factors have also contributed to the inequality that evolved between the two sexes. In terms of physical strength and body size, women obviously are the weaker sex. In primitive societies, this differential led to the formation of an unequal power structure based on the division of labor between the two genders (Buss, 1995). However, the tendencies of modern women toward passivity and control through weakness appear to result more from suppression, social bias, and institutionalized male attitudes than from biological determinants (Firestone & Catlett, 1999).

Until as recently as the 1960s, a large majority of women lived with the socially constructed identity of being the "second sex" and were relatively powerless in determining the course of their lives. Therefore, they had to adopt indirect means of control—such as passive manipulations and negative power plays—in an attempt to maintain some sense of their identity.[4] The long-standing power differential between men and women has also contributed to women's unconscious alignment with the defensive attitudes, strategies, and values of other defended females in relation to both men and women. This inequality has acted to strengthen the mother-daughter bond as a survival mechanism. The accumulation of these defensive machinations over time has played a significant role in shaping modern society and is at the core of couple and family relations (Bullough, Shelton, & Slavin, 1988; Hirsch, 1981; Rich, 1976; Roiphe, 1996).

Despite relatively recent changes in the structure of the family unit, a mother's role is still that of primary caregiver, a dynamic that has a powerful effect on her children and her partner. According to Chodorow (2004),

> It is clearly the case that for virtually all women, the internal and external relation to the mother is developmentally central.... It helps us to have this pattern in mind and to know that for many women, a projective and introjective filtering of the mother-daughter relationship will be centrally constitutive of their sense of female self and femininity. (p. 121)

As explained in previous chapters, some degree of frustration is inevitable in a child's early interactions with parents; however, immature or rejecting mothering compounds the problem by arousing exaggerated degrees of anger and emotional hunger in the child. In most cases, these feelings have no acceptable outlet; they are suppressed and eventually manifested in the building of defensive behaviors, the holding back of wanting, and the inhibition of loving responses (Firestone, 1990a; Rheingold, 1964).[5]

Women who had intrusive mothers who violated their personal boundaries are often damaged in their ability to develop independence and autonomy as adults. This limitation is primarily the result of being raised by emotionally immature mothers who attempted to merge their identities with their daughter's (Fenchel, 1998; Rubin, 1983; Westkott, 1997). When a mother seeks to fulfill herself through her children rather than through her relationship with her husband or other adult friends, her daughter feels drained of her emotional resources and becomes angry at her mother's invasiveness and control.

"Many girls react to their mother's exaggerated focus by repressing their anger and becoming more passive and compliant.... Paradoxically, the more the daughter resents the mother and suffers [from her rejection], the more she tends to imitate her behavior" (Firestone et al., 2006, pp. 92–93). For example, when a daughter is hurt and angered by her mother, her reactions are transformed into a type of withholding that is similar to her mother's personality traits and patterns of defense. In taking on as her own the negative qualities that are causing her pain, she attempts to maintain the connection or fantasy bond with her mother.

No woman consciously wants to imitate the ways her mother hurt her; in fact, she is often critical of her mother's inadequacies. According to Paula Caplan (2000), "Three of the major fears a daughter has in relation to her mother are the fear of losing her love, the fear of her death, and the fear of being like her" (p. 28). However, the process of identifying with and introjecting her mother's destructive behaviors and attitudes is largely an unconscious phenomenon. As Van Buren (2007) observed in female patients, "Mergers with the dangerous [maternal] figure are often translated into somatic suffering and parallel ideation of lack of self-worth and self-denigration. Alternatively, identification with the vengeful mother is manifested in hatred and destructive feelings toward helpless aspects of the self" (p. 35).

The developmental task of individuation is a difficult transition for both genders. The son, in differentiating himself from the mother, gradually shifts his identification to the father (Bernstein, Freedman, & Distler, 1993; C. Gilligan, 1982).[6] The daughter remains finely tuned to the mother, or, as Chodorow (1978) asserted, "A girl never gives up her mother as an internal or external love object" (p. 127). Thus, each step in a woman's development toward maturity is accompanied by conflict. On the one hand, she is strongly motivated to seek independence, express her love and sexual desire in a close relationship, and to have her own children; on the other hand, she is compelled to hold back this natural evolution in order to maintain the maternal connection (Firestone & Catlett, 1999).

As noted, the mother's influence as a role model—that is, the imprinting of her qualities and behavior patterns on the daughter's personality—are manifested throughout the daughter's lifetime. Subsequently, when they become adults, these daughters pass along the same characteristics to their own daughters, through both direct instruction and the processes of identification and imitation (Firestone & Catlett, 1999). In this way, women's strengths and weaknesses are transmitted from one generation to the next.

In this chapter, we explore the dynamics involved in the dark side of mother-daughter relationships and the crippling effects of the imagined merger with the mother on women's lives and relationships. Understanding the universality of maternal ambivalence can help women change the critical views and negative traits that they incorporated and thereby make a better adjustment. For example, as they relinquish hostile, stereotypic attitudes both toward themselves and the man in their lives, they can achieve higher levels of self-differentiation and experience increasing fulfillment in their intimate relationships.

NEGATIVE EFFECTS OF THE MOTHER-DAUGHTER BOND

The destructive effect of the mother-daughter bond on the daughter's life is threefold.

1. The mother's negative and rejecting attitudes are internalized and incorporated into the woman's self-concept. Women who were rejected, overly criticized, or otherwise emotionally or physically abused maintain these same destructive attitudes toward themselves and treat themselves much as they were treated (Firestone, 1990a). They continue to manifest anxious and insecure attachment patterns in their adult relationships. They lack self-confidence, anticipate rejection, and often become overly self-protective. They tend to distrust closeness and maintain a certain degree of emotional distance in their associations.
2. The mother's point of view about life and her defensive adaptation tend to be emulated by her daughter. Women consciously and unconsciously imitate their mother's style of coping with the world. For example, if their mother manifested a victimized orientation, they often manifest tendencies to relate to life as passive victims. If their mother perceived men as weak, indifferent, degrading, or hostile, they internalize these views as part of the anti-self system. As a result, many women fail to distinguish between the incorporated maternal view and their own point of view.
3. The mother's negative traits are displaced and projected by the daughter onto the world at large and contribute to a fearful and potentially paranoid point of view. Women who have been hurt or rejected by their mother tend to become especially afraid and distrustful of other women. They fear them and are overly anxious about their own competitive feelings because they expect retaliation. They shy away from competition with women and are particularly afraid of surpassing their mothers or other rivals. They expect other women to be critical, demeaning, or outright vicious to them.

As an exercise, the women in our pilot study attempted to re-create and express their mother's viewpoints about significant aspects of their lives in the dialogue format. They came to recognize many of their mother's negative traits in themselves and worked to differentiate from the critical, cynical attitudes and the negative characteristics they had imitated.

One of the most common traits or behavior patterns that is passed from mother to daughter is withholding, where a woman is controlling in her basic orientation to life, and in particular her sexuality. Both men and women are predisposed to becoming withholding when faced with maternal rejection and painful childhood trauma. However, we have found that the daughter's tendency to imitate her mother in this regard and to hold back her natural feelings of sexuality is usually more pronounced than the son's. When a mother represents herself as a woman who is asexual or who doesn't want sex, there are direct repercussions in her daughter's intimate relationships. In describing this dynamic, psychoanalyst Jessica Benjamin (1988) asserted, "Certainly the little girl whose femininity is formed in the image of a desexualized mother may well feel this lack of an emblem of desire" (p. 91).

Maria was determined to get away from Budapest; as soon as she finished school, she traveled to Italy and then to America. In the United States, she found employment, became a citizen, and settled down. She fell in love and entered into a committed relationship, and over the next five years, she flourished. The life that she had forged for herself brought her joy and satisfaction. Then Maria's mother came to the United States to visit her, and even though there was no animosity between mother and daughter, Maria began to notice disturbing changes in herself. In a discussion group, she explored the reasons for her troubling behavior.

MARIA: I was so happy before my mother came. And I was looking forward to her visit; I thought she would be glad to see what I had made of myself since leaving Hungary. Michael and I have always had a very romantic relationship, and also very sexy. We joke about how in spite of being together for over five years, we still feel like newlyweds. But after my mother's visit, all of that started to change. I became more and more distant from Michael. It's like I pulled into myself. I became less and less interested in being sexual. I put on weight and felt like a blob. It's like I lost my passion. I felt like those women I grew up with back in Hungary, like my mother or one of her friends.

R. FIRESTONE: What would your mother or one of those women say to you; about your relationship with Michael?

MARIA: That's interesting. I think she would say something like: "So what's so amazing about your life? You've fallen in love? Yeah, I know what that's all about. I also fell in love—with your father, and look what an asshole he turned out to be! He was a mean, abusive bastard. Those were his true colors. And it's only a matter of time before Michael's true colors show. All men are assholes. Sure, I'd like to believe in love; who wouldn't. But it just isn't real! Being loving is just not in a man's nature."

R. FIRESTONE: How would you answer back to those voices?

MARIA: "You don't know anything. You are just a narrow-minded, angry woman. You don't know anything about men or love—or life, for that matter. Just because you married an asshole doesn't mean all men are like that. Michael is a loving, sensitive person. He loves me and cares about me. Your views about men are archaic and they're hostile. And they aren't my views. I know what the world is like; and I know what men are like."

R. FIRESTONE: What would she say about sex?

MARIA: That's easy to imagine. Since she divorced my dad, she hasn't been sexual; it's obvious what she thinks: "You have a nice sex life? You disgust me! Sex is disgusting. It isn't something that a woman wants; it's what a woman has to put up with if she is married. And you shouldn't be having sex if you aren't married. You say you like it and you want it? I never wanted it. I was happy when I didn't have to do it anymore. And I don't ever want to have to do it again!"

And my answer back to those voices would be: "Yes, I like sex. I want sex. I love sex. It makes me feel good. It's pleasurable and fun and I love having it with Michael. And it's not about having sex, the way that you think about it; it's about making love. About making someone feel good and them making you feel good. And about expressing your loving feelings physically. And if that disgusts you, then you are the one who is sick. You are denying one of life's basic pleasures. You're the one who's got it all wrong!"

In our experience, we have found that, as women attempt to emerge from the mother-daughter bond, they experience an unconscious fear that their independent actions and mature expression of sexuality will threaten this fantasy bond. They may even go so far as to give up their sexuality to maintain this connection. At times, a decline in sexual desire indicates the woman's attempt to take on a sameness with her mother, which contributes to feelings of self-hatred and depression.

Women who develop patterns of withholding have unconsciously reverted to a more immature, undifferentiated state in which they tend to lose empathy and genuine feeling for their partner. They are once again their mother's daughter—guilty about sex, distrustful of men, and self-hating. In renouncing their real pursuits, women often rely increasingly on maternal substitutes and the symbolic reinstatement of the bond with the mother. Through this process of imitation, many women eventually re-create the life of their mother in their own adult relationships—a life of self-denial, of holding back from gratifying their children's wants and needs, and, perhaps most important, a life in which there is little or no sexual intimacy.

NEGATIVE EFFECTS OF THE MOTHER-DAUGHTER BOND ON WOMEN'S RELATIONSHIPS WITH CHILDREN

> Winnicott (1965) said that babies achieve their "true self" through "good mothering." However, this is more easily said than done, since mothers are also the children of their own mothers, with their own range of early ordeals and traumas.
>
> —Estela Welldon, *Playing With Dynamite*

Because having a child of one's own symbolizes a separation from one's own mother, it is an event that can trigger considerable anxiety. Assuming responsibility for the well-being of another person implies that one is an adult and signifies a permanent and final end to childhood (L. Holmes, 2008). Many women react to this crucial step in the individuation process by clinging to more dependent, childlike patterns of behavior, both during the pregnancy and following the birth of their baby. Stereotypic views of expectant mothers have traditionally supported this regression to a less mature state and to tendencies to resort to self-indulgent behaviors during pregnancy. After the baby is born, the focus of care suddenly shifts, and the new mother is now expected to be mature and to nurture and take care of her baby. The abrupt transition from being taken care of to being the caregiver often precipitates regressive behavior and is a significant factor in postpartum depression (Firestone, 1990a).

New mothers often have feelings of fear and anger about motherhood that they try to suppress because they consider these emotional reactions to be unacceptable. Berry Brazelton (1973), pediatrician and developmental psychologist, observed this tendency when he interviewed first-time mothers. These interviews were conducted before the baby was born and revealed "anxiety which often seemed to be of . . . pathological proportions. . . . The unconscious material was so loaded and so distorted, so near the surface, that before delivery one felt an ominous direction for making a prediction about the woman's capacity to adjust to the role of mothering" (p. 260).[7]

Another complication frequently arises soon after the delivery, when mother and child return home. Traditionally, the new grandmother, most often the mother's mother, comes to help with the baby. Instead of relieving anxiety and helping out practically, this visit often causes additional tension and can actually trigger regressive trends in the new mother. Catherine talks about her mother's visit after her first child was born:

> When I had my first baby, my mother came to stay with me for a week to help me out. I tried and tried to breastfeed Leo, but I couldn't. My milk wouldn't come in, so finally after trying everything, I had to put Leo on formula. The very day my mother left, my milk came in and I was able to breastfeed him.
>
> The thing that is so amazing is that my mother was unable to breastfeed any of her children. She told me that when she tried to feed me, her milk wouldn't flow. That is such a strange thing to hear from your mother. And I have siblings who are much younger than I am, so I remember watching her trying to breastfeed them. The same thing happened. The scene was horrible: the baby was crying and hungry, she was frustrated and getting more and more agitated. The whole thing was traumatic; and judging from my experience with my own breastfeeding, it had a huge impact.

Women who grow up with a withholding mother gradually come to disengage from the part of themselves that was in pain. In doing so, they also become removed to varying degrees from feelings of compassion for themselves and for others. As parents, they tend to move in and out of feeling for their children. When they revert to a more detached, inward state, they are blocked from being able to respond sensitively to the behavioral cues of their offspring. Therefore, they consistently fail to repair painful disruptions that occur in those relationships.

Indeed, to the extent that the mother has unresolved trauma in her own development, she will tend to be misattuned to her baby regardless of her love for the child or her desire to be nurturing. She also has a pronounced tendency to re-create the same trauma in her children that she experienced. If she suffered physical abuse, she will tend to be abusive physically; if she was a victim of emotional abuse, she will unconsciously tend to repeat that destructive style of relating. For example, in her work with women, Estela Welldon (1988) observed,

> The woman who struggled through her own childhood with a punitive mother, in submission to her own superego, identifies with the aggressive mother and may easily attack the disappointing and depriving child. . . . That awful parental voice or action we tried so carefully to avoid re-emerges forcefully in our dealings with our own children, and immediately we feel a sense of guilt and shame. . . . Our goal is to become our own person, our "true self" which will enable us to let our children do the same. (p. 69)

Only by understanding and working through the unresolved trauma of her childhood on an emotional level can a mother avert the potentially damaging effect of her maternal responses.

ANXIETY AND GUILT AROUSED BY MOVEMENT AWAY FROM THE MOTHER-DAUGHTER BOND

There are crucial points in a woman's life that signify moving away from the mother: when she pursues a mature sexual relationship, when she marries, and when she becomes a mother herself. Each step in the movement toward differentiation and separation from the mother creates a sense of fear and guilt.[8] Hudson and Jacot (1995) described the effect that these feelings have on a daughter's sexual development and her relationships: "Heterosexual intimacy taps automatically into deep reservoirs of unresolved hostility, blame and depression" (p. 9). These powerful emotions, in turn, often cause women to retreat during this critical juncture, revert to a sameness with the mother, and engage in behaviors that provide an illusion of safety and diminish the intensity of their anxiety and guilt.

When a man and a woman become close, there is an emotional conflict of interest between them.[9] A woman moving toward intimacy with a man is symbolically moving away from the mother-daughter bond; in effect, she is replacing her mother. At these times, she often feels anxious or guilty. In the same situation, the man is symbolically going toward his mother and restoring the fantasy bond with her. In our observations of couples, we found that this conflict of interest is one of the primary factors responsible for disrupting the ongoing relationship (particularly the sexuality) between men and women.

This conflict within the woman between her desire for closeness and sexual intimacy with a man and her unconscious longing to hold on to her mother accounts for the fact that, while both men and women can be emotionally and sexually withholding, there is a gender difference in relation to sexuality. For example, many women feel anxious and pull away after a particularly close and satisfying sexual experience because it disrupts the connection with the mother, whereas most men are not only gratified but eager to repeat the activity, partly because it has symbolized a reunion with their mother.

In addition, the attainment of sexual maturity; being in a loving, committed relationship; and becoming a mother can arouse a woman's long-standing fear of her mother's jealousy, envy, and vindictiveness. Based on interviews with more than 2,500 women, Rheingold (1967) concluded that many women fear punishment from the mother "for feminine self-fulfillment—indeed, for just being a female" (p. 96). In our experience, we have found that at significant points in a woman's personal development, separation anxiety and fear of the mother's retaliation are a common experience. Indeed, a daughter's fear and guilt in relation to an envious mother can cause her to turn her back on fundamental personal and vocational goals. She may sabotage her relationships or career success if she surpasses the level of her mother's achievements.

In describing maternal envy, Kim Chernin (1985) wrote,

> We have arrived at the underside of the mother/daughter bond, the unsweetened bitterness of it. To envy one's child, to want what she has, to feel that her having it has been at one's own expense—what a cruel and terrible irony it is to envy her the very opportunities one longed so urgently to give her. (p. 87)

Similarly, in *The Second Sex,* Simone de Beauvoir (1952) portrayed the feelings experienced by mothers who envy and resent their daughter's independence and are fearful of separating from her.

> Real conflicts arise when the girl grows older; as we have seen, she wishes to establish her independence from her mother. This seems to the mother a mark of hateful ingratitude; she tries obstinately to checkmate the girl's will to escape. ... The pleasure of feeling absolutely superior ... can be enjoyed by woman only in regard to her children, especially her daughters; she feels frustrated if she has to renounce her privilege, her authority. ... She is doubly jealous: of the world, which takes her daughter from her, and of her daughter, who in conquering a part of the world robs her of it. (p. 519)

Women's Fear and Guilt in Relation to Symbolic Substitutes

The original guilt and fear of loss that daughters experience in relation to surpassing and separating from their mothers are often transferred to other women who serve as symbolic substitutes for the maternal figure. For example, a woman may feel guilty about achieving intimacy and happiness with a man in relation to a close woman friend who is unsuccessful in her pursuit of men, self-denying, or seemingly uninterested in having a romantic relationship. Furthermore, many women feel uncomfortable with competitive feelings and are afraid of retaliation from their peers, often to the point where they withdraw from the competition.

Women in our discussion groups have repeatedly talked about their fear of other women: their criticism, their competitive feelings, and their outright aggression. It not only causes them to retreat from competition but to compensate with exaggerated friendliness. They develop servile attitudes and behaviors toward the women they fear. Often they are more concerned about what other women are thinking about them than they are about the man in their lives. In competitive situations, this fear causes many women to regress, to become childish, and to retreat from actively pursuing their goals and priorities. The imagined danger interferes with the process of differentiation and women's ability to maintain their unique identity.[10]

We have also found that women tend to take their cues from other women in terms of their emotional state—for example, in their tendency to be self-denying. Rather than competing actively in her personal life or for success in the practical world, a woman will often move toward the level of the lowest common denominator within her circle of women friends or associates. She is particularly affected by women who are withholding, who manipulate through weakness, who play the victim, and who engage in various forms of self-destructive behavior. Such women cause her to feel guilty about differentiating herself from them, and she responds adversely to this unconscious social pressure by giving up her own drive to excel or find gratification. I refer to this type of negative social pressure as "The Women's Club." It is a common phenomenon in the lives of women and contributes to a cultural pattern of control through weakness (Firestone & Catlett, 1999).

"The Women's Club"

> In the final analysis, difficulties mothers and daughters face in negotiating separation-individuation issues must take into account both intrapsychic and cultural factors, which are inextricably interwoven, mutually reinforcing, and difficult to separate from each other.
>
> —Harriet Lerner, *Women in Therapy*

Most women are afraid to be a nonconformist in relation to other women—that is, to stand apart from the "sisterhood."[11] When this fear is operating, a woman can be described as belonging to "The Women's Club," a group whose "members" subscribe to negative stereotypic views of men and follow prescribed ways of relating to them.

The distorted societal attitudes of the Women's Club exert a strong pull on women to believe that they are justified in feeling victimized or exploited by men. Indeed, cynical and/or condescending views about men are often accepted as foregone conclusions. When these negative attitudes are expressed, they are rarely, if ever, challenged by others, even by those women who may disagree. Many women manifest a paradoxical combination of inferiority and superiority in relation to men, both in their attitudes about them and in their style of relating to them. They alternate between building up their mate and tearing him down and often ridicule him behind his back while chatting with friends.

Women in our discussion groups have delineated a number of these stereotypic views and identified them as reflecting their mother's spoken and unspoken attitudes toward men.

> All men want is sex. They don't want to make a commitment.
> Men don't have feelings.
> Men are inferior to women in emotional intelligence.
> Men are idiots and need to be educated by women about feelings.
> If a man does show emotion or tenderness, it means that he is weak.
> Men can be easily controlled by women.
> Men are wimpy, childish, and pathetic because they can be controlled.
> Men don't care about women or children.
> Men are insensitive and don't know how to take care of a child.
> Men are harsh and punitive and too rough in handling kids.
> Men just don't understand women.
> Men don't know how to communicate with women; they speak a different language; they are from a different planet.

The women also verbalized their mother's prescriptions or advice about how to handle a man in an intimate relationship:

> You've got to build up a man, make him feel really special.
> You've got to laugh at his jokes.
> You've got to pretend that he's more intelligent than you.
> You've got to make him feel important.
> You just have to play the game and then you'll have him eating out of your hand.
> Men are good at practical matters, so defer to his decisions in those areas.
> It's his job to take care of you; if he doesn't take care of you, he's not a real man.
> It's his job to make you happy; if you're unhappy, it's his fault.
> You can control him in subtle ways, give him the silent treatment, cry, pout, fall apart, threaten to leave him or threaten to hurt yourself.
> Men are tough; they can take it. You don't have to worry about hurting them. They're invulnerable, whereas you're fragile and can be easily hurt.

In these discussion groups, when women disclosed their critical attitudes and manipulative strategies in relation to men, many of the men initially defended their mates and resisted acknowledging the destructive behaviors that were being exposed. Their reactions indicated the collusive nature of the fantasy bond that is formed within a couple.

It is possible to change destructive stereotypic thinking and alter these traditional cultural patterns. On a social level, the feminist movement has contributed much to women's struggles to achieve personal freedom and equal status with men; nevertheless, some proponents of this movement have expressed radical views that disparage men and are intrinsically damaging to both men and women. It is not necessary for women to adopt superior, hostile attitudes toward men in order to fight against the inequities that still exist in our society. This posture only leads to animosity between the sexes.

> Women need not sacrifice their sexuality or their love for men to attain equality; to do so would be self-defeating. Many can and do pursue their rights without turning against that part of themselves that is basically loving and naturally drawn to men. (Firestone & Catlett, 1999, p. 220)

DIFFERENTIATION AND THE MOTHER-DAUGHTER BOND

In the accepting atmosphere of our group discussions, women were able to reveal their destructive thoughts and feelings toward men, to challenge these attitudes by answering back from their own point of view, and to act in opposition to their mother's maladaptive prescriptions for living. To a large extent, they have achieved the freedom that Peg Streep (2009) referred to in her chapter "Stilling the Voice of the Mother Within": "The daughter no longer 'identifies' with the maternal voice but is separated from it.... In the process, the internalized voice is out, dealt with, 'de-dramatized,' and its mythic power dissolved" (p. 164).[12]

In one group discussion, Natalie made use of voice therapy methodology to explore the views of men that she realized she had incorporated from her mother:

> I've been thinking about what my mother thinks about men. This would be a good opportunity for me to try to get into her point of view and really see what she thinks. So, let's see; it would go something like: "So you think you can have a relationship with a nice man? You can't, you know why? You're never going to find anyone nice because there are no men like that. They're all horrible. They all want to make a fool of you. They all do."
>
> That's definitely my mother's distrust of men and her warnings to me. There's another way that my mother thought about my father and about all men, actually. The way that voice goes is: "Look at how pathetic he is! What does he want from you anyway? Can't he be okay on his own? He always wants you around to do something with him, or to do something for him. It's so disgusting!"
>
> This point of view goes into a nasty way that I have of seeing Dave, and I act on it, too. Sometimes I act so much like my mother that I can't stand myself afterwards. There are a thousand examples I could give. Take last week. We were going to go away for the weekend and Dave was having a really busy week at work. So on Wednesday, he asked if I could help him

pack the next night. I was actually happy that he asked; it's something I enjoy doing and I was glad to be able to help him and make his life easier. Plus, we always have fun when we do something like that together. But on Thursday, when he asked if I was ready to start packing, I felt annoyed. I said something like, "Well, I still have to pack for the kids and for myself, but I guess I could help you." If I were to say the voice that was inside me, it would be really furious and would go something like this: "Who the fuck does he think he is? Does he think he's the only person on this earth? Does he think the world revolves around him? Can't he pack for himself? He's such a baby! What the hell does he need you for? Jesus Christ! Just tell him to pack for himself. Can't he see you're busy? Can't he see you have to pack for the kids? What is he thinking? He's so fucking selfish! Doesn't he think about anybody but himself?"

That was my attitude, and I was so irritated at him and so angry that I could have torn him to shreds. By the time I was done packing for the kids, it was late and that made me even more frustrated. Then when I went to our bedroom, he had this irritating comedy show on TV and by now I had completely lost my senses. I was thinking: "What idiot would watch a show like this? It's so mindless and brainless. And here it is already midnight and we haven't gone to bed yet and we have to wake up early. What's he thinking about?"

All of this was directed at Dave. Even though I didn't say these things out loud, they were communicated in my attitude, which, of course, he picked up. We packed and when we were done, I looked around at the room and thought, "My God! Look at this room! It's a pigsty!" By the time I got to bed, my neck and shoulders were in so much pain from tension. When we were in bed, Dave reached out and put his arm around me. I felt like I would explode. If I said it as a voice, it would be: "Why on earth would he want to have sex right now? He always wants sex. That's the last thing in the world you want, to have sex right now. Can't he see that? What an idiot!"

When I woke up the next morning, I had calmed down but I felt horrible. I was in a bad place. So I asked Dave to talk with me. I told him about the mood I had been in the night before. I described the things I had been thinking and feeling; you know, the way I see things when I'm in that mood. It's interesting because as I was talking, every tension and pain that I had in my neck and shoulders went away during that five-minute conversation.

You know, it would be one thing if Dave were a jerk or inconsiderate, but he's actually a very vulnerable person who is sweet to me almost all of the time. And also, it was painful because he told me there are times when he actually watches what he says because he's afraid of triggering me into a bad mood. And I thought, how could I be scaring another person like that, especially someone I love? That's like terrorism on my part.

SUMMARY

The destructive aspects of mother-daughter relationships impose profound limitations on each woman's sense of self, on her sexuality, and on her ability to love and be loved. We have observed considerable progress in women as they have come to understand the division within themselves between their strivings toward independence and sexual fulfillment and the debilitating psychological tie to their mothers. As they have broken with this fantasy bond and have changed negative traits that are imitative of their mothers, they have allowed themselves to experience more satisfaction in their relationships and have manifested a stronger identity.

Subscribing to the Women's Club seriously impairs a woman's potential for independence, equality, sexual satisfaction, and happiness. By understanding the nature of the imagined merger with her mother and mother substitutes, women can change the aversive characteristics, behaviors, and modes of relating they have incorporated and can enjoy more fulfilling lives. They can truly find themselves. In relating to the man in their lives, they can be strong and equal and enjoy a genuine sense of partnership.

To summarize, both men and women face difficult tasks in challenging their defenses and differentiating from the negative aspects of their parents that they internalized during their formative years. The last two chapters about family dynamics have explored the harmful aspects of each parent-child dyad, focusing attention on how sons and daughters are often diverted from their natural developmental pathways; how they incorporate their parents' maladaptive traits, attitudes, and behaviors; and how they replicate these patterns in their adult associations. Our analysis provided examples of people who used voice therapy methods to become aware of and separate from the internalized parental attitudes that were harmful to their emotional health and sense of self. Understanding the diverse problems that men and women face in differentiating from early attachment figures has increased our pool of knowledge about the significant milestones and crises in the individuation process and has stimulated our thinking about ways of potentially overcoming these obstacles. Learning to deal with the destructive side of their personalities and understanding the sources of their aggression led to positive changes that relieved people's guilt feelings, whereas previously their critical, angry attitudes had served to fuel feelings of self-hatred and restricted their movement toward higher levels of differentiation.

9

DEATH ANXIETY AND DIFFERENTIATION

> Since the terror of death is so overwhelming we conspire to keep it unconscious. "The vital lie of character" is the first line of defense that protects us from the painful awareness of our helplessness. Every child borrows power from adults and creates a personality by introjecting the qualities of the godlike being. If I am like my all-powerful father I will not die. So long as we stay obediently within the defense mechanisms of our personality, what Wilhelm Reich called "character armor" we feel safe and are able to pretend that the world is manageable. But the price we pay is high.
>
> —Sam Keen, foreword to *The Denial of Death*

The fear of death is the most profound terror experienced by human beings. The contemplation of the obliteration of the ego, the total loss of self, the cessation of one's existence in any knowable or recognizable form is traumatizing on the deepest level. The way people deal with their death anxiety is one of the primary determinants of the course of their psychological life. The terror surrounding the awareness of death necessitates the formation of defenses that function to deny existential realities on an unconscious level. These defenses, formed in early childhood, seriously interfere with the process of individuation and the natural course of one's development toward independence and autonomy.

People do not consciously decide to defend themselves, nor do they weigh the issue of whether to adopt psychological defenses from a rational mind-set; most people accommodate to death anxiety with little awareness that they are progressively withdrawing from life. One of the most effective ways of doing this is to relinquish the goals and priorities that express one's unique individuality. Because a person's wants and special passions, to a large extent, define who one is, to give them up is tantamount to giving up one's basic identity. It is as though, in a magical way, diminishing the self and gradually eliminating life can preclude death. This self-protective stance cuts people off from feeling for themselves and denies the need for affiliation with others.

Ernest Becker (1973/1997) drew attention to this defensive solution to the existential dilemma: "The irony of man's condition is that the deepest need is to be free of the anxiety of death and annihilation; but it is life itself which awakens it, and so we must shrink from being fully alive" (p. 66). It takes considerable courage for people not to shrink from the awareness of death and instead to be fully alive, because in moving toward increased independence and self-fulfillment, they experience the existential terror that is lying dormant just below conscious awareness. Thus, the fear aroused by the knowledge of mortality is at the core of an individual's resistance to change and differentiation.[1]

THE RELATIONSHIP BETWEEN SEPARATION ANXIETY AND THE FEAR OF DEATH

One emotion inherent in separation anxiety that is also present in the fear of death is an intense fear of being alone and isolated. The fear aroused by separation anxiety is determined by both evolutionary and developmental factors. In terms of our evolution as a species, this fear can be traced back to the time when our survival was dependent upon being part of the tribe and not cut off from the group.

In terms of our personal development, this fear can be traced to early childhood when we first experienced separation anxiety. Even in the most ideal parental environment, children are subjected to the inevitable frustrations that are part of the developmental process. However, when the infant or child is the victim of immature, inadequate, or hostile parenting, the traumatic impact of extensive frustration on the total reactivity of the infant causes undue psychological pain; a defended posture is the only escape. In describing the emotional turmoil of these early years, Ernest Becker (1973/1997) rightly observed,

> There can be no clear cut victory or straightforward solution of the existential dilemma he [the child] is in.... What we call the child's character is a *modus vivendi* achieved after the most unequal struggle any animal has to go through; a struggle that the child can never really understand.... To grow up at all is to conceal the mass of internal scar tissue that throbs in our dreams. (pp. 28–29)

As described in Chapter 2, at the stage in the developmental sequence when children become aware of mortality—first their parents' and then their own—their illusion of self-sufficiency and omnipotence is shattered. They feel insecure and manifest a wide range of reactions to this realization. Many cut off their feelings, become distant from their parents and siblings, develop phobias, express anger and hostility, and, in general, regress to a more infantile level of functioning. Unable to bear the prospect of losing the self through death, children retreat to a prior level of development, to a stage when they were unaware of their mortality. In her seminal work, *The Discovery of Death in Childhood and After,* Sylvia Anthony (1971/1973) observed, "Denial of personal mortality is only one among several ways in which the child gradually becomes able to assimilate emotionally and intellectually the realities of his physical and social environment" (p. 163).

Children utilize the defenses they formed prior to learning about death to quell the paralyzing panic they feel when they first grasp the full meaning of their predicament. Throughout the life span, people continue to rely on those defenses to deny or negate the reality of their personal mortality. The initial panic and terror still exist in their unconscious and necessitate the maintenance of the original psychological defenses that have severely limiting and negative consequences for their lives.

These existential fears are the driving force behind an individual's retreat to a defended posture. Any negative event or reminder of death, such as a rejection, illness, or accident, can arouse death anxiety and precipitate defensive reactions and regression to a less mature level of functioning. Positive events also play a significant role in triggering unconscious death fears. This seemingly paradoxical reaction is understandable when death anxiety is taken into account, because any experience that reminds an individual that he or she possesses strength, independence, personal power, or intrinsic value as a person will make him or her acutely conscious of his or her life and its inevitable loss.

THE CORE CONFLICT

As noted, the core conflict within each individual is centered on the choice between contending with emotional pain or defending against it. The universal dilemma is whether to live with existential awareness or to disengage from the self (Firestone & Catlett, 2009a). Most people choose some degree of denial and suffer the consequences in a loss of personal identity, freedom, and autonomy. One cannot circumvent emotional pain and suffering and repress the existential dilemma without imposing serious limitations on one's personal development.[2]

With the formation of defenses, a person becomes split between having an alliance with death and an alliance with life. In aligning oneself with death, one chooses destructive, inward patterns of defense that preclude love and compassion and shrink one's life space. In contrast, aligning oneself with life enables one to experience a full range of feelings, both positive and negative. Less defended individuals feel more alive and have the opportunity to experience more freedom and independence. They have a better chance to differentiate from destructive developmental influences, realize their unique personality, and fulfill their human potential (Firestone & Catlett, 2009a).

TWO VIEWS OF DEATH ANXIETY AND INDIVIDUATION

> Not everyone is as honest as Freud was when he said that he cured the miseries of the neurotic only to open him up to the normal misery of life.
>
> —Ernest Becker, *The Denial of Death*

In the field of psychology there are two views regarding the impact of death anxiety on human affairs: the "healthy" view and the "morbid" view. Proponents of the healthy view consider existential concerns and the "fear of death as morbid and pathological (Templer, 1970, 1972)" (Florian & Kravetz, 1983, p. 600). They assert that the fear of death is not natural and that the child who receives the necessary nurturing will develop a sense of basic security and will not be subject to "morbid" fears of losing support, being annihilated, or dying. The opposing view, labeled the morbid view by advocates of the healthy view, perceives the fear of death as a "significant characteristic of natural and normal human experience (Kastenbaum & Aisenberg, 1972; Lepp, 1968; Zilboorg, 1943)" (Florian & Kravetz, 1983, p. 600). Proponents of this view contend that although "early...experiences may heighten natural anxieties and later fears...nevertheless, the fear of death is natural and is present in everyone" (Becker, 1973/1997, p. 15).[3]

A corollary derived from the first proposition—the "life satisfaction" point of view proposed by Hinton (1975), Yalom (1980), and others—asserts that death anxiety is a manifestation of unfulfilled strivings in life and is "inversely proportional to life satisfaction" (Yalom, 1980, p. 207). In contrast to these clinicians, my investigations support the proposition that conscious death anxiety is exacerbated by the degree of individuation and self-actualization. The more invested in life one is, the more one fears the reoccurrence of a conscious manifestation of the dread that was suffered as a child in relation to death issues. I have observed that death anxiety increases as people relinquish defenses, refuse to conform to familial and societal standards, reach new levels of differentiation of self, and expand their lives.

Proponents who conceptualize death anxiety as inversely proportional to life satisfaction are referring to what I (R. Firestone) have defined as existential guilt—that is, regret stemming from holding back from one's investment and fulfillment in life. All people exist within a narrow range of experience bounded on the one side by neurotic guilt, which refers to individuation and movement toward self-affirmation, and on the other by existential guilt, which refers to giving up one's priorities and withdrawing from life.

Ernest Becker and several other theorists subscribe to the view I propose here—that the process of individuation intensifies the fear of death (Becker, 1973/1997; Maslow, 1971; O. Rank, 1941; Tillich, 1952). In *The Courage to Be,* Tillich (1952) asserted, "It has been observed that the anxiety of death increases with the increase of individualization" (p. 50). In several works, Maslow (1971) discussed the close relationship between the fear of death and the fear of standing alone, as an individual, apart from the crowd. He claimed that this fear manifests itself during a person's most fulfilling or peak experiences, when he or she has a sense of being separate from the group.

> We fear our highest possibilities (as well as our lowest ones). We are generally afraid to become that which we can glimpse in our most perfect moments....We enjoy and even thrill to the godlike possibilities we see in ourselves in such peak moments. And yet we simultaneously shiver with weakness, awe, and fear before these very same possibilities. (p. 34)

Findings from terror management researchers McCoy, Pyszczynski, Solomon, and Greenberg (2000) have shown that people tend to conform to the worldview of the society in which they live as a way of buffering or relieving death anxiety. According to McCoy et al., "Independence from social consensus [and] creation of a truly individualized worldview... are difficult to achieve" (p. 58) because they precipitate unconscious death fears. Similarly, Piven (2004a) has observed "The clinical literature is replete with instances where individuation in adulthood continues to threaten death and annihilation. Experiencing one's own feelings and ideas, acting upon one's own desires against anonymous conformity, even sexual pleasure itself can [be threatening]" (p. 174).

HOW DEFENSES AGAINST DEATH ANXIETY AFFECT DIFFERENTIATION

> Character armor garrisons the ego but impedes motility. We repress ourselves from fear of death; we deny reality, and cocoon ourselves in a womb-like, fragile web of illusions. We cannot individuate if we remain tied to illusions. If we are too deluded and cocooned to embrace reality, then we are in fact killing ourselves.
>
> —Jerry Piven, "Transference as Religious Solution to the Terror of Death"

People's defensive reactions to death anxiety are apparent on three different levels of experience: a personal level, an interpersonal level, and a societal level.

1. On a personal level, people's defended responses limit their lives in ways that can be considered microsuicidal. This tendency to, in a sense, prematurely give up one's life encompasses myriad destructive behaviors ranging from addiction, progressive self-denial, and withholding or renunciation of personal and vocational goals to isolation and withdrawal into an inward lifestyle and, finally, to actual self-harm and suicide. As noted in Chapter 3, internalized voices regulate these behaviors at each step along the continuum of self-destructiveness.
2. On the level of interpersonal relationships, people's defended responses predispose an avoidance of intimacy, including a restriction of sexuality. The acting out of these defenses limits the expansion of each partner's boundaries, thereby precluding differentiation. The less defended partners are, the more they are able use an intimate relationship to further develop themselves as individuals.
3. At the societal level, people's fear reactions intensify the need to subordinate themselves to authority figures and to conform to the conventions, beliefs, and mores of a particular institution, religious group, or nation. It appears that when individuals live out their lives enmeshed in this type of "other power" described by Erich Fromm (1941) in *Escape From Freedom,* they never (or rarely) experience the "shiver of weakness" to which Maslow alluded. People are terrified

to emancipate themselves from the beliefs and cultural worldviews which are upheld by their family and thus tend to unquestioningly conform to society's conventions, cultural norms, and social mores. As Becker (1973/1997) emphasized in his discussion of the individuation process,

> Most people play it safe: they choose the beyond of standard transference objects like parents, the boss, or the leader; they accept the cultural definition of heroism and try to be a "good provider" or a "solid" citizen.... Almost everyone consents to earn his immortality in the popular ways mapped out by societies everywhere, in the beyonds of others and not their own. (p. 170)

In merging their identity with that of the group, individuals become polarized against other groups whose beliefs or worldviews differ from and threaten their own. This collective societal defense against death anxiety, which is a major causative factor in ethnic strife, religious wars, and warfare in general, is described in depth in Chapter 10, "The Impact of Cultural and Social Factors on Differentiation."

EFFECTS OF DEFENSIVE REACTIONS TO DEATH ANXIETY ON THE SELF

> The common denominator of all negative ways of dealing with anxiety is a shrinking of the area of awareness and of activity.... We are afraid to die, and therefore we are afraid to live.... The avoidance of anxiety then means a kind of death in life.
>
> —Joseph Rheingold, *The Mother, Anxiety, and Death*

In accommodating to painful existential realities, people progressively lose feeling for themselves and others. The extent to which they move in and out of this nonfeeling state is largely dependent on whether they are living according to the dictates of their voice. In retreating to a more inward, self-protective lifestyle, people tend to act from both the childlike and parental components of the anti-self system.

People's voices support their self-nurturing, addictive behaviors in an effort to diminish unconscious death anxiety. Repetitive behaviors, rituals, and routines, such as TV watching, video games, overwork, or cybersex, function to dull people's sensitivity to painful emotions and lend a false air of certainty and permanence to a life of uncertainty and impermanence. People who are addicted to substances or routines often retreat from activities and interests that would imbue their life with meaning and strengthen the self. In continuing to gratify themselves in this manner, many individuals fail to pursue goals that are expressions of their basic personality, thus seriously compromising their creativity as well as their personal lives.

People who exist in an inward state come to rely on fantasy rather than on external stimuli to gratify their wants and needs. They often avoid making their dreams real because actual achievement interferes with the fantasy of success. As Eric Hoffer (1955/2006) observed, "We do not really feel grateful toward those who make our dreams come true; they ruin our dreams" (p. 97).

Microsuicide: Death of the Spirit

I have conceptualized microsuicide as a form of progressive self-denial in which people increasingly deny themselves gratifications in real life. This particularly insidious defense against death anxiety has, until recently, been largely neglected in psychological literature.[4] Microsuicide encompasses behaviors and lifestyles that are self-induced and that threaten an individual's physical health, emotional well-being, and/or personal goals (Firestone & Seiden, 1987).

The idea that self-destructive and suicidal behavior can alleviate fears of death and dying may at first seem paradoxical, yet the phenomenon has been a topic in literature and philosophy for centuries. For example, F. Scott Fitzgerald (1920/1960) succinctly described how people utilize self-denial as a defense to help them adapt to their inevitable fate as they grow older:

> The years between thirty-five and sixty-five revolve before the passive mind as one unexplained, confusing merry-go-round.... For most men and women these thirty years are taken up with a gradual withdrawal from life, a retreat... to a life with less, when we peel down our ambitions to one ambition, our recreations to one recreation, our friends to a few to whom we are anesthetic; ending up at last in a solitary, desolate strong point that is not strong where... by turns frightened and tired, we sit waiting for death. (p. 110)

When discussing the microsuicidal process, people have described having voices such as, "Why invest in a life that you must certainly lose?" "Why invest in a relationship where you might be rejected and eventually lose the person?" "Why go through all that pain? Why not just give up?" Although a majority of these voices exist below conscious awareness, they nonetheless strongly influence the acting out of microsuicidal behavior. By deadening themselves while they are still alive, the transition from life to death becomes less apparent.

Microsuicide can be thought of as a death of the spirit. All aspects of giving up oneself, one's sense of reality, and one's goal-directed activity represent a defensive, self-destructive orientation toward life, which, when it becomes severe, can lead to neurotic or psychotic symptom formation. Family systems theorist Murray Bowen (Kerr & Bowen, 1988) contended, "Chronic psychosis and depression can be thought of not just as diseases, but as symptoms of having given up too much self to the relationship system [family or couple system]" (p. 87). According to Bowen, these disorders represent attempts to manage anxiety; similarly, we see them as efforts to alleviate existential dread and terror.

The process of progressively relinquishing one's desires and interests over an extended period of time creates a state of emptiness and futility. This lack of purpose can lead to depressed states, acts of self-injury, and, at the extreme, suicide, which represents the ultimate triumph of the anti-self over the self.

EFFECTS OF DEFENSIVE REACTIONS TO DEATH ANXIETY ON RELATIONSHIPS

> Love signals our eventual final death. . . . Like love, life itself is something we won't let go of, but which we refuse to accept anyway. . . . Loving is not for the weak. . . . There is an alternative escape route that many people take: to not love the partner too much.
>
> —David Schnarch, *Constructing the Sexual Crucible*

Moving toward closeness and mature sexuality is tantamount to separation from the illusory connection with the mother or primary caregiver. In fact, one of the most difficult concepts for people to accept is that genuine love destroys the imagined connection that has imbued them with a sense of safety, security, and immortality since early childhood. As noted earlier, men and women often react to this symbolic separation by retreating to a defended, less differentiated state. Their anxiety about being separate and alone is compounded by their sharpened awareness of existential concerns. The increase in death anxiety that is aroused by loving and being loved precipitates an unconscious defensive response wherein people feel compelled to withdraw from genuine intimacy to the safety of the fantasy bond.

In the beginning phases of a relationship, some people unconsciously anticipate the arousal of anxious feelings and retreat from becoming too involved. They preemptively withdraw from or reject someone whom they feel strongly attracted to. Self-protective voices triggered by the mere possibility of love, such as "Don't be vulnerable! Don't be a fool! You're just going to get hurt!" cause these individuals to reverse their initial positive response and pull back to the safety of their comfort zone.

An increase in both the conscious and unconscious awareness of death affects the quality of relationships. Conscious death awareness is triggered by actual experiences that pertain to death, such as rejection, illness, or financial setback, whereas closeness and love usually precipitate unconscious death anxiety. Both types of death anxiety can be aroused in the process of experiencing love and tenderness in an intimate relationship.

Mary and Roger

Mary planned a romantic evening with her husband, Roger. They went out to dinner and then home to watch a movie she had chosen for them to watch together, *The Notebook*. Throughout the film, Mary and Roger were touched by the story of the couple's relationship. Mary was especially moved by the husband's response after his wife was diagnosed with Alzheimer's disease. He remained devoted to her through her declining years, even though she rarely knew who he was. Toward the end of the movie, when the wife was dying, the elderly couple had a brief but very meaningful exchange and then fell asleep in each other's arms. As she watched this scene unfold, Mary realized that this was the couple's final good-bye, and she was overcome by deep sadness.

That night, Mary and Roger felt close as they talked about their emotional reactions to the film and the personal meaning it held for them in terms of their love for one another and the future that they faced together. However, the next morning, Mary was cool and distracted. Roger noticed that she seemed different than she had the night before. In this example, Mary had reacted adversely on an unconscious level to the reminder of death she had seen in the film.

The seemingly perverse, hostile, or provoking behaviors that people direct toward those who love them become more understandable in relation to death anxiety. Fear that results from an intensified awareness of death creates the need to control one's interpersonal world. Once death anxiety is aroused, people's unconscious goal is to alter the other person's loving feelings toward them in order to create enough emotional distance to reduce or relieve any anxiety or dread they may experience. Control and withholding are the principal methods used to accomplish these goals. For example, in their intimate relationships, people may seek to maintain this type of control by holding themselves back from engaging in spontaneous emotional exchanges with their mate, by strategizing about the frequency of having sex, or by placing other limits on what they are willing to give and to accept. Both control and withholding are regulated by the voice process.[5]

SYMBOLIC AND LITERAL IMMORTALITY AS DEFENSES AGAINST DEATH ANXIETY

> Everything that man does in his symbolic world is an attempt to deny and overcome his grotesque fate.
>
> —Ernest Becker, *The Denial of Death*

Denial is a major defense against death anxiety; people attempt to deny death through both symbolic and literal means. *Symbolic immortality* is a way to imagine extending one's life and meaning through the use of defensive adaptations. *Literal immortality* manifests itself in various religious beliefs that people use to negate the scientific conclusion that humans die like other species and that there is no objective proof of an afterlife (Firestone & Catlett, 2009a).

Symbolic Immortality

Three of the most common manifestations of symbolic immortality are vanity, living on through one's children, and living on through one's works. One has the illusion of being able to transcend death by leaving a legacy or imprint that lives on after one dies.

Vanity and Narcissism

Vanity is a fantasized positive image of the self that is used to compensate for feelings of inadequacy and inferiority. It represents remnants of the child's imagined invincibility, magical thinking, and omnipotence that exist in the unconscious. This fantasy process is utilized as a survival mechanism in times of stress or when one becomes consciously threatened by the fallibility of one's physical nature and the impermanence of life. This process facilitates the universal sentiment that death happens to someone else, never to oneself.

People who are vain think of themselves as superior to others and capable of performing at unreasonably high levels; however, when their performance falls short of perfection, severe self-castigation and demoralization often result. They are willing to withstand the pressure of having to maintain vanity in their desperate attempt to avoid feeling *ordinary* and subject to death as ordinary people are (Firestone & Catlett, 2009a). Unrealistically high self-esteem or feelings of exaggerated self-importance are governed by seemingly positive voices that build up the person to unrealistic heights, then tear him or her apart for failing to live up to this inflated image. As a result, the self becomes weaker, more fragile, and progressively more susceptible to attack from without and within and consequently even more reliant upon the buildup.

Narcissists are self-centered and exhibit a startling lack of interest in or concern for others. According to Lowen (1985), narcissism denotes "an exaggerated investment in one's image at the expense of the self. Narcissists are more concerned with how they appear than what they feel" (p. ix). There is some overlap between the two traits: narcissists tend to be vain, whereas a vain individual may not necessarily be classified as a narcissistic personality (Morey & Jones, 1998). However, both share a deep concern with the image of how they are perceived, both have problems with self-esteem regulation, and both desperately attempt to build themselves up in an effort to rebuild their self-esteem when it is threatened by reminders of death. Both tend to conform, more than the average person, to cultural worldviews in order to give their lives significance and enhance their feelings of self-worth (Schmeichel et al., 2009).

Others are motivated to accumulate power in a misguided attempt to maintain a sense of specialness; similarly, some use wealth to strengthen their imagination of being invulnerable to death. There are negative consequences in upholding these types of defenses—in this case, the overriding need to acquire power, money, and prestige. Paradoxically, the more power or wealth accrued for this defensive purpose, the greater is one's sense of insecurity and fear about the future (Firestone & Catlett, 2009b).

Living On Through One's Children—Gene Survival

The existential impact that the birth of a child has on a parent is complex and even contradictory. In becoming a parent, especially a first-time parent, one senses that this milestone in adulthood signifies being one step closer to old age and death. At the same time, in loving their child and feeling their child's love for them, parents are giving value to their life and that of their offspring, both of which arouse their death anxiety. Feeling for a child also reawakens parents' suppressed separation anxiety and fears of death from their own childhood.

On the other hand, children represent a symbolic triumph over death by perpetuating their parents' identity into the future, a concept referred to as *gene survival.* According to Lifton (1979), gene survival "is epitomized by family continuity, living on through—psychologically speaking, *in*—one's sons and daughters and their sons and daughters, with imagery of an endless chain of biological attachment" (p. 18).

When parents employ this form of symbolic immortality and refuse to see their offspring as separate persons, they are inadvertently teaching their children to form a fantasy bond so that both parent and child can feel secure in an insecure and uncertain world. To protect this fantasy from potential threat, parents often fail to provide conditions in which their child's personality and unique qualities can emerge. Instead they bring the child into their own defensive structure and prevent the child from developing his or her own potentialities. To accomplish this, parents often exert subtle forms of psychological control over their children through the use of rules that emphasize obligation over choice and image over real concern (Barber & Harmon, 2002). They also may label and categorize a child—in effect, assign a specific identity to the child as a way of accomplishing this primarily unconscious goal. "To the extent that children resemble their parents in appearance, characteristics, and behavior, they are their parents' legacy, providing evidence to the world after the parents die that their lives were meaningful" (Firestone, 1994b, p. 230).[6]

These parents also tend to believe that their children "belong" to them and experience feelings of exclusivity and possessiveness in relation to them. This illusion of fusion is costly, however, because the child feels too guilty to individuate and live his or her own life. Even as adults, when people pursue priorities, interests, and goals that are distinctly different from those of their family, they often sense that they have failed to fulfill an expected symbolic function in relation to them. They experience a form of survivor guilt (Lifton, 1968/1991; Lifton & Olson, 1976) as they have made it impossible for their parents to live on through them or their progeny. They are symbolically breaking the continuity between the successive generations within their family constellation, in effect, leaving their parents to die bereft of this comforting illusion (Firestone & Catlett, 2009a).

Living On Through One's Works

Creativity has been conceptualized by O. Rank (1972/1936), Becker (1973/1997), and Lifton (1979) as a mode of symbolic immortality. The unending succession of beautiful works of art, architecture, music, and literature that have survived through time to inspire people in the world today does offer a certain feeling that this could indeed be a means to continue one's existence. Creative contributions can also be manifested in dedication to a life of scientific inquiry or service to others. This level of devotion is admirable; however, when it is motivated by a search for symbolic immortality, the person is often compelled to devote all of his or her time and energy to his or her life project and, in the process, neglects personal concerns or family life or fails to develop other facets of his or her personality.

Moreover, the illusion that one can truly live on through one's creative works is doomed to failure. The notion of symbolically continuing on through a tangible piece of work cannot completely allay the basic anxiety we are trying to avoid in relation to the finality of death, the separation from our imaginative powers, and the cessation of our conscious awareness as we know it. In reality, there is no living on through our creative endeavors or service to humanity. In fact, at death, we are forever separated from the work that has been the closest to us.

Literal Immortality

In an earlier work, I (R. Firestone) proposed, "Traditional religious ideologies offer protection against death anxiety through an imagined connection with an all-powerful figure and emphasize the submission of the believer's will to that of a god" (Firestone, 1985, p. 268). Religious doctrines based on self-sacrifice and the concept of original sin support the voice process in each believer. They strengthen the anti-self system, provide rationalizations for self-denial, and contribute to a passive orientation toward life that is basically subservient. People who see death as a punishment and cling to the belief in a punitive yet forgiving god use this ideology to feel unworthy and powerless in their own right. At the same time, they tend to feel righteous and powerful in imagining that they are connected to their God either directly or through doing God's work.

Thus, the fantasy bond represented by religious dogma is directly analogous to the good parent/bad child dichotomy of the original fantasy bond with one's parents. "The process of investing someone outside oneself with strength and goodness to the detriment of one's own sense of worth is the same in both cases. Both connections provide relief from one's existential fears by offering a sense of immortality" (Firestone, 1985, pp. 249–250). The belief in a life after death based on the immortality of the soul can be conceptualized as a more sophisticated version of the child's earliest fantasies of omnipotence and magical control over events in the external world, including control over death.

Psychological damage results from using these beliefs as a defense mechanism, despite the comfort and security they offer. For example, the dogma of selflessness promoted by these philosophies reinforces destructive voices underlying people's feelings of shame about having natural desires, wants, and needs. Also, because these ideologies often equate thought with action, they basically operate as a form of thought control, necessarily supporting the suppression of aggressive thoughts and feelings. Having no acceptable outlet, these negative emotions are manifested in destructive acting-out behavior toward either oneself or others.

Over many millennia, religious dogma from both Western and Eastern cultures that support people's tendencies to deny the body or diminish the ego or self have contributed to a collective denial or negation of death. Since the fifth century, when St. Augustine reinterpreted the creation myth, theologians throughout the Western world have proposed that the punishment for Adam's act of disobedience was death and held out the promise that if people deny sexual desire and bodily pleasure, their soul will triumph over the body and survive death (Pagels, 1988).[7]

Secular attitudes toward sexuality and the human body derived from these traditional religious beliefs cause untold damage to people in their sexual lives. Researchers in terror management theory (Goldenberg, Cox, Pyszczynski, Greenberg, & Solomon, 2002; Goldenberg, Pyszczynski, Greenberg, & Solomon, 2000; Goldenberg, Pyszczynski, McCoy, Greenberg, & Solomon, 1999) have proposed that these beliefs provide a buffer against death anxiety. "Although virtually all cultures restrict and disguise sexual behavior in some ways, some seem more restrictive than others" (Goldenberg et al., 2002, p. 318). Goldenberg et al.'s (2002) findings suggest that "Rules and restrictions for sexual behavior protect individuals from confrontation with their underlying animal nature that frightens us because of our knowledge that all creatures must someday die" (p. 318). These conventional restrictions reinforce the shame that many people feel about their bodies as well as their guilt about taking pleasure in sexual activity.

There is also a sense of betrayal in knowing that one is trapped in a body that will eventually fail and die. The tendency to renounce sexual pleasure and deny oneself happiness in an intimate relationship can be attributed to the fact that sexual experiences are inextricably linked to the body, which is subject to deterioration and, eventually, death. As noted, some people may become sexually withholding to escape an awareness of being connected to their body. As E. Becker (1973/1997) affirmed, "The sexual conflict is thus a universal one because the body is a universal problem to a creature who must die. One feels guilty toward the body because the body is a bind, it overshadows our freedom" (p. 164).

Throughout history, religion has provided explanations about the mysteries of the universe and stories about life's origins and endings. Huston Smith, author of *Why Religion Matters,* contended that the world's religions address "the ultimate questions human beings ask—what is the meaning of existence?" (H. Smith, 2009, loc. 4167–4172). In addition, it has served numerous other functions—counseling and guidance, charitable works, solace for the sick and dying, uplifting music, social affiliation—for its 6 billion believers. When one examines the religions of the world, one notes that all offer similar guidelines and ethical principles about how to lead a good life. The essential problem is the hypocrisy in the way that they are practiced. Where religious doctrines differ is in their cosmologies—that is, their myths about creation and the afterlife. Their destructiveness lies in the fervor and aggression with which their believers try to defend these differences (see Chapter 10).

FACING DEATH WITH EQUANIMITY AND APPROPRIATE FEELING

> As long as man is an ambiguous creature he can never banish anxiety; what he can do instead is to use anxiety as an eternal spring for growth into new dimensions of thought and trust.
>
> —Ernest Becker, *The Denial of Death*

In studying aspects of this human dilemma, my associates and I have observed three types of destructive thought patterns or voices that are based on people's defensive adaptations to the fear of death: (1) those consisting of rationalizations (seemingly reasonable motives for retreating from life-affirming activities); (2) those involving existential guilt (self-attacking thoughts and recriminations for a life unlived); and (3) those involving prohibitions and warnings to avoid investment in life and love.

In a focus group that explored existential issues, Kristen wanted to investigate the anger and the cynicism she felt following the death of a close friend, Joe, who was a childhood friend of her husband. She revealed the following voices:

KRISTEN: "You thought this was it, did you? You thought that now that you are all happy with someone who loves you, you've got it made. You thought that your struggle was over, and it was just happily ever after from here on. Well, it's not! You're such an idiot! [Angry and loud.] Your struggle may be over, but you're not safe just because you're happy now. What about when Stan gets older? Joe just died; when is Stan going to die? Next year? And how are you going to deal with it when it happens? You could barely deal with Joe's death and he wasn't anywhere near as important to you as Stan is. You're not going to be able to deal with Stan's death whenever it happens. You should just get away. Get out now! Cut and run! Go somewhere else.

Nothing matters, anyway. There's nobody to save you; you're not safe! In the end, you're going to die just like Joe did. So what are you doing with your life? Whatever you do, don't get too close to anyone because they are just going to die just like Joe did. Let this be a warning to you!"

I get a strong feeling of running; I want to get away. But from what? Death; it's like I will be able to get away from death. It's like I somehow believed that there was something special about my relationship with Stan; that it was so different, so loving, so special, that it was safe. So when Joe died, it was like a blow to me. I was actually shocked that death could happen in my life with Stan! I know that it's a childish way of looking at things, but it really is a feeling of being protected from death, saved from it.... [Cries.]

R. FIRESTONE: How would you answer that attack?

KRISTEN: I feel like I'm sitting on so many feelings. [Begins to cry and sobs deeply for several minutes.] "I don't want to die, that's how I really feel. I want to live!"

I *do* know that life is not permanent, no matter who you're with, no matter how you live, no matter what kind of a person you are. Those voices saying that I can't take it are clearly my mother's attitudes about wanting to be protected from death. I feel like I *can* take it. I *can* stand the feelings of loving and losing. I *can* take a chance on love, even though my mother ran from it. Those voices I had about "Nothing matters. What's the use?" I recognize those feelings as the way I felt in my childhood. Those are old, childish feelings.

When I look realistically at my life, I feel happy, and I feel that life is precious, Stan is precious to me, and other people are too. When I feel close to Stan and my life means so much to me, just the thought of things changing is so

> torturous. Then when I hear bad news, like about Joe dying, first I feel so much fear and sadness, but then I get more and more removed from myself. It's hard for me to stay in the state of feeling about these things and not get caught up in all the voices that torture me and distract me and cut me off from my feelings. I don't want to do that. I know that's a waste of time. Right now I feel really, really sad. But I feel that it's worth it to live life, in spite of it being so sad.

All people fear and mourn the loss of the people they love, and, in some cases, these feelings seem to be more unbearable than imagining one's own death. There is a poignant sadness that often arises when people contemplate the potential loss of loved ones or themselves. Expressing deep feelings of sadness and sorrow about these existential realities appears to have an ameliorative, rather than disturbing, effect on those who are open to this emotional experience. As was true for Kristen, the process of feeling one's sadness, sorrow, and grief helps dispel self-hating thoughts and other painful ruminations about death (Firestone & Catlett, 2009a).

The more people are able to differentiate themselves from early destructive influences and strengthen their authentic selves, the more they become aware of death, and the more they have to learn to deal with these painful feelings. As death fears surface in the course of their everyday lives, people can face the reality of their mortality; identify and express the accompanying feelings of fear, sadness, and anger; and communicate their thoughts and feelings to others rather than retreat into a defensive posture. Giving up well-established defenses and dispelling destructive illusions is not only possible but essential to living one's life fully.

LEARNING TO LOVE

In a previous book, I [R. Firestone] wrote, "If death anxiety is the poison, then love is the antidote" (Firestone & Catlett, 2009a, p. 285). In relation to the existential dilemma facing all of us, loving and being loved make human existence bearable. There are few experiences in life that make us feel more alive, that are more critical to our personal development, and that give our lives more meaning than genuinely loving and caring for another person. In order to develop psychologically and spiritually, one needs to learn how to love; to continue to search for love throughout life; and to remain open, vulnerable, and positive and to not become self-protective, cynical, or despairing when love fails (Firestone et al., 2006).

Individuals can challenge their unconscious reactions to the fear of death by being close in an intimate relationship while resisting the urge to form a fantasy bond to relieve their death anxiety. They can sweat through the anxiety inherent in combining genuine love and physical intimacy while maintaining their individuality. In doing so, they can gradually increase their tolerance for loving and being loved without becoming overwhelmed by primitive fears and existential anxieties.

Kristen, the woman in the previous example, composed a poem to express how experiencing love was central to her discovering who she was as a person.

Life Story

Born to a woman and a man
Who never knew me...nor I them *or* me.
Nourished to grow in years
Yet not in understanding—an absolute
That should run parallel to the changing self.

With a heavy load and an open heart
I stumbled on this life. A place where I could unpack myself
Each item handled with care, to be studied
So as to understand how I came to be...

To be loved! How is it to be loved?
When a man touches your cheek
And his eyes reacting to his overwhelming emotional feeling
Of absolute contentment
Do you give yourself worth?

Or when a child reaches out with a face that could brighten
The whole world and with eyes that reflect excitement and admiration,
Do you acknowledge it and set yourself free?

And when a friend whose open heart understands your pain
And who looks at you with complete acceptance,
Do you look back and say "I love you, too?"

So as I look up into the beautiful night sky
A moment comes where that feeling of love explodes within me
And I realize that the understanding is who I am
And the challenge is who I'll be.

SUMMARY

In this chapter we have shown that, in attempting to elude death anxiety, people give up their lives to varying degrees, ration or restrict enriching experiences, and develop defenses that preclude possibilities for further personal growth. They utilize both literal and symbolic defenses to deny the reality of death in their unconscious and unintentionally pass on this destructive legacy to their children and future generations. We observed that loving or being loved makes people acutely conscious of their existence; they experience a heightened awareness of themselves and an enhanced sense of being and becoming. Paradoxically, these positive feelings come with a price—that of a particularly poignant appreciation of a life that one knows is terminal (Firestone & Catlett, 2009a).

We have explained how certain attitudes and belief systems support the defenses against death anxiety that provide an illusion of immortality, whereas other events and circumstances challenge them. For example, religious beliefs, an imagined fused identity in personal relationships, vanity, and fantasies of omnipotence help maintain the illusion. Conversely, negative events, such as rejection, separation, sickness, and signs of aging, as well as positive events, such as loving, respectful relationships and accomplishments that emphasize one's unique identity, disrupt it. When these internal fantasy processes are dispelled, the original suppressed fear reaction is activated, which tends to arouse anger toward the source of the disruption.

The hypothesis that death anxiety increases in direct proportion to the degree of individuation explains the fears underlying people's fundamental resistance to becoming independent and autonomous. It accounts for people's fear of change, the stubbornness with which they cling to the negative identity formed in the family of origin, and their periodic regressions related to unusual achievement or fulfillment. We have found that the process of identifying and challenging defenses that are at the core of this resistance can move an individual toward a more autonomous way of being and living.

Altering defenses that impede the differentiation process offers the potential for additional positive eventualities. In the examined life, there is the possibility for powerful changes that can become part of a continuous progression toward a more meaningful and fulfilling existence (Firestone & Catlett, 2009a). As people become increasingly emancipated from destructive remnants of their past, they are better able to confront death with equanimity, to be more aware, to live in the present, to experience both the joy and pain of existence without resorting to defenses or comforting illusions. In being more open and vulnerable, they are able to more fully embrace love and life.

As we emphasized throughout this chapter, when the defended, less-differentiated individual is faced with the fact of personal mortality, he or she tends to progressively retreat from activities and pursuits that are expressions of his or her authentic self in a futile attempt to take control over death. However, the less-defended, more-differentiated person faces issues of mortality, no matter how painful they may be. Realizing life's finitude from an undefended state of mind can heighten the awareness of the preciousness of each moment, increasing the likelihood of investing more of oneself in one's unique personal goals and relationships (Firestone, 1988, 1994b; Firestone & Catlett, 2009a). It can spur us on to greater creativity; inspire us to further separate from destructive vestiges of our past; enhance our sense of wholeness, integration, and integrity; and make us more compassionate toward the rest of humankind who share our fate.

10

THE IMPACT OF CULTURAL AND SOCIAL FACTORS ON DIFFERENTIATION

Society, unlike biochemical processes, does not escape human influence. Man is what brings society into being.

—Frantz Fanon, *Black Skin, White Masks*

Each person faces a fundamental struggle against tremendous odds to retain a sense of self as a unique individual. We are not only affected by the psychological and existential challenges that have previously been described in this book, but we also exist in a cultural structure that imposes serious restrictions on some of our most human qualities—the capacity for sustaining personal feeling, the desire for meaning and developing one's creativity, and the ability to live in harmony with other people, particularly one's closest associations. Society exerts its influence through explicit and implicit demands for sameness and uniformity that tend to reinforce the anti-self system in each person. These conventional attitudes and social mores support the formation of the fantasy bond in couples and families and encourage the socialization of children into accepted norms, many of which are limiting or harmful to their emotional well-being.

The defenses of individual members of a society combine to produce cultural attitudes, mores, and institutions, which, in turn, act back on each person through social pressure. The resultant causal feedback loops, structures, and complex systems (Forrester, 1994) interfere with people's movement toward differentiation and deprive them of the vital experiences necessary for pursuing personal freedom and fulfilling their true potential (Firestone, 1985, 1997a; Giddens, 1991; Habermas, 1984; Lasch, 1979; Marcuse, 1955/1966).[1] For example, the popular culture places more value on role-playing and image than on real experience and authenticity.[2] This strengthens the defensive façade that many people form in the family and supports them as they sacrifice parts of their authentic self for an externally imposed identity.

In this chapter, we explore the ways in which cultural worldviews and religious beliefs help maintain each person's defensive solution to the issue of death. This, in turn, leads to prejudice, derogation, and violent acts against those who directly or indirectly challenge these established defenses by holding to different views and customs. We compare harmful practices that exist within social systems with those operating in family systems in examining how each can violate the fundamental rights of the individual and can negatively influence the socialization of children. In challenging the enemy—both within and without—we show how one can strive to be nonconformist in the best sense of the word, neither defiant nor rebellious. The process of differentiating from negative parental introjects and restrictive elements in society enables people to develop their personal power and to live according to their own values and principles.

INSTITUTIONAL DEFENSES AGAINST DEATH ANXIETY

> What people want in any epoch is a way of transcending their physical fate, they want to guarantee some kind of indefinite duration, and culture provides them with the necessary immortality symbols or ideologies; societies can be seen as structures of immortality power.
>
> —Ernest Becker, *Escape From Evil*

Social mores and cultural practices in which people embrace various causes, groups, and ideologies in their search for immortality and security represent an adaptation to the fear of death. Individuality and personal expression are sacrificed when people adhere to conventional or societal defenses that protect them from directly facing the fact of their personal mortality. Two major forms of defense that have evolved into specific cultural systems can be delineated: (1) nationalism, idolization of leadership, and mindless allegiance to the group cause and (2) religious dogma, including the belief in an afterlife, reincarnation, or union with a universal consciousness.

Nationalism, Totalitarianism, and the "Ultimate Rescuer"

Nationalism, totalitarianism, and other isms, such as communism and capitalism, can foster a deep dependency in people who are searching for comfort, security, and relief from ontological anxiety. Any cause, whether potentially good or evil, is capable of engendering this reaction. James Gilligan (2007) has defined nationalism as

> a form of prejudice that privileges members of one's own nation and discredits those who belong to others.... Once religion—the divine right of kings—lost its credibility as the source of legitimacy, another basis had to be found.... With belief in nationalism came the belief that governments, or states, derived their legitimacy from the nation they represented and defended. The concept of nationhood and the nation-state thus replaced the now-defunct concepts of God, religion, and the divine right of kings. (p. 39)

The fear of death drives people not only to reinforce the fantasy bond with family but also to extend it to society in the form of group identification. The primitive feelings that initially characterized the illusion of fusion with one's parents are transferred onto new figures and ideologies (Firestone, 1994b). Conformity to the belief system of the culture and adherence to its collective symbols of immortality protect one against the horror of facing the objective loss of self. In merging one's identity with that of the group or nation, each person feels that, although he or she may not survive as an individual entity, he or she will live on as part of something larger that will continue to exist after he or she is gone.

The sense of being connected to a group provided by being part of a patriotic movement is compelling and exhilarating because of the sense of power it bestows on the individual. According to Falk (2004), nationalism represents a collective illusion, a fusion of one's narcissistic, grandiose image with the image of greatness embedded in the national group. "Nationalism can be viewed as defensive group narcissism" (p. 99). Falk went on to explain that nationalism, patriotism, and fascism "may result from an unconscious displacement of the personal narcissism of each of the individuals belonging to the group onto the national group, and of an identification with the group as a mirror image of one's own grandiose self" (p. 99).

Although most people rely on this defense, few are emotionally disturbed to the extent that the existence of a group with different views would cause them to strike out with aggressive or violent acts. However, the majority can be induced into a state of intense hatred or rage by a leader who has pathological needs and the ability to manipulate their fear and insecurity to achieve power (Fromm, 1941; Shirer, 1960).

People tend to be easily swayed by the opinions of others, particularly by charismatic, authoritarian leaders who promise them certainty and safety (Firestone & Catlett, 2009a). In this form of death denial, the leader of the group becomes the "ultimate rescuer," and the cause becomes a bid for immortality. According to Kaiser (Fierman, 1965), the individual's compelling need to submit his or her will to another person or group through a "delusion of fusion" represents the universal neurosis.

To the degree that people are defended, they have difficultly living an independent existence according to their own value system. To counteract the tendency toward conformity and to uphold one's principles in the face of such influences, one needs determination and a personal code of morality.

Religious Doctrine

For the most part, religious dogma consists of consensually validated concepts of existential truth. As noted, traditional religious beliefs of both Western and Eastern cultures, each with their own promise of eternal life, can be conceptualized as contributing to a collective defense against death anxiety. Believers are strongly motivated by the desire to transcend a body that must die, by the idea of a soul or spirit that survives physical death, and by the anticipation of a union with an all-powerful being.

Religious dogmatism generally supports a process of self-limitation and self-abrogation; restricts or suppresses people's natural desires, particularly their sexuality; and incidentally contributes to an increase in violence and immoral acting-out behavior (Prescott, 1996; Vergote, 1978/1988). Fundamentalist religious groups tend to be more fanatic than other more intrinsically spiritual groups in this regard, creating rules and passing punitive laws that suppress sexuality and often oppress women.

Nevertheless, there are variations in the hostile tendencies of religious sects and nation-states dominated by religious groups; some are more extremist and aggressively attached to their beliefs, while others are more peace-loving and tolerant toward people of different persuasions.[3] The more people subscribe to religious dogma that is rigid, restrictive, and inflexible, the greater their hatred and malice toward nonbelievers. Throughout history, this level of fanaticism has resulted in atrocities such as the Inquisition, ethnic cleansing, and terrorism. In fact, in some religious factions, individual sacrifice in war is a basic tenet of their doctrine: a heroic death in a religious war guarantees entry into the afterlife. Yet, on some level, most people still remain uncertain and insecure despite their adherence to strong and rigid belief systems. These socially constructed defensive solutions never fully succeed in resolving life's unresolvable problems. If they did, there would be no reason for people to sacrifice themselves in war to preserve their religious group's particular symbols of immortality.

ORIGINS OF ETHNIC STRIFE, WARFARE, AND TERRORISM

Distinctive cultural practices have contributed to the development of tendencies toward cooperation, as well as conformity, in humans throughout the era of evolutionary adaptation (Henrich & Boyd, 2001).[4] So, too, have cultural, racial, religious, and ethnic differences among the peoples of the world contributed to unique and fascinating cultural variations; nonetheless, these differences have also been responsible for arousing insidious hostilities that could threaten life on the planet (Firestone, 1996). Although issues of economics and territoriality also foster hatred and aggression between nations, at this point in history, religious differences and ethnic hatred constitute the more significant threat. The rapid advance of our technological ability and its destructive potential is outrunning our rationality. Unless we understand the nature of the psychological defenses that play a major part in people's intolerance and savagery, the human race will be threatened by unending conflict, or even extinction (Firestone, 1996, 1997a).

Prejudice and Racism

Prejudice and racism obviously contribute considerable impetus to the intolerance exhibited by many nations. In his classic work, *The Nature of Prejudice,* Allport (1954) described a number of causative factors of prejudice, emphasizing that "Violence is always an outgrowth of milder states of mind.... It is apparent, therefore, that under certain circumstances there will be stepwise progression from verbal aggression to violence, from rumor to riot, from gossip to genocide" (p. 57).

One basis for prejudice and racism is the defense of disowning one's own negative or despised characteristics by projecting them onto others in an attempt to maintain self-esteem. This is operating on a societal level when people of one ethnic group dispose of their self-hatred by projecting it onto the people of another and perceiving them as subhuman, dirty, impure, and inherently evil (Erikson, 1969; Fanon, 1967; Keen, 1986; Newman, Duff, & Baumeister, 1997). Therefore, the removal of this imperfection, impurity, and evil is seen as a valid means by which to perfect themselves and cleanse the world.

The degree of prejudice and intolerance that individuals express toward those of different ethnicity, religious persuasion, or racial background is influenced by the extent to which they rely on the fantasy bond as a source of security. Attachment theorists Fonagy and Higgitt (2007) explained that malignant prejudice "is associated with disorganization of the attachment system" (p. 71). People who have been significantly damaged in early family interactions are generally more defended or rigid regarding their beliefs than their less damaged counterparts and tend to react with fear and aggression when confronted by racial and cultural differences (Erlich, 1973).

If the personality makeup of most of the people in a society or nation is rigid and intolerant, their social mores and conventions tend to reinforce a general movement toward a prejudicial view of others. Entire societies are capable of becoming progressively more hostile, paranoid, or psychologically disturbed in much the same manner that a defended individual can become mentally ill. Indeed, the more a society is built on insecurity and inflexible belief systems, the more "sick" it becomes, and the more danger it poses to world peace (Firestone, 1997a).

Empirical Studies

Over the past three decades, researchers in terror management theory (TMT) have conducted over 300 empirical studies designed to test Ernest Becker's hypotheses. Their findings have validated his central thesis that an awareness of one's death tends to "induce high levels of anxiety and raise the need for managing the impinging terror by validating the worldviews and values that a culture provides" (Florian & Mikulincer, 1998, p. 1104). According to Pyszczynski (2004),

> One of our earliest and most widely replicated findings [in TMT research] is that reminders of death increase nationalism and other forms of group identification, making people more accepting of those who are similar to themselves and more hostile toward those who are different. (p. 837)

Other research investigating the antecedents of prejudice (S. Solomon, Greenberg, & Pyszczynski, 1991) found that much of our social behavior is "directed toward sustaining faith in a shared cultural world view"—which provides the basis for our self-esteem—"and maintaining a sense of value within that cultural context" (p. 118). S. Solomon, Greenberg, and Pyszczynski (2000) asserted,

> Mortality concerns contribute to prejudice because people who are different challenge the absolute validity of one's cultural worldview. Psychological

> equanimity is restored by bolstering self-worth and faith in the cultural worldview, typically by engaging in culturally valued behaviors and by venerating people who are similar to oneself, and berating, converting, or annihilating those who are different. (p. 203)

This extensive research, which shows increased reliance on cultural worldviews as a result of experimentally manipulating an awareness of death, has provided support for my hypotheses regarding increased dependence on collective or societal defenses that result from reminders of mortality associated with real events in one's life (Mikulincer & Shaver, 2001; S. Solomon et al., 1991). In discussing the social and political implications of TMT research, J. Greenberg et al. (1990) concluded,

> People's beliefs about reality [and their cultural expressions of such beliefs] provide a buffer against the anxiety that results from living in a largely uncontrollable, perilous universe, where the only certainty is death. (p. 308)
>
> Enthusiasm for such conflicts [religious wars and ethnic conflict] among those who actually end up doing the killing and the dying is largely fueled by the threat implied to each group's cultural anxiety-buffer by the existence of the other group. (pp. 309–310)

THE PARALLEL BETWEEN THE VIOLATION OF HUMAN RIGHTS IN SOCIAL SYSTEMS AND IN FAMILY SYSTEMS

> If it is not only power and coercion that enslave man, then there must be something in his nature that contributes to his downfall; since this is so, the state is not man's first and only enemy, but he himself harbors an "enemy within."
>
> —Ernest Becker, *Escape* From *Evil*

An analogy can be drawn between social systems and family systems. From an ethical standpoint, the functions of a society or government can be compared with those served by the family in terms of the extent to which they either support or violate the rights of the individual (Firestone & Catlett, 1999).

The key consideration when analyzing the functions of a social system is what the state is offering its citizens—that is, to what extent does it provide for the welfare of its constituents? The ideal society would be concerned with the economic security of its members and the protection of their personal freedom and basic human rights (Rawls, 1999).[5] Philosophically, it would value the life and well-being of each person over the survival of the social system or government itself. In a speech to Congress urging the passage of his New Deal programs during the Great Depression, Franklin D. Roosevelt gave words to these values and concerns: "The test of our progress is not whether we add more to the abundance of those who have much; it is whether we provide enough for those who have too little" (cited by Seton, 2011). Granting preeminence to the individual rather than to the state or any of its institutions is logical as well as ethical because systems are merely abstractions, whereas people are living entities.

In contrast, when protection of a government or political system takes precedence over the rights of the individual, the needs of most citizens are not served, resulting in general economic and personal suffering. In *The Good Society,* Bellah, Madsen, Sullivan, Swidler, and Tipton (1991) highlighted one of the consequences of this favoritism in their description of the economic suffering of the homeless:

> The problem of homelessness, like many of our problems, was created by social choices.... [For example] government urban-renewal projects that revitalized downtowns while driving up rents and reducing housing for the poor, economic changes that eliminated unskilled jobs paying enough to support a family, the states' "deinstitutionalization" of the mentally ill and reduced funding of local community mental health programs, have together created the crisis of homelessness. (p. 4)

Similarly, in *The Shame of The Nation: The Restoration of Apartheid Schooling in America,* Kozol (2005) exposed how discriminatory government policies and Supreme Court decisions have interfered with the rights of many individuals to obtain an "equal education under the law." Kozol cited a Harvard study showing that "during the past 25 years... 'there has been no significant leadership towards the goal of creating a successfully integrated society built on integrated schools and neighborhoods'" (loc. 279).

> The last constructive act by Congress was the 1972 enactment of a federal program to provide financial aid to districts undertaking efforts at desegregation, which, however, was "repealed by the Reagan administration in 1981." The Supreme Court "began limiting desegregation in key ways in 1974"—and actively dismantling existing integration programs in 1991. (loc. 282–286)

Totalitarian states are an extreme representation of the philosophy that the system is to be valued over the individual. They are tyrannical in nature in that they forcefully demand conformity and submission. The efforts of their political leaders are often directed toward categorizing persons as a means of manipulation and control (Marcuse, 1955/1966; Popper, 1966).[6] Vaclav Havel (1990) described the "self-momentum" of impersonal power manifested in authoritarian systems as "the blind, unconscious, irresponsible, uncontrollable, and unchecked momentum that is no longer the work of people, but which drags people along with it and therefore manipulates them" (p. 166). Sadly, many of the people who are living under this type of regime willingly submit rather than accept the frightening responsibility of freedom. In effect, they are in collusion with the social system.

Institutionalized Stereotypes About Gender and Age

Gender stereotyping and sexual restrictiveness, which are widespread in our society, create animosity between men and women and undermine personal relationships. For example, the sexist attitudes and stereotypic views of gender roles disseminated through the media, educational institutions, and other forms of public discourse seriously restrict people's thinking and adversely affect their behavior. Social psychologist Geis (1993) concluded, "Gender stereotypes, operating as implicit expectations, bias perception and treatment of women and men and the results of the discriminatory perceptions and treatment—sex differences in behavior and achievement—then seemingly confirm that the stereotypes were true all along" (p. 37).

Similarly, Carol Gilligan has censured sexist views that are circulated through both popular media and professional texts: "You divide human beings into these two incoherent categories, and then you say that's somehow the way men and women are, and it's absolutely false for both" (personal communication, August 2008). The resultant distorted perceptions of what constitutes "real" masculinity and "true" femininity contribute to parents' differential treatment of boys and girls. Society promulgates certain values and views that limit the psychological development of children by encouraging compliance and conformity.[7]

Stereotypic attitudes that define age-appropriate roles and behaviors in a severely restrictive manner tend to reinforce microsuicidal tendencies in many older individuals.[8] Despite our society's focus on remaining youthful, popular concepts of maturity support the gradual retreat from energetic activities as one grows older. Each withdrawal is supported by social mores, institutions, and the media: early retirement, diminished participation in sports and other physical activities, a waning interest in sex and a decline in sexual relating, loss of contact with old friends, and a dwindling social life. At the same time, people tend to engage in more sedentary or self-nourishing activities, and many come to experience their lives as boring and tedious.

In describing how older people are devalued in advertisements, television, and other media, McIntosh (1995) commented, "The old tend to be viewed as expendable, as having lived long enough and, perhaps, as having outlived their usefulness" (p. 190). Because their opinions and ideas appear to be largely ignored, these attitudes of ageism contribute to the belief among many of the elderly that they don't matter. Terror management theorists Martens, Greenberg, Schimel, and Landau (2004) have attributed ageism, in part, to people's fear of death:

> If TMT is correct and we want very much to live in the most secure and death-free way possible, then elderly people are always a potential threat to our equanimity. Elderly people have an uncanny way of exposing the existential dilemma we all can understand on some level, and yet want very much to be free of. They are a living symbol of time running out, of faculties fading, of potentially frightening biological facts. (p. 1534)

To counteract this form of negative social pressure, suicidologist John McIntosh (1990) urged, "As a society we must improve our attitudes toward the elderly and aging and change our stigmatizing beliefs surrounding mental health problems and the receiving of mental health services" (p. 307). Martens et al. (2004) proposed an antidote to the tendency to isolate and stigmatize older people:

> A possibility for reducing…ageism…might be broadening our values and what makes our lives meaningful. If people value in themselves qualities that are strengths of the elders, such as wisdom, a sense of humor about the dark side of life, or achieving close and rich relationships…perhaps people will have less to fear in elderly people.…Perhaps people and culture can still imbue elders with more value than appears to be currently the case. (p. 1533)

Indifference to the Rights of the Individual

In addition to society's damaging effect on the elderly and on potentially harmonious relations between men and women, our legal system often fails to preserve the human rights they are mandated to protect. For example, the court is a social institution with the responsibility of defending the safety of children by establishing and enforcing definitions of child maltreatment and neglect.[9] Child welfare agencies operate as bureaucratic extensions of the social system for the purpose of supporting children; yet, at times, these institutions ignore or overlook the welfare of children in support of the primacy of the biological family in the child-care role.

The idealization of the family, regardless of the degree of its dysfunction, also makes it possible for many people to avoid critical issues that are vital to children's mental health. In "Trauma and Its Challenge to Society," McFarlane and van der Kolk (1996) asserted that the larger society appears to have "a stake in believing that the trauma is not really the cause of the victims' suffering" (p. 27). These attitudes have significant, detrimental effects on children's ability to develop and to move toward individuation and independence (Firestone & Catlett, 1999). The results are evident in the high rates of homicide and suicide, drug addiction, depression, and random acts of violence among adolescents. In *Raising Children in a Socially Toxic Environment,* James Garbarino (1995) pointed out how society's indifference to childhood trauma has created an environment of "social toxicity" in relation to children:

> The social world of children, the social context in which they grow up, has become poisonous to their development.…They're [the toxic elements] easy enough to identify: violence, poverty and other economic pressures on parents and their children, disruption of relationships, nastiness, despair, depression, paranoia, alienation—all the things that demoralize families and communities. These are the forces in the land that pollute the environment of children and youth. (pp. 4–5)

Like the "good" society, the ideal family would attempt to gratify the physical, economic, and emotional needs of the individual and in particular, enhance the personal development of children. There would be a minimum number of rules and restrictions, allowing for optimal freedom and autonomy (Firestone, 1990a; Garbarino, 1995).[10]

In contrast, the less-than-ideal family tends to function in a manner that exerts excessive control over each person through unnecessary restrictions, manipulations, and power plays while denying the fact that such controls exist. Just as social systems and institutions ignore issues of human rights, many families intrude on, disrespect, and violate the boundaries of their members—that is, their right to live and develop as autonomous individuals.

Forensic psychologist Felicity de Zulueta (1993) has described how the combined pressures from family and society wear away the real self of each individual and disrupt social relationships.

> When cultural and parental conditions fail to give us a sense of worth, the self knows only how to survive. The "other" must become the "object" of a self that needs to be in control. Reminders of inner weakness and pain must be banished, even at the cost of destruction of the self or dehumanization of the other. (p. 135)

Dictatorial power structures in the family are mirrored in a societal framework and in the political arena. On a societal level, when power is corrupted—when it is used to control, intimidate, or oppress others—there is a corresponding increase in the incidence of social violence and other forms of "social evil." For example, several theorists, among them James Gilligan (2001) and Donald Dutton (1995), have called attention to the fact that the epidemic of violence in the United States, a major public health problem, is closely related to both *familial* and *social* conditions that evoke unbearable feelings of shame. They each attribute the origins of shame to early abuses within the family, in particular sexual abuse. J. Gilligan (2001, 2011) explained how societal inequities, indifference, and oppression trigger overwhelming feelings of shame, which lead to reactive violence, especially in individuals who have been profoundly damaged early in life:

> Every time we divide one group of human beings from another on the scale of superior versus inferior, we are shaming people at the bottom, who are placed in an inferior position. That's a recipe for violence because people don't like to be treated as inferior. (J. Gilligan, personal communication, August 2008)

> It is not poverty, racism, sexism, or age-discrimination, as such, that actually cause violence. It is, rather, that each correlates with violence because each increases the statistical probability that individuals exposed to these social forces will be subjected to intolerable and potentially self-destroying

> intensities of shame, from which they do not perceive themselves as having any means of rescuing themselves except by violence. (J. Gilligan, 2001, p. 66)

ASPECTS OF THE SOCIALIZATION PROCESS THAT PREDISPOSE CONFORMITY

> The family is, in the first place, the usual instrument for what is called socialization, that is, getting each new recruit to the human race to behave and experience in substantially the same way as those who have already got here.
>
> —R. D. Laing, *The Politics of Experience*

The struggle to become a person in the face of negative elements existing in the family and in society begins in infancy and continues throughout the life span. As noted in Chapter 2, children are inevitably damaged early in their lives in the process of being socialized (Briere, 1992; Firestone, 1990a; A. Miller, 1980/1984). They are first exposed to the distinctive indoctrination into the microculture of the family in which they are raised. Erich Fromm (1944) described these negative influences in "Individual and Social Origins of Neurosis":

> The child does not meet society directly at first; it meets it through the medium of his parents, who in their character structure and methods of education represent the social structure, who are the psychological agents of society, as it were. What, then, happens to the child in relationship to his parents? It meets through them the kind of authority which is prevailing in the particular society in which it lives, and this kind of authority tends to break his will, his spontaneity, his independence. But man is not born to be broken, so the child fights against the authority represented by his parents; he fights for his freedom not only *from* pressure but also for the freedom to be himself, a full-fledged human being, not an automaton. (pp. 381–382)

In many families, the socialization of children takes the form of lecturing, nagging, or even attacking the child. Children may receive severe tongue lashings when they fail to live up to parental expectations. They tend to internalize the harsh tone accompanying these punitive, often humiliating object lessons as parents repeatedly issue their warnings and prohibitions. The emotional attitudes implicit in these warnings are internalized by the child and subsequently form the core of his or her voice attacks and self-recriminations (Firestone, 1990a). There are parents who believe that to be properly socialized, children must be forced to submit to parental authority for their own good. Societal attitudes and legal sanctions often reinforce these beliefs (Garbarino & Gilliam, 1980).[11] Parents who attempt to force their child to submit or who issue unreasonable ultimatums set up conditions that often lead to destructive power struggles.

In the interest of properly raising their child, many well-meaning parents make evaluative, judgmental pronouncements about their children's behaviors. They often evaluate behavior as good and bad; for example, "You're bad if you don't listen," or "You're good if you don't cry." These categorical statements or attributions support the formation of a narrow view of human nature, demand children's obedience, and discourage them from developing their own standards and values (Grolnick, Deci, & Ryan, 1997).[12] R. D. Laing (1969/1972) underscored the insidious power that the process of attribution has over children's lives:

> For example, a naughty child is a role in a particular family drama. Such a drama is a continuous production. His parents tell him he *is* naughty; because he does not do what they tell him. What they tell him he *is*, is far more potent than what they tell him to do. (p. 80)

To varying degrees, most people fail to emancipate themselves from the detrimental effects of the socialization process. They engage in the defensive behaviors that their families and society condone at the price of their integrity and individuality, and thus they are limited as thinking and feeling people.

THE PROBLEM OF BEING A NONCONFORMIST

Being a free person or nonconformist requires maturity and the ability to remain in an individuated mode of functioning. In this state, one is relatively free of self-criticism and lives with a sense of internal harmony. Everyone has savored this state at one time or another, but often this phenomenon is short-lived because, as noted, in finding oneself and liking oneself, one has a self to lose (Firestone, 1988).

The challenge of maintaining one's integrity and standing behind one's values and principles is made even more difficult within society, where the need to belong and to be accepted can override a person's investment in his or her own principles (Baumeister, 2005). In reality, significant prejudices, repercussions, and retaliations are often directed against people who espouse views that differ from those of the majority. After observing political movements in societies around the world, Rollo May (1981) concluded,

> A pressure toward conformism infuses every society. One function of any group or social system, as Hannah Arendt has pointed out, is to preserve homeostasis, to keep people in their usual positions. The danger of freedom to the group lies exactly at that point: that the nonconformist will upset the homeostasis, will use his or her freedom to destroy the tried and true ways. (p. 191)

The nonconformist is threatened with rejection, aggression, or expulsion because his or her opinions and beliefs arouse the group's existential terror. According to

Baumeister (2005), the "more prevalent and powerful source of anxiety... [is] *social isolation.* It consists of fears of ending up alone" (p. 257). This anxiety, which is akin to the fear of death, has its roots in our evolutionary history. As Baumeister and Leary (1995) have suggested, "A general pattern may well be that cultures use social inclusion to reward, and exclusion to punish, their members as a way of enforcing their values. As is well known, many early civilizations equated exile with death" (p. 521).[13]

Because people fear exclusion to such an extent, they "conform, comply, obey, ingratiate, improve their appearance, and manage their impressions to others in order to be included and feel like they belong" (Williams, Cheung, & Choi, 2000, p. 749). In one experiment, Williams (Williams et al., 2000; Williams & Jarvis, 2006) explored the phenomenon of "cyberostracism"—a form of Internet bullying. In the experiment, which was conducted on a computer, each subject was invited by two other players to participate in a simulated game of "cyberball." After several turns of passing the ball back and forth to the other players, the subject was systematically excluded from play and his or her presence was completely ignored by the other two players. In follow-up interviews, subjects reported experiencing a significant decrease in self-esteem, and several reported feelings of depression as a result of the virtual (not actual) ostracism. Williams concluded that his "Internet ostracism paradigm is similar in some ways to Asch's (1956) conformity, Tajfel's (1970) minimal group, and Milgram's (1974) obedience paradigms. In these classic studies, the researchers "were all surprised that, even in their baseline conditions, people conformed to clearly wrong answers, developed senses of 'we and they,' and obeyed authority figures to the point of hurting someone" (Williams et al., 2000, p. 760).

Social norms have been defined as jointly negotiated rules for social behavior, including societal expectations for specific role-determined behaviors (Cialdini & Trost, 1998). Guilt reactions are often precipitated in individuals whose behaviors and lifestyles depart from accepted societal standards and norms. In previous works (Firestone, 1988, 1997a), I (R. Firestone) have conceptualized this form of guilt as "neurotic guilt." Drawing on O. Rank's (1936/1972) work, Becker (1964) defined neurotic guilt as "the action-bind that reaches out of the past to limit new experiences, to block the possibility of broader choices" (p. 186). He attributed the cause of this constriction of life to the "early indoctrination" of the child. My views concerning neurotic guilt are similar to Rank's and Becker's thinking. It is my contention that neurotic guilt reactions arise when a person chooses self-actualization over conformity. When people choose to go against their inhibitions and fully embrace life, they must deal with both the fear and guilt aroused by affirming their individuality and personal power.

Each successive stage in the individuation process is marked by guilt at leaving one's parents behind as well as fear at having to face the world alone. In fact, guilt reactions are often a sign of an unconscious desire to hold on to the fantasy connection with one's parents. Guilt about moving in a direction that is different from, or more fulfilling than, experiences in one's family is often expressed in voice attacks or self-critical thoughts such as, "Who do you think you are?" "You always want your own way!" and "You only think of yourself."

Elena's story is an example of how people typically react when they choose a path that is different from that of their peers.[14] After her second child was in preschool, Elena decided to go back to work. It had been a difficult decision for her to make. She and her husband were comfortable financially and did not need her second income. Most of her friends were devoting themselves to raising their children. Elena's husband was supportive of her whether she chose to resume her career or stay at home. Elena decided that in order for her to be personally fulfilled, she needed to have a professional life along with a family life. Here she recounts an experience she had soon after she resumed her career:

> The other day I was at a business lunch and a woman was at a table near me with her new baby, having lunch with some of her girlfriends. They were all oohing and awing over the baby and when the waitress came over, she joined in. I swear they went on for about fifteen minutes. At first I was irritated by the whole scene but then I just sort of forgot about it. Later that afternoon, I was feeling down, really against myself.
>
> When I tried to figure out what had happened to change my mood, I thought of the scene in the restaurant. I wondered why I had had such a strong reaction to something that didn't even involve me. What had it triggered in me? Had it triggered voice attacks? When I thought about that, I had some clarity. I knew what the voices were:
>
> "See those women? They are doing what you should be doing: you should be focusing on your kids instead of prancing around trying to have a career. Who do you think you are? You are so irresponsible and self-centered. You should be like those women. They are dedicated to their children. They know that having a career isn't meaningful; they know that you're just superficial and self-centered. All you care about is yourself."
>
> "And what about Carlos? You are depriving him of the kind of life he should be having. You should be at home raising the children! Sure, he says he's okay with your decision. But you have just manipulated him into going along with you. No real man would be okay with this situation! Those women have made their husbands happy. They have done the right thing."
>
> I couldn't believe that all of those attacks came from just watching the way those women were with that baby. I saw them as doing what I am supposed to be doing with my life. I recognized a lot of the voices as coming from my mother. Then I became aware that her point of view is even vicious toward me.
>
> "So you think you can show me up? You think that being a mother isn't good enough? Are you saying you are better than those women? Are you saying you are better than me? Don't fool yourself! This is just a big cover-up. The truth is that you are a terrible mother and you know it. That's why you don't want to stay home with your children. It's not about your career at all. Otherwise, you would be happy to do what you are supposed to do. You

> would be happy being home with your kids. You would find satisfaction in what every woman is supposed to do!"
>
> You know, there is such a strong feeling that that's what I'm supposed to be, what a woman is supposed to do. I should be building my entire life around my children and making a home for my family. Then there are other voices, the ones that aren't angry; they are persuasive and reasonable sounding:
>
> "If you just do what you are supposed to do, you won't have to feel so out-of-place. You'll fit in. You won't have to be out there in the business world, competing with men. Life will be easy. Besides, that's where your husband really wants you. He doesn't want you mixing with men; he wants you tucked away at home. And do you blame him? Why can't you offer him that security?"
>
> Even though Carlos is nothing but encouraging of my career, I still have these voices telling me that I am betraying him by going back to work. It's like it's part of the old-fashioned marriage deal: keep the woman at home, otherwise she will stray. My answer to those voices is:
>
> "You have it completely wrong! Just because my career is important to me doesn't mean that I don't love my children or that I'm not a good mother. And it certainly doesn't mean that I don't love Carlos and that I am not a good wife. My family loves me for who I am, and that includes being a woman with a career. My husband benefits from me being a strong, independent person and so do my children. Just because you limited yourself and hid behind the role of mother so that you didn't have to be your own person doesn't mean that I have to. You had it wrong, not me!"
>
> I definitely have a lot of fear and guilt about changing this part of my life, about going out into the world and being involved in creative work again. It's interesting to me that those voices were so loud and strong, telling me to stay in my role, and I believe that kind of attitude is still pretty dominant in my family. It's even dominant among my friends and I believe that it's true about our society, too.

According to terror management theorists Arndt, Greenberg, Solomon, Pyszczynski, and Schimel (1999), "Creativity by definition involves doing something other than what is prescribed by prevailing norms" (p. 29). In research that investigated the relationship between creativity and "an individual's construction of a unique personality," Arndt et al. cited O. Rank's (1932/1989) earlier study of creative individuals, who "must ultimately...carve their own individuality out of the collective ideology that prevails and that they themselves have accepted, like the sculptor who carves his figures out of raw stone" (p. 368). Arndt et al. referred to Becker's (1973/1997) work when they wrote,

> To the extent that the expression of the creative will is the vehicle through which people engage in the process of individuation, creative engagement may threaten the delicate balance between the needs to stick out and fit

> in. . . . The motive to fit in leads to culturally appropriate behavior that consensually validates one's beliefs and is thus likely to increase faith in one's worldview and one's value, which, in turn, affords protection from mortality concerns. (p. 20)

Guilt reactions can predispose serious consequences and regressions that limit each person's destiny. However, utilizing the techniques of voice therapy to verbalize the self-recriminations that underlie one's guilt evokes feelings of compassion and support for one's self and personal point of view. In contrast, when voice attacks are not identified and challenged, they permeate a person's thoughts and lead to him/her submitting to their injunctions. By identifying the external forces that discourage individuation and differentiation and that support the forces within each person that represent the anti-self, people can move toward a more creative, fulfilling life and deal more effectively with their tendencies toward conformity and self-limitation (Firestone, 1988).

On a broader societal level, people can challenge harmful institutional practices and work toward building a more inclusive global community based on mutual concern and true interdependence. As Robert Bellah and his colleagues (1991) advocated in concluding their book *The Good Society,*

> If we are fortunate enough to have the gift of faith through which we see ourselves as members of the universal community of all being, then we bear a special responsibility to bring whatever insights we have to the common discussion of new problems, not because we have any superior wisdom but because we can be, as Vaclav Havel defines his role, ambassadors of trust in a fearful world. When enough of us have sufficient trust to act responsibly, there is a chance to achieve, at least in part, a good society. (p. 286)

SUMMARY

In this chapter, we described how cultural prerogatives, social mores, and the institutions of society function to reinforce people's defense systems, promote attitudes of conformity, and, to a large extent, interfere with the movement toward differentiation. We showed how nationalism and religious dogma serve as powerful buffers against death anxiety. Essentially, these institutionalized defenses offer an illusory connection to the group, nation, leader, or higher power that imbues one with a sense of immortality. People who have come to rely on the fantasy bond for this form of security are intolerant of other groups who hold differing worldviews or religious beliefs, because these views threaten their own solution to the death problem. Each group's or nation's hostile reactions to the imagined danger posed by the out-group have contributed to the recurring ethnic cleansing, warfare, and terrorism that endanger life on this planet.

We went on to delineate negative aspects of the socialization process in the nuclear family that encourage unquestioning obedience and conformity in children. We showed how individuals, following this initial training and acculturation, encounter new programming within the cultural complex of society. To varying degrees, its institutions, cultural attitudes, and social mores can represent a serious assault on the self. Societies, like families, can either support or oppose individuality. Oppressive families set up the individual to accept social systems that are undemocratic or totalitarian in nature.

Most people sacrifice their personal strengths and subjugate themselves to other persons and ideologies in their search for security. They forsake reality for illusion, choose role-determined behavior and symbols in place of real experiences, sacrifice individuality for a fantasy of fusion, and reject their unique and separate identity for a life of conformity and submission. They hold on to religious beliefs that promise eternal life and, in so doing, increasingly turn their backs on their actual lives.

Faced with painful existential truths, most people despair or become cynical; they withdraw from close relationships or form an alliance with death by giving up their lives prematurely. All people utilize psychological defenses to ward off existential pain; however, some rise to the challenge posed by ontological threats and continue to pursue a creative, individualistic life (Firestone, 2000). People essentially give meaning to their lives by investing emotionally in personal relationships, activities, interests, and causes that express their true identity. As people strive toward higher levels of differentiation and achieve true maturity, they feel integrated and centered in themselves. They have integrity when they refuse to blindly conform to conventional attitudes.

It is imperative to come to understand how fear negatively impacts families as well as institutions and how people can be manipulated in terms of their fears. To overcome prejudice, racism, and hostilities associated with ethnic differences, we need to develop a more inclusive worldview and a truly compassionate attitude toward people everywhere. In the wake of 9/11, Michael Salzman (2001) reported findings from terror management studies that suggested a cautious hope for the future. In an experiment that aroused subjects' awareness of death, those who held an inclusive worldview did not endorse degrading, punitive attitudes toward people from different ethnic backgrounds; instead, they endorsed even more tolerant, compassionate attitudes than they did prior to the experiment: "TMT researchers have found that when subjects whose world-views valued tolerance and respect for diversity are exposed to the mortality-salience condition, they bolstered that world-view and actually exhibited greater tolerance.... This is cause for optimism" (p. 350).

To be successful in the differentiation process, we must face up to existential issues, overcome the negative effects of our upbringing, and learn to live without comforting illusions or soothing psychological defenses. "An individual *can* overcome personal limitations and embrace life in the face of death anxiety. Such a person would find no need for ethnic hatred or insidious warfare" (Firestone, 1997a, p. 289).

11

LEADERSHIP, POWER, AND DIFFERENTIATION

> The essential strategy of leadership in mobilizing power is to recognize the arrays of motives and goals in potential followers, to appeal to those motives by words and action, and to strengthen those motives and goals in order to increase the power of leadership, thereby changing the environment within which both followers and leaders act.
>
> —James Burns, *Leadership*

Unresolved dependency needs, the residual desire for love, care, and protection, and the resultant tendency to subordinate ourselves to others all combine to oppose self differentiation. If one is in an unfamiliar situation and lacks an understanding of the pertinent parameters of the new circumstance, one is likely to turn to others who appear to be more self-confident or action-oriented or who seem to be more knowledgeable about the situation. One evening after disembarking from an airplane at a new destination, I strode off in what I thought was the direction of the terminal. Because I was one of the first passengers off the plane and tend to be assertive by nature, the other passengers followed me until our large procession was intercepted by an airline official who sent us in the correct direction.

What happened that evening is not that uncommon; in fact, it is typical of the behavior of most individuals in a group or crowd. Even in circumstances where a perceived authority figure is in error, most people tend to simply follow his or her lead without thinking, just as the passengers did. A number of psychological processes account for this phenomenon, including imitation, emotional contagion (the ripple effect), synchronicity, social connectivity, and the power of suggestion, among others (Bandura, 2001; Bandura & Walters, 1963; Barsade, 2002; Christakis & Fowler, 2009; N. Miller & Dollard, 1941). In addition, elements of transference and attachment behavior were operating, even during this brief interaction at the airport (S. Freud, 1921/1955; Popper & Mayseless, 2003). It is widely recognized that all people, not just patients in psychotherapy, tend to transfer the feelings they had toward early attachment figures onto others, particularly those individuals they perceive as worthy of respect, authority figures, or people who possess status or power.

Transference reactions are also responsible, in part, for many of the behaviors that individuals engage in when they become part of a group, a phenomenon that Trotter (1916) attributed to a "herd instinct" in humans. These exaggerated responses have been studied in depth since the publication of Freud's (1921/1955) essay, "Group Psychology and the Analysis of the Ego," which was informed by Gustave LeBon's 1897 work, *The Crowd.* LeBon had observed,

> The sentiments and ideas of all the persons in the gathering [crowd] take one and the same direction, and their conscious personality vanishes. (p. 9) In a crowd every sentiment and act is contagious, and contagious to such a degree that an individual readily sacrifices his personal interest to the collective interest. (p. 13) In crowds the foolish, ignorant, and envious persons are freed from the sense of their insignificance and powerlessness, and are possessed instead by the notion of brutal and temporary but immense strength. (p. 25)

The actions that people are prepared to take when they have merged their identity with that of the group can have diverse manifestations, ranging from acts of patriotism, humanitarianism, or nonviolent protest to acts of criminality or violence. What actually transpires when individuals are in the "hypnotic" state of operating on the basis of the group mind is dependent upon many variables, including the motives (for good or evil) of the leader and his or her followers, the leader's goals, and the means employed to attain these goals.

In his critique of Trotter's idea of a herd instinct, Freud emphasized the impossibility of being able to "grasp the nature of a group without taking into account the importance of the leader" (Eizirik, 2001, p. 160). Leadership is necessary in any group or organization because a capable leader is essential in coordinating projects and people without encountering confusion and chaos (Paul, Costley, Howell, & Dorfman, 2002; Wren, 1995). Even a small group of like-minded individuals seek direction in making significant decisions. Indeed, "leadership, as such, is a universal phenomenon" (Bass, 1997, p. 130). Successful leaders facilitate the accomplishment of the agreed-upon goals of group members because they are competent and decisive and tend to have the vision, drive, and ability to translate plans into action. Clearly, in any organization, good leadership is a highly valuable asset, whereas destructive leadership is detrimental or even disastrous.

Equally important are the personality traits, abilities, and values of the constituents or followers. Any analysis of the personal qualities that characterize effective, ethical leaders must take into account the situation and the personalities of those being led. Leadership cannot be studied in a vacuum. As Ciulla (2004) asserted, "Leadership is not a person or a position. It is a complex moral relationship between people, based on trust, obligation, commitment, emotion, and a shared vision of the good" (p. xv).[1] Indeed, a well-functioning democracy requires the active participation of informed, educated citizens who have an independent point of view and a humane, ethical approach to life.

Unfortunately, individuals who are immature or less individuated are more likely to betray themselves by subverting their values, relinquishing their capacity for critical thinking, and submitting to a leader, group, or cause, with little or no awareness that they are doing so. The effect is a progressive limitation on their lives and a surrendering of their unique point of view and sense of self.

Because each of us experiences remnants of our child selves that drive us to seek care and guidance, on an unconscious level, we tend to feel that we cannot survive unless we are connected to someone who is more powerful—an ultimate rescuer or savior (Firestone, 1994b; Firestone & Catlett, 2009b). The more fearful people become, the more they cling to this type of illusion, which results in the idealization of leaders and an exaggeration of their strengths and abilities.

The results of this defensive adaptation can be observed in unhealthy, dysfunctional leader-follower interactions in business and in politics and in the destructive consequences of such relationships in both arenas. In describing this phenomenon, Lipman-Blumen (2005b) noted,

> Many of us look to leaders who project an aura of certainty—real or imagined—that we lack within ourselves. And if they are not *actually* knowledgeable and in control, we convince ourselves that they truly are, to satisfy our own desperate need. (p. 53)

In describing reciprocal follower-leader relationships, Vaclav Havel (1990) emphasized "All power is power over someone, and it always somehow responds, usually unwittingly rather than deliberately, to the state of mind and the behavior of those it rules over" (p. 182).[2]

LEADERSHIP

> Discussions of leadership are often hopelessly intertwined with issues of authority. And, if Western philosophy has had one central preoccupation, it has been with the emancipation of the individual from externally imposed forms of authority and control.
>
> —Bernard M. Bass and Paul Steidlmeier, *Ethics, Character, and Authentic Transformational Leadership*

According to leadership expert Warren Bennis (2007), "In the best of times, we tend to forget how urgent the study of leadership is. But leadership always matters, and it has never mattered more than it does now" (p. 2). Many of the early approaches to leadership conceptualized the personality traits of the leader as being critical in the analysis of leader effectiveness, notably the "great man" or "qualities" model originally described by Thomas Carlyle. Inspired by the popularity of intelligence tests in the early twentieth century, proponents of the great man approach proposed that successful leaders possess certain universal traits that distinguish them from ordinary people.[3]

In recent years, leadership theorists and researchers have begun to pay more attention to leadership as "a *process* rather than a property or a *thing*" (Wood, 2005, p. 1103). According to Wood, "'successful leaders' are not simple, locatable social actors.... Instead, leadership *is* movement, open and dynamic process...a creative process of becoming" (pp. 1117–1118).[4]

Dimensions of Positive Leadership

Leadership is a multidimensional concept that may or may not have positive ethical implications. Leadership and the effect that leaders have on the people they influence can be evaluated from two perspectives: (1) pragmatic: is the leader effective in achieving certain prescribed goals? (2) ethical or moral: does the leader meet appropriate standards of responsibility and compassion in regard to human concerns? The question of ethics applies to both the means employed by the leader and to the end results.

Many of the basic qualities that contribute to leadership potential—competence, authenticity, a creative vision or goal, high energy level, and even a genuine desire to serve people—are essentially neutral in relation to moral or ethical considerations. These personality characteristics, while admirable in their own right, might also be utilized to accomplish destructive goals or acted upon in a manner that is harsh, authoritarian, demeaning, or demoralizing to others (Firestone & Catlett, 2009b).[5]

The ethical position of any leader can be determined by answering a fundamental question: Does the leader meet the needs of his or her followers without causing harm to people either inside or outside the group or organization? Leaders who are both effective and ethical possess personal integrity. They are emotionally mature, have the ability to integrate emotions and rational thought, have little or no vanity or narcissism, appreciate the uniqueness and humanity of each individual, value the means as well as the ends, and have a strong service orientation.

Leaders can be evaluated from an ethical perspective by using the same criteria that Becker (1971) used to assess the dimensions of an ideal or good society. Becker's first criterion is that the ideal society or government meet the needs of its constituency, maintain the welfare of the citizens, and protect the society against outside threat. Therefore, the ethical leader would serve his or her constituency by striving to fulfill people's basic needs, both physical and economic, without inflicting harm on anyone in the process. In the political world, the good leader would tend to be bipartisan in the sense that he or she would serve the needs of the majority while respecting and upholding the needs of the minority.

Contemporary Models of Leadership Development

In recent years, many corporations have increasingly instituted systematic training programs to help them meet the compelling "need to have more people in the organization thinking like leaders." According to Ciulla (2005), "In most large American companies, leadership programs have become a regular part of training and development" (p. 325). Burns (1978) has indicated that, in the past, many such programs—for example, those of the transactional leadership model—sought only "to train persons to manage and manipulate other persons, rather than to *lead* them" (p. 446).

More recently, however, the emphasis has been on educating the whole person to become a leader. The terms *leadership* and *education* have become strongly associated with each other in the thinking of a significant number of people who are influential in the world of business and politics. According to Bass (1997), transformational leaders enlarge and elevate "followers' motivation, understanding, maturing, and sense of self-worth" (p. 130). Education in both the transformational and servant-leadership models not only facilitates participants' professional development but also contributes to their personal growth by focusing on issues of integrity, values, and ethics, and particularly in the servant-leadership model, the focus is on service to others. In the servant-leadership model, the leader is servant first, and service to all stakeholders is given precedence even over profit as the bottom line (Greenleaf, 1970).[6]

Over the past 40 years, the servant-leadership approach has become integrated into numerous programs directed toward helping participants move from dependence to independence to interdependence. There is a strong emphasis on developing self-awareness and on honestly acknowledging defensive agendas that one might be bringing to the table. As Anzalone (2007) emphasized in describing the self-awareness component of servant-leadership training, "The path to self-knowledge is not always a smooth one. Uncovering the demons that lurk beneath the surface leads to growth, but it can be unsettling" (p. 800). This process is similar in many respects to that of uncovering destructive thoughts and attitudes in voice therapy.

Why People Tend to Retreat From a Position of Positive Leadership

Occupying a leadership position heightens one's sense of aloneness. Being the ultimate decision maker can give those in power an exaggerated sense of pressure in relation to the responsibility they hold for themselves and others. Nevertheless, they alone are the final recourse and are accountable for the outcomes of their decisions. All of these issues emphasize the reality to the leader that he or she is the lone person at the top, thereby increasing his or her separation anxiety and death anxiety.

Leadership experts McKee and Boyatzis (2005) have described several reasons that people are resistant to pursuing and maintaining a position of leadership in politics and business. They observed, "Leaders are under a steady flow of stress related to the exercise of power and its responsibility" (loc. 3490). The dependency load inherent in being a strong leader who is responsible for a company's productivity and the welfare of employees as well as the self-control required to deal effectively with enumerable crises are all part of that stress. As McKee and Boyatsiz noted, "Unchecked or unbalanced behavior in leadership positions, especially when people arouse their self-control in order to be effective, will result in damage over time" (loc. 3544).

Fledgling leaders often start off with egalitarian, humanitarian values and ideologies but are later overwhelmed and then undermined by their strong emotional reactions to their newfound prestige and status. The exhilaration of having control over others can become addictive, enhancing feelings of elation while diminishing feelings of insecurity and inferiority. This dynamic can lead to a compelling need to maintain and increase one's status and power for the sake of satisfying these addictive tendencies. However, the combination of this need on the leader's part and the negative reactions from the citizenry often makes these leaders suspicious and increasingly paranoid.[7]

Paradoxically, as leaders accumulate power, they necessarily become more dependent upon others to manage the broadening range of their responsibilities; this leaves them in a position of being somewhat helpless and vulnerable. In the event that these leaders are faced with clashes among their subordinates or threatened by outside enemies determined to destroy their power base, they typically resort to even more drastic means of control, domination, and violent retaliation. Although these examples represent extreme reactions to the accumulation of power, they point to an understanding of some of the factors that negatively impact leaders in general.

POWER

In exploring the dynamics of power, one needs to understand how power structures originate, develop, and function. For the past two millennia, social scientists, psychologists, historians, and philosophers have grappled with ethical questions concerning the use and misuse of power. Their descriptive accounts have dealt with both the positive and negative effects that powerful individuals have had on historical events, current world affairs, religious movements, government institutions, politics, the business world, and individual members of society (Firestone & Catlett, 2009b).

In defining the word *power,* Max Weber (cited by Burns, 1978) proposed that it "is the probability that one actor within a social relationship will be in a position to carry out his own will despite resistance, regardless of the basis on which this probability rests" (Burns, 1978, p. 12). Historically, power has often been viewed with misgiving and suspicion or given a negative, even evil, connotation—and rightfully so. Examples of the destructive use of power dominate the history of humankind. James Madison, in an 1829 speech to the Virginia Constitutional Convention, declared that, "The essence of government is power, and power, lodged as it must be in human hands, will ever be liable to abuse" (universitymovers.com). Postmodern views about power in relation to the concepts of good and evil are frequently expressed in derogatory terms such as *harsh, exploitive, fascist, sadistic,* and *Machiavellian.* Nevertheless, as McClelland (1975) duly noted, "Power must have a positive face too. After all, people cannot help influencing one another; organizations cannot function without some kind of authority relationships" (p. 257).

According to Lammers and Galinsky (2009), "In Western philosophy there are two philosophical traditions that have opposing views on power" (p. 69). The first view can be traced back to Aristotle, who contended that "power differences are something positive and legitimate because they allow order and stability. . . . This view on power is coined the *functionalist view*" (p. 69). The second view originated with

Plato, who argued that "power differences are something negative and inherently illegitimate. . . . This view is often termed the *conflict theory* of power" (p. 69).[8]

Power per se is neither positive nor negative; rather, it is neutral or amoral. It is the specific types of power that people tend to develop over time and the methods whereby they utilize the power they have accumulated, to either inspire or to dominate, which can be evaluated from psychological, cultural, and ethical perspectives.

In the psychological literature, power has often been defined as the "ability to control resources, one's own and others" (Lammers & Galinsky, 2009, p. 67). The meaning attributed to power or the way it is conceptualized varies across cultures. Generally speaking, individualistic Western societies perceive power "as being associated with assertive and individual action," whereas the more collectivist cultures in the Far East associate power with "responsibility and personal restraint" (Lammers & Galinsky, 2009, p. 80). Lammers's and Galinsky's statements agree in substance with the first author's (R. Firestone's) point of view regarding the numerous ways in which people from societies around the world conceptualize power. Nevertheless, there are probably more commonalities than differences among diverse cultures with respect to the meanings attributed to power and the ways in which it is exercised. As Burns (1978) asserted, "Power is ubiquitous; it permeates human relationships. It exists whether or not it is quested for. It is the glory and the burden of most of humanity" (p. 15).

Although power has often been misused, in documenting the impact that "anti-Machiavellian" individuals have had throughout history in upsetting illegitimate power structures, Howard Zinn (2003) declared,

> There have always been people who did think for themselves, against the dominant ideology, and when there were enough of them history had its splendid moments: a war was called to a halt, a tyrant was overthrown, an enslaved people won its freedom, the poor won a small victory. Even some people close to the circles of power, in the face of overwhelming pressure to conform, have summoned the moral strength to dissent, ignoring the Machiavellian advice to leave the end unquestioned and the means unexamined. (p. 27)

Sources of Power

Every society or group values specific personality traits or achievements of its members; thus, individuals with these traits have considerable influence or power within that group. Strength of character, integrity, charisma, athletic ability, and positive physical attributes such as beauty or good looks are all potential sources of power. People can accrue power through wealth and popularity and by demonstrating their competence and knowledge in a given field. They can also acquire power by living according to a certain belief system or set of ethical principles or by being dominating, intimidating, aggressive, or violent.

The French sociologist and social critic Pierre Bourdieu (1985) has proposed that the status or position occupied by individuals within the areas of their work, family, and sociopolitical life is largely determined by

> the distribution of the powers which are active within each of them. These are, principally, economic capital (in its different kinds), cultural capital and social capital, as well as symbolic capital, commonly called prestige, reputation, renown, etc., which is the form in which the different forms of capital are perceived and recognized as legitimate. (p. 197)

In some instances, the traits or abilities of a leader that make him or her popular and powerful are more difficult to identify. This type of individual seems to possess an elusive personal quality or combination of attributes, such as charisma, kindness, and warmth, that have a broad appeal, transcending the interests and values of any specific group or miniculture. For example, George Stephanopoulos, in recalling his early encounters with President Bill Clinton, could only describe this indefinable quality in terms of his own feeling reactions to the new leader: "I was moved by more than what he stood for or how much he knew. It was how I felt around him" (cited by Lord & Brown, 2004, loc. 127–131).

People have the tendency to idolize and deify powerful figures, war heroes, celebrities, famous trend makers, as well as their leaders. This idealization is often manifested even when these individuals do not exhibit any evidence of moral principles, which has a negative influence on their supporters as well as on society at large. The halo effect from desirable characteristics that originally earned an authority figure power and influence enables people to deny reality and continue to follow leaders who have become inadequate or even potentially destructive. As Lipman-Blumen (2005b) observed, this form of idealization is illusory, yet "illusions are the umbilical cord linking leaders and followers. Leaders understand their followers' need for illusions. So do their entourages, who promote illusions about the leader's omnipotence and omniscience" (p. 51).

Types of Power

> The more power the leaders have, the greater their responsibility for what they do and do not do.
>
> —Joanne B. Ciulla, "The State of Leadership Ethics and the Work That Lies Before Us"

It is important to make a distinction between power that is acquired as a by-product of one's personal development, assertiveness, movement toward increased individuation, and healthy striving for love, satisfaction, and meaning and the amassing of power as a part of one's defensive adaptation. There are two principle types of power: (1) personal power, which is characteristic of well-differentiated, emotionally healthy individuals and is based on strength, confidence, and competence that they gradually accrue over the course of their development, and (2) negative power, which can be both overt and covert in its manifestations over others.

In terms of the self-parenting system described in Chapter 2, people who exhibit overt negative power are identified with the parental side of the parent-child dichotomy. It is characterized by aggressive tendencies and is exercised through the use of force or coercion to control others. It can be manifested within a relationship or become a significant part of a political or social movement. Individuals who employ covert negative power are identified with the childish side of the parent-child dichotomy. This type of power is based on passive aggression and is evident in behaviors such as weakness, incompetence, and self-destructive tendencies that manipulate others in the interpersonal world by arousing their feelings of fear, guilt, and anger.

Personal Power

Personal power represents a positive, natural striving for satisfaction and meaning in life, exercised in the honest attempt to realize one's unique potentialities and transcendent goals; its primary aim is mastery of self, not others.[9] In a previous work (Firestone & Catlett, 1989), we defined personal power as "direct, goal-oriented behavior using all of one's resources. It is persuasive and logical rather than manipulative in relation to other people. It is strong rather than oppressive or hostile" (pp. 184–185). The exercise of this form of power is likely to be more service-oriented and humane than other forms of power.

From a developmental perspective, the processes of personal growth, individuation, and differentiation can be seen as providing opportunities for accumulating personal power. As children move from a position of dependence to one of independence and develop increased assertiveness, autonomy, and confidence in their abilities, they accrue more personal power. People who have developed a good deal of personal power have generally relinquished parental or childish modes of relating and have assumed full adult responsibility for their lives. They are, for the most part, independent or interdependent rather than pseudoindependent or overly dependent on others. These individuals tend to participate in life rather than standing by as passive onlookers. They are inner directed rather than outer directed and strive to live honestly, according to their own principles.

Personal power is essentially strength of character and integrity. People who possess it are generally comfortable with and accepting of their angry emotions. They express their anger directly rather than through passive-aggressive, victimized behavior. Their ability to effectively deal with their anger contributes to their strength and confidence and their ability to influence others. They are neither defiant nor submissive, because these negative behaviors are directed by external influences rather than by motivation from within. They are not afraid of pursuing what they want in life and tend to be action-oriented. They pursue their own personal and vocational goals and do not shy away from competition when the situation arises; however, neither do they compete merely for the sake of competing.

In a previous work (Firestone & Catlett, 2009b), we described why individuals who possess personal power are rare in U.S. society: First, many people relinquish power, because, on an unconscious level, they anticipate the anxiety that would be aroused if they were to become fully individuated—that is, autonomous and responsible adults. Instead, they prefer to depend on more familiar, indirect, or manipulative forms of power that they utilized as children to get what they wanted without risking self-assertion. Second, as individuals strive to achieve goals and thereby develop personal power, they will find themselves in competitive situations where their strivings incidentally conflict with or hurt others. This often arouses anxiety that can be traced to inappropriate and sometimes punitive reactions to competition experienced within the original family. Third, some people retreat from pursuing personal power because of a learned social prejudice that views power as exploitive, corrupt, and selfish.

> Each person has the right to pursue personal power—to choose a specific direction in life and to engage in actions directed toward fulfilling his or her particular goals. One has the right to challenge conventions, social mores and systems of conformity and to work toward changing attitudes, prejudices, or laws that are unjust.... Contrary to much conventional thinking, the pursuit of personal power is essentially respectful and need not intrude on the rights of others. (Firestone & Catlett, 2009b, p. 319)

In this context, nothing could be healthier or more ethical than a person seeking the full development of his or her potential and pursuing his or her own goals in a direct manner.

Covert Negative Power

Covert negative power is exercised through behaviors that manipulate others by eliciting their feelings of guilt, anger, pity, or fear. This type of power is indicative of preserving a childish orientation toward life and remaining relatively undifferentiated (Kerr & Bowen, 1988). Individuals who use this form of destructive power tend to be passive rather than proactive. They often have problems accepting or expressing their angry feelings; instead, they feel victimized and self-righteous and are, to varying degrees, suspicious or paranoid. They act as though they are weak and powerless, and they complain, criticize, and blame others for their failures or unhappiness. Instead of engaging in mature, coping behavior, they often feel frustrated, ineffective, and overwhelmed by external situations.

People who try to get what they want indirectly through negative power are generally fearful of competitive situations. They tend to retreat from goal-directed behavior or withdraw from pursuing a potentially gratifying relationship when there are indications of opposition or rivalry. "Instead of recognizing competitive feelings, they censor the emotions, turn on themselves, and become demoralized, thereby giving up personal power. When they back away from competing for what they want, they lack integrity and are unable to honestly communicate their wants and desires" (Firestone & Catlett, 2009b, pp. 319–320). Examples of this duplicity can be seen in men or women who profess that they want intimacy and love, yet who reject real opportunities to meet potential prospects or seem unable to sustain relationships that appear to be going well.

The exercise of covert negative power is a common occurrence within many relationships and families. It can be conceptualized as a form of terrorism in which one person is made accountable for the misery and unhappiness of another. In *Intimate Terrorism,* Michael Miller (1995) elaborated on a form of negative power, maneuvers of "ambivalence" or subtle passive-aggressive responses that "evoke childhood anxieties" in the other person:

> I have seen couples in therapy who create a regime of terror through the use of saintliness, rationality, complacency, ambivalence... endless explanations, lying, telling the truth, and silence. They deny or withdraw responses the partner has come to expect or they invade the partner's body, will, or experience. (p. 38) In the competition of wills that intimate terrorism sets in motion, there are no winners. (p. 42)

People who lead chronically addictive lifestyles or who are self-destructive or threaten suicide are especially effective in eliciting fear responses in their loved ones. Although covert negative power may bring about the desired results, the cost to the perpetrator is immense. By definition, covert negative power precludes self-differentiation, because in order to manipulate or control another through weakness, a person has to necessarily sacrifice his or her own personal power and autonomy.

In business, employees who demonstrate this subtle type of power tend to be dysfunctional and nonproductive, which contributes to instability in the company and a decline in morale. For example, the passive-aggressive worker who procrastinates or performs below his or her level of competency has a direct negative impact on the project and exerts social pressure that depletes coworkers' enthusiasm and vitality. Similarly, people who act weak or powerless in their personal lives tend to provoke or elicit help and caretaking responses from others, thereby sapping their energy and liveliness.

These individuals often prefer to complain about their leaders, bosses, or their government rather than taking appropriate action. However, maintaining a victimized position has an ethical implication in that it supports passive attitudes in others, thus undermining those who are more motivated to take action to change an unjust institution or to institute needed reforms.

Overt Negative Power

There are people who actively and persistently seek out and obtain dominance through the use of overt negative power. In describing the personalities of leaders who exercise this type of power, Wilson-Starks (2003) noted that many have unresolved psychological issues, including fears of the unknown, fear of failure, feelings of inadequacy, and lack of confidence or extreme overconfidence. For example, Liechty (2005) described how business executives who wield negative power "unapologetically bilk and destroy the companies they are hired to lead. . . . In politics, these are the people for whom no malevolent act is out of bounds in the name of gaining and holding power" (para. 2).

The vanity and narcissism of such individuals offer them a sense of being special and, as such, exempt from natural forces. When they assume a leadership role, this imagined specialness operates in conjunction with their successful domination of their followers to buffer feelings of death anxiety. However, this process never succeeds in completely eliminating the fear of death, and the individual's need for power becomes increasingly compelling, often leading to disastrous outcomes in business, recessions in the world of finance, or serious crimes against humanity on the international scene.

In the business world, executives and managers who exercise overt negative power clearly have detrimental effects on the organizations they oversee. Even though these destructive managers are sometimes effective over the short term, many companies with this type of management eventually encounter difficulties in sustaining a pattern of consistent growth over the long term.

In the political sphere, the ideals motivating democratic socialist, and communist ideologies appear to be similar and benevolent: the desire for reform, the need to create a more egalitarian society, and the wish to help the poor and disadvantaged. However, even when the goals of a government and its leaders are benign and concerned with the welfare of people, the means by which they try to achieve these ends can be cruel and inhumane. Destructive world leaders can have staying power, often inflicting suffering on multitudes of people over many decades (Mao Tse-tung, Pol Pot of the Khmer Rouge, Muammar Gadhafi, and Joseph Stalin, among others). When these individuals exercise overt negative power through force, military might, or coercion, they inflict considerable harm on others and seriously infringe on their human rights. By playing on the fears of their constituents, totalitarian governments and tyrannical leaders strive to establish, maintain, and increase their power base. Leaders who use such abusive force or threats of retaliation and punishment to accomplish their goals tend to eventually destabilize the larger society, depress its economy, and oppress its citizens.

Manifestations of Positive Power in the Family

In the ideal couple relationship, each partner is a differentiated person who has developed personal power. Neither utilizes overt or covert power plays in dealings with the other. Each feels congenial toward the other's aspirations and does not interfere, intrude, or manipulate to control the relationship. Both partners recognize that the motives, desires, and goals of the other are as valid as their own and conceptualize their own personal freedom and the freedom of the other as a congruent, not contradictory, value (Firestone & Catlett, 1999). Healthy relationships are characterized by each partner's independent striving for personal development and self-realization. In the type of relationship that is growth-enhancing, partners refrain from exerting proprietary rights over one another. Each is respectful of the other's boundaries, separate points of view, goals, and aspirations.

In the ideal family, the adults aspire to provide a respectful and supportive environment in which each child can develop personal power during the socialization process. From a developmental perspective, the processes of separation, individuation, and personal growth are seen as providing opportunities for a child to accumulate personal power. Parents offer the appropriate amount of care necessary at each successive stage of the child's development, but not a surplus. By encouraging their children's initiative and supporting their taking steps that lead to individuation, parents promote each child's movement from a position of dependence to one of independence. In the process, children develop increased assertiveness, autonomy, and confidence in their abilities and accrue more personal power. Even though these parents experience a certain amount of anxiety and pain as they let their children go, these emotions are usually counterbalanced by feelings of satisfaction and pride as each child moves toward greater independence.

Negative Power Plays in Family Interactions

Issues of power and control enter into all family relationships. There are several ways that power struggles within couples can upset the stability and harmony of family life: through the disturbances in parent-child alliances, the establishment of inappropriate cross-generational or emotionally incestuous coalitions, and the triangulation of a child into the marital conflict (Lindahl, Malik, Kaczynski, & Simons, 2004). In his observations of family life, Murray Bowen (Bowen, 1978; Kerr & Bowen, 1988) found that the triangulated child typically becomes the focus or receptacle for his parents' chronic anxiety, which helps to defuse the conflict between them. However, as a result, the child often has more difficulty than his or her nontriangulated siblings in differentiating from the family. According to Bowen, "Anxiety that is not bound in the parental generation will usually focus on a child. Families differ in the particular sibling positions that are vulnerable to draw the most intense child focus" (Kerr & Bowen, 1988, p. 211).

Bowen proposed that less-differentiated parents experience more chronic anxiety, are more likely to triangulate a child, and are more susceptible to being triangulated themselves than those who are more differentiated. In families where there is an imbalance of power (domineering/submissive polarization or triangulation of a particular child), the effects can often be observed in a triangulated child who, as an adult, lacks personal power and utilizes covert or overt power to achieve his or her goals.[10]

Parents who exhibit characteristics of an authoritarian personality tend to exercise overt negative power in socializing their children (Tedeschi & Felson, 1994). They establish rigid standards regarding appropriate and inappropriate behavior and often use physical punishment, humiliation, coercion, emotional blackmail, and other manipulations of psychological control to keep their children in line (Barber,

2002).[11] These families tend to be autocratic and cultlike in how they operate in that they demand submission to an irrational authority and conformity to arbitrary and unreasonable rules. In a previous work (Firestone, 1997a), I described this type of family.

> When the parental atmosphere is immature, frightened, hostile or overly defended, the family takes on the quality of dictatorship or cult, wherein powerful forces operate to control other family members, fit them into a mold, "brain wash" them with a particular philosophy of life, and manipulate them through guilt and a sense of obligation. (p. 285)

Children who are raised in this way become either defiant or compliant. As adults, they tend to manifest authoritarian personality traits and are easily manipulated and exploited by charismatic or power-struck leaders.

In some cases, parents project the self-hatred they feel about their weaknesses onto their children and sadistically punish these imagined weaknesses in the child. The child internalizes the sadism and then, as an adult, extends the same treatment to others who are vulnerable or in a subordinate position in relation to him or her. This phenomenon was observed in the extreme in *Schutzstaffel* Nazi security guards who took pleasure in punishing concentration camp prisoners for minor infractions, particularly in relation to cleanliness. In effect, these guards were punishing their despised child-selves. In post–World War II Germany, these destructive attitudes became so prevalent in child-rearing practices that legislation was instituted against *Kinderunfreundlichkeit* (antagonistic, sadistic behavior toward children) in an effort to control such actions in parents and the general public (Meyer, 1991).

On the other hand, parents who have a victimized orientation or a childish approach to life typically employ covert power for controlling their children. They also extend their self-nurturing attitudes toward their offspring by being overprotective, permissive, or catering. This type of indulgence does not allow children to experience the inevitable frustrations of life or to develop the skills necessary for dealing with them. Instead, it creates a victimized orientation in the child that contributes to acting-out behavior.

The Corruption of Power

On a societal level, when power is corrupted—when it is utilized to control others, to intimidate or oppress them—there is a corresponding increase in the incidence of social violence and other forms of "social evil." In this context, evil can be defined as "the inflicting of harm or suffering on another human being" (Baumeister, 1997, p. 305). Baumeister also noted, "Evil does not exist in terms of solitary actions by solitary individuals. Perpetrators and victims—and in many cases, bystanders or observers, too—are necessary to the vast majority of evil acts" (p. 375). The propensity in each individual to be corrupted by power was clearly demonstrated in Zimbardo's Stanford prison experiment (Zimbardo, 2004; Zimbardo & White, 1972), where ordinary students were randomly assigned the role of either prisoner or guard. Those who played the role of guards became increasingly punitive and sadistic to the point where the experiment had to be prematurely terminated after only five days. The compliance with the experimenters' (authority figures') directives exhibited by a majority of the student participants underscores their lack of integrity—that is, their failure, when under stress, to act upon their own principles. This tendency is generally characteristic of individuals who are not well differentiated.

In politics and business, the corruption of power is facilitated when individuals remain bystanders rather than taking action toward reform or when they become whistle-blowers. Yet, as Kellerman (2004) pointed out,

> nay-sayers and second guessers are frowned on in most corporate cultures.... It's human nature... [to protect] our basic needs for safety, security, and certainty and also... our need to belong. To become a whistle-blower is to put all of these at risk. (p. 154)

People are ultimately accountable for their government's policies, for the goals that their leaders pursue, for the actions taken on their behalf, and, most important, for the means their leaders use to maintain their power base and achieve their goals (Firestone & Catlett, 2009b; Kellerman, 2004).

Why People Often Follow Corrupt Leaders

Throughout history, average citizens, who are unlikely to promote or engage in widespread aggressive acting-out behavior or warfare, have been led into this behavior by leaders who have exercised either overt negative power or covert negative power—for example, manipulating the populace by inducing fear in them. This influence is possible when citizens are passive and lean more toward the childish, dependent side of the parent-child dichotomy. Many people are so drawn to the personality of this type of authority figure that they ignore the reality of his or her failings or remain indifferent to the immoral means by which he or she accomplishes his or her goals. Even in circumstances where a leader is clearly in error, most people tend to follow his or her lead without thinking.

Corrupt or destructive leaders often have charisma as well as elements of authoritarianism and paranoia in their personality structure, and these traits tend to be reminiscent of their followers' parents and early family life. The defenses that followers develop as children in reaction to authoritarian parenting practices strongly influence their responses as adults to authority figures. According to Post (2004), "Damage to the self-concept during early childhood development tends to leave individuals permanently psychologically scarred, with an enduring need to attach themselves to a powerful, caring other" (p. 195). As adults, they may unconsciously seek out and endorse the type of leader whom they believe has the power to meet this need. Post (2004) referred to this transference phenomenon when he asserted that there are "crucial aspects of the psychology of the leader that, like a key, fit and unlock certain aspects of the psychology of their followers" (p. 188).[12] In *The Authoritarian Specter,* Altemeyer (1996) reported findings from studies showing that

> Both leaders and followers can be "authoritarian." Hitler, for example, believed his authority to do what he wanted superseded all human rights, laws, treaties, etc. He was an authoritarian leader. Millions of Germans in turn gladly accepted his authority over the state and everything in it. They were authoritarian followers. (pp. 310–311)

Lipman-Blumen (2005a) has contended that, for many citizens, charismatic authority figures appear to fill still another set of psychological needs—this time *existential* needs:

> The tension between the certainty of our death and the uncertainty of when and how it will occur gives rise to what philosophers have called "existential angst." The consoling hope that our existence will have served some meaningful purpose allows us to live without paranoia and despair. Toxic leaders feed this hope by persuading us that we belong to "The Chosen." (p. 2)

As noted previously, it is our contention that the fear of death drives individuals to support authoritarian, charismatic leaders in their search for security and immortality. The fantasy of being merged with someone or something larger than oneself imbues one with a sense of omnipotence, invincibility, and immunity to death. These feelings tend to exist on a preconscious or unconscious level. Most people know that, in reality, a powerful figure is not a savior and that loyalty to such a person does not guarantee survival. Nevertheless, in circumstances of imminent threat or danger, when an awareness of death is unavoidable, people appear to prefer a charismatic, authoritarian leader whose promises of certainty and stability alleviate their fear.

This hypothesis has been supported by empirical research conducted by terror management theorists (Cohen, Ogilvie, Solomon, Greenberg, & Pyszczynski, 2005; Cohen, Solomon, Maxfield, Pyszczynski, & Greenberg, 2004). These researchers concluded that reminders of death, which were experimentally induced, influenced people's choice of a more dogmatic, charismatic leader over a more task-oriented leader, particularly in uncertain times and under conditions of fear such as those that prevailed following the events of 9/11.[13]

DIMENSIONS OF RESPONSIBLE FOLLOWERSHIP

The word *follower* has a negative connotation for many people. However, a more objective or positive understanding of the term acknowledges both the necessity and value of the follower in leader-follower interactions (Avolio, 2007).[14] It is natural and adaptive for people to seek help and guidance from leaders in areas where they have little or no expertise.

> Independent followers depend on a leader to the extent that they lack a particular skill, knowledge, or capability or the necessary traits or requirements for organizing and maintaining an effective enterprise. Because they possess dignity and a strong sense of self, they tend not to prevail on a leader in a manner that would elicit a parental response. They are not excessively dependent nor do they subordinate their personality to an authority figure. The ideal follower is neither defiant nor submissive in his/her basic orientation to others. Just as there should be no surplus power in ethical leadership, so too there should be no surplus dependency on the part of the ethical follower. (Firestone & Catlett, 2009b, p. 298)

As followers, differentiated individuals would reject leaders who were disrespectful to them as humans. For example, although financial adversity may make it necessary to remain in a job where one is not treated with respect, whenever possible, one would seek another position rather than accept derogation or mistreatment. Independent followers would hold leaders to high standards practically and ethically and would reject those who failed to live up to their promises, demanding that they meet the physical and economic needs of their constituents.

SUMMARY

In this chapter, we described how individuals tend to subordinate themselves to others whom they see as more competent and powerful than they see themselves. This propensity acts as a strong deterrent to the process of differentiation. Next, we outlined the traits and abilities that characterize effective, ethical leaders—personal qualities that are also exemplified in individuals who have achieved a high level of self-differentiation. In examining contemporary models of leadership, we noted the recent emphasis on developing leaders who are fully adult and autonomous and who place a high value on serving their constituents and employees. We explored the reasons why people tend to retreat from assuming a leadership position and why leaders who originally were humanitarian often become destructive as they try to consolidate their power base.

In delineating the fundamental types of power—personal power and negative power—we described how each type is manifested in people's relationships and in business and politics. We examined the power dynamics operating within families and showed how early negative conditioning can predispose tendencies to follow leaders who are exercising overt negative power. We suggested that these destructive leaders often use their positions to bolster an inflated self-image, defend against feelings of insecurity and inferiority, or deny their vulnerability to death. Their charismatic, narcissistic leadership styles resonate with their followers' feelings of inadequacy and insecurity, leaving the door open for the manipulation of their fears and uncertainties, especially during times of crisis.

We suggested that responsible followership is necessary to break out of the destructive symbiosis or fantasy bond that people tend to form with a leader or group. Both leaders and their followers must become aware of the diverse defensive machinations they engage in that help sustain the exercise of overt negative power in both the business and political spheres. Learning to identify individuals who seek out and obtain power through destructive means is critical to maintaining one's independence and equality and helps one resist becoming part of a compliant followership.

To remain free of the social pressure exerted by destructive influences within the larger society, people must learn to discriminate between trends and policies that lead to authoritarian, restrictive practices and those that are congruent with principles that enhance individual freedom for all citizens. Because the very nature of human relating necessitates leader-follower associations, understanding the destructive role played by psychological defenses in both leaders and followers is imperative to furthering one's personal journey toward differentiation.

12

THE DIFFERENTIATED PERSON

> Your time is limited, so don't waste it living someone else's life. Don't be trapped by dogma—which is living with the results of other people's thinking. Don't let the noise of others' opinions drown out your own inner voice. And most important, have the courage to follow your heart and intuition.
>
> —Steve Jobs, commencement speech at Stanford University, June 15, 2005

Becoming a differentiated person is a lifelong project. It involves separating from internalized negative elements within one's personality that interfere with the fulfillment of one's unique potential. It entails emancipating oneself from illusory connections and other defenses that one developed in adapting to painful circumstances in childhood. It means learning to accommodate to the anxiety and guilt aroused by having one's own point of view and living according to one's own ideals and ethical principles.

In this chapter, we describe the person who is highly differentiated from both a philosophical and psychological perspective. The first author's work combines a philosophical basis regarding the ethics of how one might choose to live with a full understanding of the ways psychological defenses interfere with the ability to formulate one's own values and ideals as well as how to live by them. This approach is rooted in sound psychological principles rather than in judgmental or moralistic precepts, yet it has been our observation that individuals who have achieved higher levels of differentiation tend to conduct their lives in a manner that is generally more ethical than those who function at lower levels of differentiation. Ethical behavior and integrity, as defined here, represent a lifestyle that facilitates harmonious positive relations with others as well as one that has an enhancing effect on a person's sense of well-being (Firestone & Catlett, 2009a).[1]

Differentiating involves identifying aversive behaviors and faulty programming in the family and in society and developing insight into the relationship between these factors and negative internal voices that cause personal distress. It involves understanding the source of these emotional problems and modifying one's negative attitudes, personality traits, and behaviors accordingly. Almost any problem or psychological malady that impedes personal growth can be overcome if one has both the motivation and courage. We have consistently found that humans have a remarkable ability to change, develop their own identity, and maintain their integrity and an ethical approach to life.

Interestingly, recent studies in the neurosciences utilizing brain-imaging techniques have demonstrated the plasticity or changeability of the brain. Findings from investigations over the past two decades have led several researchers to describe psychoanalysis and other long-term talk therapies as "brain-changing" processes (Doidge, 2007).[2] Indeed, people can change the way they think and act; they can progressively liberate themselves from outmoded defenses and negative parental introjects. The process of unlearning old, inappropriate behaviors combined with learning new and more adaptive ones empowers the individual to live a free, more fulfilling life rather than continuing to repeat negative aspects of one's early programming.

THEORETICAL AND CLINICAL PERSPECTIVES ON IDENTITY FORMATION AND DIFFERENTIATION

Historically, several theorists, beginning with Freud, have proposed conceptual models to better understand important dimensions of human development, identity formation, and the process of differentiation. Family systems theorist Murray Bowen (Bowen, 1978; Kerr & Bowen, 1988) hypothesized

> the existence of an instinctually rooted life force (differentiation or individuality) in every human being that propels the developing child to grow to be an emotionally separate person, with the ability to think, feel, and act for himself. . . . Differentiation describes the process by which individuality and togetherness are managed by a person and within a relationship system. (Kerr & Bowen, 1988, p. 95, 95n)

Bowen defined differentiation on two levels: (1) internally, people's levels of self-differentiation are determined "by the degree to which they are able to distinguish between the feeling process and the intellectual process . . . and the ability to *choose* between having one's functioning guided by feelings or by thoughts" (p. 97), and (2) interpersonally, a high level of differentiation is

> reflected in the ability to be in emotional contact with a difficult, emotionally charged problem and not feel compelled to preach about what others "should" do, not rush in to "fix" the problem, and not pretend to be detached by emotionally insulating oneself. (p. 108)

Basically, the well-differentiated person is able to maintain emotional closeness with others while achieving an autonomous self. Bowen's clinical experience suggested that "a person must be self-sustaining and living independently of his family of origin to be successful at modifying his basic level of differentiation in relationship to the family" (Kerr & Bowen, 1988, p. 98).

Adults who are highly differentiated are less emotionally reactive than their less-differentiated counterparts. They are better able to take the "I" position in relating to others, preserve a firm sense of self, and remain true to their own principles and values. According to Gerson (2010),

> Anxiety is most disabling to dyads in which the members have the least differentiation from one another. Differentiation of self is characterized by the ability to control anxiety.... The differentiated person takes a moment to assess the danger and thus reduces the emotionally contagious response to it. (p. 34)

Because these individuals are comfortable with intimacy, they refrain from using fusion or distancing maneuvers as defensive mechanisms to regulate their anxiety in a close relationship. In addition, they are better able to deal with uncertainty and ambiguity and remain relatively calm or neutral when conflicts arise with a mate, parents, children, friends, or coworkers (Skowron & Friedlander, 1998).[3]

Erik Erikson (1963, 1968) delineated eight developmental stages or identity "crises" that begin in infancy and continue through the adult years. In "Reflections on the Last Stage—and the First," Erikson (1984) explained,

> Each stage is dominated by both a syntonic and a dystonic quality—that is: Mistrust as well as Trust and Despair as well as Integrity are essential developments, constituting together a "crisis" only in the sense that the syntonic should systematically outweigh or at least balance (but never dismiss) the dystonic. (p. 155)

One of Erikson's most significant works dealing with differentiation can be found in *Identity: Youth and Crisis* (1968). Erikson believed that adolescents must search for their own political and religious ideology and value system because these would provide a positive focus and sense of commitment to their future career and personal pursuits. Moreover, he felt that "a youthful ideology affords young people with an instrument of individuation and self-definition" (Burston, 2007, p. 152). To avoid becoming stuck or fixated at this level of development, which Erikson observed to be the case with many adults at that time (1950s and 1960s), teenagers need positive role models, older adults whose values include helping to improve the well-being of other people. From Erikson's perspective, "To avoid the dangers of sterility and rigidity, the postadolescent conscience can (and must) become less fixated on abstract principles and more focused on the contributing concretely to the welfare of others" (Burston, 2007, p. 152).[4]

Arnett (2004) and his colleagues (Arnett, Ramos, & Jensen, 2001) proposed a new stage of identity formation that encompasses the years between 19 and 29—a stage they refer to as "emerging adulthood." According to these researchers, this time period has only recently been conceptualized as a distinct stage of human development and is due to a shift in certain demographic trends in the population.

Arnett et al. (2001) have suggested that there is now a "new norm" for this age group, one that is characterized by "years of experimentation and exploration of a variety of life possibilities as enduring decisions are delayed for many young people into the mid-to-late twenties" (p. 69). "They [the young people] view this process, of deciding on their beliefs and values, as a key part of becoming an adult" (p. 78).

To some extent, Maslow's (1968) hierarchy of the needs that motivate human behavior parallels Erikson's and Arnett's stages of identity formation and self-development. According to Maslow, as people fulfill their more "basal" desires or needs, they continue to move toward growth and eventually approach self-actualization, an outcome that is similar to Erikson's Stages 7 and 8 and that represents the ideal culmination of the "emerging adulthood" stage described previously.

Interestingly, Maslow (1968) described the self-actualizing adult subjects that he studied as manifesting a

> greater wholeness and integration, which is what self-acceptance implies. The civil war within the average person between the forces of the inner depths and the forces of defense and control seem to have been resolved in my subjects and they are less split. As a result, more of themselves is available for use, for enjoyment and for creative purposes. (p. 141)

In discussing "low-order" and "high-order" meanings associated with Maslow's ascending levels of need fulfillment, Israel Orbach (2008) depicted the self-actualized person as being authentic and having personal integrity: "Authentic being is creating and constructing one's life on the basis of what one thinks, feels, and desires and not on conventions, norms, fashions, or expectations of others" (p. 283).

CHARACTERISTICS OF THE DIFFERENTIATED PERSON

Individuals with a high degree of self-differentiation can be described as having developed a unique personal point of view, a realistic identity separate from any labels or definitions internalized from childhood. Because they know themselves and have an accurate self-concept, these individuals are aware of both the positive and negative aspects of their personalities. They have an accurate, balanced perspective in relation to themselves and others. This allows them to be more receptive to criticism and to respond to feedback with interest and objectivity. They do not use critical feedback to fuel voice attacks; instead, they utilize pertinent information to plan constructive changes in behavior.

Moving toward a more creative, individualistic life involves achieving a high level of emotional maturity. People who have attained this level of maturity tend to live primarily in the adult ego state even though they may occasionally revert to a more undifferentiated, defended parent/child mode of functioning. They have a strong emotional investment in living and are acutely sensitive to events in their lives that impinge on their sense of well-being or that hurt the people closest to them. In fact, they appear to be more vulnerable, yet also more resilient than most, in relation to emotionally painful situations.

In Western culture, vulnerability is typically perceived as negative. For example, the thesaurus lists these synonyms for vulnerable: a weak position, defenseless, helpless, exposed, at risk, in danger. Many people adhere to this definition and conduct their lives so as to avoid risk or exposure to potentially painful feelings. Being vulnerable to feeling and the possibility of being hurt or humiliated is actually a more adaptive, powerful position to take and increases the probability of achieving gratification and satisfaction in life. Living on this level necessitates a high degree of self-acceptance, inner strength, and the capacity to deal with frustration.

In being able to fully experience their emotional reactions, more-differentiated individuals are better able to cope with anxiety and stress and are far less susceptible to childlike regression and neurotic symptoms than they would otherwise be. They tend to not react overdramatically to negative events in life, nor are they obsessed by destructive ruminations based on the voice. They are uncritically accepting of their irrational feelings and, in particular, their anger. The ability to tolerate anger enables them to control its expression and to manifest it appropriately rather than to internalize it or act it out in aversive or aggressive behavior.

Emotionally differentiated individuals tend to experience an inner harmony and a self-affirming approach to life. They are not preoccupied with the past or the future; instead, they focus on the here and now, which allows them to respond with appropriate affect to both the positive and negative aspects of life. In being attuned to their emotions, they retain their vitality and excitement, not only adding dimensions to their personality but also supporting their creative potential. They tend to be open and empathic in their interactions and are generally more warm, respectful, and kind, especially to those people closest to them.

In addition, their characteristic lack of exclusivity allows these individuals to extend their caring feelings to people beyond their immediate surroundings. They exhibit a concern with the suffering of all people and are likely to be involved in efforts to help. Their altruism is expressed in a sensitive, feeling response to another person's needs and wants in an understanding and timely manner. Giving freely of oneself with one's time and energy counteracts voice attacks, increases feelings of self-esteem, and makes a person feel worthwhile.

Individuals who are honest with themselves tend to be upfront and forthright in their communications and do not mislead or confuse others with double messages. They speak truthfully about their wants and desires as well as their thoughts, feelings, and opinions. In being direct and open about themselves, they also take responsibility for their feelings and do not complain, blame, or dump their problems on others.

The evolved individual tends to live in reality and avoids forming a fantasy bond in his or her adult associations. In general, these individuals pursue genuine companionship and love in their present-day relationships instead of reliving the past by projecting elements of earlier attachments into their new associations. They are willing to take a chance on love by risking the possibility of being hurt or rejected and, as a result, become increasingly tolerant of intimacy. In addition, they appreciate the importance of sexuality and regard sex as a natural extension of physical affection. When entering into a serious relationship, they are able to sustain a genuine feeling of love; that is, they value their partner's goals separate from their own needs and interests and respect the other's personal independence and sovereignty.

As parents, differentiated individuals have a realistic view of their children, which includes their positive and negative qualities rather than a fantasized family image of them. In the ideal family, accurate perceptions of both children and parents are openly discussed. Each person is careful to refrain from reacting defensively to feedback from other family members. Freedom of speech is upheld, and no topics are forbidden; parents support children speaking up, saying what they see, and asking questions about so-called taboo subjects. No feelings are unacceptable; children are free to express pain or unhappiness without feeling guilty about betraying the idealized picture of the family (Firestone, 1990a).

Individuals who have emancipated themselves from the negative aspects of family life are freer to formulate their own system of values and ideals. They tend to find that their values are closely related to personal pursuits and goals that hold deep meaning for them (Deci & Ryan, 2008). In an essay titled "The Life We Choose," Jennifer Cantor (2008) articulated what is involved in living by one's own values and ideals rather than conforming to restrictive mores and conventional beliefs.

> Passive conformity to social norms and expectations undercuts our freedom to decide what constitutes the good life. Every social category—race, class, gender, profession—contains within it judgments about the good, and to remain open to possibility and free ourselves from foreclosure often entails an Eriksonian-style crisis that may make the difference between a life lived with integrity and one that ends in despair. (p. 74)

Individuals who are highly differentiated appreciate the fact that the unknown and ambiguous are realistic parts of life, and they usually have a strong need to search for meaning beyond their everyday existence. In being involved in transcendental goals that go beyond the sphere of their personal and family life, they gain a sense of purpose and of valuing themselves that cannot be achieved by any other means.

Searching for personal meaning in life and embracing transcendent goals enable people to realize their unique human potentialities, closely following their true destiny. They are able to preserve rather than distort or block out experience, while maintaining feeling contact with themselves, compassion for others, and a deep appreciation of the richness of life.

Finally, differentiated individuals face death straightforwardly and feel their sadness about the future loss of themselves and their loved ones. They experience the reality of death as the ultimate equalizer and, as a result, maintain an inclusive worldview regarding no one as inferior or superior or of higher or lower status. In relation to religion, there is an appreciation that when there is an absence of fact, each person has the right to choose and adhere to beliefs about the origin and nature of life, the way to live, and issues relating to death or rebirth (Firestone, 1997a). In formulating their own belief system, these individuals take into consideration and attempt to understand the views and opinions of others. However, they do not accept outside ideas uncritically; instead, they develop their own conclusions, all the while recognizing their own fallibility.

As noted earlier, differentiation ultimately means being human to the fullest extent. The individual who is adult, independent, and autonomous maintains personal integrity. He or she is nondefensive, vulnerable, empathic, respectful, and generous. Obviously, no one can live up to all of these criteria; an individual can be well developed in certain areas of functioning and less developed in others. The personal qualities delineated here represent an ideal to aspire to.

MOVING TOWARD A HIGHER LEVEL OF DIFFERENTIATION

How does one become more distinct and vivid as a separate person, more vulnerable in one's relationships, and less inward and defended? What are the prerequisites for moving toward increased personal power, self-determination, and genuineness?

Our approach to differentiation involves the use of voice therapy techniques that expose critical attitudes toward the self and others, challenge defenses, and advocate the implementation of corrective suggestions to overcome obstacles to self-realization. The therapeutic process also involves a form of feeling release therapy in which people are encouraged to fully express their emotions.

In addition, as noted in the Preface over the past 35 years, the authors have been involved in seminars and group processes with over 100 individuals who have explored methods for interrupting the cycle of self-limitation that comes from living out early psychological programming. The participants in the observational study, which includes three generations of individuals, have provided valuable insights into human development and behavior. Initially, as the participants became increasingly aware of their own feelings, they developed more sensitivity and compassion for others. They confronted behaviors in one another that they found to be unpleasant or hurtful. In particular, they were critical of personality traits that were demeaning of others, such as attitudes of superiority, contempt, sarcasm, dishonesty, phoniness, and cynicism. Any attempt to manipulate the group process—for example, through domineering power plays or childish, victimized complaints—was vigorously challenged. This type of feedback along with corrective suggestions motivated people to alter their destructive responses and to develop better relationships. As they relinquished the defensive patterns, deadening routines, and painkillers that had been limiting their lives, they became better able to talk at a deeper level and even more candidly about relationships, sexuality, competitive feelings, and interactions with their children. From these conversations, we were able to begin to identify conditions that were conducive to optimal human development and to healthy psychological functioning.

In this open forum, these people have come to understand how their defenses hurt both themselves and their loved ones. They have challenged negative ways of evaluating themselves and have become more open to the possibility of change. They have been able to give up many of their addictive habit patterns and defensive styles of interacting. In their couple relationships, they have, to a large extent, come to recognize and take back projections of their self-attacks onto their partners. The dynamics of this sensitive group process have challenged these people's tendencies toward distancing behaviors and isolation.

For example, Brad (Chapter 4) described how these talks have contributed to his understanding of the differentiation process and have increased his motivation to free himself of negative influences from the past:

> I would describe the process of differentiating as an exorcism of sorts. It's like you are exorcising the negative images of yourself and the alien points of view of yourself when you take actions that contradict them. It really is powerful like an exorcism; that's the best way I can describe it. That's what I felt in becoming more sociable. I grew up convinced that I was what my family called me: cold and heartless. I lived a very isolated life; after my divorce I lived alone and basically all I did was work.
>
> Then I got involved with Amy and met her friends, and I really liked them. But no matter how apparent it was that they liked me, I stubbornly held on to my identity that I was cold and sort of a loner. When my new friends confronted me about this, I had to acknowledge that they felt warmly toward me. I made a conscious decision to counter my old identity and act according to what I knew: that they liked me and that I liked them. I participated in more activities with them, I included myself more, I joked around more, I wasn't so serious, I actually had fun. Now I hardly ever have that attack that I'm cold and a loner. I'm a sociable person and I have friendships with many people who I feel deeply about.
>
> Another self-attack that I dealt with turned out to be what was driving me to be a workaholic. When I got feedback from people in the group about having vanity about being a business executive, it forced me to look deeper into myself. I realized that it was a compensation for my father's view that I was a "worthless shit." He called me that all the time. And it was also a response to my mother's buildup that I was her special boy who would make her proud.
>
> When the subject of my vanity came up, first I was very angry but after thinking about it for a while, I realized that the people in the group weren't against me. I could feel that they had a compassionate point of view toward me. It was the opposite of my father's criticisms of me; they cared about me. I was able to listen to their feedback with interest and reflect on it. Their warmth and objectivity toward me actually affected my attitude toward myself, and I realized that my only feeling of worth was tied up with being a businessman. I could see the ways that I was overly involved in running every facet of my business. I was able to relax my control and to stop micromanaging everybody. I was able to have a more balanced life; there was more to me than just being an executive. And I wasn't connected to my parents. I didn't have to prove to my father that I wasn't a lazy shit and I didn't have to be my mother's son, "the successful entrepreneur." In under-

> standing that link, I didn't have to "perform" for either of them anymore. Needless to say, there's less pressure. You know, it's changed my whole life.

Virtually everyone who participated in these seminars and groups made strides in separating from the negative identity they had incorporated early in life. For example, Lou changed from being combative and distrustful, as his father had been, to becoming a sensitive and warm individual. Mary, who had been labeled "the stupid one" in her family, came to know herself as an intelligent woman who functioned well in the corporate business world. Sam, whose father, a doctor, repeatedly forewarned medical worse-case scenarios, went from being preoccupied with negative predictions about his health to living in the moment, free of pessimistic speculations about his future. Sara, who was held back in her aspiration to become a filmmaker, went on to a successful career in film.

In describing voice therapy methods and the group process that we have utilized in facilitating the process of differentiation, we do not wish to imply that this is the only path people could or should follow in attempting to achieve emancipation from internalized negative influences.[5] We only hope that these insights might inspire others to give more value to their experience, pursue their own form of self-actualization, and search for their own personal meaning in life.

FACILITATING THE PROCESS OF DIFFERENTIATION

It is possible to achieve a high level of differentiation if individuals have the courage to face the truth about how they defend themselves and limit their life experience. A key element in this process of liberation is breaking past and present fantasy bonds or illusions of connection. One must challenge both the self-nurturing and self-punishing aspects of this process. To become independent and centered in oneself, individuals must relinquish self-soothing addictions and routine habit patterns, challenge their negative voices, and control the self-destructive and hostile behaviors that these voices instigate.

However, breaking with well-established defensive behaviors is anxiety provoking and at first can lead to intensified voice attacks. But if people refuse to live out the negative prescriptions of their internalized voices—if, in a sense, they do not obey the introjected parent—, they will eventually adapt to their new circumstances. When people persist in this endeavor, voice attacks decrease over time, much like parents who gradually accommodate to the independence of their children as time passes. When ignored, the voice becomes weary of nagging and can become quieted.

Paradoxically, people unconsciously fear the loss of the constant companionship of their destructive voices. Just as self-assertion and movement toward independence from emotional ties with the family disrupt a vital support system, separation from introjected parental voices severs a critical symbolic tie.

In distinguishing one's point of view from negative aspects of one's internalized parent, one becomes involved in a process of continually finding oneself rather than defining oneself. Identity is essentially a flexible and evolving variable rather than a fixed or stable entity. Thus, the project of coming to know oneself, discovering one's likes and dislikes, wants and priorities, dreams and fantasies, becomes a fascinating, lifelong enterprise.

Psychotherapy Applied to the Process of Differentiation

Although some people develop themselves and formulate their personal goals and values within a self-help format, significant movement for many may necessitate participation in some form of psychotherapy. Psychotherapy can be defined as a powerful personal interaction wherein a trained person attempts to offer psychological assistance to another. Within this unique relationship, there is a renewed opportunity for personality development that exceeds and transcends virtually any other mode of experience. In the ideal clinical situation, the therapist's primary concern is the particular personality of the client and the client's personal freedom and potential for self-realization. To this end, the therapist is sensitized to and able to access clients' special points of identity, a process that helps clients give value to themselves.

The psychotherapist is mindful that humans exist in a state of conflict between the active pursuit of their goals in the real world and an inward, self-protective defense system. Therapy brings these two alternatives to the foreground by emphasizing the client's sense of self in opposition to the invalidation of self caused by maintaining defenses. The therapist is aware that resistance to a better life is at the core of the neurosis itself and is expressed in every aspect of a defended person's lifestyle. This is the dilemma of therapy that the therapist and client face together.

A number of methods employed in our approach to psychotherapy help clients increase their capacity for feeling and separate from negative parental introjects. As previously mentioned, some type of feeling release therapy in addition to voice therapy is valuable in this regard.

Feeling release sessions allow for the full expression of clients' deepest feelings, which is accompanied by emotionally integrated insights into present-day problems in life. People give free rein to feelings that are often primal in nature—that is, intense expressions of the emotions suffered in childhood trauma. In exploring their thoughts, feelings, and memories, they gain a new perspective on the connection among early childhood experiences, present-day behavior, and defensive ways of living. They come to see how, on an unconscious level, they have been avoiding positive experiences because they might reactivate old fears, painful memories, or primitive feelings of death anxiety that they suffered as children. In identifying the primal elements in their present-day reactions, they are better able to reflect on their emotions, consider the consequences of their actions, and react more rationally. This awareness helps diminish the intensity of these feelings and defuse the melodrama and overreactions, enabling people to respond more appropriately when strong feelings of anger, hurt, sadness, or fear are aroused.

In addition, people learn that anger is a normal and inevitable reaction to frustration and is proportional to the degree of frustration experienced rather than being based on rationality. They discover that their angry feelings can be a source of energy and vitality when accepted as an inherent part of their emotional makeup, and they learn to utilize their aggression constructively. They come to understand that anger, like all feelings, must be allowed free rein in consciousness, while actions must be subject to both ethical and reality considerations.

In voice therapy, as clients verbalize their negative thoughts in the voice format and release the accompanying affect, they develop insight into the connection between their parents' attitudes and the destructive point of view they have incorporated as their own. In identifying their voice attacks as representing an alien viewpoint, they regain a sense of themselves, which provides an impetus for altering their negative traits on an action level.

Feeling release therapy and voice therapy techniques access two different aspects of a client's experiences. In intense feeling release sessions, clients experience the fear, pain, sadness, and reactive anger that they suffered as children from the child's point of view, whereas in voice therapy sessions, clients experience the maladaptive thoughts and attitudes toward themselves from their parent's point of view. Both procedures help clients identify the sources of their self-destructive thinking, allowing them to generate a coherent narrative about their lives.

Effective psychotherapy techniques not only result in significant changes in people's behaviors and lifestyles, but, as noted earlier, neuroscience suggests that therapy can also alter synaptic connections in the brain. According to Doidge (2007), "Psychoanalysis is in fact a neuroplastic therapy" (loc. 3504). In his book *The Brain That Changes Itself,* Doidge cited the work of Erik Kandel, who asserted, "There is no longer any doubt that psychotherapy can result in detectable changes in the brain" (loc. 3755).

The psychotherapy experience provides the potential for a deeper awareness of one's emotions—both painful feelings of sorrow, anger, fear, shame, and envy as well as pleasurable ones of happiness, love, and appreciation of life. It allows one to feel more centered and dispels self-critical thoughts, self-hating ruminations, and distortions of others. In helping to strengthen a person's point of view, psychotherapy supports the development of one's capacity for creative and judicious thinking.

When Alisa was in her late 20s, she entered therapy. She complained of feeling lost and confused. She had fallen into a job working at a nursery school and had been involved in a series of short-term, unsuccessful relationships. She said that she always ended up feeling like she was losing her identity in these relationships and had to get out, only to end up in another relationship where she was soon experiencing the same feelings.

Alisa's mother had been physically rejecting and emotionally absent. When it came to the functions of mothering, she largely left Alisa in the care of a nanny. She was averse to physical contact with Alisa, especially in situations where she considered Alisa to be unclean or dirty. She was clearly ill at ease whenever Alisa was emotional, and on those occasions, rather than offering comfort and reassurance, she would withdraw from her daughter. Alisa's father was gregarious and outgoing, and originally he was Alisa's source of warmth and love. He said that Alisa was the "sunshine of his life." However, he doted on her much as he would on a girlfriend. He was an emotionally unstable man and he had a sexualized focus on his daughter that was intense and inappropriate. He was often under the influence of drugs and alcohol, and at those times, he would be sexually inappropriate with her. Alisa grew up to be distrustful and afraid of women and seductive with men.

In the beginning of therapy, Alisa did not know how to relate to her male therapist. She had learned to figure out what a man wanted and then provide it. But the therapy situation was different: Her therapist didn't want anything from her; he simply encouraged her to learn how to be herself. This was an entirely different perspective for Alisa.

In deep feeling release sessions, Alisa was able to relive and investigate the traumatic events in her childhood and access the pain, fear, and loneliness that she had suppressed. She felt her anger toward her mother for all but abandoning her and at her father, who used her to satisfy his perverted needs. Alisa used voice therapy techniques to identify voices she had incorporated from her mother, such as those that accused her of being disgusting and dirty. She identified voices from her father that built her up as being "the most amazing person on earth" and then tore her down as being "nothing but a slut."

As Alisa progressed in therapy, faced her anger, and answered back to her voices, she began to have a feeling for herself as a worthwhile, loving woman. She realized that she liked teaching children and enrolled in college to get a degree in education and child development. She developed a stronger sense of who she was, and eventually she entered into a relationship with a man who was secure in himself and was not looking to her for confirmation of his masculinity. This enabled her to maintain her identity while appreciating him for who he was. By the time Alisa completed therapy, her life was very different than it had been when she began the therapy process.

The Therapeutic Value of Friendship

One loyal friend is worth ten thousand relatives.

—Euripides, *Orestes*

Friendship implies mutuality and equality and, as such, has therapeutic value because it stands in opposition to the obligatory kind of relating that exists within a fantasy bond. Genuine friendship involves closeness without bondage or illusions of security and enables a person to feel the truth of his or her separateness. It is characterized by a lack of exclusiveness and possessiveness, wherein each person is respectful of the other's boundaries, goals, and aspirations (Firestone & Catlett, 1989). It provides companionship that is open and nonintrusive, factors that lead to self-awareness and encourage a person to emerge from an inward posture. When one feels compatible with one's friend, well liked and sought after, it leads to good feelings about oneself and at the same time tends to minimize anger, resentment, and cynicism toward others. A meaningful interaction with a close friend on a daily basis diminishes voice attacks and interferes with the propensity to be self-denying and self-hating. All of these factors play a positive role in supporting the self system.

When moving toward increased maturity and individuation, it is important to surround oneself with positive influences and to be open to imitating admirable characteristics in one's friends and other positive role models. In our experience, we found that many people who, as children, lacked a positive role model were able, as adults, to emulate positive behaviors of a close friend who served as a new role model.

For example, Kirk, who grew up in a turbulent environment and tended to be agitated and overreactive, admired the calmness with which his friend Paul responded to stress. He also liked Paul's warmth and easy affection. Over the years, Kirk gradually assimilated these tendencies into his own behavioral repertoire to the point where they became part of his own personality. In addition, Kirk adopted some of Paul's ideals, values, and principles—in particular, his generosity and compassionate view of people. For Kirk, this close friendship was indeed therapeutic. The processes of identification and imitation continue throughout life, enabling us to take on and internalize an admired friend's values, goals, and other positive attributes, thereby strengthening our self system.

As part of the process of self-development, it is advisable to single out and associate with people and circumstances that are conducive to one's development as well as to be aware of and avoid destructive influences. Ever since Josh was a child, he had had a problem with his temper. As an adolescent, he was involved in more violent acting-out behavior. Finally, in his late teens, an incident occurred in which he attacked and seriously injured another man, and both he and his victim had to be hospitalized. That same summer, Josh had the opportunity to join some family friends for an extended vacation in Europe. His father was seriously worried about his son's acting-out behavior and encouraged him to take advantage of the chance to leave his present situation and change the circumstances of his life.

Josh himself was concerned about the destructive direction in which his life was heading, so he accepted the offer. The new social environment was very different from the one Josh had come from. At home, Josh spent most of his time with his peers, and there was considerable use of hard drugs and alcohol. In the new group he interacted with his peers and some of their parents; there was no drug use and only social drinking. His friends at home were tough, suspicious, and defended, whereas the people he was traveling with were warm, easy going, and open. They did not judge Josh, and he found himself at ease in their company. Josh admired some of the young people who were his age and enjoyed talking with them. As time passed, Josh began to see himself in a different light—not as the angry, violent, out-of-control kid he had always been seen as. He was coming to know a side of himself that was compassionate, insightful, and caring. As his aggressive tendencies subsided, he began to like himself, and he was surprised at how good he felt.

Toward the end of the summer, Josh realized that going home would mean returning to an environment that supported the negative side of his personality. He decided to move to where his new friends lived so he could be near people who supported the positive side of who he was. With the encouragement of his new friends, he also chose to go into therapy to deal with the deeper issues underlying his anger and violent behavior, because he wanted to strengthen the changes that he had been making. He wanted to be able to remain the person he was getting to know himself to be no matter what the circumstances of his life.

SUMMARY

Years of clinical experience, as well as our observational study of individuals and their families referenced throughout this book, have led to a better understanding of familial and social factors that either contribute to or detract from an individual's psychological well-being. In the course of these explorations, we developed a methodology for challenging the destructive influences that make up the internalized anti-self system.

In this chapter we delineated the characteristics of the differentiated, emotionally mature individual who functions primarily in the adult ego state. We described how people can aspire to these qualities in their everyday lives and move toward a more satisfying and freer existence. They can overcome even the most serious limitations and evolve as independent, autonomous individuals if they are willing to challenge fantasy bonds, confront their deepest emotions, and take action to alter their defenses and self-limiting behaviors.

However, faced with the fact of mortality and the subsequent terror, many individuals refrain from truly investing in life-affirming activities and, in effect, form an alliance with death by declining to pursue what is most meaningful to them. In other words, they withhold from themselves and others their most prized goals and priorities. This defense causes a significant amount of the misery in personal associations. People often withhold genuine expressions of love and appreciation or the unique personal attributes that originally drew their loved ones to them. Instead they tend to form a fantasy bond and sacrifice real exchanges for habit patterns and routines that offer an illusion of sameness and security. The lure of this illusory comfort is addictive and is at the core of people's resistance to change.

To the extent that people maintain these defenses and illusions, they relinquish their opportunity to live a full life. In this sense, defensive reactions to personal trauma and death anxiety constitute the most powerful and insidious enemy of differentiation. Furthermore, people's defensive attitudes and behaviors are at the core of their aggression toward others, polarizing one group of people against others who hold different customs and beliefs and eventually result in violence. This manifestation constitutes a threat to humankind's continued existence on the planet. As Becker (1971) emphasized, "It seems clear that comfortable illusion is now a danger to human survival" (pp. 198–199).

To counter defensive lifestyles, we stress the importance of living a life of self-exploration and accepting a changing identity and emphasize the therapeutic value of friendship. Our work indicates the potential value of a psychotherapy experience and describes how voice therapy and feeling release therapy techniques can improve one's mental outlook and expand one's life.

Living a differentiated adult existence leaves one keenly aware of one's aloneness and of the uncertainty and ambiguity of life. At the same time, this experience is alive with a potential for personal gratification, self-expression, and virtually unlimited possibilities. The choice to lead an undefended life is well worth fighting for. The feeling of freedom inherent in experiencing oneself as a separate person is both rewarding and exhilarating.

NOTES

PREFACE

1 The title, *The Self Under Siege,* was suggested by a series of videotaped lectures by Rick Roderick (1993) titled "The Self Under Siege: Philosophy in the 20th Century," produced by the Teaching Company. In the study guide, Roderick introduced the course with this statement:

> We all strive to have a "theory" or narrative about our selves, we want to have a meaningful story about our lives that affirms our humanity. In short, we want them to *mean* something. The complex systems under which we live (economic, technological, global) have put the self "under siege," overloaded with information and images that offer no meaning for us. We have difficulty making any sense out of our lives. (Lecture 1)

In a review of the lectures, Stamenkovic (2009) summarized Roderick's main thesis as follows: "Basically, modern and post-modern philosophy fails to give a proper solution to the 'great and overriding problem' and provide us with a satisfactory theory about the self: 'a narrative story to connect disconnected episodes in our lives' (Roderick, 1993: LO1)" (p. 116).

CHAPTER 1

1 One source of variation that results in the uniqueness of the newborn's genetic makeup (and not a simple combination of DNA copies of the mother's and father's genetic material) can be found in the crossover and other gene recombinations that occur during the first cell division within the embryo. Calling attention to recent research in epigenetics, Wenner (2009) noted that selective imprinting of the mother's and the father's genes on the genetic makeup of the infant can be expressed phenotypically—that is, in the infant's traits and behaviors that endure through its life span. Therefore, "We can no longer think of ourselves as rough composites of our parents but rather as intricate puzzles crafted from thousands of maternal and paternal pieces over the course of evolution" (p. 59). As one example, "When passing on DNA to their offspring, mothers silence certain genes and fathers silence others. These imprinted genes usually result in a balanced, healthy brain, but when the process goes awry, neurological disorders can result" (p. 54).

2 Murray Bowen (1978) originally defined "differentiation of self" as a concept that "defines people according to the degree of fusion, or differentiation, between emotional and intellectual functioning" (p. 362). In constructing his Differentiation of Self Scale, Bowen stated that he wanted to convey the idea that "people at one level have remarkably

different life styles from those at other levels" (p. 364). In distinguishing between levels of solid self and pseudo-self in an individual, Bowen went on to note,

> The solid self says, "This is who I am, what I believe, what I stand for, and what I will do or will not do" in a given situation (p. 365). In periods of emotional intimacy, two pseudo-selfs will fuse into each other, one losing self to the other, who gains self. The solid self does not participate in the fusion phenomenon. (pp. 364–365)

According to Skowron and Friedlander (1998), individuation and differentiation of self, while having some similarities, still refer to different processes.

> Individuation, from an object-relations perspective . . . involves the achievement of independence and a unique sense of identity. Differentiation of self is the capacity to maintain autonomous thinking and achieve a clear, coherent sense of self in the context of emotional relationships with important others. (p. 237)

3 According to Kochanska and Aksan (2006), "Early conscience is an important early personality system, coherently organized, relatively stable over time, and subject to individual differences that emerge as a result of a complex interplay between children's temperamental individuality and socialization in the family" (p. 1587). Also see Fowles and Kochanska (2000), who found that for fearless children, only attachment security and maternal responsiveness predicted conscience development. This study established child temperament as a moderator of socialization in early moral development and lovelessness in psychopathic individuals as an index of the failure of the socialization pathway (via attachment) to conscience in fearless children.

Findings from another study by Shaw, Gilliom, Ingoldsby, and Nagin (2003) showed that the second and third year of a boy's life is a critical period for the subsequent development of conduct problems. This negative trajectory is correlated with differential parental responses and the child's temperament. Parental hostility, elevated levels of maternal depressive symptoms, mother's rejection, and high ratings of child fearlessness predicted persistent behavior problems in older boys.

4 It appears that Kevin's mother was largely unaware of the effect she was having on her son. Her frightening facial expression, aggressiveness, lack of awareness, and failure to repair the resulting misattunments all pointed to the development of a disorganized/disoriented attachment pattern between the mother and son. See Judith Solomon and Carol George's (2011) recent compilation of research and theoretical advances in this area in *Disorganized Attachment and Caregiving*. In a chapter in the same volume, Giovanni Liotti (2011) emphasized,

> Besides being intrinsically multiple, incoherent, and very likely compartmentalized in its content—so that the construction of a single representation of self and caregiver is hindered—the IWM [internal working model] of disorganized attachment may be selectively and defensively excluded, (i.e., segregated; Bowlby, 1980) from conscious scrutiny. (p. 386)

The dissociated or segregated views that Kevin initially expressed were indicative of the defensive exclusion Liotti depicted.

5 Fonagy, Gergely, Jurist, and Target (2002) referred to the alien part of the self in their description of borderline personality disorder as one outcome of disorganized attachment in childhood:

> In the case of chronically insensitive or misattuned caregiving, a fault is created in the construction of the self, whereby the infant is forced to internalize the representation of the object's [caregiver's] state of mind as a core part of himself.... But in such cases the internalized other remains alien and unconnected to the structures of the constitutional self. (p. 11)

6 Philosophers, psychologists, biologists, and neuroscientists have long struggled to describe what the self is. Strawson (1999) posed the following question:

> What, then, is the ordinary, human sense of the self, in so far as we can generalize about it? I propose that it is (at least) the sense that people have of themselves as being, specifically, a mental presence; a mental someone; a single mental thing that is a conscious subject of experience, that has a certain character or personality, and that is in some sense distinct from all its particular experiences, thoughts, and so on, and indeed from all other things. (p. 3)

Brook (1999) emphasized, "More specifically, it is when I am experiencing my thoughts by thinking them, my desires by feeling them, my perceptions by having them, my actions by doing them, etc., that I am aware of myself as a self" (p. 40).

Affective neuroscience descriptions of the self include Jaak Panksepp's (1998), which contended that

> it is generally agreed that the self is experienced as a stable mental presence that provides a sense of felt affective unity and continuity to humans, commonly with strong cognitive overtones.... Of course, the fundamental nature of the self remains a matter of controversy. (p. 566)

Damasio (1999) focused on the problem of self in a biological/neurological context:

> In the very least, then, the neurobiology of consciousness faces two problems: the problem of how the movie-in-the-brain is generated, and the problem of how the brain also generates the sense that there is an owner and observer for that movie. (p. 11)

In this work, Damasio defined what he refers to as the "core self," stating,

> I would venture that virtually all of the machinery behind core consciousness and the generation of core self is under strong gene control.... The development of the autobiographical self is a different matter.... When we talk about the self in order to refer to the unique dignity of a human being, when we talk about the self to refer to the places and people that shaped our lives and that we describe as belonging to us and as living in us, we are talking, of course, about the autobiographical self. The autobiographical self is the brain state for which the cultural history of humanity most counts. (pp. 229–230)

Schore (2011) cited evidence in support of his proposition

> that the early developing right brain generates the implicit self, the structural system of the human unconscious.... The concept of a singly unitary "self" is as misleading as the idea of a single unitary "brain." The left and right hemispheres process information in their own unique fashion and represent a conscious left brain self system and an unconscious right brain self system. (pp. 75–76)

Other researchers have described the narrative self. In his book *The Mindful Therapist,* Dan Siegel (2010) posed the question,

> When we have a sense of our self as a witness of our ongoing mental life and even our ability to be aware, we are observing the flow of the mind and the creation of a sense of self. But who, then, is observing?... Enter the narrator. (p. 113)

Ochs and Capps (1996) stressed the fact that "Narrative and self are inseparable. Self is here broadly understood to be an unfolding reflective awareness of being-in the-world, including a sense of one's past and future" (pp. 20–21).

> Developing a sense of one's self as separate from others is considered a cornerstone of human cognition and well-being.... From 8 to 18 months, the normally developing child gains a sense of "me" as a coherent, continuous, and discrete being over time. (pp. 28–29)

The dialogical self has been described by Cote and Levine (2002), who have asked whether there is

> such a thing as a "unified" self, or is it more appropriate to think of the self as a multiple, organized set of cognitive schema, each likely to be sensed as more or less meaningful by a person and others, depending on the situation? (loc. 626–632)

The Russian dialogical school inspired by the literary scientist Mikhail Bakhtin (1921/1973, 1981; see Hermans & Dimaggio, 2004, p. 1) has developed the concept of the sociological self, which is closely aligned with the narrative self but also is substantially different. The dialogical self "is made up of various positions, voices or characters, each of them functioning as a partly independent agency that generates specific memories, thoughts, and stories" (p. 2). Salgado and Hermans (2005) noted that "the self has been characterised as a continuous dialogue and interplay between different I-positions, each one with a specific voice. Consequently, each person is devised as a polyphonic society of mind" (p. 3).

In attempting to identify the psychological and neurological underpinnings of radically different points of view taken by the self at any moment in time, Lewis and Todd (2004) posed a thorny theoretical question: "How can one be both subject and object in the same dialogue?" (p. 45). See "Toward a Neuropsychological Model of Internal Dialogue," by Marc D. Lewis and Rebecca Todd (Hermans & Dimaggio, 2004), and Robert Neimeyer's (2006) "Narrating the Dialogical Self: Toward an Expanded Toolbox for the Counseling Psychologist."

Finally, there are philosophical descriptions of the self. In *Being No One,* Metzinger (2003) described the phenomenal self as "A process—and the subjective experience of being someone emerges if a conscious information-processing system operates under a transparent self-model" (p. 1). "In conscious experience there is a world, there is a self and there is a relation between both—because in an interesting sense the world appears to the experiencing self" (p. 5). Ramachandran (2011) described seven aspects of the self: unity, continuity, embodiment, privacy, social embedding, free will, and self-awareness. "These seven aspects, like legs of a table, work together to hold up what we call the self" (p. 253).

7 Erikson (1959) proposed,

> Ego identity... could be said to be characterized by the more or less actually attained but forever-to-be-revised sense of the reality of the self within social

> reality; while the imagery of the ego ideal could be said to represent a set of to-be-strived-for but forever-not-quite-attainable ideal goals for the self. (p. 160)

"The term 'identity' expresses such a mutual relation in that it connotes both a persistent sameness within oneself (selfsameness) and a persistent sharing of some kind of essential character with others" (p. 109). Erikson (1964) indicated the way in which personal identity was related to the society in which an individual lived: "Identity does not connote a closed inner system impervious to change, but rather a psychosocial process which preserves some essential features of the individual as well as his society" (p. 96).

CHAPTER 2

1 Separation and individuation have long been conceptualized as linked in the sense that the degree of separation was seen as proportional to the degree of individuation. According to classical psychoanalytic theories of separation-individuation, as articulated by Blos (1967), "In order to achieve individuation, the adolescent has to let go of the internalized childhood image of the parent" (cited by Meeus, Iedema, Maassen, & Engels, 2005, p. 90). Researchers Kroger and Haslett (1988); Lopez, Watkins, Manus, and Hunton-Shoup (1992); and Lucas (1997) have tested hypotheses to determine "whether the degree of separation from the parents is predictive of the degree of identity development [or individuation]" (Meeus et al., 2005, p. 91). However, Meeus and colleagues have proposed that "separation and identity development are two processes, which run in parallel" and reported findings from a large study (2,814 Dutch adolescents) to support their hypothesis (p. 91).

2 As noted in Chapter 1, interactions between the genes and the environment as well as epigenetic influences need to be considered in determining the phenotypic makeup of the infant and in investigating how both nature and nurture impact the emerging self. According to Meaney (2010),

> The recent integration of epigenetics into developmental psychobiology illustrates the processes by which environmental conditions in early life structurally alter DNA, providing a physical basis for the influence of the perinatal environmental signals on phenotype over the life of the individual. (p. 41)

Jacobson (2009) has asserted,

> Emerging lines of research from epigenetics suggest that not only can nature alter nurture, but nurture, in turn, has the power to modify nature.... Environmental experiences, particularly those related to stress, have the capacity to alter biological and genetic mechanisms associated with increased risk of problem behavior. (p. 2)

Based on three decades of research with animal and human subjects, Tremblay and Szyf (2010) have concluded,

> Epigenetic mechanisms are especially important because they provide a powerful explanation for maternal transmission of behavior disorders that extend beyond the traditional genetic transmission explanations. The mother, through her maternal behavior, can affect DNA methylation of critical genes in the offspring. (p. 497)

Citing Harlow's studies of monkeys and their wire mothers as well as research with vervet and rhesus monkeys who were cross-adopted, Champagne (2010) and Jacobson (2009) have provided us with numerous examples of epigenetic effects in primates. Also reported were findings from postmortem brain-imaging studies of human subjects conducted by McGowan et al. (2009) demonstrating epigenetic changes in the brains of patients who had committed suicide. These researchers found "DNA hypermethylation of the rRNA promoter region in the hippocampus" (Jacobson, 2009, p. 2) of patients who suffered child abuse and neglect and who died by suicide as compared with those who experienced sudden, accidental death. This finding supported "the hypothesis that epigenetic changes due to social and environmental experiences are related to behavioral traits" (Jacobson, 2009, p. 2). Also see Champagne's (2010) research on the effects of low childhood socioeconomic status on gene expression that "may increase the likelihood of physical and psychiatric illness" (p. 306).

3 Contact with another person or persons is one of the prerequisites for the development of the self. See Steeves (2003), who argued, "The burgeoning consciousness of the infant will not necessarily 'develop' into human intentionality on its own, but rather requires the presence of a Significant Other who is human" (pp. 13–14).

Lockley (2011) has observed,

> Rare cases of feral children and abnormal development severely compromise the quintessential human traits of language, self consciousness and their experience of the world.... Without language and self consciousness, the child's psychological experience would not be fully or healthily human. (para. 3)

In *The Interpersonal World of the Infant,* D. Stern (1985) clarified how the infant's "emergent self," through repeated interactions with the mother or primary caregiver, gradually evolves into a "core self" and later a "subjective self" and lastly a "narrative self," which emerges around three years of age. Similarly, L. Stern (1991) pointed out that "Some theorists emphasize the self as fundamental for relationships (e.g., Erikson, 1963) while others emphasize relationships as fundamental for the self (e.g., Kohut, 1977; Winnicott, 1960 [1965])" (p. 112).

4 In describing specific stimuli that impinge on the infant, both overly exciting and aversive, D. Stern (1985) delineated

> all the influences that disrupt the organized perceptions of self: overstimulation, situations that disrupt the flow of tonic perceptions that maintain the sense of self (being thrown too high in the air with too long a fall); experiences of self/other similarity that confound the self/other boundary cues; maternal understimulation that reduces certain tonic and phasic self-experiences. (p. 199)

5 Stimuli from the environment that are assessed by the infant or young child as either dangerous or life-threatening are received and processed through a bidirectional circuitry described by Stephen Porges (2011) in his explanation of the polyvagal theory. Porges emphasized that, in order for individuals

> to effectively switch from defensive to social engagement strategies, the mammalian nervous system needs to perform two important adaptive tasks: (1) assess risk, and (2) if the environment is perceived as safe, inhibit the more primitive limbic structures that control fight, flight, or freeze behaviors. (p. 273)

Neuronal perception or neuroception describes a process that takes place outside of conscious awareness, "that is capable of distinguishing environmental (and visceral) features that are safe, dangerous, or life-threatening" (p. 273).

6 For a historical-evolutionary view of parental ambivalence, see Hrdy (1999, 2009). Hrdy (1999) asserted,

> Maternal ambivalence is treated today as if it were a deep secret only just being unveiled.... Far from being surprised or shocked, we should be asking ourselves how we failed to expect these ambivalent emotions in their every nuance. There are good reasons *why* infant demands sometimes seem so insatiable, and there are equally good reasons *why* mothers sometimes find such servitude overwhelming and resist them. There are also sound evolutionary reasons why such tensions would have an important impact on the developing child's view of the other people in his or her world. For what Bowlby termed the baby's "internal working model" of relationships would in fact constitute the best predictor any developing human could have about what to expect. (p. 391)

7 Research in attachment theory has shown that the child whose parent or caregiver is withholding or emotionally unavailable often develops an anxious/avoidant attachment pattern with that parent, whereas children raised by an emotionally hungry, overly protective, or intrusive parent tend to develop an anxious/avoidant pattern of attachment with that parent. According to Hazan and Shaver (1994),

> The typical caregiver of an anxious/ambivalently attached infant, observed in the home, exhibited inconsistent responsiveness to the infant's signals, being sometimes unavailable or unresponsive and at other times intrusive.... [Their infants] appeared both anxious and angry and were preoccupied with their caregivers to such a degree that it precluded exploration.... Caregivers of avoidantly attached infants consistently rebuffed or deflected their infants' bids for comfort, especially for close bodily contact.... These infants... avoided contact with their caregivers, and kept their attention directed toward the toys. (p. 6)

Also see Gergeley (2007), who noted that sensitive, attuned parents or caregivers tend to "repeatedly present their infants during affect-regulative interactions with empathic emotion displays that imitatively 'mirror' their baby's momentary affect-expressions (including the empathic mirroring of negative affect displays as well") (p. 61). Experiments testing this hypothesis and reactions of infants categorized as avoidantly and ambivalently attached to their mothers are described in Gergeley's chapter.

8 During the first 18 months of life, important neuronal connections are being laid down in the infant's brain, especially in the right hemisphere. According to Schore (2009),

> In light of the observations that the emotion-processing human limbic system myelinates in the first year-and-a-half... and that the early-maturing right hemisphere... which is deeply connected into the limbic system—is undergoing a growth spurt at this time, attachment experiences specifically impact limbic and cortical areas of the developing right cerebral hemisphere. (p. 194)

However, according to Badenoch (2008), in the context of a harsh or alarming interaction with a parent,

> Stress may cause excessive pruning of neural connections between the hemispheres... making it difficult for this child to generate words for feelings or create a meaningful and containing story of inner experience, especially since Mother lacks the resources to shape her own story or give words to her child's experience. (p. 136)

9 In repairing a misattunement with their child, parents can talk with the child about what happened, which allows the experience to become part of the child's explicit or procedural memory system—part of the "autobiographical" self. Research has demonstrated that individuals who have integrated a coherent narrative of their childhood and made sense out of these misattuned experiences, as determined by the Adult Attachment Interview (George, Kaplan, & Main, 1984), are more likely to form a secure attachment with their own children (Fonagy, Steele, & Steele, 1991).

10 In discussing how infants are able to "read" the intentions of the caregiver, Siegel (2001) noted,

> The mind of the child appears to develop a core manner in which the mental states of other individuals become represented within the neural functioning of the brain.... One form of neural map is the way in which the brain creates images of other minds. (p. 82)

> We can propose that within the child's brain is created a multisensory image of the emerging caregiver's nonverbal signals. These nonverbal signals reveal the primary emotional states of the individual's [caregiver's] mind. (p. 84)

Writing from an evolutionary perspective, Hrdy (2009) proposed that within the brains of early Homo sapiens, a "novel nervous system" probably developed that

> would in turn have been exposed to selection pressures that favored the survival of any child born with slightly better aptitudes for enlisting, maintaining, and manipulating alloparental [substitute caregiver] ministrations. In this way, natural selection would lead to the evolution of cognitive tendencies that further encouraged infants to monitor and influence the emotions, mental states, and intentions of others. (p. 121)

11 The discovery of mirror neurons has significantly modified our view of human nature. According to Iacoboni (2009),

> Traditionally, our biology is considered the basis of self-serving individualism, whereas our ideas and our social codes enable us to rise above our neurobiological makeup. The research on mirror neurons, imitation, and empathy, in contrast, tells us that our ability to empathize, a building block of our sociality... and morality... has been built "bottom up" from relatively simple mechanisms of action production and perception. (pp. 666–667)

> An fMRI study of imitation and observation of facial emotional expressions (Carr, et al., 2003) tested the hypothesis that empathy is enabled by a large-scale neural network composed of the mirror neuron system, the limbic system, and the insula connecting these two neural systems. Within this network, mirror neurons would support the simulation of the facial expressions observed in other people, which in turn would trigger activity in limbic areas, thus producing in the observer the emotion that other people are feeling. (p. 665)

According to D. Siegel (personal communication, September 4, 2009),

> When you can see an act of intention, you create a map of that intention in the perceiver's own experience. What this tells us is that we are hardwired to perceive the mind of another being. But the mirror neuron system works with the

superior temporal cortex and other areas to actually do more than just imitate behavior. It simulates internal states.

12 See "Attachment and Self-Understanding: Parenting With the Brain in Mind," in which Siegel (2004) proposed hypotheses, based on extensive brain-imaging studies, about how attachment relationships shape neural connections in the infant's developing brain:

> This shaping process, for example, may enable parent-child interactions to alter the genetically programmed ways in which the brain matures and sculpts those fundamental processes, such as regulating emotions, responding to stress, remembering our past, and even developing our abilities to empathize with others (mindsight).... In this way, secure attachment relationships may promote resilience and well-being by supporting the integrative capacities of the child's developing brain. (pp. 29–30)

13 Regarding childhood neglect, see Perry's (2002) observations of Romanian orphans who suffered severe neglect during the first year of life and showed significant loss of cortical function in the fronto-temporal areas of the brain. Perry's observations are similar to those of Schore (2003a), who cited extensive studies in neurobiology showing that "an impairment of the orbito-frontal cortex is a central mechanism in the behavioral expression of violence" (p. 269). Schore observed, "There is a link between neglect in childhood and antisocial personality disorders in later life" (p. 268). Schore linked this damage to subsequent aggressive states and violent behavior. According to Schore,

> Physically abused infants show high levels of negative affect, while neglected infants demonstrate flattened affect.... But the worst case scenario is, not infrequently, found in a child who experiences both abuse and neglect.... There is agreement that severe trauma of interpersonal origin may override any genetic, constitutional, social, of psychological resilience factor. (pp. 268–269)

With respect to the long-term effects of neglect, maltreatment, and other toxic environmental factors on adult functioning, it has been demonstrated that the number of adverse childhood experiences is proportional to the severity of adult medical and psychological disorders (Chapman et al., 2004).

14 Regarding incorporation or introjection of a parent's maladaptive point of view under conditions of stress, two important psychological processes, identification and introjection, which are critical in terms of the child's development, are also responsible for "the inclusion of a systematized 'parental' point of view within the self" (Firestone, 1988). Neurologically, Lewis and Todd (2004) suggested that in punitive, stressful situations, the child may shift his or her attention in a way that facilitates the incorporation of parents' point of view.

> For example, a blend of anxiety and rage felt toward a parent can shift to rage directed at the self, with only a small piece of the appraisal (i.e., its object) being replaced.... The neurological fault line that subserves such changes [may include] the... orbitofrontal and anterior cingulate systems. (Left and right-hemisphere differences may also play a central role in the switching of subjectivities.) (p. 53)

In explaining self-determination theory, Grolnick et al. (1997) have made a distinction between the processes of identification and introjection in relation to assimilating external (parental and societal) values and regulations. They described introjection as resulting in less adaptation and poorer emotional health than identification or integration. For example, in introjected regulation,

> Externally imposed regulations have been "taken in" by the person but are maintained in essentially their original form. The resulting source of regulation is within the person, but it has not been integrated with the self and is thus a source of tension and inner conflict. Regulation is not perceived as one's own, but instead as controlling and coercive. (p. 141)

15 A number of other theorists have elaborated on the concept of the fantasy bond, including Hellmuth Kaiser (Fierman, 1965), Karpel (1976, 1994), Shapiro (2000), Wexler and Steidl (1978), and Willi (1975/1982). See studies by Silverman, Lachmann, and Milich (1982), who presented subjects with the subliminal message "Mommy and I are One" on the tachistoscope, which functioned to ameliorate severe symptoms in schizophrenic and other less disturbed individuals. Interpretations of the findings from this research have become controversial in the field of psychology. See Chirban's (2000) findings and interpretations that discriminated between "oneness experiences," which are progressive and transformative, and "oneness fantasies," which are based on longings for merger with figures from the past and so become generally regressive.

16 Nagy (1948/1959) suggested that children's awareness of the irreversibility of death develops between the ages of 5 and 9 years. Others place it at an earlier age, between ages 3 and 7, or even earlier (Hoffman & Strauss, 1985; Rochlin, 1967; Speece & Brent, 1984), and Robert Kastenbaum (2000) has cited a case in which this more complete understanding of death appeared to occur in a toddler at the age of 16 months.

17 Sylvia Anthony (1971/1973) reported that many children had a fantasy that reuniting with the mother would imbue them with immortality:

> In all these instances, anxiety is clearly about death as separation from the love-object, and the defence has taken the form of a belief or hope of union in death; indeed, unconsciously of a closer union in death than was possible in life. (p. 151)

Some children who have suffered unusual trauma and early loss may be unable to successfully rid themselves of morbid thoughts about death and may develop generalized anxiety, panic disorders, phobias, obsessive-compulsive disorder, asthma, or other psychosomatic complaints (Furer & Walker, 2008; Kosloff et al., 2006; Monsour, 1960; Noyes, Stuart, Longley, Langbehn, & Happel, 2002; Randall, 2001; Strachan et al., 2007).

18 For example, Arndt et al. (2002) found that

> death primes that were presented outside of conscious awareness…increased worldview accessibility immediately.…These results support the idea that nonconscious knowledge of mortality is embedded in an associative network that also contains interconnections with beliefs that function to protect individuals from these concerns. (p. 320)

Also see Pyszczynski et al. (1999), who pointed out,

> People manage their potential for terror without having to actually experience that terror, just as people and other animals can learn to engage in actions to avoid fear-producing stimuli without experiencing the affect that such situations would engender in the absence of such avoidance responses. (p. 836)

CHAPTER 3

1 For further suggestions and journaling exercises that can be used to identify destructive thoughts or voices, see *Conquer Your Critical Inner Voice* (Firestone et al., 2002).

2 The first author conceptualizes the voice as a dynamic representation of what attachment theorists refer to as "internal working models." In his initial description of the development of insecure attachment patterns between parent and infant, Bowlby (1980) explained that, in many of these cases, the associated cognitive working model may become "defensively excluded" from the infant's awareness, leading to mixed models of self and other. In her work, Bretherton (2005) noted,

> He [Bowlby] proposed that the dominance of the more readily accessible (conscious) working models over the defensively excluded models should not be considered as absolute. Fragments of contradictory nonconscious or partially conscious subordinate model(s) may leak into awareness, and activate fragments of attachment behavior, and associated moods, or dreams. Alternatively, two or more contradictory working models may oscillate in becoming conscious, explaining the activation of erratic interpersonal behavior. (p. 20)

Bretherton (1996) also observed that "insecure individuals develop working models of self and attachment figure in which some schema or schema networks [cognitive processes] may be dissociated from others" (p. 14), as is characteristic of children categorized as having formed a disorganized/disorientated attachment to a parent or caregiver. We suggest that defensively excluded negative working models (critical voices about the self and others) can be triggered by a wide range of circumstances in one's adult attachment.

Also see early descriptive accounts of the concept of internal working models in Bretherton et al. (1990) and Main et al. (1985). According to attachment theorists Bakermans-Kranenburg and van IJzendoorn (1993), internal working models or "current 'state of mind' with respect to attachment relationships also determine parents' sensitivity to their infants' attachment behavior, and, in turn, shape the infant's own internal working models of attachment" (p. 870). Maternal insensitivity or lack of attunement tends to predispose the formation of negative internal working models or destructive thought processes.

Internal working models have been assessed in parents, utilizing the Adult Attachment Interview (AAI; George et al., 1984). According to research conducted by Fonagy et al. (1991) and, later, Roisman, Madsen, Hennighausen, Sroufe, and Collins (2001), "Across a wide variety of samples, parents' AAI classifications consistently have been shown to relate to the quality of their own infants' attachments as inferred from the Strange Situation, the premiere behavioral assessment of attachment in infancy" (Roisman et al., 2001, p. 157). Also see Fraley's (2002) meta-analysis of 27 studies that examined the continuity of internal working models from infancy to young adulthood.

Based on findings from brain-imaging studies that examined neural correlates of internal working models, Schore (2000) proposed,

> The right brain contains the "cerebral representation of one's own past" and the substrate of affectively laden autobiographical memory.... These findings suggest that early-forming internal working models of the attachment relationship are processed and stored in implicit-procedural memory systems in the right cortex, the hemisphere dominant for implicit learning. (p. 32)

Fonagy et al. (2002) referred to another mechanism in the brain that they called the interpersonal interpretative mechanism (IIM). "We see the IIM as an overarching hypothetical neural structure, a processing system for social information that underlies reflective function or mentalization. . . . The development of the IIM is facilitated by sensitive and attuned early care" (p. 125). According to Fonagy and his colleagues,

> The interpersonal learning environment within which the IIM can develop probably requires a minimum level of contingent responding. . . . Thus, *the experience of mis-attunement (or noncontingency), which causes all of us to internalize an "other within the self" (the part of the self we will be calling the "alien self")* [italics added], goes in some cases beyond what the infant can tolerate and still feel a sense of coherent, continuous identity. . . . For other people [with disorganized attachment], the alien experience within the self remains an inassimilable core that creates an even more powerful need for integration through later attachment relationships but that also gets in the way of forming and maintaining such relationships. (pp. 129–130)

Fonagy and Target (2005) have also suggested, "If the attachment relationship is indeed a major organizer of brain development, it is even more important to understand the processes that underpin the trans-generational transmission of attachment patterns" (p. 333). The voice, as described in this chapter, can be hypothesized to be one of the processes referred to by Fonagy and Target.

3 Extensive research on adult romantic attachments tends to support the first author's observations regarding how the voice process functions to maintain the fantasy bond or an illusion of fusion between partners in an intimate relationship. For example, Mikulincer and Shaver (2007) asserted,

> We have repeatedly discovered associations between individual differences in attachment-system functioning and people's perceptions of others (e.g., what one thinks about the availability, supportiveness, personal traits and intentions of a relationship partner) and the self (what one thinks about one's own value to relationships partners, "lovability," and ability to handle challenges and threats). (loc. 2681–2686)

Similar to the voice process, these perceptions or beliefs about oneself and one's partner (described by Mikulincer and Shaver) may operate to maintain preoccupied or dismissing styles of relating in couple relationships. See Mikulincer and Shaver's meta-analysis and summary of findings linking attachment orientations with self-esteem, self-competence, recalled parental behaviors, and appraisals of social support (pp. 156, 157, 159, 173, 174, 179, 180, Tables 6.1–6.4).

S. Johnson and Whiffen (1999) asserted that the function of working models is to make predictions about adult romantic attachments that would tend to support the formation of a fantasy bond within the new relationship. "Insecure models may predispose people to selectively attend to and defensively distort information. . . . An anxious partner [may think] . . . 'He is distant. He doesn't love me and I am unlovable'" (p. 373).

Researchers have hypothesized that internal working models and the associated attachment strategies or behaviors in childhood and adulthood may constitute a universal phenomenon, albeit with a number of variations. For example, in a large cross-cultural study involving more than 17,000 subjects from 62 cultures, Schmitt et al. (2004) concluded,

> In nearly all cultures, people possess basic cognitive-emotional attitudes that constitute romantic attachment Models of Self and Other. These internal working models likely exist as pancultural constructs, forming independent dimensions that underlie romantic attachment types across cultures. . . . However, secure romantic attachment was significantly lower than dismissing, preoccupied, or fearful romantic attachment across several cultures. [For example], we

> found that East Asian cultures were particularly high on preoccupied romantic attachment. This result may reflect the fact that in many East Asian cultures, psychological validation (in this case romantic validation) is heavily dependent on the opinion of others. (pp. 397–398)

4 Regarding Bretherton's findings, the voice can be conceptualized as the intrapsychic mechanism primarily responsible for the intergenerational transmission of negative parental attitudes, beliefs, and defenses that mediate partners' styles of relating (secure, preoccupied, or dismissing) in intimate relationships. In describing the first author's theoretical model, P. van Horn (personal communication, August 1999) noted, "Firestone has made a convincing case that difficulties in intimate adult relationships can be traced to internal working models of self and other and to *the thoughts* about self and other that are inspired by those models."

Shaver and Clark (1994) contended that children who grow up with a negative internal model of themselves and their attachment figure often become adults who have low self-esteem and a basic distrust of relationship partners. Also see Collins, Ford, Guichard, and Allard's (2006) study linking working models of attachment with attribution processes in intimate relationships. Findings from this study supported the hypothesis that

> individuals with negative self-images and pessimistic models of relationships may be predisposed to construe events in negative ways.... Insecure working models make it difficult for individuals to interpret their partner's behavior in the most favorable light, which may undermine their ability to achieve feelings of security. (p. 216)

5 Other theories, including attribution theory and conceptual models of implicit and explicit attitudes, have some similarities to my (R. Firestone's) thinking with respect to the division of the mind and the irrationality of the voice process. See "A Model of Dual Attitudes" by Wilson, Lindsey, and Schooler (2000), who argued that people can have both implicit and explicit attitudes toward the same object. Similarly, people might have two or more implicit attitudes that are activated automatically, depending on the context. Also see Seymour Epstein's (1994) cognitive-experiential self theory, which depicts two systems of information processing and response in human beings. Epstein noted,

> The transformation that occurs in people's thinking when they are emotionally aroused provides a dramatic illustration of a very different way of thinking from the way people think when they are unemotional. People, when they are highly emotional, characteristically think in a manner that is categorical, personal, concretive, unreflective, and action oriented. (p. 710)

CHAPTER 4

1 In the professional literature, separation theory has been described by Bassett (2007) in an article, "Psychological Defenses Against Death Anxiety: Integrating Terror Management Theory and Firestone's Separation Theory," and in a chapter by Morrant and Catlett (2008) in *Existential and Spiritual Issues in Death Attitudes*.

2 Regarding the integration of existential systems of thought with psychodynamic and cognitive-behavioral approaches, Lampropoulos, Spengler, Dixon, and Nicholas (2002) argued that "the basic assumptions of the S-P [scientist-practitioner] model about methodological, open-minded, and evidence-based practice not only justify, but strongly suggest the use of integrative/eclectic therapies" (p. 1235). Castonguay and Goldfried's (1994)

"Psychotherapy Integration: An Idea Whose Time Has Come" is one of the landmark articles in the movement toward integration.

Other theories that are to some extent integrative include the self-psychology of Heinz Kohut (1977), Daniel Stern's (2004) approach depicted in *The Present Moment in Psychotherapy and Everyday Life,* Robert Langs's (1997) practice of depth psychotherapy as described in *Death Anxiety and Clinical Practice,* Jerry Piven (2004b) in "Death, Neurosis, and Normalcy: On the Ubiquity of Personal and Social Delusions," and the works of Andre Green (1999), Donald Winnicott (1958), and Harold Searles (1961). Also see Elliot, Watson, Goldman, and Greenberg's (2004) description of the integrative aspects in Greenberg's practice of process-experiential (PE) therapy: "In brief, PE therapists see human beings as constituted by multiple parts or voices.... Therapy often involves supporting a growth-oriented voice in its conflict with a more dominant negative voice that attempts to maintain the stability of familiar but negative states" (loc. 101–106).

T. Ogden (2005) set forth a conceptualization of the neurotic process in melancholia similar in some respects to the first author's (R. Firestone's) hypothesis regarding the defensive functions of neurosis in relation to separation and early object loss, as well as to existential realities. Ogden wrote,

> The individual replaces what might have become a three-dimensional relatedness to the mortal and at times disappointing external object with a two-dimensional (shadow-like) relationship to an internal object [a fantasy bond] that exists in a psychological domain outside of time (and consequently sheltered from the reality of death). In so doing, the melancholic evades the pain of loss, and by extension, other forms of psychological pain, but does so at an enormous cost—the loss of a good deal of his own (emotional) vitality. (loc. 1050–1057)
>
> Thus, the melancholic experiences a conflict between, on the one hand, the wish to be alive with the pain of irreversible loss and the reality of death, and on the other hand, the wish to deaden himself to the pain of loss and the knowledge of death. (loc. 1149–1152)

3 Voice therapy is similar in certain respects to Aaron Beck's (Beck, Rush, Shaw, & Emery, 1979) and Judith Beck's (1995) cognitive therapy (CT). For example, both therapeutic approaches attempt to access destructive voices or "automatic thoughts" that influence maladaptive behavior. Treatment outcome studies (A. Beck, 2005; Butler, Chapman, Forman, & Beck, 2006; Forman, Herbert, Moitra, Yeomans, & Geller, 2009) have demonstrated the effectiveness of CT and cognitive-behavioral therapy (CBT). Butler et al. noted, "Large effect sizes were found for CBT for unipolar depression, generalized anxiety disorder, panic disorder... social phobia, post traumatic stress disorder, and childhood depressive and anxiety disorders" (p. 17). According to A. Beck (2005), extensive research has shown CT and CBT to be more successful than drug treatment in reducing anxiety: "Meta-analyses indicate that CT/CBT protocols are more effective in reducing panic and anxiety symptoms than pharmacological treatments" (p. 956).

Also see Epstein's (1994) cognitive-experiential self-theory, in which "the task of therapy is to change the maladaptive schemata in the experiential system and to promote synergistic (rather than conflictual) need fulfillment" (p. 717).

Ryan and Deci's (2008) self-determination theory addresses resistance and other motivational issues in psychotherapy, proposing that when clients "have a more *internal perceived locus of causality* for treatment, they will be more likely to integrate learning and behavioral change, resulting in more positive outcomes" (p. 187). Ryan and Deci have described "introjects [as] frequently derived from clients' experiences of conditional regard during development... and are buttressed by the resulting sense of contingent self-worth.... Such cases often require identifying and challenging these introjects" (p. 189).

As noted earlier, other methodologies have certain elements in common with voice therapy, including emotion-focused therapy (EFT) developed by L. Greenberg (2011), who conceptualized the individual "as a complex, ever-changing, organized collection of various part-aspects of self. These self-aspects or 'voices' interact to produce experience and action" (p. 52). For an example of EFT, see L. Greenberg's description of his adaptation of the Gestalt two-chair dialogue in "A Case of Anxiety," in which the patient deals with her "critical" voice:

> In EFT, the goal in treating anxiety is to access and restructure the underlying maladaptive emotion scheme.... Her "critical" voice told her that she was wasting time and that she should be more efficient and put in more effort. As the critical voice was elaborated, it said,... "You are not trying hard enough." "It doesn't matter if you spend 8 hours [on your work] because you will still do poorly." (pp. 105–109)

4 Cognitive therapist Judith Beck (1995) has emphasized that gaining access to emotions helps in identifying the "hot cognitions"—the core schema or previously unconscious beliefs about self, others, and the world. Also see "Facilitating Emotional Change: The Moment-by-Moment Process" by L. Greenberg, Rice, and Elliot (1993). Their approach, emotion-focused therapy (EFT), focuses primarily on eliciting emotion by directing the client to amplify his or her self-critical statements. Greenberg and his colleagues direct the therapist as follows:

> For example, if the client says "you're worthless" or sneers while criticizing, direct the client to "do this again...," "do this some more..."; "put some words to this...." This operation will intensify the client's affective arousal and help access core criticisms. (p. 205)

"It is only then that they become accessible to new input and change" (p. 6). Greenberg et al. believe that "Affect is thus a core constituent of the human self and establishes links between self and the environment and organizes self-experience. In a sense, feelings are ultimately the meeting place of mind, body, environment, culture, and behavior" (p. 54).

5 Regarding the adult mode or ego state, the ability to remain in an "adult ego state" (Berne, 1961; Firestone, 1988) appears to depend primarily on an individual's level of self-differentiation (separation from the fantasy bond with the family of origin) (Bowen, 1978; Hellinger, 1998; Karpel, 1994; Kerr & Bowen, 1988; Schnarch, 1991; Willi, 1978/1984, 1999). Transactional analysts have observed that "the Adult is still the least well understood of the three types of ego states" (Berne, 1961, p. 76). Berne proposed that the adult is best conceptualized as "the residual state left after the segregation of all detectable Parent and Child elements" (p. 76). The present author (R. Firestone) has suggested that the adult state is perhaps the least well understood because even mature, well-adjusted individuals find it difficult to remain in the adult mode for extended periods of time.

6 In addressing this difficulty, Bromberg (2009) noted that traditional psychoanalytic interpretations are usually ineffective with clients who are unaware of the division within, as well as clients who have tendencies to dissociate under stress:

> In certain areas of every individual's personality the experience of intrapsychic conflict is difficult to *bear* much less resolve, and for some people this incapacity goes back to early childhood because the mind's ability to access and safely tolerate two or more disjunctive self-states at the same time was virtually foreclosed at that time. But for *any* patient, in those areas where the natural dialectic

> between conflict and dissociation is either compromised or shut down, conflict-interpretations are useless or even worse. (p. 355)

See P. Ogden, Minton, and Pain (2006) and Bonnie Badenoch (2008, 2011), which provide methods for dealing with clients' tendencies to dissociate during the process of working through trauma-related emotions in psychotherapy.

7 Although transference reactions generally are minimal in the practice of voice therapy, it is important to closely monitor negative therapeutic reactions, in particular those that often occur in clients with borderline personality disorders and in those assessed as having formed a disorganized attachment with an early caregiver. According to Liotti (2004),

> When the patient is guided by an IWM [internal working model] of disorganized attachment in construing the therapist's behavior, the therapeutic relationship may become unbearably dramatic, changeable and complex for both partners. Untoward counter-transferential reactions, or premature termination of an otherwise promising treatment, may be the unfortunate consequence of the reactivation of a disorganized IWM within the therapeutic relationship. (p. 484)

8 For other resources with in-depth descriptions of voice therapy methodology and examples of corrective suggestions, the reader is referred to "Voice Therapy" in *What Is Psychotherapy? Contemporary Perspectives* (Firestone, 1990c), "Prescription for Psychotherapy" (Firestone, 1990b), *Voice Therapy: A Psychotherapeutic Approach to Self-Destructive Behavior* (Firestone, 1988), and *Combating Destructive Thought Processes: Voice Therapy and Separation Theory* (Firestone, 1997a).

CHAPTER 5

1 According to Snyder, Castellani, and Whisman (2006), studies show,

> Maritally discordant individuals are overrepresented among individuals seeking mental health services, regardless of whether they report marital distress as their primary complaint.... In brief, couple distress... is among the most frequent primary or secondary concerns reported by individuals seeking assistance from mental health professionals. (pp. 318–319)

2 Tedeschi and Felson (1994) have asserted that there are "high levels of coercive behavior, including bodily force, verbal and physical punishment, physical isolation, and deprivation of resources" (pp. 290–291) in American families, in relations between partners, and in parent-child interactions. For descriptive accounts of destructive maneuvers that many partners engage in, see Michael Vincent Miller (1995).

3 Regarding behaviors that elicit fear, anger, and guilt in the other, M. Miller (1995) observed how these behaviors function to cement the fantasy bond within the couple: "Symptoms, including phobias, addictions, and physical problems, also have similar strategic value in regulating the degree of being tied together yet far apart" (p. 123).

4 John Gottman (1979; Gottman & Krokoff, 1989; Gottman & Silver, 1999) delineated four behaviors that are diagnostic predictors of eventual divorce: defensiveness, stonewalling or filibustering, criticality, and contempt. Contempt was found to be the most serious indicator of potential divorce and could be clearly discerned during brief (15- to 20-minute) videotaped interactions between partners in an experimental situation that required collaboratively performing an assigned task. In these studies, partners were observed contradicting their positive statements toward the other with nonverbal negative messages through

frowns, sneers, expressions of disgust, a tense or impatient tone of voice, inattention, and leaning away from the other person.

5 Regarding gender role expectations, Aries (1997) reported research showing considerable agreement among people about the characteristics of men and women:

> Men are characterized by a cluster of instrumental traits: they are seen to be leaders, to be dominant, aggressive, independent, objective, and competitive. Women, in contrast, are characterized by a cluster of affective traits: they are seen to be emotional, subjective, tactful, and aware of the feelings of others. (p. 96)

These stereotypes tend to persist partly because of a phenomenon that Geis (1993) referred to as the "fundamental attribution error." The error occurs when people attribute the behavior of another person to his or her "internal personality dispositions" (p. 29). Geis has asserted, "Committing the fundamental attribution error, we assume that high-status behavior is dispositional in men and subordinate behavior in women" (p. 38).

6 For an in-depth discussion of these dynamics, see Jurg Willi's *Couples in Collusion* (1975/1982) and *Ecological Psychotherapy* (1999).

7 Tendencies toward withholding may be correlated with a deactivation of the attachment system that occurs in individuals who are categorized as avoidant or dismissing in their style of relating to a romantic partner. According to Mikulincer, Shaver, and Pereg (2003), in these cases, the primary goal is to

> keep the attachment system deactivated so as to avoid frustration and further distress caused by attachment-figure unavailability. This goal leads to the denial of attachment needs, avoidance of closeness, intimacy and dependence in close relationships; maximization of cognitive, emotional, and physical distance from others; and strivings for self-reliance and independence. (p. 85)

Or, in the present authors' terms—a pseudoindependent stance.

8 It is difficult to directly assess the effects that death salience has on proximity-seeking in adult romantic relationships because behaviors that exemplify attachment behavior may be based on any number of conscious and unconscious motives: one might be seeking genuine closeness or an imagined closeness or fantasy bond. For example, Mikulincer and Florian (2000) reported findings from terror management theory research showing that reminders of death led to increased scores on a measure of the importance of the biological mode of symbolic immortality. "Whereas the two insecure groups reacted to death reminders with more severe judgments of transgressions, secure people showed a heightened sense of symbolic immortality and desire for intimacy" (p. 271).

> Secure people hold a positive sense of the self and adequate coping skills that allow them to manage distress without defensively distorting their cognitions. . . . In our terms, these characteristics, which reflect an internalized secure base (Bowlby, 1988), may act as a cognitive shield against the terror of death and may abolish the need to validate cultural worldviews and to derogate persons and opinions that threaten these worldviews. (p. 262)

However, Mikulincer and Florian (2000) also noted that "although intimacy may promote growth, it sometimes could be a regressive response that leads people to excessively immerse themselves into another person at the expense of a sense of individuality" (p. 272).

9 A number of attachment theorists have proposed three hypotheses to explain mate selection: (1) the similarity hypothesis, (2) complementary hypothesis, and (3) attachment

security. In a meta-review of self-report assessments regarding both real and hypothetical partners, B. Holmes and Johnson (2009) found a preponderance of studies that confirmed the complementary hypothesis for couples involved in long-term relationships: "for example, Collins and Read (1990) and Simpson (1990) both found that individuals low in comfort with closeness (i.e., avoidant) tended to be paired with individuals high in fear of abandonment (i.e., anxious)" (p. 842).

10 See "Overview" by Schachner, Shaver, and Mikulincer (2003) in *Attachment Processes in Couple and Family Therapy* (S. Johnson & Whiffen, 2003), in which the authors review research related to projection, distortion, and internal working models in adult attachments:

> Mikulincer and Horesh (1999) found that avoidant individuals' perceptions of others are colored by defensive projection of their own unwanted traits ("unwanted-self" traits) onto others and then distancing themselves from others partly because of these projected traits.... Mikulincer and Horesh (1999) also found that anxious individuals tend to project their own "actual-self" traits onto others and then view themselves as overly similar to these others. (p. 32)

Noller and Feeney (1994) found that, during the first two years of marriage, one partner's higher scores on the attachment anxiety and avoidance dimensions predicted less accuracy in decoding a spouse's negative and positive facial expressions.

According to Collins et al. (2006), internal working models are closely related to attribution processes in intimate relationships. Rholes, Simpson, Tran, Martin, and Friedman (2007) reported findings related to information processing, attributions, and internal working models that suggested

> that highly anxious individuals might maintain their negative model of self in relationships by selectively attending to information about their negative behaviors/characteristics.... The partners of highly anxious and highly avoidant persons may remain dissatisfied with their relationships in part because they selectively attend to the negative qualities of their insecure partners. (p. 437)

Another common dynamic that involves distortion can be found in couples where the desires of insecure/preoccupied individuals

> for close proximity to and fusion with relationships partners [encourage them]... to project their negative self-views onto relationship partners, thereby creating an illusory sense of similarity and union. Thus, paradoxically, a negative view of others is guided partly by the anxious person's negative self-views, combined with an intense longing for "twinship" (Kohut, 1984) and connectedness. (Mikulincer & Shaver, 2007, p. 171)

11 Regarding provocation, attachment researchers have noted,

> New relationships probably call at first on fairly general working models of others, but particular partners, or particular "button-pushing" behaviors [provocations] on the part of particular partners, may evoke specific representations [internal working models], along with the fears and defenses associated with them. (Mikulincer & Shaver, 2007, p. 168)

Provocation is also related to the second of the three copying processes described by Lorna Smith Benjamin (2003), who investigated the mechanisms responsible for the repetition of defensive behavior patterns from childhood in a new adult relationship.

> Problem patterns are linked to learning with important early loved ones via one or more of three copy processes: (1) Be like him or her; (2) Act as if he or she is still there and in control; and (3) Treat yourself as he or she treated you. (p. vii)

12 Regarding societal expectations about marriage, see Ester Perel's (2006) book, *Mating in Captivity,* in which the author (at times somewhat cynically) points out the double messages or "diametrically opposed attitudes" toward marriage operating within our culture:

> The legacy of Puritanism, which locates the family at the center of society, expects marriage to be reasonable, sober, and productive. You work, you save, and you plan. You take your commitments seriously. But alongside this very American notion of individual responsibility and moderation is the equally apple-pie notion of individual freedom. We believe in personal fulfillment: in life, liberty and the pursuit of happiness. We relish the freedom to spontaneously satisfy our desires.... An entire industry of hedonism hovers on the outskirts of marriage, a constant reminder of all we've sacrificed in exchange for the muted sexuality of marital love. (loc. 1512–1516)

CHAPTER 6

1 For in-depth descriptions of voice therapy methodology applied in couple relationships, see Chapter 13, "The Therapeutic Process in Couples Therapy," and Chapter 14, "A Pilot Study Applying Voice Therapy With Four Couples: Clinical Material From a Series of Specialized Group Discussion," in *Fear of Intimacy* (Firestone & Catlett, 1999); Chapter 9, "Voice Therapy Applied to Problems in Sexual Relating, in *Sex and Love in Intimate Relationships* (Firestone, Firestone, & Catlett, 2006); and "Methods for Overcoming the Fear of Intimacy" in D. J. Mashek and A. Aron (Eds.), *Handbook of Closeness and Intimacy* (Firestone & Firestone, 2004).

2 The Firestone Voice Scale for Couples (FVSC) assesses the frequency of destructive thoughts the subject is currently experiencing toward self, toward his or her partner, and about relationships in general. The initial version of the FVSC consists of 98 items reflecting destructive thought patterns that are associated with intimate interpersonal relationships. Reliability and validity have not yet been established for this instrument. Another instrument, the Behavioral Checklist for Partners (Firestone & Catlett, 1999), is composed of items derived in part from the personal qualities that one can develop in oneself and seek in a potential partner.

Other measures, including the Experiences in Close Relationships Inventory, Revised (Fraley, Waller, & Brennan, 2000), and the Differentiation of Self Inventory (DSI; Skowron & Schmitt, 2003), have been developed to assess people's internal working models with respect to intimacy. For example, in "Assessing Interpersonal Fusion: Reliability and Validity of a New Differentiation of Self [DSI] Fusion With Others Subscale," Skowron and Schmitt (2003) noted,

> On an interpersonal level, more differentiated individuals are comfortable with intimacy in close relationships and, therefore, the need to regulate feelings of anxiety with fusion or emotional cut off in relationships is decreased.... Fusion is characterized by over-involvement with significant others in decision-making and difficulty formulating opinions or perspectives independent of one's parents or significant others. (p. 210)

3 By acting out complementary parent/child or dominant/submissive roles, people are able to elicit the specific voice attacks that they are experiencing internally. Tansey and Burke (1985) defined this unconscious process of defensive projective identification as follows: "Projective identification, although having intrapsychic characteristics, represents an interactional phenomenon in which the projector unconsciously attempts to elicit thoughts, feelings, and experiences within another individual which in some way resemble his own" (p. 46).

The other phenomenon described in this chapter, that of one partner creating new voice attacks in the other, is also made possible due to projective identification, a process that has been seen as both defensive and communicative (Greatrex, 2002). The transmission of critical thoughts and feelings from one person to a significant other occurs because of the function of mirror neurons in the brain, "which may be fundamental to the observation and communication of intention" (Greattrex, Introduction section, para. 2).

T. Ogden (1982) has emphasized the fact that "the projector subjectively experiences a feeling of oneness with the recipient with regard to the expelled feeling, idea, or self-representation" (p. 34). In this sense, projective identification may be conceptualized as a defense that reinforces the illusion of fusion or fantasy bond with one's mate. Sigmund Freud (1915/1957) called attention to this phenomenon: "It is a very remarkable thing that the *Ucs* [unconscious] of one human being can react upon that of another without passing through *Cs* [consciousness]" (p. 194). As an example, Scharff and Scharff (1991) and Zinner (1976) have suggested that through the process of projective identification, feelings of sexual inadequacy in one partner can be defensively and unconsciously transferred to the other.

Also see *The Embedded Self: An Integrative Psychodynamic and Systemic Perspective on Couples and Family Therapy* by Jane Gerson (2010) and *Self Within Marriage: The Foundation for Lasting Relationships* by Richard M. Zeitner (2012). Zeitner has explained the dynamics involved in the loss of each partner's self that occurs within many marriages and/or close relationships:

> In which a partner demands to be loved by the other, thus appropriating the identity of the partner, while simultaneously intruding and projecting into that partner those rejected and disavowed parts of the self. Thus, the second partner's self and sense of agency are usurped, while he is sometimes unaware that it is the partner who has contributed to loss of self. The second partner may feel trapped within a relationship in which love is both given and taken, but for the prices of separateness and selfhood. (p. 140)

Zeitner's descriptive accounts portray numerous examples of couple relationships characterized by the formation of a fantasy bond or imagined connection between the partners.

Recently, neuroscientists have begun to examine possible pathways by which projective identification may take place and have suggested ways in which the emotional state of one person is transmitted to the mind of another, effecting changes in patterns of neuronal firing in the brain of the other person. The process takes place below the level of conscious awareness. Specifically, Schore (2003b) has proposed that the process of projective identification is correlated with right hemisphere attachment trauma and the primitive defense of dissociation: "I suggest that an infant with an early history of 'cumulative trauma'... must excessively utilize defensive projective identification in order to cope with all-too-frequent episodes of interactive stress that disorganize the developing self" (p. 68).

4 Other interventions focus on eliciting and challenging destructive thinking in relationships that interfere with sexual relating. In cognitive-behavioral therapy, Aaron Beck (1988) educates couples who are experiencing sexual problems that the "first step in reducing the mutual anger in your relationship... [is to] determine to what degree your own mental workings contribute to the problem" (p. 261).

Object-relations therapy for couples (Scharff & Scharff, 1991) proposes that the conflicts experienced by couples may function to exacerbate "the object relations difficulties in their internal worlds" (p. 34). According to the Scharffs, in these cases, the process of projective identification operates to maintain and intensify the problem. The goal of object relations therapy with couples is similar in some respects to that of voice therapy—that is, to encourage the reinternalization of projected material, or, in our terms, encourage the taking back of negative projections based on the voice. Also see Scharff and Scharff (1997), which explains how healing may take place in therapy.

Regarding the release of feeling in voice therapy with couples, in recent years, clinicians conducting couple therapy have employed techniques to help facilitate the release of feelings (L. Greenberg, 2002; S. Johnson, 1999; S. Johnson & Denton, 2002; M. Solomon, 2001). L. Greenberg (2002) gives examples of negative voices that support cycles of anger and hurt that escalate in many couple relationships. Emotion-focused therapy, based on attachment theory, has been effectively used to treat distressed couples and partners reporting low sexual desire and sexual arousal disorders (S. Johnson, 2002; S. Johnson & Greenberg, 1995).

In his "crucible model" of marital and sex therapy, based on family systems theory, David Schnarch (1991) proposed that low levels of self-differentiation in each partner contribute to disturbances in a couple's sex life, noting that partners involved in committed relationships have sexual difficulties because they are operating at relatively low levels of self-differentiation. He observed that partners with low levels of self-differentiation cling to a conventional form of "other-validated" intimacy, based on the need for fusion, rather than "self-validated" intimacy, based on the ability to tolerate separateness and existential aloneness. He also argued that a committed sexual relationship provides the crucible in which partners can "grow up" by differentiating themselves emotionally from their family of origin.

5 Maintaining a therapeutic stance in working with couples requires the therapist to make use of benevolent forms of projective identification to facilitate deep, enduring change. For a succinct discussion of how nondefensive projective identification can be utilized in this context, see Greatrex (2002), who described the process of change as follows:

> In the complicated clinical enactment based on projective identification, painful representational schemas of early life impose themselves on the conscious awareness of both analyst and patient with an awesome and involuntary spontaneity. I am suggesting that in our relatively open posture, we analysts are willing to let the patient direct our associations, and we do so by matching or identifying with the feelings the patient projects. (Projective Identification and the Reflexive Function as Agents of Change section, para. 2)

Schore (2003b) has acknowledged what the therapist was up against in striving to maintain the therapeutic stance: "The patient does not project an internal critic [critical inner voice] into the therapist, but rather the therapist's internal critic, stimulated by the patient's negative affective communications, resonates with the patient's and is thereby amplified" (pp. 90–91).

CHAPTER 7

1 In explaining the rationale that directed the research into differential effects of the four family dyads on children, Russell and Saebel (1997) noted that "both parent sex and child sex contribute so that relationships in the four dyads of mother-son, mother-daughter, father-son, and father-daughter are distinct" (p. 111).

Although Russell and Saebel's research yielded only weak correlations between outcome variables and the four parent-child dyads, other researchers, including Cowan, Cowan, and

Kerig (1993), have reported that gender differences in parenting style do appear to have differential effects on boys and girls. Similarly,

> "Gender theory" (e.g., Ferree, 1990; Thompson & Walker, 1989, West & Zimmerman, 1987) presents an analysis of differences between family roles and behavior of mothers and fathers in terms of gender.... Gender schema theory (Bem, 1985) is another theoretical account that provides a basis for expecting combined effects of parent sex and child sex on parent-child relationships.... Gender schema theory also posits that these cultural definitions [of gender] are acquired early in childhood. It stands to reason, then, that differences would be expected not only between mother-child and father-child relationships, but also among the individual dyads. (Russell & Saebel, 1997, pp. 114–115)

2 Oren, Englar-Carlson, Stevens, and Oren (2010) reported findings from contemporary research that support Lamb's (1986) original findings regarding fathers' involvement in child-rearing and family activities: "Children with involved fathers are more confident, are better able to deal with frustration, have higher grade point averages, and are more likely to mature into compassionate adults" (loc. 1211–1214). "Fathers can serve as sensitive, supportive, and gently challenging companions for children in their attempts to move beyond the family to explore the world" (loc. 1221–1229). These authors examined the concept of "generative fathering" built on Erikson's concept of generativity, which describes fathers who respond readily and consistently to a child's developmental needs over time. Also see "An Assessment Paradigm for Fathers and Men in Therapy Using Gender Role Conflict Theory," by James M. O'Neil and Melissa L. Lujan (2010).

Regarding father-son and father-daughter relationships, Pleck (2010) cited research supporting the essential father hypothesis. Fathers have a "unique and essential role in child development, especially for boys who need a male role model to establish a masculine gender identity" (loc. 1097–1102).

In general, longitudinal studies have found that children of both genders who have a strong attachment and are consistently involved with their fathers have better self-esteem, a greater sense of competence, and better intellectual development and academic success. Father-child interaction has been shown to promote a child's physical well-being, perceptual abilities, and competency for relatedness with others, even at a young age (Krampe & Fairweather, 1993). In a 26-year longitudinal study on 379 individuals, researchers found that the single most significant childhood factor in developing empathy is paternal involvement.

In a meta-analysis of numerous studies investigating parental acceptance and rejection, Rohner and Veneziano (2001) found that "perceived paternal love and caring were as predictive of sons' and daughters' life satisfaction—including their sense of well-being—as maternal love and caring" (p. 393). They also reported studies by Amato (1994) showing that "father love is sometimes implicated to a greater extent than mother love in adult offsprings' overall psychological health and wellbeing" (p. 394).

3 Regarding father-daughter relationships and daughters' adolescent and adult adjustment, Dresner and Grolnick (1996) found that women "displaying intimate relationships perceived their fathers as having been more accepting than women who evidenced either enmeshed (merger) or superficial relationships. Further, their autonomy was linked to perceived support for independence by both their mothers and fathers" (p. 25). Flouri and Buchanan (2003) found that "father involvement at age 16 protected against adult psychological distress in women" (p. 63). Flouri and Buchanan (2002) also reported findings showing that "closeness to fathers and mothers in adolescence is linked with good relationships with partners in adult life and that closeness to fathers in turn is, to a great

extent, due to high father involvement in childhood, especially for daughters. Protecting fathers' involvement, and especially fathers' involvement with daughters, can be an effective way to promote well-adjusted family relationships in both adolescence and adult life" (p. 196).

In a 26-year longitudinal study involving 379 individuals, Krampe and Fairweather (1993) found that the single most important childhood factor in developing empathy is paternal involvement. Also see Sharpe (1994), including interviews with or letters from daughters and fathers. The topics explored during the interviews include early childhood experiences, approval and achievement, violence, sexuality, effects on future relationships with men, specific experiences of father absence, lone fathers and stepfathers, role reversal, and dependency through aging (loc. 120–124).

4 Although there is agreement in the literature that father-daughter relationships take many forms of interaction, nevertheless, a literature review of father-daughter research shows an emphasis on the abusive or absent father (Downs & Miller, 1998; Hetherington, 1972; Oates, Forrest, & Peacock, 1985), and results focus on the impact these relationships have on a woman's adult relationships. The psychological premise most commonly cited in research is that women with abusive or absent fathers have difficulty with men and often choose husbands who abuse or abandon them. However, a greater percentage of women experience fathers who are not abusive or absent (Secunda, 1990).

Belsky, Steinberg, and Draper (1991) found that adolescent girls in father-absent homes tend to show precocious sexual interest in boys, express negative attitudes toward males and masculinity, and show relatively little interest in maintaining sexual and emotional ties to one man. Also see Maureen Rank (2011). The author cited Daniel Trobisch, who in his study of German women concluded that only about 15% of the women he interviewed grew up enjoying effective fathering (Rank, 2011, loc. 79–83).

Comings, Muhleman, Johnson, and MacMurray (2002) investigated possible genetic precursors of Belsky's observation that girls exposed to a stressful environment, especially when due to father absence in the first seven years of life, showed an early onset of puberty, precocious sexuality, and unstable relationships as adults (p. 1046). These researchers examined possible effects of the variant X-linked androgen receptor gene, which predisposes the father to behaviors that include family abandonment, and how it may be passed to their daughters, causing early puberty, precocious sexuality, and behavioral problems (p. 1046). They concluded that father-daughter allele-sharing may account for some, if not the majority, of the variance in the previously observed association between fathers' absence and age of menarche and behavioral problems in their daughters (p. 1050).

5 H. Kaplan (1995) conjectured that

> the continuous and repeated mutually pleasurable intimate physical and emotional contact that small children normally enjoy with their mothers, fathers, and other family members... *are inadvertently mildly erotically arousing to infants and young children, and sensuously pleasurable for their parents... and that these experiences form the psychologic origins of normal sexual fantasies and desires.* (p. 41)

Kaplan's implication was not that these mutually pleasurable experiences harm children in the way sexually abusive or incestuous experiences do. However, she did argue that "this hypothetical normal sexual 'imprinting' process can go awry and result in linking sex with fear and/or in the acquisition of and fixation on atypical and possibly disadvantageous sexual fantasies and desires" (p. 42).

6 In a "Ten-Year Research Update Review: Child Sexual Abuse," Putnam (2003) reported that "adjusted prevalence rates are 16.8% and 7.9% for adult women and men, respectively.... Depression in adults and sexualized behavior in children are the best-documented

outcomes" (p. 269). C. Johnson (2004) reported in *The Lancet* that child sexual abuse is a worldwide problem affecting 2% to 62% of women and 3% to 16% of men as victims.

7 Kindlon and Thompson (1999) pointed out that a recent survey "found that boys were 50 percent more likely to be physically abused than were girls. Fathers, in particular, were much more likely to hit a teenage son than a teenage daughter" (loc. 1269–1275). In relation to gender role expectations for boys, Blazina and Watkins (2000) reported that "boys and men are dealt with more harshly than girls and women when they deviate from traditional societal gender role prescriptions" (p. 126).

> A growing number of theorists have suggested that many men experience a psychic woundedness related to overly harsh disindentification, separation/individuation issues and gender role socialization. It comes in part from the traditional message that boys' separation/individuation process is synonymous with and implies disavowing needing others. These boys feel the strain of gender role conflict even at this young age when they are mandated to renounce yearnings for unmet emotional needs and instead portray themselves as solely self-reliant. (p. 130)

8 Kindlon and Thompson (1999) described how these stereotypes shape the socialization process in relation to boys:

> Whether unintentionally or deliberately, we tend to discourage emotional awareness in boys. Scientists who study the way parents shape their children's emotional responses find that parents tend to have preconceived stereotypic gender notions even about infants (like the father we know who bragged to us that his son didn't cry when he was circumcised). Because of this, parents provide a different emotional education for sons as opposed to daughters. (loc. 546–552)

9 Levant and Pollack (1995) asserted that it is not inherent in men's nature to prove their image of masculinity. "Men need to prove their manhood... because men are socialized to believe that their masculinity is something they have to prove" (loc. 458), not because, as Freud believed, they are "engaged in a constant struggle against what he called their 'feminine' or 'passive' side" (loc. 465–468).

10 A meta-analysis of almost 6,000 children conducted by Fearon, Bakermans-Kranenburg, van IJzendoorn, Lapsley, and Roisman (2010) found that boys, in particular, who were insecurely attached to their mothers had more behavior problems as adolescents and as adults than those who were securely attached to their mothers. Also see Rose and Rudolph (2006) for an analysis of the specific vulnerabilities of girls and boys in peer relationships, a precursor to later adult relationships.

11 Gurian (1996) acknowledged the difficulty that some mothers encounter in striving to allow their sons the freedom to develop independently of them and to seek their own way in life:

> A mother's "letting go" of her son does not mean the mother and son love each other less. It simply means she psychologically releases him from dependency on her and herself from dependency on him. This letting go is difficult, especially for single moms who do not have a community of emotionally healthy men around them or who have unreasonable emotional and social expectations of ex-husbands and other men, making it difficult for them to let their sons go into male culture.... Any mother who does not let go of a son risks that the son will grow up through adolescence punishing her or saving her feelings

> [idealizing her] and punishing women and society later in his adult male life. (loc. 1102–1111)

Regarding parentification and emotional hunger, it is interesting that "fathers who experienced a role reversal with their own mother were more likely to marry women who were in a role reversal with their son at 2 years of age" (Macfie, McElwain, Houts, & Cox, 2005, p. 61).

12 Regarding intrusiveness, emotional incest, and parentification and other "denied processes," Hooper (2007) contended that some family systems may engender an inappropriate overlap in subsystems, with members participating in roles that are traditionally reserved for other members (e.g., parents in childlike roles and children in parental roles), a phenomenon that facilitates parentification. Furthermore, in these families, boundaries can often be seen as distorted, rigid, or nonexistent (p. 220).

13 Men and women often have different reactions to becoming a parent. Crockenberg and Leerkes (2003) found that "new mothers whose parents failed to convey to them that they were loved and valued reported sadness and hopelessness throughout the transition to parenthood" (p. 89). An interesting related finding was that a new mother's memory of paternal rejection was strongly correlated with insensitive treatment of her infant (in those mothers who had postpartum depression).

CHAPTER 8

1 Findings from attachment research suggest that girls whose mothers were able to provide them with a secure attachment are likely, as adult women, to develop secure attachment bonds which include a caregiving behavioral system that serves "two major functions: (1) to meet the dependent partner's need for security by responding to signals of distress or potential threat (providing a *safe haven*); and (2) to support the attached person's autonomy and exploration when not distressed (providing a *secure base*)" (Collins & Ford, 2010, p. 236).

2 In these cases, the mother's responses are likely to be based on unresolved issues from her own childhood, which are unconsciously projected onto her daughter, leading to a preponderance of maladaptive responses. For example, Chodorow (1991) observed that many mothers appeared to lack a well-defined sense of self and unconsciously imposed their own anxiety and guilt on their daughters regarding separation issues:

> A kind of guilt that Western women express seems to grow out of and to reflect lack of adequate self/other distinctions and a sense of inescapable embeddedness in relationships to others.... The reason is that the mother-daughter relation is the one form of personal identification that, because it results so easily from the normal situation of child development, is liable to be excessive in the direction of allowing no room for separation or difference between mother and daughter. (pp. 58–59)

3 Negative elements in the mother-daughter bond and deficient maternal care may be correlated with subsequent emotional disturbances in adolescent girls. For example, "compared to boys, they show more depression and have poorer emotional wellbeing,... exhibit more negative self-appraisal,... and are more likely to encounter their first psychological disturbances" (L. Stern, 1991, p. 114). One survey on obesity and overweight (Swallen, Reither, Haas, & Meier, 2005) involving 4,743 adolescents found that "Girls were significantly more likely than boys to report poor general health, functional limitations, many illness symptoms, depression, and low self-esteem" (p. 344).

4 See Bullough, Shelton, and Slavin (1988). The authors cited H. R. Hays's (1964) anthropological findings regarding the origins of a patriarchal social structure, which they perceived as originating in and being supported by men's defensive reaction to their fear of women.

> Hays found that in preliterate cultures there was almost a universal fear of women's sexual functions. This fear was institutionalized in sanctions and restrictions not unlike similar restrictions in more sophisticated societies.... Though an occasional woman or even small groups of women protested male assumptions, they were never powerful enough to change them. Generally, in fact, punishment for challenging the traditional male view and the rewards for accepting it served to encourage women to accept their subordination. Since they could not change it, they reaped the rewards from playing a subordinate role. Only when enough women could begin to challenge this view, as they did in the nineteenth century, do we see any real evidence of change. (pp. 14–15)

Anne Roiphe (1996) cautioned readers not to turn insights about patriarchy into a "conspiracy" of "They 'Against' Us":

> When we speak of the patriarchy we speak of a social organization, a means of distributing power and kinship relations within society. We can look at how the patriarchy works, at kings, fathers, heads of departments, CEOs, etc. But the women's movement transformed the patriarchy into something harder to observe and pin down, a "they." ... This invisible conspiratorial "they" became a trope to which stuck all kinds of female anger.... The problem is that this anger, stronger in one woman than another because of her personal experience, is aimed at the one who should be her love object, her partner, her shelter as she should be his. It makes it difficult to love and be loved and support a child in a family if rage is blazing in the hearth. (pp. 61–63)

It is important also to consider cultural differences in exploring mother-daughter relationships, patriarchy, the feminist movement, and the process of individuation. For example, in a study by Rastogi and Wampler (1999), the authors concluded, "While intergenerational family therapy theories ... emphasize autonomy over dependence in family relationships the current findings support a more ethnic-focused examination of interdependence" (p. 334).

5 Regarding inhibited desire and withholding in couple relationships and marriage, see Chapter 8, "The Mother-Daughter Bond," in *Compassionate Child-Rearing* (Firestone, 1990a) and *The Fear of Being a Woman* (Rheingold, 1964). Rheingold observed that some women unilaterally withdraw from their husbands almost "from the beginning of the marriage.... This detachment from marriage and motherhood is a fundamental defense" (p. 462). One of Rheingold's patients put it this way, "It was better to pretend you didn't want something than to be heart-broken" (p. 464).

Elizabeth Debold (1991) has also described the results of women's suppression of desire as follows:

> The ideals that they [women] take in and hold in their minds—ideals reflecting the construct of femininity—split their feelings for hunger, passion and play from their knowing. The result of this is a series of losses that live in the psyche, caught and frozen at the age where they were severed from consciousness. (p. 181)

C. Gilligan (1991) proposed that therapy could offer girls a solution for the split described by Debold, thereby reawakening wanting and desire:

> Therapists are in a key position to strengthen healthy resistance and courage, to help women recover lost voices and tell lost stories, and to provide safe houses for the underground...and [to facilitate] a political resistance which exposes false relationships and brings relational violations out into the open, to a healthy resistance to disconnection...the resistance which is rooted in *wanting* and having honest relationships. (p. 27)

6 Regarding gender differences in children related to separating from the primary identification with the mother, according to C. Gilligan (1982, 1991, 1995, 2011), both boys and girls encounter difficulties in individuating and separating from the maternal figure at different stages in their development. Both sacrifice aspects of self in order to fit into a patriarchal social order. With respect to girls' and boys' preservation of an emotionally healthy connection with the mother, Gilligan (1995) pointed out,

> In studies of girls' psychological development, my colleagues and I have witnessed the onset of dissociative processes at adolescence. Girls at this time face a relational crisis or developmental impasse which has its parallel in the relationship crisis of boys' early childhood....This is the time when girls are pressed from within and without to take in and take on the interpretive framework of patriarchy and to regulate their sexuality, their relationships, their desires and their judgments in its terms. As for boys in early childhood, this internalization of a patriarchal voice leads to a loss of relationship or a compromise between voice and relationships, leaving a psychological wound or scar. The asymmetry I have posited between boys' and girls' development finds confirmation in the considerable evidence showing that boys are more psychologically at risk than girls throughout the childhood years and that girls' psychological strengths and resilience are suddenly at risk in adolescence. (p. 120)

Also see *Female Identity Conflict in Clinical Practice* (Bernstein, Freedman, & Distler, 1993), particularly Chapter 1 on "Gender-Specific Attribution of Identity" (Bernstein & Freedman, 1993).

7 As noted, Rheingold (1964, 1967) observed similar fears in over 2,500 pregnant women he interviewed during his 12-year experimental study. He found that the mother's ambivalence usually continued unabated long after the child was born, although the more negative aspects were either completely forgotten or partially repressed. With respect to the effects on children of mothers who develop postpartum depression or who have suffered recent trauma or loss, see Andre Green's (1983/1986) essay "The Dead Mother." Here Green described a situation in which the infant's mother becomes depressed because of a profound loss in her own life:

> Thus, if the Oedipus complex is reached and even bypassed, the dead mother complex will give it a particularly dramatic aspect. Fixation to the mother will prevent the girl from ever being able to cathect the imago of the father, without the fear of losing the mother's love; or else if love for the father is deeply repressed, without her being able to avoid transferring onto the father's imago a large part of the characteristics that have been projected onto the mother. (p. 157)

Expanding on Green's concept of the "dead mother," Van Buren (2007) suggested that it contributes to the development of withholding patterns and a general withdrawal from life:

> Green is talking about a pathological organization that overcomes loss by stopping the vibrations of life....I think the sense of nothing, doubtful existence,

> or precarious going on being, is intensely related to the feeling of abjection; i.e., to have lost or never to have found the belief in one's own existence or being. The complex of the dead mother ties us to her certain deadness, the avoidance of the feelings of lack, loss and mortality is managed; for she is always there, unchanging since she never dies.... The more massive the embrace is felt, the more life is arrested, and the more the risks of emerging from the dead mother are felt to be life-threatening. Perhaps some of the processes of encapsulation related to psychological withdrawal and deadness can be understood in this way. (p. 24)

Fortunately, a father's involvement often provides the means of escape from the prison of the dead mother complex. For example, Crockenberg and Leerkes (2003) have shown that the father's involvement and warmth can ameliorate the aversive effect that the depressed or emotionally unavailable mother can have on the infant or small child. These researchers found that in many young women, "remembered paternal acceptance served as a buffer against the potentially negative impact of maternal postpartum depression on maternal sensitivity" (p. 91). Also see Lucy Holmes's (2008) chapter, "The Object Within: Childbirth as a Developmental Milestone," in *The Internal Triangle.*

8 Regarding the guilt that many women experience in relation to pursuing a heterosexual relationship, marriage, and/or a career, see "Feminine Guilt and the Oedipus Complex" (Chasseguet-Smirgel, 1970); *Mother, Madonna, Whore* (Welldon, 1988); and "Work and Success Inhibitions" in *Women in Therapy* (Lerner, 1988).

9 Other theorists have written about the conflict of interest existing between men and women in forming a relationship. Hudson and Jacot (1995) emphasized that a "less familiar feature of female development... [which] is a potent source of mutual incomprehension between the sexes... and has its point of origin in the rivalry, fantasied or real, between the small girl and her mother" (p. 8). They concluded,

> As she cannot express her anger towards her mother without threatening her own identity, the small girl's anger will also tend to translate itself into depression.... For women, in other words: Heterosexual intimacy taps automatically into deep reservoirs of unresolved hostility, blame and depression. (p. 9)
>
> Less obvious is the implication that women will be more likely than men to become depressed in marriages and intimacies that are going well. Again the statistical evidence is confirmatory: among the happily married, women are five times as likely to be depressed as men.... [This indicates that] a significant source of a woman's discontent lies within herself. (p. 10)

10 Regarding women's competitiveness, several years ago, I (R. Firestone) observed this phenomenon in a discussion group composed of professional colleagues. The group was initially made up of four men and one woman. The woman participant was active and lively. One evening, a new woman member was introduced. Almost immediately and in subsequent sessions, the first woman participant became quiet and faded into the background. At first, the new woman flourished, was quite outspoken, and attracted attention from the men participants. Later, this pattern was repeated when two more women, one at a time, joined the group. Each previously new member, in turn, withdrew from her active participation in the group. Subsequently, in exploring the reasons for this odd turn of events, the women revealed a basic fear of standing out and competing with the newcomers, which they had acted on without conscious awareness. The unconscious material that these women brought out is supportive of our hypothesis that women fear other women and often retreat from the symbolic competition with their mothers or mother substitutes.

11 In describing how other women support and reinforce a woman's fear of differentiation and nonconformity, Rheingold (1964) observed,

> Being an individual means emancipation from maternal domination, and that entails reprisal.... The conformity factor operates to cause the woman to try to replicate the marriage of her mother. She must keep house as mother did, she must respond sexually (or not respond) as mother did, and treat her husband in the same way, and she must rear her children by the same practices. Still other wives conform to an abstract idea of what marriage should be, constructed of the opinions of mother and other women. (p. 465)

12 In descriptive accounts similar to those of Streep (2009), L. Kaplan (1984) wrote about young girls who often experienced parental prohibitions and perfectionistic attitudes as "internal voices":

> Prohibitions and commandments then will continue to be experienced as coming from outside the self, or as alien inner voices. One of the major complaints of the anorectic is that she cannot rid herself of the sense that she always acts on the commands of others. "There is another self, a dictator who dominates me.... A little man screams at me when I think of eating." (p. 269)

CHAPTER 9

1 In a previous work, I (R. Firestone, 1997a) explained the core resistance to progress in psychotherapy as based on the fear of disrupting psychological defenses that function to protect one from emotional pain, separation anxiety, and existential dread. On an unconscious level, people are afraid that if they were to dismantle their defenses, they would be overwhelmed by the same anguish and terror they endured in childhood, both at the time their defenses were formed and again when they first discovered death and dying.

This theoretical approach has been supported by extensive studies conducted over the past three decades by terror management theorists and researchers. Sheldon Solomon, Tom Pyszczynski, Jeff Greenberg, and their colleagues have demonstrated people's increased reliance on defense mechanisms as a result of experimentally manipulating their death awareness. In elucidating the myriad effects that these defenses have on human behavior and choices, their work has reinforced Becker's (1973/1997) thesis that an awareness of death impels people to first construct and then immerse themselves in cultural worldviews and institutions that deny death. See Arndt, Greenberg, Pyszczynski, and Solomon (1997) and S. Solomon, Greenberg, and Pyszczynski (2004).

2 Regarding the core conflict, for an exploration of other findings in terror management research, see "Tales From Existential Oceans: Terror Management Theory and How the Awareness of Our Mortality Affects Us All" by Jamie Arndt and Matthew Vess (2008). Regarding the basic dilemma facing all humans, Arndt and Vess commented,

> From this [Becker's] perspective, the existential dilemma is conceptualized as the conflict between our biological proclivity to survive and our cognitive capabilities to be aware that death is inevitable. The human ability for symbolic, temporal, and self-referenced thought comes with the price of knowing that death is stalking us all and can catch up to us at any time. Such knowledge has the potential to arouse overwhelming feelings of terror... and thus, the core proposition of TMT [terror management theory] is that people need to manage this anxiety.... TMT, in a nutshell, seeks to explain how we symbolically try to avoid "being there" when it [death] happens. (pp. 911–912)

From the present authors' perspective, the core conflict involves the choice between defensively avoiding death and living with awareness of one's personal mortality.

3 Viewing death anxiety as proportionally related to degree of individuation also facilitates an understanding of clients' fear of change, negative therapeutic reactions related to significant improvement, and the anxiety associated with the termination of therapy. As McCarthy (1980) put it,

> If the goal of the psychoanalytic work is the patient's freedom and autonomy, and the patient retains the unconscious fears that autonomy equals death or the loss of the self, then the positive outcome of the analysis may be as anxiety-provoking as the original inner conflicts. (p. 193)

4 Regarding microsuicidal behavior, including various forms of mental illness, terror management researchers Pyszczynski, Solomon, and Greenberg (2003) described studies that involved experimentally raising death salience in normal individuals and in those with phobias and obsessive-compulsive disorder. They reported,

> These findings are consistent with the notion that phobic and obsessive-compulsive individuals transform overwhelming anxiety about death into specific and, hence, controllable fears and obsessive-compulsive activities, respectively. In so doing, they "manage" terror somewhat, but this defensive death-denying shrinking of life to an avoidance of spiders or washing of hands is ultimately limiting and unsatisfying. That is why Yalom [1980] describes mental illness as clumsy death denial. (p. 120)

Yalom (1980), Searles (1961), and Karon and VandenBos (1981) have also linked early loss of a parent, difficulty in mourning the loss, and an inability to manage death anxiety to the onset of schizophrenia in early adulthood. For example, Yalom described several sources of death anxiety in schizophrenic patients:

> A third source of intense death anxiety emanates from the nature of the schizophrenic patient's early relationship to mother—a symbiotic union from which the patient has never emerged but in which he or she continues to oscillate between a position of psychological merger and a state of total unrelatedness.... Furthermore, the schizophrenic patient perceives that the symbiotic relationship is absolutely necessary to survival. (pp. 151–152)

Yalom's hypotheses regarding the schizophrenic patient's maintenance of *psychological merger* with the mother is similar in some respects to the first author's understanding of the fantasy bond, the imagined merger with the mother or primary caretaker, as a core defense against death anxiety. See Chapter 5 in *Beyond Death Anxiety* (Firestone & Catlett, 2009a).

5 In exploring the dynamics underlying defensive behaviors that insecurely attached individuals utilize to buffer death anxiety, Mikulincer, Florian, and Hirschberger (2004) proposed the idea that close relationships can function to ameliorate the fear of death. They reviewed "empirical data showing that the quest for love and closeness acts as an additional death-anxiety buffering mechanism" (p. 287). Specifically, Mikulincer and Florian (2000) found that individuals with insecure attachment patterns have different responses to experimentally aroused death awareness than do those with secure attachments. They noted that avoidant individuals "may search for impersonal defensive shields (e.g., worldview validation) that may protect them from mortality concerns without depending on the help of significant others" (p. 271). Anxious-ambivalent persons "have serious doubts

about their inner forces and others' intentions, [and] they probably can only search for the defensive path of worldview validation" (p. 271).

6 Regarding symbolic immortality in terms of gene survival, David Cooper (1970/1971) depicted the effects on children of well-meaning parents who exert subtle forms of psychological control over their children in order to ensure their similarity to them (the parents). Cooper also described family taboos against children experiencing their individuality and separateness. In one illustrative narrative, he wrote about a young boy's first startling realization of his true aloneness and his existence as a person separate from parents and family:

> There are numerous taboos in the family system that reach much further than the incest taboo and taboos against greed and messiness. One of these taboos is the implicit prohibition against experiencing one's aloneness in the world. (p. 13)
>
> A boy called Philip, at the age of six years, lived with his parents in a hotel owned by relatives. All his life he had been assiduously cared for. *He had never been left alone* [italics added] for a moment. But then one day, playing in the gardens, he rested his hands on a white-washed birdbath and looked into the mossy water reflecting the sky. With a shock, he looked up at the sky, seeing it for the first time as if initiated into awareness of its reality by its reflection.
>
> Then he realized in a moment of suffocation, which was also a moment of liberation, his total contingency and aloneness in the world. He knew that from that moment onward he could call to no-one, and that no-one could call to him in any way that would deflect the trajectory of his life project, which he now knew he had already chosen—although of course the details would have to be filled in.
>
> His mother called out that supper was ready. He went in to eat, but for the first time he knew that he was no longer his mother's child but was, in fact, his own person. The point is that Philip could not say one word about his experience to anyone else in his family that would not be contorted into *their* terms or into some joke about *their* boy. (pp. 14–15)

7 Regarding literal immortality and St. Augustine's interpretation of the creation myth, see Elaine Pagels's (1988) *Adam, Eve, and the Serpent.* Beginning with her analysis of scriptures discovered in the Dead Sea Scrolls, Pagels's scholarly recounting of early Christianity demonstrated that the basis of the belief that people are born bad probably originated in the fifth century in the teachings of Augustine, who reinterpreted the creation myth. Augustine believed that, because Adam and Eve disobeyed God, the human race inherited a nature irreversibly damaged by their sin. Pagels noted that Augustine identified sexual desire as evidence of, and penalty for, original sin, thereby implicating the whole human race.

CHAPTER 10

1 For a philosophical discussion of the circularity of the complex relationship that exists between the individual and society, see Anthony Giddens (1991). Postmodern psychologists, including social constructivists, place considerable importance on historical, cultural, and social processes in explaining this interaction. For example, Gergen (2001) noted,

> [Cultural] psychologists have proposed that the very conceptions of the self, cognition, emotion, and so on are born within cultural traditions.... In this case, the self is a matter of how one is constructed in various relationships, to possess an emotion is to perform appropriately in a culturally constituted scenario,

> and to possess a memory is to take part in a process of communal negotiation and sanction. (p. 810)

Developmental psychologist Urie Bronfenbrenner (1994/2004) has proposed a *bioecological paradigm* of human development to highlight the complexity of the linkages between genetic inheritance and familial, societal, and historical factors that impact the growing child.

Regarding the numerous ways in which modern institutions, beliefs, and social mores restrict or oppress the individual, see Habermas (1984), who asserted that the loss of personal freedom is one of the major consequences of the repressive nature of secular beliefs that are inherent in capitalism. According to Habermas, capitalism has its roots in the Protestant ethic:

> The take-off of capitalist development drew upon the qualities of a way of life that owed its methodical rationality to the unifying power of the ascetic ethic that was generalized within Protestantism. . . . By the very negation of the will to self-preservation on earth in favor of the preservation of the eternal soul, *Christianity* asserted the infinite value of each man, an ideal that penetrated even non-Christian or anti-Christian systems of the Western world. True, the price was the repression of the vital instincts and, since such repression is never successful, an insincerity that pervades our culture. (p. 351)

A more popular version of the interplay between the individual and society can be found in Christakis and Fowler (2009). Their book elucidates the science of social networks, which "provides a distinct way of seeing the world because it is about individuals *and* groups, and about how the former actually become the latter" (loc. 554–561). Also see Watts (2004) and Brafman and Brafman (2008).

2 See "Are the Beautiful Good in Hollywood? An Investigation of the Beauty-and-Goodness Stereotype on Film" by S. Smith, McIntosh, and Bazzini (1999) as one example. These researchers empirically demonstrated a previous finding showing that "the entertainment media has been implicated as a source of this stereotype, primarily by portraying physically attractive characters as 'good' and unattractive characters as 'bad'" (p. 70).

3 A number of theorists have described religious motivations that are largely nondefensive in nature. For example, R. Beck (2004) contrasted "defensive religious belief" (fundamentalism, the belief that sacred texts are literally true) with "existential religion" ("faith stances that fully recognize our existential situation but which actively refuse to believe as a means to repress existential terror") (p. 210). Becker (1975) has also noted that the degree of inherent malevolence or benevolence arising from the death-denying function of a given culture can be evaluated by determining its overall effect on human lives.

> If each historical society is in some ways a lie or a mystification, the study of society becomes *the revelation of the lie.* The comparative study of society becomes *the assessment of how high are the costs of this lie.* Or, looked at from another way, cultures are fundamentally and basically *styles of heroic death denial.* . . . What are the costs of such denials of death. . . . These costs can be tallied roughly in two ways: in terms of the tyranny practiced within the society, and in terms of the victimage practiced against aliens or "enemies" outside it. (p. 125)

4 Cultural anthropologists Henrich and Boyd (2001) found several cultural practices that, in combination with the psychological processes of imitation and conformity, have functioned to increase humans' prosocial tendencies, such as cooperating and sharing, even with non-kin others. Utilizing their "cultural evolutionary model," they explained how "norms for cooperating and punishment are acquired via two cognitive mechanisms:

(1) payoff-based transmission—a tendency to copy the most successful individual; and (2) conformist transmission—a tendency to copy the most frequent behavior in the population" (p. 79).

5 See Rawls's (1999) *A Theory of Justice,* where he outlined his theory of distributive justice and how it would be applied (in an ideal world) to social institutions. Specifically, Rawls proposed that "in a just society the liberties of equal citizenship are taken as settled; the rights secured by justice are not subject to political bargaining or to the calculus of social interests" (pp. 3–4). In defining his second "principle of difference," Rawls emphasized that "the second holds that social and economic inequalities, for example inequalities of wealth and authority, are just only if they result in compensating benefits for everyone, and in particular for the least advantaged members of society" (p. 13).

6 See volume 1 of *The Open Society and Its Enemies,* in which Karl Popper (1966) described one of the sources of the political cliché "might makes right" in terms of the totalitarian state or nation:

> [Plato] constantly reiterates that what threatens to harm the city is morally wicked and unjust.... This is the collectivist, the tribal, the totalitarian theory of morality: "Good is what is in the interest of my group; or my tribe; or my state...." The state itself can never be wrong in any of its actions, as long as it is strong. (p. 107)

7 Stereotypic thinking in both public and professional discourse has been challenged by Janet Hyde (2005) and Alice Eagly (1995). Eagly and Diekman (2006) have proposed that "stereotypical interpretations, for example, that women's sentimental or risk-averse qualities underlie gender gaps in attitudes and voting, obscure their true origins. Our research findings suggest that these origins are deeply embedded in the gender division of labor" (p. 32). Two other works, *Joining the Resistance* by Carol Gilligan (2011) and *The Deepening Darkness: Patriarchy, Resistance, and Democracy's Future* by Carol Gilligan and David A. J. Richards (2009), have challenged the accuracy of gender stereotypes while delineating the harmful effects of patriarchy.

8 Regarding stereotypic attitudes toward the elderly that are prevalent in society, Brafman and Brafman (2008) cited a number of studies demonstrating that "negative stereotypes about aging contribute to memory loss and cardiovascular weakness, and even reduce overall life expectancy by an average of 7.5 years" (loc. 1167–1171). See McHugh (2003) and R. Butler's (2008) revealing commentary regarding one tragic consequence of ageism in our society: "Within 24 hours following the 9/11 terrorist attacks, animal advocates were on the scene rescuing pets, yet older and disabled people were abandoned in their apartments for up to seven days before ad hoc medical teams arrived to rescue them" (p. 10).

9 Specifically in relation to neglect, Rachel Kelly (2007) recommended "a universally recognized operational definition of child neglect that focuses on children and their individual needs." She cited research showing that "Child protective agencies and professional child protection workers tend to look for immediate physical harm.... By recognizing neglect only when there is 'imminent harm,' the law fails to recognize or intervene in the majority of neglectful situations" (p. 157).

In a report published by *The Lancet* exposing the underreporting of child maltreatment, Gilbert et al. (2009) called attention to the fact that "Every year, about 4–16% of children are physically abused and one in ten is neglected or psychologically abused.... However, official rates for substantiated child maltreatment indicate less than *a tenth* of this burden" (p. 68). Other surveys have shown that the prevalence of neglect increased throughout the 1990s. Interpreting these findings, Jones, Finkelhor, and Halter (2006) suggested that

> the failure of neglect to decline nationally...is something of an enigma. One possibility is that neglect is harder to prevent or has not been subject to the same intervention efforts or other social change factors that have helped with physical and sexual abuse. (p. 116)

10 Regarding the "ideal family," see Garbarino's (1995) discussion of "What Makes a Family Successful," in *Raising Children in a Socially Toxic Environment* (pp. 52–59).

11 Garbarino and Gilliam (1980) reported,

> There is clear legal sanction for the use of physical force against children. The Texas legislature, for example, in 1974 enacted legislation containing the following statement: "The use of force, but not deadly force, against a child younger than 18 years is justified: (1) if the actor is the child's parent or step-parent...(2) when and to the degree the actor believes the force is necessary to discipline the child." (p. 32)

12 See Grolnick et al. (1997) in Grusec and Kuczynski (1997). These researchers asserted, "Insofar as socializers force behaviors onto children they may, unwittingly, stifle the very assimilatory tendencies required for successful socialization" (p. 135).

13 Tendencies toward conformity are driven by still another fear that intensifies the anxiety associated with threats of social exclusion: fears about loss of identity or one's sense of self. For example, as described in the present chapter, Williams et al. (2000) tested whether people would be affected by ostracism even under artificial circumstances. In Study 1, participants were asked to use mental visualization while playing a virtual tossing game on their computer with two others (who were actually computer generated and controlled). The more the participants were ostracized, "the more they reported feeling bad, having less control, and losing a sense of belonging. In Study 2, ostracized participants were more likely to conform on a subsequent task" (p. 748). Also see Zadro, Boland, and Richardson (2006) and Hornsey and Jetten (2004). Bond and Smith (1996) found that "Collectivist countries tended to show higher levels of conformity than individualist countries" (p. 111).

14 Glick and Fiske (1996) found that women who question stereotypic attitudes and/or "reject traditional sexist roles and responsibilities...confront simultaneously both hostile and benevolent sexism" (p. 507). According to Holiday and Rosenberg (2009),

> There are pressures from within and outside groups to behave in ways that match the female stereotype. It means a woman must accept and internalize characteristics attributed to stereotypically feminine women in U.S. culture, and then behave as she is "supposed to" behave. (loc. 1730–1733)

For a description of the conventional role expectations to which Elena was unwilling to conform, see *The Erotic Silence of the American Wife* by Heyn (1993). In this controversial book, Heyn observed the detrimental effects on children of women who sacrificed themselves and their priorities in adopting the role of wife and mother:

> "Good" as it applies to the Perfect Wife inevitably modifies and diminishes the word "self"—as in self-sacrifice, self-abnegate, self-restraint, self-denial—the prefix always restraining or containing in a effort to make that woman's self a little less *something*."...Her virtue exists in direct proportion to how much of her self is whittled away. (Cited by Debold, Wilson, & Malave, 1993, p. 93)

CHAPTER 11

1 Regarding leader-follower relationships, see Davidovitz, Mikulincer, Shaver, Izsak, and Popper's (2007) article, "Leaders as Attachment Figures." Also see Siegel and McCall's (2009) "Mindsight at Work: An Interpersonal Neurobiology Lens on Leadership," in which the authors noted that "the wisest leaders invite self-leadership in others—enabling and encouraging their differentiation while cultivating their linking communication with one another" ("Integration and the Triangle of Well-being" section, para. 2).

2 Regarding Havel's statement, Karp and Helgo (2009) asserted that "the identity and behavior of the leader is, thus, as much formed by the group as he or she forms the group in his or her recognition of others" (p. 883). Vroom and Jago (2007) reported a study showing that "leaders confronted with ineffective teams behaved in a much less considerate and supportive manner than those confronted with effective teams. Leader behavior can therefore be an effect of subordinate behavior as well as a cause of it" (p. 19).

3 In an effort to integrate the earlier "universal traits" theory of leadership with more contemporary interactional theories, Zaccaro (2007) argued that "combinations of traits and attributes, integrated in conceptually meaningful ways, are more likely to predict leadership than additive or independent contributions of several single traits" (p. 6). Other theorists, including Stogdill (1948), have contended that different situations require different qualities and abilities in a leader.

4 Wood (2005) proposed, "The 'essence' of leadership is not the individual social actor but a relation of almost imperceptible directions, movement and orientations having neither beginning nor end" (p. 1115). In applying Wood's concept to the training and development of leaders, Karp and Helgo (2009) suggested that "leadership is perhaps better understood as a dynamic process which occurs between people rather than depending on the individual characteristics of the leader—appointed or not.... Leadership is a development process not suitable for everyone" (pp. 883–884).

According to Riggio (2008), "The practice of leadership, just like the practice of medicine, or law, or any other profession, is a continual learning process.... The motivation to develop and the ability to accept constructive criticism are prerequisites for positive change to actually occur" (p. 387). Hackman and Wageman (2007) cited Sternberg's (2007) assertion that "continuous learning almost always requires that leaders overcome inherently self-limiting aspects of their existing mental models" (p. 46). Also see works by Bruce Avolio (2005, 2007) and Murphy and Reichard (2011).

5 Regarding the ethics of leadership, Bass and Steidlmeier (1998) have proposed, "For many moral analysts, leadership is a many-headed hydra that alternatively shows the faces of Saddam Hussein and Pol Pat as well as the faces of Nelson Mandela and Mother Theresa" (p. 1). Also relevant are Neubert, Carlson, Kacmar, Roberts, and Chonko (2009) and Moore (2007). According to Moore, "Two cognitive mechanisms (displacement of responsibility and diffusion of responsibility) *minimize the role of the individual* in the harm that is caused by an individual's actions" (p. 130).

6 The basic tenets of the servant-leadership model have been articulated for the general public by Stephen Covey (1999) and Wheatley and Kellner-Rogers (1998). Also see Senge, Kleiner, Roberts, Ross, and Smith (1994) and Greenleaf's (1970) original essay on the servant-leadership model, where he stated, "It begins with the natural feeling that one wants to serve, to serve first.... The best test is: Do those served grow as persons, do they, while being served, become healthier, wiser, freer, more autonomous, more likely themselves to become servants?" (p. 4). Page and Wong (2000) suggested that "to learn servant leadership, individuals need to undergo a journey of self-discovery and personal transformation" (p. 69).

7 The accumulation of power by an individual who achieves a high position of leadership may also contribute to a decreased sensitivity to the needs of followers. For example, in four studies investigating power and perspective-taking, Galinsky, Magee, Inesi, and

Gruenfeld (2006) found, "Power was associated with a reduced tendency to comprehend how other individuals see the world, think about the world, and feel about the world" (p. 1072).

8 In articulating the relationship between power and leadership, Galinsky, Jordan, and Sivanathan (2008) proposed,

> Power and leadership are *not* synonymous and they diverge on a number of important dimensions: First, power's influence is derived from the ability to provide or withhold resources or administer punishments.... In contrast, the influence of leadership emerges not from the lure of incentives but by inspiring through rhetoric and being the exemplar of desired behavior.... Second, power and leadership often differ on the ultimate purpose or goal of wielding one's influence. Power's influence is often directed towards satisfying personal desires. In contrast, leaders exert influence to help the group reach a shared goal. (p. 285)

9 Lammers, Stoker, and Stapel (2009) have made an important distinction between personal power and social power:

> Personal power is power over oneself and freedom from the influence of others. People who experience a substantial amount of personal power are unconstrained by, and independent from, others.... Social power, on the other hand, is associated with interdependence rather than with independence.... It is therefore strongly linked with the need for responsibility. (p. 1544)

Lammers et al. (2009) cited the research of Van Dijke and Poppe (2006), who "showed that, in general, people prefer to increase their personal power (i.e., independence from others) but have no special desire for social power (over others)" (p. 1544).

10 In describing power relations in couples and families, Langner and Keltner (2008) pointed out that, in many couples, a certain form of social power may be exercised in which one partner exerts influence over the other person through the allocation of resources and punishments. Findings from two studies demonstrated that "being subject to a partner's elevated social power...was associated with increased negative emotion" (p. 848) in the other person.

11 Regarding psychological control in family constellations, Walling, Mills, and Freeman (2007) found that "sensitivity to hurt and disapproval of negative emotion were associated with more frequent reported use of psychological control" (p. 642) by both mothers and fathers. The authors proposed that parents' hostility and perfectionistic attitudes are also linked to the use of psychological control in relation to their children.

12 One example of the dynamics operating in cases where the key (leader) fits the lock (followers) can be found in an article by Hing, Bobocel, Zanna, and McBride (2007), "Authoritarian Dynamics and Unethical Decision Making: High Social Dominance Orientation Leaders and High Right-Wing Authoritarianism Followers." The researchers attempted to answer an important and timely question regarding unethical behavior in organizations: "When dilemmas require trade-offs between profits and ethics, do leaders high in social dominance orientation (SDO) and followers high in right-wing authoritarianism (RWA) make decisions that are more unethical than those made by others?" (p. 67). Preliminary results from four studies provided an affirmative answer to this question, leading the researchers to conjecture, "We suspect that something special is created when a leader driven by dominance over others and lacking empathy is paired with a follower driven by obedience to authority and lacking independence" (p. 78).

We suggest that individuals with lower levels of differentiation may be more susceptible to adopting a right-wing authoritarian (RWA) position. James Gilligan's (2011) recent book, *Why Some Politicians Are More Dangerous Than Others,* cited relevant research showing a significant correlation between scores on the RWA Scale and the party affiliation of state senators: "all Republicans scored above the mean on the RWA Scale, whether they were from Red or Blue States" (p. 143).

13 Findings from two studies (Cohen et al., 2004, 2005) supported the hypothesis that "people would show increased preference for a charismatic political candidate and decreased preference for a relationship-oriented political candidate in response to subtle reminders of death" (Cohen et al., 2004, p. 846). The 2005 (Cohen et al., 2005) study showed specifically that more registered voters who were reminded of death (experimental condition) said they intended to vote for George W. Bush (perceived as the more charismatic, action-taking leader), whereas more voters who were not reminded of death (control condition) said they intended to vote for John Kerry (perceived as more rational or laid-back by voters).

14 According to Avolio (2007), "Leadership theory and research has reached a point in its development at which it needs to move to the next level of integration—considering the dynamic interplay between leaders and followers" (p. 25). Lipman-Blumen (2005c) has suggested that, as followers, we need

> to take responsibility for ourselves, as well as for others... to cultivate new coping strategies. In fact, soberly recognizing that the leader's assurances are little more than grand illusions is a necessary condition for confident constituents—and the society in which they live—to survive and flourish. (p. 14)

CHAPTER 12

1 See the definition of ethical behaviors in Chapter 3, "A Moral Perspective on Relationships," in *The Ethics of Interpersonal Relationships* (Firestone & Catlett, 2009b).

2 Doidge (2007) explained that it was Freud who first proposed the law that "neurons that fire together wire together, usually referred to as Hebb's law.... Freud stated that when two neurons fire *simultaneously,* this firing facilitates their ongoing *association*" (loc. 3594–3599). "He observed that memories are not written down once, or 'engraved,' to remain unchanged forever but can be altered by subsequent events and *re-transcribed*... [and] could take on an altered meaning for patients years after they occurred" (loc. 3613–3618). "To be changed, Freud argued, memories had to be conscious and become the focus of our conscious attention, as neuroscientists have since shown" (loc. 3618–3622).

> Analysis helps patients put their unconscious procedural memories and actions into words and into context, so they can better understand them. In the process they plastically re-transcribe these procedural memories, so that they become conscious explicit memories, sometimes for the first time, and patients no longer need to "relive" or "reenact" them, especially if they were traumatic. (loc. 3697–3702)

3 A number of assessment instruments have been developed to determine levels of self-differentiation and adult functioning, including the Differentiation of Self Inventory (Skowron & Friedlander, 1998), which assesses four dimensions of differentiation: "Emotional Reactivity (ER), 'I' Position (IP), Emotional Cutoff (EC), and Fusion with Others (FO)" (Skowron & Schmitt, 2003, p. 214); the Pathology of Separation-Individuation

(Lapsley & Horton, 2002); and the Personal Authority in the Family System Questionnaire Manual (Bray, 2004).

4 Erikson's stages of identity formation differ from those formulated by S. Freud (1905/1955). In a seminal work, "Three Essays on the Theory of Sexuality," Freud depicted the mature, emotionally healthy adult as having successfully progressed through four psychosexual developmental stages—oral, anal, phallic, and latency—to arrive at the genital stage, which is attained by "mature" individuals at some point during late adolescence or early adulthood.

5 Regarding another possible path toward increased differentiation, research has shown that mindfulness and other meditative practices are effective as adjuncts to psychotherapy for improving both physical and mental health. The practice may also facilitate personal development and movement toward individuation. Siegel (2010) described how mindfulness practice can integrate and strengthen neuronal connections in both therapists' and clients' minds: "Our job as mindful therapists is to cultivate mindsight in ourselves so we can detect chaos and rigidity and then identify which neural areas need to be freed to differentiate and link toward integration" (loc. 4181–4190). Regarding mindfulness practices incorporated into psychotherapy, see *The Brain-Savvy Therapist's Workbook* by Bonnie Badenoch (2011) and "The Use of Meditation in Psychotherapy: A Review of the Literature" by Greg Bogart (1991).

Jack Kornfield (1993) has written a thought-provoking and balanced perspective on meditation practice:

> For most people meditation practice doesn't "do it all." At best, it's one important piece of a complex path of opening and awakening.... Meditation and spiritual practice can easily be used to suppress and avoid feeling or to escape from difficult areas of our lives.... Does this mean we should trade meditation for psychotherapy? Not at all. Therapy isn't the solution either. Consciousness is!... The best therapy, like the best meditation practice, uses awareness to heal the heart and is concerned not so much with our stories, as with fear and attachment and their release, and with bringing mindfulness to areas of delusion, grasping and unnecessary suffering. (pp. 67–68)

REFERENCES

Allport, G. W. (1954). *The nature of prejudice.* New York, NY: Basic Books.

Altemeyer, B. (1996). *The authoritarian specter.* Cambridge, MA: Harvard University Press.

Amato, P. R. (1994). Father-child relations, mother-child relations and offspring psychological well-being in adulthood. *Journal of Marriage and the Family, 56,* 1031–1042.

Anthony, S. (1973). *The discovery of death in childhood and after.* Harmondsworth, England: Penguin Education. (Original work published 1971)

Anzalone, F. M. (2007). Servant leadership: A new model for law library leaders. *Law Library Journal, 99,* 793–812.

Aries, E. (1997). Women and men talking: Are they worlds apart? In M. R. Walsh (Ed.), *Women, men, and gender: Ongoing debates* (pp. 91–100). New Haven, CT: Yale University Press.

Arieti, S. (1974). *Interpretation of schizophrenia* (2nd ed.). New York, NY: Basic Books.

Arndt, J., Greenberg, J., & Cook, A. (2002). Mortality salience and the spreading activation of worldview-relevant constructs: Exploring the cognitive architecture of terror management. *Journal of Experimental Psychology: General, 131,* 307–324.

Arndt, J., Greenberg, J., Pyszczynski, T., & Solomon, S. (1997). Subliminal exposure to death-related stimuli increases defense of the cultural worldview. *Psychological Science, 8,* 379–385.

Arndt, J., Greenberg, J., Solomon, S., Pyszczynski, T., & Schimel, J. (1999). Creativity and terror management: Evidence that creative activity increases guilt and social projection following mortality salience. *Journal of Personality and Social Psychology, 77,* 19–32.

Arndt, J., & Vess, M. (2008). Tales from existential oceans: Terror management theory and how the awareness of our mortality affects us all. *Social and Personality Psychology Compass, 2,* 909–928.

Arnett, J. J. (2000). Emerging adulthood: A theory of development from the late teens through the twenties. *American Psychologist, 55,* 469–480.

Arnett, J. J. (2004). *Emerging adulthood: The winding road from the late teens through the twenties.* New York, NY: Oxford University Press. [Amazon Kindle version]

Arnett, J. J., Ramos, K. D., & Jensen, L. A. (2001). Ideological views in emerging adulthood: Balancing autonomy and community. *Journal of Adult Development, 8,* 69–79.

Asch, S. E. (1956). Studies of independence and conformity: A minority of one against a unanimous majority. *Psychological Monographs, 70* (9, Whole No. 417).

Avolio, B. J. (2005). *Leadership development in balance: Made/born.* Mahwah, NJ: Lawrence Erlbaum.

Avolio, B. J. (2007). Promoting more integrative strategies for leadership theory-building. *American Psychologist, 62,* 25–33.

Bach, G. R., & Deutsch, R. M. (1979). *Stop! You're driving me crazy.* New York, NY: Berkley Books.

Badenoch, B. (2008). *Being a brain-wise therapist: A practical guide to interpersonal neurobiology.* New York, NY: W. W. Norton.

Badenoch, B. (2011). *The brain-savvy therapist's workbook.* New York, NY: W. W. Norton.

Bakermans-Kranenburg, M. J., & van IJzendoorn, M. H. (1993). A psychometric study of the Adult Attachment Interview: Reliability and discriminant validity. *Developmental Psychology, 29,* 870–879.

Bakhtin, M. M. (1973). *Problems of Dostoevsky's poetics* (2nd ed.). (R. W. Rotsel, Trans.). Ann Arbor, MI: Ardis. (Original work published 1929)

Bakhtin, M. M. (1981). *The dialogic imagination: Four essays.* Austin, TX: University of Texas Press.

Bandura, A. (2001). Social cognitive theory: An agentic perspective. *Annual Review of Psychology, 52,* 1–26.

Bandura, A., & Walters, R. H. (1963). *Social learning and personality development.* New York, NY: Holt, Rinehart, and Winston.

Barber, B. K. (Ed.). (2002). *Intrusive parenting: How psychological control affects children and adolescents.* Washington, DC: American Psychological Association.

Barber, B. K., & Harmon, E. L. (2002). Violating the self: Parental psychological control of children and adolescents. In B. K. Barber (Ed.), *Intrusive parenting: How psychological control affects children and adolescents* (pp. 15–52). Washington, DC: American Psychological Association.

Barsade, S. G. (2002). The ripple effect: Emotional contagion and its influence on group behavior. *Administrative Science Quarterly, 47,* 644–675.

Bass, B. M. (1997). Does the transactional-transformational leadership paradigm transcend organizational and national boundaries? *American Psychologist, 52,* 130–139.

Bass, B. M., & Steidlmeier, P. (1998). Ethics, character, and authentic transformational leadership. Binghamton, NY: Center for Leadership Studies. Retrieved from http://binghamton.edu/BassSteid.html

Bassett, J. F. (2007). Psychological defenses against death anxiety: Integrating terror management theory and Firestone's separation theory. *Death Studies, 31,* 727–750.

Baumeister, R. F. (1997). *Evil: Inside human violence and cruelty.* New York, NY: Henry Holt.

Baumeister, R. F. (2005). *The cultural animal: Human nature, meaning, and social life.* New York, NY: Oxford University Press.

Baumeister, R. F., & Leary, M. R. (1995). The need to belong: Desire for interpersonal attachments as a fundamental human motivation. *Psychological Bulletin, 117,* 497–529.

Beck, A. T. (1988). *Love is never enough.* New York, NY: Harper & Row.

Beck, A. T. (2005). The current state of cognitive therapy: A 40-year retrospective. *Archives of General Psychiatry, 6,* 953–959.

Beck, A. T., Rush, A. J., Shaw, B. F., & Emery, G. (1979). *Cognitive therapy of depression.* New York, NY: Guilford Press.

Beck, J. S. (1995). *Cognitive therapy: Basics and beyond.* New York, NY: Guilford Press.

Beck, R. (2004). The function of religious belief: Defensive versus existential religion. *Journal of Psychology and Christianity, 23,* 208–218.

Becker, E. (1964). *The revolution in psychiatry: The new understanding of man.* New York, NY: Free Press.

Becker, E. (1971). *The birth and death of meaning: A perspective in psychiatry and anthropology* (2nd ed.). New York, NY: Free Press.

Becker, E. (1975). *Escape from evil.* New York, NY: Free Press.

Becker, E. (1997). *The denial of death.* New York, NY: Free Press. (Original work published 1973)

Bellah, R. N., Madsen, R., Sullivan, W. M., Swidler, A., & Tipton, S. M. (1991). *The good society.* New York, NY: Vintage Books.

Belsky, J., Steinberg, L., & Draper, P. (1991). Childhood experience, interpersonal development, and reproductive strategy: An evolutionary theory of socialization. *Child Development, 62,* 647–670.

Bem, S. L. (1985). Androgyny and gender schema theory: A conceptual and empirical integration. In T. B. Sonderegger (Ed.), *Nebraska Symposium on Motivation: Vol. 32. Psychology and gender* (pp. 179–226). Lincoln, NE: University of Nebraska Press.

Benjamin, J. (1988). *The bonds of love: Psychoanalysis, feminism, and the problem of domination.* New York, NY: Pantheon Books.

Benjamin, L. S. (2003). *Interpersonal reconstructive therapy: Promoting change in nonresponders.* New York, NY: Guilford Press.

Bennis, W. (2007). The challenges of leadership in the modern world. *American Psychologist, 62,* 2–5.

Berne, E. (1961). *Transactional analysis in psychotherapy: A systematic individual and social psychiatry.* New York, NY: Grove Press.

Bernstein, D., & Freedman, N. (1993). Gender-specific attribution of identity. In D. Bernstein, N. Freedman, & B. Distler (Eds.), *Female identity conflict in clinical practice* (pp. 1–16). Northvale, NJ: Jason Aronson.

Bernstein, D., Freedman, N., & Distler, B. (Eds.). (1993). *Female identity conflict in clinical practice.* Northvale, NJ: Jason Aronson.

Beutler, L. E. (1997). Foreword. In R. W. Firestone, *Combating destructive thought processes: Voice therapy and separation theory* (pp. xi–xvii). Thousand Oaks, CA: Sage.

Blazina, C., & Watkins, C. E., Jr. (2000). Separation/individuation, parental attachment, and male gender role conflict: Attitudes toward the feminine and the fragile masculine self. *Psychology of Men and Masculinity, 1,* 126–132.

Bloch, D. (1978). *"So the witch won't eat me": Fantasy and the child's fear of infanticide.* New York, NY: Grove.

Bloch, D. (1985). The child's fear of infanticide and the primary motive force of defense. *Psychoanalytic Review, 72,* 573–588.

Blos, P. (1967). The second individuation process of adolescence. *Psychoanalytic Study of the Child, 22,* 172–186.

Bogart, G. (1991). The use of meditation in psychotherapy: A review of the literature. *American Journal of Psychotherapy, 45,* 383–412.

Bond, R., & Smith, P. B. (1996). Culture and conformity: A meta-analysis of studies using Asch's (1952b, 1956) line judgment task. *Psychological Bulletin, 119,* 111–137.

Boszormenyi-Nagy, I., & Spark, G. M. (1984). *Invisible loyalties: Reciprocity in intergenerational family therapy.* New York, NY: Brunner/Mazel. (Original work published 1973)

Bourdieu, P. (1985). The social space and the genesis of groups. (R. Nice, Trans.). *Social Science Information, 24,* 195–220.

Bowen, M. (1978). *Family therapy in clinical practice.* New York, NY: Jason Aronson.

Bowlby, J. (1980). *Attachment and loss: Vol. 3. Loss: Sadness and depression.* New York, NY: Basic Books.

Bowlby, J. (1982). *Attachment and loss: Vol. 1. Attachment* (2nd ed.). New York, NY: Basic Books.

Bowlby, J. (1988). *A secure base: Clinical applications of attachment theory.* London, England: Routledge.

Bradbury, T. N., & Fincham, F. D. (1990). Attributions in marriage: Review and critique. *Psychological Bulletin, 107,* 3–33.

Brafman, O., & Brafman, R. (2008). *Sway: The irresistible pull of irrational behavior.* New York, NY: Doubleday. [Amazon Kindle version]

Bramley, W. (2008). *Bewitched, bothered and bewildered: How couples really work.* London, England: Karnac.

Bray, J. H. (2004). *Personal Authority in the Family System Questionnaire manual* (2nd ed.). Houston, TX: D-Boy Productions.

Brazelton, T. B. (1973). Effect of maternal expectations on early infant behavior. *Early Child Development and Care, 2,* 259–273.

Bretherton, I. (1996). Internal working models of attachment relationships as related to resilient coping. In G. G. Noam & K. W. Fischer (Eds.), *Development and vulnerability in close relationships* (pp. 3–27). Mahwah, NJ: Lawrence Erlbaum.

Bretherton, I. (2005). In pursuit of the internal working model construct and its relevance to attachment relationships. In K. E. Grossmann, K. Grossmann, & E. Waters (Eds.), *Attachment from infancy to adulthood: The major longitudinal studies* (pp. 13–47). New York, NY: Guilford Press.

Bretherton, I., Ridgeway, D., & Cassidy, J. (1990). Assessing internal working models of the attachment relationship. In M. T. Greenberg, D. Cicchetti, & E. M. Cummings (Eds.), *Attachment in the preschool years: Theory, research, and intervention* (pp. 273–308). Chicago, IL: University of Chicago Press.

Briere, J. N. (1992). *Child abuse trauma: Theory and treatment of the lasting effects.* Newbury Park, CA: Sage.

Bromberg, P. M. (2009). Truth, human relatedness, and the analytic process: An interpersonal/relational perspective. *International Journal of Psychoanalysis, 90,* 347–361.

Bronfenbrenner, U. (2004). Ecological models of human development. In M. Gauvain & M. Cole (Eds.), *Readings on the development of children* (2nd ed., pp. 37–43). New York, NY: Freeman. (Original work published 1994)

Brook, A. (1999). Unified consciousness and the self. In S. Gallagher & J. Shear (Eds.), *Models of the self* (pp. 39–47). Exeter, England: Imprint Academic.

Bullough, V. L., Shelton, B., & Slavin, S. (1988). *The subordinated sex: A history of attitudes toward women* (Rev. ed.). Athens, GA: University of Georgia Press.

Burns, J. M. (1978). *Leadership.* New York, NY: Harper & Row.

Burston, D. (2007). *Erik Erikson and the American psyche: Ego, ethics, and evolution.* Lanham, MD: Jason Aronson.

Buss, D. M. (1995). Psychological sex differences: Origins through sexual selection. *American Psychologist, 50,* 164–168.

Butler, R. (2009). Combating ageism: A matter of human and civil rights. *International Psychogeriatrics, 21,* 211–211.

Butler, A. C., Chapman, J. E., Forman, E. M., & Beck, A. T. (2006). The empirical status of cognitive-behavioral therapy: A review of meta-analyses. *Clinical Psychology Review, 26,* 17–31.

Cantor, J. (2008). The life we choose. *The Candidate Journal, 3,* 72–75.

Caplan, P. J. (2000). *The new don't blame mother: Mending the mother-daughter relationship.* New York, NY: Routledge.

Carnelley, K. B., Pietromonaco, P. R., & Jaffe, K. (1994). Depression, working models of others, and relationship functioning. *Journal of Personality and Social Psychology, 66,* 127–140.

Carr, L., Iacoboni, M., Dubeau, M. C., Mazziotta, J. C., & Lenzi, G. L. (2003). Neural mechanisms of empathy in humans: A relay from neural systems for imitation to limbic areas. *Proceedings of the National Academy of Science, 100,* 5497–5502.

Cassidy, J., & Mohr, J. J. (2001). Unresolvable fear, trauma, and psychopathology: Theory, research, and clinical considerations related to disorganized attachment across the life span. *Clinical Psychology: Science and Practice, 8,* 275–298.

Castonguay, L. G., & Goldfried, M. R. (1994). Psychotherapy integration: An idea whose time has come. *Applied and Preventive Psychology, 3,* 159–172.

Champagne, F. A. (2010). Epigenetic influence of social experiences across the lifespan. *Developmental Psychobiology, 52,* 299–311.

Chapman, D. P., Whitfield, C. L., Felitti, V. J., Dube, S. R., Edwards, V. J., & Anda, R. F. (2004). Adverse childhood experiences and the risk of depressive disorders in adulthood. *Journal of Affective Disorders, 82,* 217–225.

Chasseguet-Smirgel, J. (1970). Feminine guilt and the Oedipus complex. In J. Chasseguet-Smirgel (Ed.), *Female sexuality: New psychoanalytic views* (pp. 94–134). London, England: Karnac Books.

Chernin, K. (1985). *The hungry self: Women, eating, and identity.* New York, NY: Times Books.

Chirban, S. (2000). Oneness experience: Looking through multiple lenses. *Journal of Applied Psychoanalytic Studies, 2,* 247–264.

Chodorow, N. (1978). *The reproduction of mothering: Psychoanalysis and the sociology of gender.* Berkeley, CA: University of California Press.

Chodorow, N. (1991). *Feminism and psychoanalytic theory.* New Haven, CT: Yale University Press.

Chodorow, N. (2001). Family structure and feminine personality. In D. M. Juschka (Ed.), *Feminism in the study of religion* (pp. 81–105). London, England: Continuum.

Chodorow, N. (2004). Psychoanalysis and women: A personal thirty-five-year retrospect. In J. A. Winer, J. W. Anderson, & C. C. Kieffer (Eds.), *Psychoanalysis and women: The annual of psychoanalysis* (Vol. 32, pp. 101–129). Hillsdale, NJ: Analytic Press.

Christakis, N. A., & Fowler, J. H. (2009). *Connected: The surprising power of our social networks and how they shape our lives.* New York, NY: Little, Brown.

Cialdini, R. B., & Trost, M. R. (1998). Social influence: Social norms, conformity, and compliance. In D. T. Gilbert, S. T. Fiske, & G. Lindzey (Eds.), *The handbook of social psychology* (Vols. 1 & 2, 4th ed., pp. 151–192). New York, NY: McGraw-Hill.

Ciulla, J. B. (2004). Introduction. In J. B. Ciulla (Ed.), *Ethics: The heart of leadership* (2nd ed., pp. xv–xvix). Westport, CT: Praeger.

Ciulla, J. B. (2005). The state of leadership ethics and the work that lies before us. *Business Ethics: A European Review, 14,* 323–335.

Cohen, F., Ogilvie, D. M., Solomon, S., Greenberg, J., & Pyszczynski, T. (2005). American roulette: The effect of reminders of death on support for George W. Bush in the 2004 presidential election. *Analyses of Social Issues and Public Policy, 5,* 177–187.

Cohen, F., Solomon, S., Maxfield, M., Pyszczynski, T., & Greenberg, J. (2004). Fatal attraction: The effects of mortality salience on evaluations of charismatic, task-oriented, and relationship-oriented leaders. *Psychological Science, 15,* 846–851.

Collins, N. L., & Allard, L. M. (2004). Cognitive representations of attachment: The content and function of working models. In M. B. Brewer & M. Hewstone (Eds.), *Social cognition: Perspectives on social psychology* (pp. 75–101). Malden, MA: Blackwell.

Collins, N. L., & Ford, M. B. (2010). Responding to the needs of others: The caregiving behavioral system in intimate relationships. *Journal of Social and Personal Relationships, 27,* 235–244.

Collins, N. L., Ford, M. B., Guichard, A. C., & Allard, L. M. (2006). Working models of attachment and attribution processes in intimate relationships. *Personality and Social Psychology Bulletin, 32,* 201–219.

Collins, N. L., & Read, S. J. (1990). Adult attachment, working models, and relationship quality in dating couples. *Journal of Personality and Social Psychology, 58,* 644–663.

Comings, D. E., Muhleman, D., Johnson, J. P., & MacMurray, J. P. (2002). Parent-daughter transmission of the androgen receptor gene as an explanation of the effect of father absence on age of menarche. *Child Development, 73,* 1046–1051.

Cooper, D. (1971). *The death of the family.* New York, NY: Vintage Books. (Original work published 1970)

Cote, J. E., & Levine, C. G. (2002). *Identity formation, agency, and culture: A social psychological synthesis.* Mahwah, NJ: Lawrence Erlbaum. [Amazon Kindle version]

Covey, S. R. (1999). *Living the 7 habits: The courage to change.* New York, NY: Simon & Schuster.

Cowan, P. A., Cowan, C. P., & Kerig, P. K. (1993). Mothers, fathers, sons, and daughters: Gender differences in family formation and parenting style. In P. A. Cowan, D. Field, D. A. Hansen, A. Skolnick, & G. E. Swanson (Eds.), *Family, self, and society: Toward a new agenda for family research* (pp. 165–195). Hillsdale, NJ: Lawrence Erlbaum.

Cozolino, L. (2006). *The neuroscience of human relationships: Attachment and the developing social brain.* New York, NY: W. W. Norton.

Cramer, B. (1997). The transmission of womanhood from mother to daughter. In B. S. Mark & J. A. Incorvaia (Eds.), *The handbook of infant, child, and adolescent psychotherapy: Vol. 2. New directions in integrative treatment* (pp. 373–391). Northvale, NJ: Jason Aronson.

Crockenberg, S. C., & Leerkes, E. M. (2003). Parental acceptance, postpartum depression, and maternal sensitivity: Mediating and moderating processes. *Journal of Family Psychology, 17,* 80–93.

Damasio, A. (1999). *The feeling of what happens: Body and emotion in the making of consciousness.* Orlando, FL: Harcourt.

Davidovitz, R., Mikulincer, M., Shaver, P. R., Izsak, R., & Popper, M. (2007). Leaders as attachment figures: Leaders' attachment orientations predict leadership-related mental representations and followers' performance and mental health. *Journal of Personality and Social Psychology, 93,* 632–650.

De Beauvoir, S. (1952). *The second sex.* (H. M. Parshley, Trans.). New York, NY: Vintage Books.

Debold, E. (1991). The body at play. In C. Gilligan, A. G. Rogers, & D. L. Tolman (Eds.), *Women, girls and psychotherapy: Reframing resistance* (pp. 169–183). New York, NY: Haworth Press.

Debold, E., Wilson, M., & Malave, I. (1993). *Mother daughter revolution: From good girls to great women.* New York, NY: Bantam Books.

Deci, E. L., & Ryan, R. M. (2008). Self-determination theory: A macrotheory of human motivation, development, and health. *Canadian Psychology, 49,* 182–185.

De Zulueta, F. (1993). *From pain to violence: The traumatic roots of destructiveness.* London, England: Whurr.

Doidge, N. (2007). *The brain that changes itself.* New York, NY: Penguin. [Amazon Kindle version]

Downs, W. R., & Miller, B. A. (1998). Relationships between experiences of parental violence during childhood and women's psychiatric symptomatology. *Journal of Interpersonal Violence, 13,* 438–455.

Dresner, R., & Grolnick, W. S. (1996). Constructions of early parenting, intimacy and autonomy in young women. *Journal of Social and Personal Relationships, 13,* 25–39.

Dutton, D. G. (1995). *The batterer: A psychological profile.* New York, NY: Basic Books.

Eagly, A. H. (1995). The science and politics of comparing women and men. *American Psychologist, 50,* 145–158.

Eagly, A. H., & Diekman, A. B. (2006). III. Examining gender gaps in sociopolitical attitudes: It's not Mars and Venus. *Feminism and Psychology, 16,* 26–34.

Eizirik, C. L. (2001). Freud's group psychology, psychoanalysis, and culture. In E. S. Person (Ed.), *On Freud's group psychology and the analysis of the ego* (pp. 155–173). Hillsdale, NJ: Analytic Press.

Elliott, R., Watson, J. C., Goldman, R. N., & Greenberg, L. S. (2004). *Learning emotion-focused therapy: The process-experiential approach to change.* Washington, DC: American Psychological Association. [Amazon Kindle version]

Epstein, S. (1994). Integration of the cognitive and the psychodynamic unconscious. *American Psychologist, 49,* 709–724.

Erikson, E. H. (1959). *Identity and the life cycle.* New York, NY: W. W. Norton.

Erikson, E. H. (1963). *Childhood and society* (2nd ed.). New York, NY: W. W. Norton.

Erikson, E. H. (1964). *Insight and responsibility: Lectures on the ethical implications of psychoanalytic insight.* New York, NY: W. W. Norton.

Erikson, E. H. (1968). *Identity: Youth and crisis.* New York, NY: W. W. Norton.

Erikson, E. H. (1969). *Gandhi's truth: On the origins of militant nonviolence.* New York, NY: W. W. Norton.

Erikson, E. H. (1984). Reflections on the last stage—and the first. *Psychoanalytic Study of the Child, 39,* 155–165.

Erlich, H. J. (1973). *The social psychology of prejudice: A systematic theoretical review and propositional inventory of the American social psychological study of prejudice.* Oxford, England: John Wiley.

Fairbairn, W. R. D. (1952). *Psychoanalytic studies of the personality.* London, England: Routledge & Kegan Paul.

Falk, A. (2004). *Fratricide in the Holy Land: A psychoanalytic view of the Arab-Israeli conflict.* Madison, WI: University of Wisconsin Press.

Fanon, F. (1967). *Black skin, white masks.* (C. L. Markmann, Trans.). New York, NY: Grove Press.

Fearon, R. P., Bakermans-Kranenburg, M. J., van IJzendoorn, M. H., Lapsley, A., & Roisman, G. I. (2010). The significance of insecure attachment and disorganization in the development of children's externalizing behavior: A meta-analysis. *Child Development, 81,* 435–455.

Felitti, V. J., Anda, R. F., Nordenberg, D., Williamson, D. F., Spitz, A. M., Edwards, V., . . . Marks, J. S. (1998). Relationship of childhood abuse and household dysfunction to many of the leading causes of death in adults: The Adverse Childhood Experiences (ACE) study. *American Journal of Preventive Medicine, 14,* 245–258.

Fenchel, G. H. (1998). Introduction. In G. H. Fenchel (Ed.), *The mother-daughter relationship: Echoes through time* (pp. xv–xviii). Northvale, NJ: Jason Aronson.

Ferenczi, S. (1955). Confusion of tongues between adults and the child. In M. Balint (Ed.), *Final contributions to the problems and methods of psycho-analysis* (E. Mosbacher & others, Trans.) (pp. 156–167). New York, NY: Basic Books. (Original work published 1933)

Ferree, M. M. (1990). Beyond separate spheres: Feminism and family research. *Journal of Marriage and the Family, 52,* 866–884.

Fierman, L. B. (Ed.). (1965). *Effective psychotherapy: The contribution of Hellmuth Kaiser.* New York, NY: Free Press.

Firestone, R. W. (1985). *The fantasy bond: Structure of psychological defenses.* Santa Barbara, CA: Glendon Association.

Firestone, R. W. (1987). Destructive effects of the fantasy bond in couple and family relationships. *Psychotherapy, 24,* 233–239.

Firestone, R. W. (1988). *Voice therapy: A psychotherapeutic approach to self-destructive behavior.* Santa Barbara, CA: Glendon Association.

Firestone, R. W. (1990a). *Compassionate child-rearing: An in-depth approach to optimal parenting.* Santa Barbara, CA: Glendon Association.

Firestone, R. W. (1990b). Prescription for psychotherapy. *Psychotherapy, 27,* 627–635.

Firestone, R. W. (1990c). Voice therapy. In J. Zeig & W. Munion (Eds.), *What is psychotherapy? Contemporary perspectives* (pp. 68–74). San Francisco, CA: Jossey-Bass.

Firestone, R. W. (1994a). A new perspective on the Oedipal complex: A voice therapy session. *Psychotherapy, 31,* 342–351.

Firestone, R. W. (1994b). Psychological defenses against death anxiety. In R. A. Neimeyer (Ed.), *Death anxiety handbook: Research, instrumentation, and application* (pp. 217–241). Washington, DC: Taylor & Francis.

Firestone, R. W. (1996). The origins of ethnic strife. *Mind and Human Interaction, 7,* 167–180.

Firestone, R. W. (1997a). *Combating destructive thought processes: Voice therapy and separation theory.* Thousand Oaks, CA: Sage.

Firestone, R. W. (1997b). *Suicide and the inner voice: Risk assessment, treatment, and case management.* Thousand Oaks, CA: Sage.

Firestone, R. W. (2000). Microsuicide and the elderly: A basic defense against death anxiety. In A. Tomer (Ed.), *Death attitudes and the older adult: Theories, concepts, and applications* (pp. 65–84). Philadelphia, PA: Brunner-Routledge.

Firestone, R. W., & Catlett, J. (1989). *Psychological defenses in everyday life.* Santa Barbara, CA: Glendon Association.

Firestone, R. W., & Catlett, J. (1999). *Fear of intimacy.* Washington, DC: American Psychological Association.

Firestone, R.W., & Catlett, J. (2009a). *Beyond death anxiety: Achieving life-affirming death awareness.* New York, NY: Springer.

Firestone, R. W., & Catlett, J. (2009b). *The ethics of interpersonal relationships.* London, England: Karnac Books.

Firestone, R. W., & Firestone, L. (2004). Methods for overcoming the fear of intimacy. In D. Mashek & A. Aron (Eds.), *The handbook of closeness and intimacy* (pp. 375–395). Mahwah, NJ: Lawrence Erlbaum.

Firestone, R. W., & Firestone, L. (2006). *Firestone Assessment of Self-Destructive Thoughts (FAST) manual.* Lutz, FL: Psychological Assessment Resources.

Firestone, R. W., & Firestone, L. (2008a). *Firestone Assessment of Violent Thoughts (FAVT) manual.* Lutz, FL: Psychological Assessment Resources.

Firestone, R. W., & Firestone, L. (2008b). *Firestone Assessment of Violent Thoughts—Adolescent (FAVT-A) manual.* Lutz, FL: Psychological Assessment Resources.

Firestone, R. W., & Firestone, L. (2012). Separation theory and voice therapy methodology. In P. R. Shaver & M. Mikulincer (Eds.), *The social psychology of meaning, mortality, and choice.* Washington, DC: American Psychological Association.

Firestone, R. W., Firestone, L., & Catlett, J. (2002). *Conquer your critical inner voice: A revolutionary program to counter negative thoughts and live free from imagined limitations.* Oakland, CA: New Harbinger.

Firestone, R. W., Firestone, L., & Catlett, J. (2003). *Creating a life of meaning and compassion: The wisdom of psychotherapy.* Washington, DC: American Psychological Association.

Firestone, R. W., Firestone, L. A., & Catlett, J. (2006). *Sex and love in intimate relationships.* Washington, DC: American Psychological Association.

Firestone, R. W., & Seiden, R. H. (1987). Microsuicide and suicidal threats of everyday life. *Psychotherapy, 24,* 31–39.

Fitzgerald, F. S. (1960). *Six tales of the Jazz Age.* New York, NY: Scribner. (Original work published 1920)

Florian, V., & Kravetz, S. (1983). Fear of personal death: Attribution, structure, and relation to religious belief. *Journal of Personality and Social Psychology, 44,* 600–607.

Florian, V., & Mikulincer, M. (1998). Terror management in childhood: Does death conceptualization moderate the effects of mortality salience on acceptance of similar and different others? *Personality and Social Psychology Bulletin, 24,* 1104–1112.

Flouri, E., & Buchanan, A. (2002). What predicts good relationships with parents in adolescence and partners in adult life: Findings from the 1958 British birth cohort. *Journal of Family Psychology, 16,* 186–198.

Flouri, E., & Buchanan, A. (2003). The role of father involvement in children's later mental health. *Journal of Adolescence, 26,* 63–78.

Fonagy, P., & Bateman, A. (2008). Mentalization-based treatment of borderline personality disorder. In E. L. Jurist, A. Slade, & S. Bergner (Eds.), *Mind to mind: Infant research, neuroscience, and psychoanalysis* (pp. 139–166). New York, NY: Other Press.

Fonagy, P., Gergely, G., Jurist, E., & Target, M. (2002). *Affect regulation, mentalization, and the development of the self.* New York, NY: Other Press.

Fonagy, P., & Higgitt, A. (2007). The development of prejudice: An attachment theory hypothesis explaining its ubiquity. In H. Parens, A. Mahfouz, S. W. Twemlow, & D. E. Scharff (Eds.), *The future of prejudice: Psychoanalysis and the prevention of prejudice* (pp. 63–79). Lanham, MD: Rowman & Littlefield.

Fonagy, P., Steele, H., & Steele, M. (1991). Maternal representations of attachment during pregnancy predict the organization of infant-mother attachment at one year of age. *Child Development, 62,* 891–905.

Fonagy, P., & Target, M. (2005). Commentary: Bridging the transmission gap: An end to an important mystery of attachment research? *Attachment and Human Development, 7,* 333–343.

Forman, E. M., Herbert, J. D., Moitra, E., Yeomans, P. D., & Geller, P. A. (2009). A randomized controlled effectiveness trial of acceptance and commitment therapy and cognitive therapy for anxiety and depression. *Behavior Modification, 31,* 772–799.

Forrester, J. W. (1994). System dynamics, systems thinking, and soft OR. *System Dynamics Review, 10,* 245–256.

Fowles, D. C., & Kochanska, G. (2000). Temperament as a moderator of pathways to conscience in children: The contribution of electrodermal activity. *Psychophysiology, 37,* 788–795.

Fraley, R. C. (2002). Attachment stability from infancy to adulthood: Meta-analysis and dynamic modeling of developmental mechanisms. *Personality and Social Psychology Review, 6,* 123–151.

Fraley, R. C., Waller, N. G., & Brennan, K. A. (2000). An item-response theory analysis of self-report measures of adult attachment. *Journal of Personality and Social Psychology, 78,* 350–365.

Freud, H. C. (2011). *Electra vs Oedipus: The drama of the mother-daughter relationship.* (M. de Jager, Trans.). London, England: Routledge. (Original work published 1997)

Freud, S. (1955). Three essays on the theory of sexuality. In J. Strachey (Ed. and Trans.), *The standard edition of the complete psychological works of Sigmund Freud* (Vol. 17, pp. 125–243). London, England: Hogarth. (Original work published 1905)

Freud, S. (1955). Group psychology and the analysis of the ego. In J. Strachey (Ed. and Trans.), *The standard edition of the complete psychological works of Sigmund Freud* (Vol. 18, pp. 63–143). London, England: Hogarth. (Original work published 1921)

Freud, S. (1957). The unconscious. In J. Strachey (Ed. & Trans.), *The standard edition of the complete psychological works of Sigmund Freud* (Vol. 14, pp. 159–209). London, England: Hogarth Press. (Original work published 1915)

Freyd, J. J. (1996). *Betrayal trauma: The logic of forgetting childhood abuse.* Cambridge, MA: Harvard University Press.

Friday, N. (1977). *My mother/my self: The daughter's search for identity.* New York, NY: Delacorte Press.

Fromm, E. (1941). *Escape from freedom.* New York, NY: Avon Books.

Fromm, E. (1944). Individual and social origins of neurosis. *American Sociological Review, 9,* 380–384.

Furer, P., & Walker, J. R. (2008). Death anxiety: A cognitive-behavioral approach. *Journal of Cognitive Psychotherapy, 16,* 167–182.

Galinsky, A. D., Jordan, J., & Sivanathan, N. (2008). Harnessing power to capture leadership. In J. B. Ciulla, D. R. Forsyth, M. A. Genovese, G. R. Goethals, L. C. Han, & C. L. Hoyt (Eds.), *Leadership at the crossroads: Vol. 1. Leadership and psychology* (pp. 283–299). Westport, CT: Greenwood.

Galinsky, A. D., Magee, J. C., Inesi, M. E., & Gruenfeld, D. H. (2006). Power and perspectives not taken. *Psychological Science, 17,* 1068–1074.

Garbarino, J. (1995). *Raising children in a socially toxic environment.* San Francisco, CA: Jossey-Bass.

Garbarino, J., & Gilliam, G. (1980). *Understanding abusive families.* Lexington, MA: Lexington Books.

Gartner, R. B. (1999). *Betrayed as boys: Psychodynamic treatment of sexually abused men.* New York, NY: Guilford Press.

Gavin, L. A., & Furman, W. (1996). Adolescent girls' relationships with mothers and best friends. *Child Development, 67,* 375–386.

Geary, D. C. (1998). *Male, female: The evolution of human sex differences.* Washington, DC: American Psychological Association.

Geis, F. L. (1993). Self-fulfilling prophecies: A social psychological view of gender. In A. E. Beall & R. J. Sternberg (Eds.), *The psychology of gender* (pp. 9–54). New York, NY: Guilford Press.

George, C., Kaplan, N., & Main, M. (1984). *Adult Attachment Interview.* Unpublished manuscript. University of California.

Gergely, G. (2007). The social construction of the subjective self: The role of affect-mirroring, markedness, and ostensive communication in self development. In L. Mayes, P. Fonagy, & M. Target (Eds.), *Developmental science and psychoanalysis: Integration and innovation* (pp. 45–88). London, England: Karnac Books.

Gergen, K. J. (2001). Psychological science in a postmodern context. *American Psychologist, 56,* 803–813.

Gerson, M. (2010). *The embedded self: An integrative psychodynamic and systemic perspective on couples and family therapy* (2nd ed.). New York, NY: Routledge.

Giddens, A. (1991). *Modernity and self-identity: Self and society in the late modern age.* Stanford, CA: Stanford University Press.

Gilbert, R., Widom, C. S., Browne, K., Fergusson, D., Webb, E., & Janson, S. (2009). Burden and consequences of child maltreatment in high-income countries. *The Lancet, 373,* 68–81.

Gilligan, C. (1982). *In a different voice: Psychological theory and women's development.* Cambridge, MA: Harvard University Press.

Gilligan, C. (1991). Women's psychological development: Implications for psychotherapy. In C. Gilligan, A. G. Rogers, & D. L. Tolman (Eds.), *Women, girls and psychotherapy: Reframing resistance* (pp. 5–31). New York, NY: Haworth Press.

Gilligan, C. (1995, Spring). Hearing the difference. *Hypatia, 10,* 120. Bloomington, IN: Indiana University Press.

Gilligan, C. (2011). *Joining the resistance.* Oxford, England: Polity Press.

Gilligan, C., & Richards, D. A. J. (2009). *The deepening darkness: Patriarchy, resistance, and democracy's future.* New York, NY: Cambridge University Press.

Gilligan, J. (2001). *Preventing violence.* New York, NY: Thames & Hudson.

Gilligan, J. (2007). Terrorism, fundamentalism, and nihilism: Analyzing the dilemmas of modernity. In H. Parens, A. Mahfouz, S. W. Twemlow, & D. E. Scharff (Eds.), *The future of prejudice: Psychoanalysis and the prevention of prejudice* (pp. 37–59). Lanham, MD: Rowman & Littlefield.

Gilligan, J. (2011). *Why some politicians are more dangerous than others.* Cambridge, England: Polity Press.

Glick, P., & Fiske, S. T. (1996). The Ambivalent Sexism Inventory: Differentiating hostile and benevolent sexism. *Journal of Personality and Social Psychology, 70,* 491–512.

Goldenberg, J. L., Cox, C. R., Pyszczynski, T., Greenberg, J., & Solomon, S. (2002). Understanding human ambivalence about sex: The effects of stripping sex of meaning [Electronic version]. *Journal of Sex Research, 39,* 310–320.

Goldenberg, J. L, Pyszczynski, T., Greenberg, J., & Solomon, S. (2000). Fleeing the body: A terror management perspective on the problem of human corporeality. *Personality and Social Psychology Review, 4,* 200–218.

Goldenberg, J. L., Pyszczynski, T., McCoy, S. K., Greenberg, J., & Solomon, S. (1999). Death, sex, love, and neuroticism: Why is sex such a problem? *Journal of Personality and Social Psychology, 77,* 1173–1187.

Gottman, J. M. (1979). *Marital interaction: Experimental investigations.* New York, NY: Academic Press.

Gottman, J. M., & Krokoff, L. J. (1989). Marital interaction and satisfaction: A longitudinal view. *Journal of Consulting and Clinical Psychology, 57,* 47–52.

Gottman, J. M., & Silver, N. (1999). *The seven principles for making marriage work.* New York, NY: Three Rivers Press.

Greatrex, T. (2002). Projective identification: How does it work? *Neuro-Psychoanalysis, 4,* [Electronic version] 187–197. Retrieved from http://bostonneuropsa.net

Green, A. (1986). The dead mother (K. Aubertin, Trans.). In A. Green, *On private madness* (pp. 142–173). London, England: Karnac Books. (Original work published 1983)

Green, A. (1999). *Fabric of affect in the psychoanalytic discourse.* (A. Sheridan, Trans.). London, England: Routledge. (Original work published 1973)

Greenberg, J., Pyszczynski, T., Solomon, S., Rosenblatt, A., Veeder, M., Kirkland, S., & Lyon, D. (1990). Evidence for terror management theory II: The effects of mortality salience on reactions to those who threaten or bolster the cultural worldview. *Journal of Personality and Social Psychology, 58,* 308–318.

Greenberg, L. S. (2002). *Emotion-focused therapy: Coaching clients to work through their feelings.* Washington, DC: American Psychological Association.

Greenberg, L. S. (2011). *Emotion-focused therapy.* Washington, DC: American Psychological Association.

Greenberg, L. S., Rice, L. N., & Elliott, R. (1993). *Facilitating emotional change: The moment-by-moment process.* New York, NY: Guilford Press.

Greenleaf, R. K. (1970). *The servant leader.* Westfield, IN: Greenleaf Center for Servant Leadership.

Grolnick, W. S., Deci, E. L., & Ryan, R. M. (1997). Internalization within the family: The self-determination theory perspective. In J. E. Grusec & L. Kuczynski (Eds.), *Parenting and children's internalization of values: A handbook of contemporary theory* (pp. 135–161). New York, NY: John Wiley.

Grotstein, J. S. (1981). *Splitting and projective identification.* New York, NY: J. Aronson.

Guntrip, H. (1961). *Personality structure and human interaction: The developing synthesis of psychodynamic theory.* New York, NY: International Universities Press.

Gurian, M. (1996). *The wonder of boys.* New York, NY: Jeremy P. Tarcher.

Habermas, J. (1984). *The theory of communicative action: Vol. 1. Reason and the rationalization of society.* (T. McCarthy, Trans.). Boston, MA: Beacon Press.

Hackman, J. R., & Wageman, R. (2007). Asking the right questions about leadership: Discussion and conclusions. *American Psychologist, 62,* 43–47.

Harter, S. (1999). *The construction of the self: A developmental perspective.* New York, NY: Guilford Press.

Havel, V. (1990). *Disturbing the peace: A conversation with Karel Hvizdala.* (P. Wilson, Trans.). New York, NY: Alfred A. Knopf.

Hays, H. R. (1964). *The dangerous sex: The myth of the feminine evil.* New York, NY: Putnam's Sons.

Hazan, C., & Shaver, P. R. (1994). Attachment as an organizational framework for research on close relationships. *Psychological Inquiry, 5,* 1–22.

Hellinger, B. (with G. Weber & H. Beaumont). (1998). *Love's hidden symmetry: What makes love work in relationships.* Phoenix, AZ: Zeig, Tucker.

Henrich, J., & Boyd, R. (2001). Why people punish defectors: Weak conformist transmission can stabilize costly enforcement of norms in cooperative dilemmas. *Journal of Theoretical Biology, 208,* 79–89.

Herman, J. (1992). *Trauma and recovery.* New York, NY: Basic Books.

Herman, N. (1999). *Too long a child: The mother-daughter dyad.* London, England: Whurr. (Original work published 1989)

Hermans, H. J. M., & Dimaggio, G. (2004). The dialogical self in psychotherapy: Introduction. In H. J. M. Hermans & G. Dimaggio (Eds.), *The dialogical self in psychotherapy* (pp. 1–10). Hove, England: Brunner-Routledge.

Hetherington, E. M. (1972). Effects of father absence on personality development in adolescent daughters. *Developmental Psychology, 7,* 313–326.

Heyn, D. (1993). *The erotic silence of the American wife.* New York, NY: Signet/Penguin.

Hing, L. S. S., Bobocel, D. R., Zanna, M. P., & McBride, M. V. (2007). Authoritarian dynamics and unethical decision making: High social dominance orientation leaders and high right-wing authoritarianism followers. *Journal of Personality and Social Psychology, 92,* 67–81.

Hinton, J. (1975). The influence of previous personality on reactions to having terminal cancer. *Omega, 6,* 95–111.

Hirsch, M. (1981). Mothers and daughters. *Journal of Women in Culture and Society, 7,* 200–222.

Hoffer, E. (2006). *The passionate state of mind and other aphorisms.* Titusville, NJ: Hopewell. (Original work published 1955)

Hoffman, S. I., & Strauss, S. (1985). The development of children's concepts of death. *Death Studies, 9,* 469–482.

Holiday, E., & Rosenberg, J. I. (2009). *Mean girls, meaner women: Understanding why women backstab, betray, and trash-talk each other.* Seattle, WA: Amazon.com.

Holmes, B. M., & Johnson, K. R. (2009). Adult attachment and romantic partner preference: A review. *Journal of Social and Personal Relationships, 26,* 833–852.

Holmes, L. (2008). *The internal triangle: New theories of female development.* Lanham, MD: Jason Aronson.

Hooper, L. M. (2007). The application of attachment theory and family systems theory to the phenomena of parentification. *Family Journal: Counseling and Therapy for Couples and Families, 15,* 217–223.

Hornsey, M. J., & Jetten, J. (2004). The individual within the group: Balancing the need to belong with the need to be different. *Personality and Social Psychology Review, 8,* 248–264.

Hrdy, S. B. (1999). *Mother nature: A history of mothers, infants, and natural selection.* New York, NY: Pantheon Books.

Hrdy, S. B. (2009). *Mothers and others: The evolutionary origins of mutual understanding.* Cambridge, MA: Harvard University Press.

Hudson, L., & Jacot, B. (1995). *Intimate relations: The natural history of desire.* New Haven, CT: Yale University Press.

Hyde, J. S. (2005). The gender similarities hypothesis. *American Psychologist, 60,* 581–592.

Iacoboni, M. (2007). Face to face: The neural basis of social mirroring and empathy. *Psychiatric Annals, 374,* 236–241.

Iacoboni, M. (2009). Imitation, empathy, and mirror neurons. *Annual Review of Psychology, 60,* 653–670.

Jacobson, K. (2009, April). Considering interactions between genes, environments, biology, and social context. *American Psychological Association Science Briefs.* Retrieved from www.apa.org/science/about/psa/2009/04/sci-brief.aspx

Johnson, C. F. (2004). Child sexual abuse. *The Lancet, 364,* 462–470.

Johnson, S. M. (1999). Emotionally focused couple therapy: Straight to the heart. In J. M. Donovan (Ed.), *Short-term couple therapy* (pp. 13–42). New York, NY: Guilford Press.

Johnson, S. M. (2002). *Emotionally focused couple therapy with trauma survivors: Strengthening attachment bonds.* New York, NY: Guilford Press.

Johnson, S. M., & Denton, W. (2002). Emotionally focused couple therapy: Creating secure connections. In A. S. Gurman & N. S. Jacobson (Eds.), *Clinical handbook of couple therapy* (3rd ed., pp. 221–250). New York, NY: Guilford Press.

Johnson, S. M., & Greenberg, L. S. (1995). The emotionally focused approach to problems in adult attachment. In N. S. Jacobson & A. S. Gurman (Eds.), *Clinical handbook of couple therapy* (pp. 121–141). New York, NY: Guilford Press.

Johnson, S. M., & Whiffen, V. E. (1999). Made to measure: Adapting emotionally-focused couple therapy to partners' attachment styles. *Clinical Psychology Science and Practice, 6,* 366–381.

Johnson, S. M., & Whiffen, V. E. (Eds.). (2003). *Attachment processes in couple and family therapy.* New York, NY: Guilford Press.

Jones, L. M., Finkelhor, D., & Halter, S. (2006). Child maltreatment trends in the 1990s: Why does neglect differ from sexual and physical abuse? *Child Maltreatment, 11,* 107–120.

Kaplan, H. S. (1995). *The sexual desire disorders: Dysfunctional regulation of sexual motivation.* Levittown, PA: Brunner/Mazel.

Kaplan, L. J. (1984). *Adolescence: The farewell to childhood.* New York, NY: Simon & Schuster.

Karon, B. P., & VandenBos, G. R. (1981). *Psychotherapy of schizophrenia: The treatment of choice.* Lanham, MD: Rowman & Littlefield.

Karp, T., & Helgo, T. I. T. (2009). Leadership as identity construction: The act of leading people in organisations: A perspective from the complexity sciences. *Journal of Management Development, 28,* 880–896.

Karpel, M. (1976). Individuation: From fusion to dialogue. *Family Process, 15*(1), 65–82.

Karpel, M. A. (1994). *Evaluating couples: A handbook for practitioners.* New York, NY: W. W. Norton.

Kastenbaum, R. (2000). *The psychology of death* (3rd ed.). New York, NY: Springer.
Kastenbaum, R., & Aisenberg, I. (1972). *The psychology of death.* New York, NY: Springer.
Keen, S. (1986). *Faces of the enemy: Reflections of the hostile imagination.* San Francisco, CA: Harper & Row.
Keen, S. (1997). Foreword. In E. Becker (1973/1997), *The denial of death* (pp. xi–xvi). New York, NY: Free Press.
Kellerman, B. (2004). *Bad leadership: What it is, how it happens, why it matters.* Boston, MA: Harvard Business School Press.
Kelly, R. (2007, April 26). Childhood neglect and its effects on neurodevelopment: Suggestions for future law and policy. *Houston Journal of Health Law and Policy, 8,* 133–161.
Kerr, M. E., & Bowen, M. (1988). *Family evaluation: An approach based on Bowen theory.* New York, NY: W. W. Norton.
Kindlon, D., & Thompson, M. (1999). *Raising Cain: Protecting the emotional life of boys.* New York, NY: Ballantine Books.
Kipnis, L. (2003). *Against love: A polemic.* New York, NY: Pantheon Books.
Kochanska, G., & Aksan, N. (2006). Children's conscience and self-regulation. *Journal of Personality, 74,* 1587–1617.
Kohut, H. (1977). *The restoration of the self.* New York, NY: International Universities Press.
Kohut, H. (1984). *How does analysis cure?* Chicago, IL: University of Chicago Press.
Kornfield, J. (1993). Even the best mediators have old wounds to heal: Combining meditation and psychotherapy. In R. Walsh & F. Vaughan (Eds.), *Paths beyond ego: The transpersonal vision* (pp. 67–69). New York, NY: Jeremy P. Tarcher/Putnam.
Kosloff, S., Solomon, S., Greenberg, J., Cohen, F., Gershuny, B., Routledge, C., & Pyszczynski, T. (2006). Fatal distraction: The impact of mortality salience on dissociative responses to 9/11 and subsequent anxiety sensitivity. *Basic and Applied Social Psychology, 28,* 349–356.
Kozol, J. (2005). *The shame of the nation: The restoration of apartheid schooling in America.* New York, NY: Crown Publishers. [Amazon Kindle version]
Krampe, E. M., & Fairweather, P. D. (1993). Father presence and family formation: A theoretical reformulation. *Journal of Family Issues, 14,* 572–591.
Kroger, J., & Haslett, S. J. (1988). Separation-individuation and ego identity in late adolescence: A two-year longitudinal study. *Journal of Youth and Adolescence, 17,* 59–79.
Laing, R. D. (1960). *The divided self.* New York, NY: Pantheon Books.
Laing, R. D. (1967). *The politics of experience.* New York, NY: Ballantine Books.
Laing, R. D. (1971). *Self and others.* Harmondsworth, England: Penguin. (Original work published 1961)
Laing, R. D. (1972). *The politics of the family and other essays.* New York, NY: Vintage. (Original work published 1969)
Lamb, M. E. (1986). The changing role of fathers. In M. E. Lamb (Ed.), *The father's role: Applied perspective* (pp. 3–27). New York, NY: John Wiley.
Lamb, M. E. (2010). How *do* fathers influence child development: Let me count the ways. In M. E. Lamb (Ed.), *The role of the father in child development* (5th ed., pp. 1–26). New York, NY: John Wiley.
Lamb, M. E., & Lewis, C. (2004). The development and significance of father-child relationships in two-parent families. In M. E. Lamb (Ed.), *The role of the father in child development* (4th ed., pp. 272–306). New York, NY: John Wiley.
Lammers, J., & Galinsky, A. D. (2009). The conceptualization of power and the nature of interdependency: The role of legitimacy and culture. In D. Tjosvold & B. Wisse (Eds.), *Power and interdependence in organizations* (pp. 67–82). Cambridge, England: Cambridge University Press.

Lammers, J., Stoker, J. I., & Stapel, D. A. (2009). Differentiating social and personal power: Opposite effects on stereotyping, but parallel effects on behavioral approach tendencies. *Psychological Science, 20,* 1543–1549.

Lampropoulos, G. K., Spengler, P. M., Dixon, D. N., & Nicholas, D. R. (2002). How psychotherapy integration can complement the Scientist-Practitioner model. *Journal of Clinical Psychology, 58,* 1227–1240.

Langner, C. A., & Keltner, D. (2008). Social power and emotional experience: Actor and partner effects within dyadic interactions. *Journal of Experimental Social Psychology, 44,* 848–856.

Langs, R. (1997). *Death anxiety and clinical practice.* London, England: Karnac Books.

Lapsley, D. K., & Horton, M. D. (2002, April). *The construct validity of pathology of separation-individuation (PATHSEP).* Paper presented at the 9th Biennial Meeting of the Society for Research on Adolescence, New Orleans, LA.

Lasch, C. (1979). *The culture of narcissism: American life in an age of diminishing expectations.* New York, NY: W. W. Norton.

LeBon, G. (1897). *The crowd: A study of the popular mind* (2nd ed.). London, England: T. F. Unwin.

Lepp, I. (1968). *Death and its mysteries.* New York, NY: Macmillan.

Lerner, H. G. (1988). *Women in therapy.* Northvale, NJ: Jason Aronson.

Levant, R. F., & Pollack, W. S. (1995). *The new psychology of men.* New York, NY: Basic Books. [Amazon Kindle version]

Lewis, M. D., & Todd, R. (2004). Toward a neuropsychological model of internal dialogue: Implications for theory and clinical practice. In H. J. M. Hermans & G. Dimaggio (Eds.), *The dialogical self in psychotherapy* (pp. 43–59). Hove, England: Brunner-Routledge.

Liechty, D. (2005). [Review of the book *The allure of toxic leaders: Why we follow destructive bosses and corrupt politicians—and how we can survive them,* by J. Lipman-Blumen]. Ernest Becker Foundation. Retrieved from http://faculty.washington.edu/neglee/hidden/hidn_5.htm

Lifton, R. J. (1979). *The broken connection: On death and the continuity of life.* New York, NY: Simon & Schuster.

Lifton, R. J. (1991). *Death in life: Survivors of Hiroshima.* Chapel Hill, NC: University of North Carolina Press. (Original work published 1968)

Lifton, R. J., & Olson, E. (1976). The human meaning of total disaster: The Buffalo Creek Experience. *Psychiatry, 39,* 1–18.

Lindahl, K. M., Malik, N. M., Kaczynski, K., & Simons, J. S. (2004). Couple power dynamics, systemic family functioning, and child adjustment: A test of a meditational model in a multiethnic sample. *Development and Psychopathology, 16,* 609–630.

Liotti, G. (2004). Trauma, dissociation, and disorganized attachment: Three strands of a single braid. *Psychotherapy: Theory, Research, Practice, Training, 41,* 472–486.

Liotti, G. (2011). Attachment disorganization and the clinical dialogue: Theme and variations. In J. Solomon & C. George (Eds.), *Disorganized attachment and caregiving* (pp. 383–413). New York, NY: Guilford Press.

Lipman-Blumen, J. (2005a, January/February). The allure of toxic leaders: Why followers rarely escape their clutches. *Ivey Business Journal,* 1–8.

Lipman-Blumen, J. (2005b). *The allure of toxic leaders: Why we follow destructive bosses and corrupt politicians—and how we can survive them.* New York, NY: Oxford University Press.

Lipman-Blumen, J. (2005c). Toxic leadership: When grand illusions masquerade as noble visions. *Leader to Leader Journal,* Issue 36, 29–36. doi: 10.1002/ltl.125.

Lockley, M. (2011). The evolution of human consciousness: Reflections on the discovery of mind and the implications for the materialist Darwinian paradigm. *Journal of Cosmology, 14.* Retrieved from http://journalofcosmology.com/Consciousness145.html

Lopez, F., Watkins, C., Manus, M., & Hunton-Shoup, J. (1992). Conflictual independence, mood regulation, and generalized self-efficacy: Test of a model of late-adolescent identity. *Journal of Counseling Psychology, 39,* 375–381.

Lopez-Duran, N. (2009, May 27). Father-daughter bond affects the daughters' romantic relationships. Retrieved from http://www.child-psych.org/2009/05/father-daughter-bonds-and-future-dromantic-relations

Lord, R. G., & Brown, D. J. (2004). *Leadership processes and follower self-identity.* Mahwah, NJ: Lawrence Erlbaum. [Amazon Kindle version]

Love, P. (with J. Robinson). (1990). *The emotional incest syndrome: What to do when a parent's love rules your life.* New York, NY: Bantam Books.

Love, P., & Shulkin, S. (1997). *How to ruin a perfectly good relationship.* Austin, TX: Authors.

Lowen, A. (1985). *Narcissism: Denial of the true self.* New York, NY: Simon & Schuster.

Lucas, M. (1997). Identity development, career development, and psychological separation from parents: Similarities and differences between men and women. *Journal of Counseling Psychology, 44,* 123–132.

Macfie, J., McElwain, N. L., Houts, R. M., & Cox, M. J. (2005). Intergenerational transmission of role reversal between parent and child: Dyadic and family systems internal working models. *Attachment and Human Development, 7,* 51–65.

Maier, M. A., Bernier, A., Pekrun, R., Zimmermann, P., & Grossmann, K. E. (2004). Attachment working models as unconscious structures: An experimental test. *International Journal of Behavioral Development, 28,* 180–189.

Main, M., & Hesse, E. (1990). Parents' unresolved traumatic experiences are related to infant disorganized attachment status: Is frightened and/or frightening parental behavior the linking mechanism? In M. T. Greenberg, D. Cicchetti, & E. M. Cummings (Eds.), *Attachment in the preschool years: Theory, research, and intervention* (pp. 161–182). Chicago, IL: University of Chicago Press.

Main, M., Kaplan, N., & Cassidy, J. (1985). Security in infancy, childhood, and adulthood: A move to the level of representation. *Monographs of the Society for Research in Child Development, 50* (1–2, Serial No. 209), 66–104.

Manlove, E. E., & Vernon-Feagans, L. (2002). Caring for infant daughters and sons in dual-earner households: Maternal reports of father involvement in weekday time and tasks. *Infant and Child Development, 11,* 305–320

Marcuse, H. (1966). *Eros and civilization: A philosophical inquiry into Freud.* Boston, MA: Beacon Press. (Original work published 1955)

Martens, A., Greenberg, J., Schimel, J., & Landau, M. J. (2004). Ageism and death: Effects of mortality salience and perceived similarity to elders on reactions to elderly people. *Personality and Social Psychology Bulletin, 30,* 1524–1536.

Mashek, D. J., & Aron, A. (Eds.). (2004). *Handbook of closeness and intimacy.* Mahwah, NJ: Lawrence Erlbaum.

Maslow, A. H. (1968). *Toward a psychology of being* (2nd ed.). New York, NY: Van Nostrand Reinhold.

Maslow, A. H. (1971). *The farther reaches of human nature.* New York, NY: Penguin.

Masterson, J. F. (1985). *The real self: A developmental, self, and object relations approach.* New York, NY: Brunner/Mazel.

May, R. (1981). *Freedom and destiny.* New York, NY: Dell.

McCarthy, J. B. (1980). *Death anxiety: The loss of the self.* New York, NY: Gardner.

McClelland, D. C. (1975). *Power: The inner experience.* New York, NY: John Wiley.

McCoy, S. K., Pyszczynski, T., Solomon, S., & Greenberg, J. (2000). Transcending the self: A terror management perspective. In A. Tomer (Ed.), *Death attitudes and the older adult: Theories, concepts, and applications* (pp. 37–63). Philadelphia, PA: Brunner-Routledge.

McFarlane, A., & van der Kolk, B. A. (1996). Trauma and its challenge to society. Traumatic stress: The effects of overwhelming experience on mind, body, and society. In B. A. van der Kolk, A. C. McFarlane, & L. Weisaeth (Eds.), *Traumatic stress: The effects of overwhelming experience on mind, body, and society* (pp. 24–46). New York, NY: Guilford Press.

McGowan, P. O., Sasaki, A., D'Alessio, A. C., Dymov, S., Labonte, B., Szyf, M., . . . Meaney, M. J. (2009). Epigenetic regulation of the glucocorticoid receptor in human brain associates with child abuse. *Nature Neuroscience, 12,* 342–348.

McHugh, K. E. (2003). Three faces of ageism: Society image and place. *Ageing and Society, 23,* 165–185.

McIntosh, J. L. (1990). Older adults: The next suicide epidemic? In D. Lester (Ed.), *Proceedings, 23rd Annual Meeting, American Association of Suicidology, New Orleans, Louisiana, April 25–29, 1990* (pp. 305–308). Denver, CO: American Association of Suicidology.

McIntosh, J. L. (1995). Suicide prevention in the elderly (age 65–99). In M. M. Silverman & R. W. Maris (Eds.), *Suicide prevention: Toward the year 2000* (pp. 180–192). New York, NY: Guilford Press.

McKee, A., & Boyatzis, R. (2005). *Resonant leadership: Renewing yourself and connecting with others through mindfulness, hope, and compassion.* Boston, MA: Harvard Business School Press.

Meaney, M. J. (2010). Epigenetics and the biological definition of gene-environment interactions. *Child Development, 81,* 41–79.

Meeus, W., Iedema, J., Maassen, G., & Engels, R. (2005). Separation-individuation revisited: On the interplay of parent-adolescent relations, identity and emotional adjustment in adolescence. *Journal of Adolescence, 28,* 89–106.

Metzinger, T. (2003). *Being no one: The self-model theory of subjectivity.* Cambridge, MA: MIT Press.

Meyer, M. (1991, December 16). Be kinder to your "kinder." *Newsweek,* 43.

Mikulincer, M., & Florian, V. (2000). Exploring individual differences in reactions to mortality salience: Does attachment style regulate terror management mechanisms? *Journal of Personality and Social Psychology, 79,* 260–273.

Mikulincer, M., Florian, V., & Hirschberger, G. (2004). The terror of death and the quest for love: An existential perspective on close relationships. In J. Greenberg, S. L. Koole, & T. Pyszczynski, (Eds.), *Handbook of experimental existential psychology* (pp. 287–304). New York, NY: Guilford Press.

Mikulincer, M., & Horesh, N. (1999). Adult attachment style and the perception of others: The role of projective mechanisms. *Journal of Personality and Social Psychology, 76,* 1022–1034.

Mikulincer, M., & Shaver, P. R. (2001). Attachment theory and intergroup bias: Evidence that priming the secure base schema attenuates negative reactions to out-groups. *Journal of Personality and Social Psychology, 81,* 97–115.

Mikulincer, M., & Shaver, P. R. (2007). *Attachment in adulthood: Structure, dynamics, and change.* New York, NY: Guilford Press. [Amazon Kindle version]

Mikulincer, M., Shaver, P. R., & Pereg, D. (2003). Attachment theory and affect regulation: The dynamics, development, and cognitive consequences of attachment-related strategies. *Motivation and Emotion, 27,* 77–102.

Milgram, S. (1974). *Obedience to authority: An experimental view.* New York, NY: Harper & Row.

Miller, A. (1984). *For your own good: Hidden cruelty in child-rearing and the roots of violence* (2nd ed., H. & H. Hannum, Trans.). New York, NY: Farrar, Straus, Giroux. (Original work published 1980)

Miller, M. V. (1995). *Intimate terrorism: The crisis of love in an age of disillusion.* New York, NY: W. W. Norton.

Miller, N. E., & Dollard, J. (1941). *Social learning and imitation.* New Haven, CT: Yale University Press.

Monsour, K. J. (1960). Asthma and the fear of death. *Psychoanalytic Quarterly, 29,* 56–71.

Moore, C. (2007). Moral disengagement in processes of organizational corruption. *Journal of Business Ethics, 80,* 129–139.

Morey, L. C., & Jones, J. K. (1998). Empirical studies of the construct validity of narcissistic personality disorder. In E. F. Ronningstam (Ed.), *Disorders of narcissism: Diagnostic, clinical, and empirical implications* (pp. 351–373). Northvale, NJ: Jason Aronson.

Morrant, C. (2003). Review of *Creating a life of meaning and compassion,* by Robert W. Firestone, Lisa Firestone, & Joyce Catlett. Unpublished manuscript.

Morrant, C., & Catlett, J. (2008). Separation theory and voice therapy: Philosophical underpinnings and applications to death anxiety across the life span. In A. Tomer, G. T. Eliason, & P. T. P. Wong (Eds.), *Existential and spiritual issues in death attitudes* (pp. 345–373). New York, NY: Lawrence Erlbaum.

Murphy, S. E., & Reichard, R. J. (Eds.). (2011). *Early development and leadership: Building the next generation of leaders.* New York, NY: Routledge.

Nagy, M. H. (1959). The child's view of death. In H. Feifel (Ed.), *The meaning of death* (pp. 79–98). New York, NY: McGraw-Hill. (Original work published 1948)

Nealer, J. (2002, July/August). Children's gender identity development: A closer look. *Family Therapy Magazine,* 24–27.

Neimeyer, R. A. (2006). Narrating the dialogical self: Toward an expanded toolbox for the counselling psychologist. *Counselling Psychology Quarterly, 19,* 105–120.

Neubauer, P. B. (1986). Reciprocal effects of fathering on parent and child. In G. I. Fogel, F. M. Lane, & R. S. Liebert (Eds.), *The psychology of men: Psychoanalytic perspectives* (pp. 213–228). New Haven, CT: Yale University Press.

Neubert, M. J., Carlson, D. S., Kacmar, K. M., Roberts, J. A., & Chonko, L. B. (2009). The virtuous influence of ethical leadership behavior: Evidence from the field. *Journal of Business Ethics, 90,* 157–170.

Newman, L. S., Duff, K. J., & Baumeister, R. F. (1997). A new look at defensive projection: Thought suppression, accessibility, and biased person perception. *Journal of Personality and Social Psychology, 72,* 980–1001.

Noller, P., & Feeney, J. A. (1994). Relationship satisfaction, attachment, and nonverbal accuracy in early marriage. *Journal of Nonverbal Behavior, 18,* 199–221.

Norman, C. (1958). *The magic-maker: E.E. Cummings.* New York, NY: Macmillan.

Noyes, R., Jr., Stuart, S., Longley, S. L., Langbehn, D. R., & Happel, R. L. (2002). Hypochondriasis and fear of death. *Journal of Nervous and Mental Disease, 190,* 503–509.

Oaklander, V. (1978). *Windows to our children: A gestalt therapy approach to children and adolescents.* Moab, UT: Real People Press.

Oaklander, V. (2006). *Hidden treasure: A map of the child's inner self.* London, England: Karnac Books.

Oates, R. K., Forrest, D., & Peacock, A. (1985). Self-esteem of abused children. *Child Abuse and Neglect, 9,* 159–163.

Ochs, E., & Capps, L. (1996). Narrating the self. *Annual Review of Anthropology, 25,* 19–43.

Ogden, P., Minton, K., & Pain, C. (2006). *Trauma and the body: A sensorimotor approach to psychotherapy.* New York, NY: W. W. Norton.

Ogden, T. H. (1982). *Projective identification and psychotherapeutic technique.* New York, NY: Jason Aronson.

Ogden, T. H. (2005). *The art of psychoanalysis: Dreaming undreamt dreams and interrupted cries.* New York, NY: Routledge. [Amazon Kindle version]

O'Neil, J. M., & Lujan, M. L. (2010). An assessment paradigm for fathers and men in therapy using gender role conflict theory. In C. Z. Oren & D. C. Oren (Eds.), *Counseling fathers* (pp. 49–71). New York, NY: Routledge. [Amazon Kindle version]

Orbach, I. (2008). Existentialism and suicide. In A. Tomer, G. T. Eliason, & P. T. P. Wong (Eds.), *Existential and spiritual issues in death attitudes* (pp. 281–316). New York, NY: Lawrence Erlbaum.

Oren, C. Z., Englar-Carlson, M., Stevens, M. A., & Oren, D. C. (2010). Counseling fathers from a strength-based perspective. In C. Z. Oren & D. C. Oren (Eds.), *Counseling fathers* (pp. 23–47). New York, NY: Routledge. [Amazon Kindle version]

Oren, C. Z., & Oren, D. C. (Eds.). (2010). *Counseling fathers.* New York, NY: Routledge. [Amazon Kindle version]

Page, D., & Wong, P. T. P. (2000). A conceptual framework for measuring servant leadership. In S. Adjibolooso (Ed.), *The human factor in shaping the course of history and development* (pp. 69–110). Lanham, MD: University Press of America.

Pagels, E. (1988). *Adam, Eve, and the serpent.* New York, NY: Random House.

Panksepp, J. (1998). The periconscious substrates of consciousness: Affective states and the evolutionary origins of the self. *Journal of Consciousness Studies, 5,* 566–582.

Park, J. (1995). *Sons, mothers and other lovers.* London, England: Abacus.

Parr, G. (Producer and Director). (1995). *Invisible child abuse* [DVD]. Santa Barbara, CA: Glendon Association.

Paul, J., Costley, D. L., Howell, J. P., & Dorfman, P. W. (2002). The mutability of charisma in leadership research. *Journal of Management History, 40,* 192–200.

Perel, E. (2006). *Mating in captivity: Unlocking erotic intelligence.* New York, NY: HarperCollins. [Amazon Kindle version]

Perry, B. D. (2001). Violence and childhood: How persisting fear can alter the developing child's brain. In D. Schetky & E. Benedek (Eds.), *Textbook of child and adolescent forensic psychiatry* (pp. 221–238). Washington, DC: American Psychiatric Press.

Perry, B. D. (2002). Childhood experience and the expression of genetic potential: What childhood neglect tells us about nature and nurture. *Brain and Mind, 3,* 79–100.

Pietromonaco, P. R., & Barrett, L. F. (2000). The internal working models concept: What do we really know about the self in relation to others? *Review of General Psychology, 4,* 155–175.

Pines, A. M. (1999). *Falling in love: Why we choose the lovers we choose.* New York, NY: Routledge.

Piven, J. S. (2002). Transference as religious solution to the terror of death. In D. Liechty (Ed.), *Death and denial: Interdisciplinary perspective on the legacy of Ernest Becker* (pp. 237–246). Westport, CT: Praeger.

Piven, J. S. (2004a). *Death and delusion: A Freudian analysis of mortal terror.* Greenwich, CT: Information Age.

Piven, J. S. (2004b). Death, neurosis, and normalcy: On the ubiquity of personal and social delusions. In J. S. Piven (Ed.), *The psychology of death in fantasy and history* (pp. 245–266). Westport, CT: Praeger.

Pleck, J. E. (2010). Fatherhood and masculinity. In M. E. Lamb (Ed.), *The role of the father in child development* (5th ed., pp. 27–57). New York, NY: John Wiley.

Pollack, W. (1998). *Real boys: Rescuing our sons from the myths of boyhood.* New York, NY: Henry Holt.

Popper, K. R. (1966). *The open society and its enemies: Vol. 1. The spell of Plato* (5th ed.). Princeton, NJ: Princeton University Press.

Popper, M., & Mayseless, O. (2003). Back to basics: Applying a parenting perspective to transformational leadership. *Leadership Quarterly, 14,* 41–65.

Porges, S. W. (2011). *The polyvagal theory: Neurophysiological foundations of emotions, attachment, communication, and self-regulation.* New York, NY: W. W. Norton.

Post, J. M. (2004). *Leaders and their followers in a dangerous world: The psychology of political behavior.* Ithaca, NY: Cornell University Press.

Prescott, J. W. (1975). Body pleasure and the origins of violence. *Bulletin of the Atomic Scientists, 10–20.* Retrieved from http://www.violence.de/prescott/bulletin/article.html

Prescott, J. W. (1996). The origins of human love and violence. *Pre- and Perinatal Psychology Journal, 10,* 143–188.

Putnam, F. W. (2003). Ten-year research update review: Child sexual abuse. *Journal of the American Academy of Child and Adolescent Psychiatry, 42,* 269–278.

Pyszczynski, T. (2004). What are we so afraid of? A terror management perspective on the politics of fear. *Social Research, 71,* 827–848.

Pyszczynski, T., Greenberg, J., & Solomon, S. (1999). A dual-process model of defense against conscious and unconscious death-related thoughts: An extension of terror management theory. *Psychological Review, 106,* 835–845.

Pyszczynski, T., Solomon, S., & Greenberg, J. (2003). *In the wake of 9/11: The psychology of terror.* Washington, DC: American Psychological Association.

Ramachandran, V. S. (2011). *The tell-tale brain: A neuroscientist's quest for what makes us human.* New York, NY: W. W. Norton.

Randall, E. (2001). Existential therapy of panic disorder: A single system study. *Clinical Social Work Journal, 29,* 259–267.

Rank, M. (2011). *Fathering matters: How great fathers empower their daughters and what to do if yours didn't.* CreateSpace. [Amazon Kindle version]

Rank, O. (1941). *Beyond psychology.* New York, NY: Dover.

Rank, O. (1972). *Will therapy and truth and reality.* (J. Taft, Trans.). New York, NY: Knopf. (Original work published 1936)

Rank, O. (1989). *Art and artists: Creative urge and personality development.* New York, NY: Knopf. (Original work published 1932)

Rastogi, M., & Wampler, K. S. (1999). Adult daughters' perceptions of the mother-daughter relationship: A cross-cultural comparison. *Family Relations, 48,* 327–336.

Rawls, J. (1999). *A theory of justice* (rev. ed.). Cambridge, MA: Harvard University Press.

Rheingold, J. C. (1964). *The fear of being a woman: A theory of maternal destructiveness.* New York, NY: Grune & Stratton.

Rheingold, J. C. (1967). *The mother, anxiety, and death: The catastrophic death complex.* Boston, MA: Little, Brown.

Rholes, W. S., Simpson, J. A., Tran, S., Martin, A. M., & Friedman, M. (2007). Attachment and information seeking in romantic relationships. *Personality and Social Psychology Bulletin, 33,* 422–438.

Rich, A. (1976). *Of woman born: Motherhood as experience and institution.* New York, NY: W. W. Norton.

Riggio, R. E. (2008). Leadership development: The current state and future expectations. *Consulting Psychology Journal: Practice and Research, 60,* 383–392.

Rizzolatti, G., Fogassi, L., & Gallese, V. (2001). Neurophysiological mechanisms underlying the understanding and the imitation of action. *Nature Review Neuroscience, 2,* 660–670.

Rochlin, G. (1967). How younger children view death and themselves. In E. A. Grollman (Ed.), *Explaining death to children* (pp. 51–85). Boston, MA: Beacon Press.

Roderick, R. (1993). The self under siege: Philosophy in the 20th century [Lecture Series]. Springfield, VA: Teaching Company.

Rohner, R. P. (1986). *The warmth dimension: Foundations of parental acceptance-rejection theory.* Newbury Park, CA: Sage.

Rohner, R. P. (1991). *Handbook for the study of parental acceptance and rejection.* Storrs, CT: University of Connecticut Press.

Rohner, R. P., & Veneziano, R. A. (2001). The importance of father love: History and contemporary evidence. *Review of General Psychology, 5,* 382–405.

Roiphe, A. (1996). *Fruitful: A real mother in the modern world.* Boston, MA: Houghton Mifflin.

Roisman, G. I., Madsen, S. D., Hennighausen, K. H., Sroufe, L. A., & Collins, W. A. (2001). The coherence of dyadic behavior across parent-child and romantic relationships as mediated by the internalized representation of experience. *Attachment and Human Behavior, 3,* 156–172.

Rose, A. J., & Rudolph, K. D. (2006). A review of sex differences in peer relationship processes: Potential trade-offs for the emotional and behavioral development of girls and boys. *Psychological Bulletin, 132,* 98–131.

Rubin, L. B. (1983). *Intimate strangers: Men and women together.* New York, NY: Harper & Row.

Russell, A., & Saebel, J. (1997). Mother-son, mother-daughter, father-son, and father-daughter: Are they distinct relationships? *Developmental Review, 17,* 111–147.

Ryan, R. M., & Deci, E. L. (2008). A self-determination theory approach to psychotherapy: The motivational basis for effective change. *Canadian Psychology, 49,* 186–193.

Salgado, J., & Hermans, H. J. M. (2005). The return of subjectivity: From a multiplicity of selves to the dialogical self. *E-Journal of Applied Psychology: Clinical section, 1,* 3–13.

Salzman, M. B. (2001). Globalization, culture, and anxiety: Perspectives and predictions from terror management theory. *Journal of Social Distress and the Homeless, 10,* 337–352.

Schachner, D. A., Shaver, P. R., & Mikulincer, M. (2003). Adult attachment theory, psychodynamics, and couple relationships: An overview. In S. M. Johnson & V. E. Whiffen (Eds.), *Attachment processes in couple and family therapy* (pp. 18–42). New York, NY: Guilford Press.

Scharff, D. E., & Scharff, J. S. (1991). *Object relations couple therapy.* Northvale, NJ: Jason Aronson.

Scharff, J. S., & Scharff, D. E. (1997). Object relations couple therapy. *American Journal of Psychotherapy, 51,* 141–173.

Schmeichel, B. J., Gailliot, M. T., Filardo, E., McGregor, I., Gitter, S., & Baumeister, R. F. (2009). Terror management theory and self-esteem revisited: The roles of implicit and explicit self-esteem in mortality salience effects. *Journal of Personality and Social Psychology, 96,* 1077–1087.

Schmitt, D. P., Alcalay, L., Allensworth, M., Allik, J., Ault, L., Austers, I., . . . Scrimali, T. (2004). Patterns and universals of adult romantic attachment across 62 cultural regions: Are models of Self and of Other pancultural constructs? *Journal of Cross-Cultural Psychology, 35,* 367–402.

Schnarch, D. M. (1991). *Constructing the sexual crucible: An integration of sexual and marital therapy.* New York, NY: W. W. Norton.

Schnarch, D. (2009). *Intimacy and desire: Awaken the passion in your relationship.* New York, NY: Beaufort Books.

Schore, A. N. (1994). *Affect regulation and the origin of the self: The neurobiology of emotional development.* Hillsdale, NJ: Lawrence Erlbaum.

Schore, A. N. (2000). Attachment and the regulation of the right brain. *Attachment and Human Development, 2,* 23–47.

Schore, A. N. (2003a). *Affect regulation and disorders of the self.* New York, NY: W. W. Norton.

Schore, A. N. (2003b). *Affect regulation and the repair of the self.* New York, NY: W. W. Norton.

Schore, A. N. (2009). Relational trauma and the developing right brain: An interface of psychoanalytic self psychology and neuroscience. In W. J. Coburn & N. VanDerHeide (Eds.), *Self and systems: Explorations in contemporary self psychology, Annals of the New York Academy of Sciences* (pp. 189–203). New York, NY: Wiley-Blackwell.

Schore, A. N. (2011). The right brain implicit self lies at the core of psychoanalysis. *Psychoanalytic Dialogues, 21,* 75–100.

Schwartz, S. J. (2005). A new identity for identity research: Recommendations for expanding and refocusing the identity literature. *Journal of Adolescent Research, 20,* 293–308.

Schwartz, S. J., Zamboanga, B. L., & Weisskirch, R. S. (2008). Broadening the study of the self: Integrating the study of personal identity and cultural identity. *Social and Personality Psychology Compass, 2,* 635–651.

Searles, H. F. (1961). Schizophrenia and the inevitability of death. *Psychiatric Quarterly, 35,* 631–665.

Secunda, V. (1990). *When you and your mother can't be friends: Resolving the most complicated relationship of your life.* New York, NY: Delacorte Press.

Senge, P. M., Kleiner, A., Roberts, C., Ross, R. B., & Smith, B. J. (1994). *The fifth discipline fieldbook: Strategies and tools for building a learning organization.* New York, NY: Doubleday.

Seton, M. (2011). Providing for those who have too little. *New England Journal of Medicine, 365,* 1169–1171.

Shapiro, D. (2000). *Dynamics of character: Self-regulation in psychopathology.* New York, NY: Basic Books.

Sharpe, S. (1994). *Fathers and daughters.* New York, NY: Routledge. [Amazon Kindle version]

Shaver, P. R., & Clark, C. L. (1994). The psychodynamics of adult romantic attachment. In J. M. Masling & R. F. Bornstein (Eds.), *Empirical perspectives on object relations theory* (pp. 105–156). Washington, DC: American Psychological Association.

Shaver, P. R., Collins, N., & Clark, C. L. (1996). Attachment styles and internal working models of self and relationship partners. In G. J. O. Fletcher & J. Fitness (Eds.), *Knowledge structures in close relationships: A social psychological approach* (pp. 25–61). Mahwah, NJ: Lawrence Erlbaum.

Shaw, D. S., Gilliom, M., Ingoldsby, E. M., & Nagin, D. S. (2003). Trajectories leading to school-age conduct problems. *Developmental Psychology, 39,* 189–200.

Shirer, W. L. (1960). *The rise and fall of the Third Reich: A history of Nazi Germany.* New York, NY: Simon & Schuster.

Siegel, D. J. (1999). *The developing mind: Toward a neurobiology of interpersonal experience.* New York, NY: Guilford Press.

Siegel, D. (2001). Toward an interpersonal neurobiology of the developing mind: Attachment relationships, "mindsight," and neural integration. *Infant Mental Health Journal, 22,* 67–94.

Siegel, D. J. (2004). Attachment and self-understanding: Parenting with the brain in mind. In M. Green & M. Scholes (Eds.), *Attachment and human survival* (pp. 21–35). London, England: Karnac.

Siegel, D. J. (2007). *The mindful brain: Reflection and attunement in the cultivation of well-being.* New York, NY: W. W. Norton.

Siegel, D. J. (2010). *The mindful therapist.* New York, NY: W. W. Norton. [Amazon Kindle version]

Siegel, D. J., & Hartzell, M. (2003). *Parenting from the inside out: How a deeper self-understanding can help you raise children who thrive.* New York, NY: Jeremy P. Tarcher.

Siegel, D. J., & McCall, D. P. (2009). Mindsight at work: An interpersonal neurobiology lens on leadership. *NeuroLeadership Journal,* Issue 2 [online journal].

Silverman, L. H., Lachmann, F. M., & Milich, R. H. (1982). *The search for oneness.* New York, NY: International Universities Press.

Simpson, J. A. (1990). Influence of attachment styles on romantic relationships. *Journal of Personality and Social Psychology, 59,* 971–980.

Skowron, E. A., & Friedlander, M. L. (1998). The Differentiation of Self Inventory: Development and initial validation. *Journal of Counseling Psychology, 45,* 235–246.

Skowron, E. A., & Schmitt, T. A. (2003). Assessing interpersonal fusion: Reliability and validity of a new DSI fusion with others subscale. *Journal of Marital and Family Therapy, 29,* 209–222.

Smith, H. (2009). *Why religion matters: The fate of the human spirit in an age of disbelief.* HarperCollins e-Books.

Smith, S. M., McIntosh, W. D., & Bazzini, D. G. (1999). Are the beautiful good in Hollywood? An investigation of the beauty-and-goodness stereotype on film. *Basic and Applied Social Psychology, 21,* 69–80.

Snyder, D. K., Castellani, A. M., & Whisman, M. A. (2006). Current status and future directions in couple therapy. *Annual Review of Psychology, 57,* 317–344.

Solomon, J., & George, C. (2011). The disorganized attachment-caregiving system: Dysregulation of adaptive processes at multiple levels. In J. Solomon & C. George (Eds.), *Disorganized attachment and caregiving* (pp. 3–24). New York, NY: Guilford Press.

Solomon, M. F. (2001). Breaking the deadlock of marital collusion. In M. F. Solomon, R. J. Neborsky, L. McCullough, M. Alpert, F. Shapiro, & D. Malan, *Short-term therapy for long-term change* (pp. 130–154). New York, NY: W. W. Norton.

Solomon, S., Greenberg, J., & Pyszczynski, T. (1991). A terror management theory of social behavior: The psychological functions of self-esteem and cultural worldviews. *Advances in Experimental Social Psychology, 24,* 93–159.

Solomon, S., Greenberg, J., & Pyszczynski, T. (2000). Pride and prejudice: Fear of death and social behavior. *Current Directions in Psychological Science, 9,* 200–204.

Solomon, S., Greenberg, J., & Pyszczynski, T. (2004). The cultural animal: Twenty years of terror management theory and research. In J. Greenberg, S. L. Koole, & T. Pyszczynski (Eds.), *Handbook of experimental existential psychology* (pp. 13–34). New York, NY: Guilford Press.

Speece, M. W., & Brent, S. B. (1984). Children's understanding of death: A review of three components of a death concept. *Child Development, 55,* 1671–1686.

Stamenkovic, D. (2009). The overpopulation of Popper's World 3: Rick Roderick's views on the excess of information in the postmodern world. *Facta Universitatis Series, Linguistics and Literature, 7,* 113–121.

Steeves, H. P. (2003, August). Humans and animals at the divide: The case of feral children. *Between the Species, 3,* 1–18.

Stern, D. N. (1985). *The interpersonal world of the infant: A view from psychoanalysis and developmental psychology.* New York, NY: Basic Books.

Stern, D. N. (2004). *The present moment in psychotherapy and everyday life.* New York, NY: W. W. Norton.

Stern, L. (1991). Disavowing the self in female adolescence. In C. Gilligan, A. G. Rogers, & D. L. Tolman (Eds.), *Women, girls and psychotherapy: Reframing resistance* (pp. 105–118). Binghamton, NY: Haworth Press.

Sternberg, R. J. (2007). A systems model of leadership: WICS. *American Psychologist, 62,* 34–42.

Stogdill, R. M. (1948). Personal factors associated with leadership: A survey of the literature. *Journal of Psychology, 25,* 35–71.

Strachan, E., Schimel, J., Arndt, J., Williams, T., Solomon, S., Pyszczynski, T., & Greenberg, J. (2007). Terror mismanagement: Evidence that morality salience exacerbates phobic and compulsive behaviors. *Personality and Social Psychology Bulletin, 33,* 1137–1151.

Strawson, G. (1999). The self. In S. Gallagher & J. Shear (Eds.), *Models of the self* (pp. 1–24). Exeter, England: Imprint Academic.

Streep, P. (2009). *Mean mothers: Overcoming the legacy of hurt.* New York, NY: HarperCollins.

Swallen, K. C., Reither, E. N., Haas, S. A., & Meier, A. M. (2005). Overweight, obesity, and health-related quality of life among adolescents: The National Longitudinal Study of Adolescent Health. *Pediatrics, 115,* 340–347.

Tajfel, H. (1970). Experiments in intergroup discrimination. *Scientific American, 223,* 96–102.

Tansey, M. H., & Burke, W. F. (1985). Projective identification and the empathic process. *Contemporary Psychoanalysis, 21,* 42–69.

Tedeschi, J. T., & Felson, R. B. (1994). *Violence, aggression, and coercive actions.* Washington, DC: American Psychological Association.

Templer, D. I. (1970). The construction and validation of a death anxiety scale. *Journal of General Psychology, 82,* 165–174.

Templer, D. I. (1972). Death anxiety: Extraversion, neuroticism, and cigarette smoking. *Omega, 3,* 53–56.

Thompson, L., & Walker, A. J. (1989). Gender in families: Women and men in marriage, work, and parenthood. *Journal of Marriage and the Family, 51,* 845–871.

Tillich, P. (1952). *The courage to be.* New Haven, CT: Yale University Press.

Tremblay, R. E., & Szyf, M. (2010). Developmental origins of chronic physical aggression and epigenetics. *Epigenomics, 2,* 495–499.

Trotter, W. (1916). *Instincts of the herd in peace and war.* London, England: Unwin.

Van Buren, J. (2007). *Mothers and daughters and the origins of female subjectivity.* London, England: Routledge.

Van Dijke, M., & Poppe, M. (2006). Striving for personal power as a basis for social power dynamics. *European Journal of Social Psychology, 36,* 537–556.

Vergote, A. (1988). *Guilt and desire: Religious attitudes and their pathological derivatives.* (M. H. Wood, Trans.). New Haven, CT: Yale University Press. (Original work published 1978)

Vroom, V. H., & Jago, A. G. (2007). The role of the situation in leadership. *American Psychologist, 62,* 17–24.

Waddington, C. H. (1957). *The strategy of the genes.* London, England: Allen & Unwin.

Walling, B. R., Mills, R. S. L., & Freeman, W. S. (2007). Parenting cognitions associated with the use of psychological control. *Child and Family Studies, 16,* 642–659.

Watts, D. J. (2004). *Six degrees: The science of a connected age.* New York, NY: W. W. Norton.

Welldon, E. V. (1988). *Mother, madonna, whore: The idealization and denigration of motherhood.* London, England: Free Association Books.

Welldon, E. V. (2011). *Playing with dynamite: A personal approach to the psychoanalytic understanding of perversions, violence, and criminality.* London, England: Karnac Books.

Wenner, M. (2009, July/August). A patchwork mind. *Scientific American Mind,* 52–59.

West, C., & Zimmerman, D. (1987). Doing gender. *Gender and Society, 1,* 125–151.

Westkott, M. C. (1997). On the new psychology of women: A cautionary view. In M. R. Walsh (Ed.), *Women, men, and gender: Ongoing debates* (pp. 362–372). New Haven, CT: Yale University Press.

Wexler, J., & Steidl, J. (1978). Marriage and the capacity to be alone. *Psychiatry, 41,* 72–82.

Wheatley, M. J., & Kellner-Rogers, M. (1998). Bringing life to organizational change. Retrieved from http://www.berkana.org/articles/life.html

Willi, J. (1982). *Couples in collusion: The unconscious dimension in partner relationships.* (W. Inayat-Khan & M. Tchorek, Trans.). Claremont, CA: Hunter House. (Original work published 1975)

Willi, J. (1984). *Dynamics of couples therapy.* (J. Van Heurck, Trans.). Claremont, CA: Hunter House. (Original work published 1978)

Willi, J. (1999). *Ecological psychotherapy: Developing by shaping the personal niche.* Seattle, WA: Hogrefe & Huber.

Williams, K. D., Cheung, C. K. T., & Choi, W. (2000). Cyberostracism: Effects of being ignored over the Internet. *Journal of Personality and Social Psychology, 79,* 748–762.

Williams, K. D., & Jarvis, B. (2006). Cyberball: A program for use in research on interpersonal ostracism and acceptance. *Behavior Research Methods, 38,* 174–180.

Wilson, T. D., Lindsey, S., & Schooler, T. Y. (2000). A model of dual attitudes. *Psychological Review, 107,* 101–126.

Wilson-Starks, K. Y. (2003). Toxic leadership. Retrieved from www.transleadership.com

Winnicott, D. W. (1958). *Collected papers: Through paediatrics to psycho-analysis.* London, England: Tavistock.

Winnicott, D. W. (1965). Ego distortion in terms of true and false self. In D. W. Winnicott, *The maturational processes and the facilitating environment: Studies in the theory of emotional development* (pp. 140–152). Madison, CT: International Universities Press. (Original work published 1960)

Winnicott, D. W. (1965). *The maturational processes and the facilitating environment: Studies in the theory of emotional development.* Madison, CT: International Universities Press.

Wood, M. (2005). The fallacy of misplaced leadership. *Journal of Management Studies, 42,* 1101–1121.

Wren, J. T. (1995). *The leader's companion: Insights on leadership throughout the ages.* New York, NY: Free Press.

Yalom, I. D. (1980). *Existential psychotherapy.* New York, NY: Basic Books.

Zaccaro, S. J. (2007). Trait-based perspectives of leadership. *American Psychologist, 62,* 6–16.

Zadro, L., Boland, C., & Richardson, R. (2006). How long does it last? The persistence of the effects of ostracism in the socially anxious. *Journal of Experimental Social Psychology, 42,* 692–697.

Zeitner, R. M. (2012). *Self within marriage: The foundation for lasting relationships.* New York, NY: Routledge.

Zilboorg, G. (1943). Fear of death. *Psychoanalytic Quarterly, 12,* 465–475.

Zimbardo, P. G. (2004). A situationist perspective on the psychology of evil: Understanding how good people are transformed into perpetrators. In A. G. Miller (Ed.), *The social psychology of good and evil* (pp. 21–50). New York, NY: Guilford Press.

Zimbardo, P. G., & White, G. (1972). *Stanford Prison Experiment slide-tape show.* Stanford, CA: Stanford University Press.

Zinn, H. (2003). *Passionate declarations: Essays on war and justice.* New York, NY: HarperCollins.

Zinner, J. (1976). The implications of projective identification for marital interaction. In H. Grunebaum & J. Christ (Eds.), *Contemporary marriage: Structure, dynamics, and therapy* (pp. 293–308). Boston, MA: Little, Brown.

Zurbriggen, E. L., & Freyd, J. J. (2004). The link between child sexual abuse and risky sexual behavior: The role of dissociative tendencies, information-processing effects, and consensual sex decision mechanisms. In L. J. Koenig, L. S. Doll, A. O'Leary, & W. Pequegnat (Eds.), *From child sexual abuse to adult sexual risk: Trauma, revictimization, and intervention* (pp. 135–157). Washington, DC: American Psychological Association.

INDEX